THE CULTURAL ONE OR THE RACIAL MANY

To Virginia

The Cultural One or the Racial Many

Religion, culture and the interethnic experience

EVANDRO CAMARA

Ashgate

Aldershot • Brookfield USA • Singapore • Sydney

Published by
Ashgate Publishing Limited
Gower House
Croft Road
Aldershot
Hants GU11 3HR
England

Ashgate Publishing Company
Old Post Road
Brookfield
Vermont 05036
USA

British Library Cataloguing in Publication Data

Camara, Evandro
    The cultural one or the racial many : religion, culture
    and the interethnic experience. - (Research in ethnic
    relations)
    1. Race relations
    I. Title
    305.8

Library of Congress Catalog Card Number: 97-74508

ISBN 1 84014 119 0

Printed and bound by Athenaeum Press, Ltd.,
Gateshead, Tyne & Wear.

Contents

Preface

This book grew out of my long-standing interest in culture and interethnic life, which has broadened and deepened over the years on account of my having lived in two different sociocultural contexts, Brazil and the United States. Despite the parallels shared by these two societies with respect to their cultural and ethnic developmental history, their differences in this regard are far more striking, and it is precisely this aspect that has nurtured my informal and academic interest in this issue, and motivated me to organize my feelings and insights into this work. I have specifically endeavored to identify and explain the cultural and ideological forces that have accounted not only for the divergences in interethnic arrangements between the two societies, but also, with reference to the U.S., for the persistence of ethnic divisions and conflict, and the resurgence of separatist trends over the last decade, in no small measure through the effect of the multiculturalist movement, notwithstanding the integrationist changes in dominant-minority relations that marked the end of the Jim Crow period in the 1960s.

During the course of writing this book I have amassed a number of debts. The project was started within the context of a postdoctoral visitorship at the University of Chicago in 1991-1992. I would like, in this connection, to acknowledge the invaluable assistance and encouragement of Martin Riesebrodt, of the Sociology Department and Divinity School at that institution, who gave unstintingly of his time and expertise towards helping me organize and develop my ideas, and thus get the work "off the ground."

I am also indebted to Martin Marger, of Michigan State University, who, at a later point in the research, read critical parts of the manuscript, and offered meticulous and very useful comments and suggestions.

The work has likewise benefitted, particularly in terms of certain key theoretical aspects, from the incisive criticisms of Craig C. Calhoun, of the University of North Carolina-Chapel Hill, for which I am grateful.

Special thanks also to the editorial staff at Ashgate-Avebury, in particular Kate Hargreave, Anne Keirby, Lindsey Wilsden, Valerie Polding, Tracey Daborn, and Pauline Beavers.

Additionally, I wish to acknowledge the assistance of Anita Vanschaik and her clerical staff at Emporia State University for expertly typing some sections of the manuscript.

In a larger sense, I owe a special debt, as regards my early graduate efforts, to Larry Reynolds, of Central Michigan University, and, regarding my years in the doctoral program and beyond, to Fabio Dasilva, of the University of Notre Dame, for having stimulated and guided my interest in the theoretical-interpretative understanding of social things.

Finally, Virginia de Oliveira-Alves, to whom this book is dedicated, has been my sternest critic and greatest benefactor. She has consistently pushed me toward greater analytical rigor and clarity of expression, and, as concerns this project, her substantive contributions to it, particularly during its initial phase, enabled me to rethink key formulations and tighten the general thesis.

The main stars in the philosophy of culture

are to be found in the heaven of theology.

Jacques Maritain

1 Cultural explanation and the question of intergroup life

The nature of intergroup relations and inequality varies significantly across multiethnic or pluralist societies, a phenomenon that has constituted a matter of long-standing and lively sociological interest. This has been especially the case in the United States, where the resurgence of sociological, anthropological, and historical scholarship in this area since the late 1960s attests to the continuing relevance of this problem in social studies and to its persisting presence in the social milieu. Some three decades after the momentous changes in the American legal system that led to the dismantling of the Jim Crow system of race segregation, discriminatory and segregationist practices as well as prejudicial feelings and attitudes against "nonwhite" minority groups still persist in American society, and even gathered strength through the 1980s. This phenomenon is, indeed, "a commonplace of empirical verification," says one observer (Gordon, 1964:114), and it invokes the same dilemma addressed by Gunnar Myrdal in the 1940s in his celebrated and now classic study *An American Dilemma*. There has been a steady reawakening of public and scholarly attention to the problem of intergroup relations, particularly as concerns race and ethnicity. This heightened societal sensitivity to this problem results precisely from the fact that, despite the progressive social, economic, and political incorporation of racial and ethnic minorities since the late 1960s, the deep cleavages which separate the dominant and subordinate ethnic groups in this society have not disappeared. Not only does race remain the main regulative principle of social relations, but also, racism continues to be a conspicuous feature of social organization. It is expressed in the presence of *de facto* inequality and segregation in the workplace, housing, the educational system,[1] and the legal system, as well as in the informal sectors of social life (Willie, 1978). It is the basis for the upsurge of ethnic consciousness among minority-group members in

1

recent years.[2] Lastly, it is seen in the racially-motivated turmoil and conflict that have erupted in the past decade on campuses and on the street, ranging from interpersonal harassment to more serious forms of conflict. In the single year of 1982, there were more than 500 documented cases of racist violence against blacks by white teenagers alone, which included "cross burnings, vandalism, arson, physical assaults, and murder" (Ofari, 1984). A specific example could be cited for 1987, the Howard Beach incident of Queens, New York, which involved the unprovoked beatings of some black teenagers by white teenagers. Of much greater proportions and more dire consequences were the April 1992 events of Los Angeles, following the acquittal of four white police officers who had been charged with extreme police brutality against a black man who had led them on a car chase on the highway. This legal outcome sparked days of full-scale rioting, looting, and burning of buildings, in which some people ended up dead and hundreds injured. The atmosphere was one of greatly exacerbated interracial tension.

The present analysis looks at this issue in a comparative framework, contrasting the cultural models of Brazil and the United States, two societies where, notwithstanding the remarkable similarity in their patterns of ethnic history and development, interethnic/interracial relations in each one have developed along clearly divergent lines. Exploring the intergroup problematic in comparative perspective can be highly effective for revealing dimensions and possibilities of social action that may remain obscured in single-case analysis. The conventional posture in comparative study, however, is to assume that, given the development of certain social institutions - for example, the economy - social practices will be manifested rather uniformly across societies. Hence, the analytical focus tends to be on the commonalities and repeatabilities of these practices in different societies.[3] In this study, the emphasis is shifted to the conceptual instability or diversity of social phenomena such as ethnic inequality and ethnic prejudice, which at first glance may be seen as homogeneous crossnationally, because of perceived structural isomorphisms that have to do with the process of economic and political evolution of the society, but in fact may be in important ways quite dissimilar, due to the historical and cultural variability between societies.

The approach emphasized here may be termed a culturalist one, in the sense that its point of departure is the concern with and focus on cultural forces and cultural change, and how these elements affect the larger architecture of integroup life. The intent has been to illuminate specifically the manner and degree in which the element of culture accounts for the emergence and maintenance of collective patterns of action, whereby cultural norms and beliefs are concretely externalized as social arrangements and practices, a service not usually provided by sociologies that treat ideas as mere epiphenomenal expressions of social structure. The present analysis addresses the specific problem of intergroup relations by considering the type of cultural system of the society, thematized here on the basis of a tripartite model of assimilation, comprising the following interrelated aspects: dominant-minority cultural interaction, cultural identity, and kinship formation (miscegenation and intermarriage). These are aspects which, despite being an integral part of the larger process of migrant-group assimilation, tend to be denied systematic attention in conventional analyses. They are introduced here as an alternative conceptual and methodological yardstick for assessing the nature and dynamics of dominant-minority ethnic relations, especially in hemispheric or crosscultural perspective. In this capacity, the culturalist position deviates from, but also complements, nonculturalist strategies, which mainly stress "structural" aspects, such as those of political economy on the one hand, or strictly quantitative ones on the other. In the race and ethnicity literature, this has meant a basic analytical bifurcation whereby the focus is directed either to social stratification aspects derived from "class" standing (e.g., Cox, 1948; Horowitz, 1964; Blauner, 1972), or from the distribution of the population among different social positions, regarding socioeconomic status, education, occupational rank, political representation (e.g., Gottfredson, 1981; Gardner, Robey, and Smith, 1985; Tuch and Martin, 1991), either in single-case or comparative context. The reduction of the dynamics of intergroup life to economic and political power relations, or its abstraction into strictly quantitative schemes, leaves much to be desired. In comparative studies, this has the effect of "homogenizing" the multiethnic experience, thus neutralizing the comparative focus through the idea that, despite the crosscultural variations stemming from the cultural and historical specificity of each society, patterns of intergroup relations in different multiethnic social systems are fundamentally similar. Riesman (1967:xxii) addresses this problem in stating that the traditional materialist position dictates that in order "to interpret reality one need not inquire into the motives of men, but rather notice that the situations they face are much alike, that the power of modern technology and science, modern economic organization, modern ideological and party organization is such that a single style of society becomes possible everywhere ...". It might be added to his commentary that this approach tends to perpetuate a false dualism between material and nonmaterial influences in social causation, as if these were mutually exclusive entities. The position taken in this analysis concerning the relationship between material and nonmaterial forces is that it is unitary, in the sense that material arrangements are essentially concrete

3

externalizations of dominant ways of thinking that have become institutionalized. The two elements are therefore assumed to be like two sides of the same coin. Arbousse-Bastide emphasizes this point: "Material elements are only signs of other realities, more difficult to grasp, but more fundamental ... material objects, from this perspective, are not meaningful or interesting except in the degree that they translate nonmaterial realities, worldviews, beliefs, prejudices, ideas" (1940:xiv; my translation). Thus, in this light, the material aspects of social life are more important in what they symbolize, not for what they are in themselves. They are indispensable signifiers or mediating aspects that facilitate the understanding of nonmaterial realities which, as noted, are even more fundamental to social knowledge and thus must be unearthed and brought to full view. To maintain a sharp distinction between material and nonmaterial elements in the understanding of social events, as traditional approaches tend to do, is to obscure the processes that help shape these events.

Regarding the matter of the formation of social phenomena - the specific phenomena in question here are interethnic conflict and inequality - traditional investigative approaches typically do not account for the forces and mechanisms responsible for establishing the character of ethnic relations in a given society, and for creating integration or separation of group interests and tendencies at the level of the society as a whole. This omission in sociological scholarship has been increasingly evidenced in recent times in societies like the United States, where the systematic formal rectification of legally and socially sanctioned injustice against minority ethnic groups, starting in the 1960s, has failed to eliminate interethnic and interracial separatism and antagonism. As already indicated, this problem has in fact intensified since the early 1980s, for reasons that will be addressed subsequently. Structural and cultural separatism, which remained the dominant feature of life in U.S. society for about 70 years, from the time of the 1896 Plessy vs. Ferguson Supreme Court decision and the installation of the Jim Crow system of race-based segregation to the 1960s, have been gaining strength again, only this time the legal mechanisms that supported the manifestation of structural and cultural separatism in the various spheres of social life have been removed. However, in parallel fashion to the former pattern, the separatist impulse continues to be stimulated officially and unofficially, indeed ever more vigorously, through the multiculturalist movement, which has been in operation and gaining momentum in the society over the past decade, and which hinges on the recognition and preservation of minority-group difference, with the end result being of this difference being crystallized as an end in itself.

4

The impact of material change

The importance of material or formal change, such as legal reform, for bringing equality and harmony to the interethnic sphere is not to be denied. Legislative reform is a crucial element in the abrogation of institutionalized arrangements and practices of segregation and discrimination, inasmuch as this type of change is normally followed by the structural assimilation of minority-group members into the occupational, political, and educational sectors of social life (see, e.g., Marger, 1991:118-9). The problem is that this phenomenon may come to be widely perceived (as in the case of U.S. society) as the definitive resolution of the long-standing interethnic problem, the dawning of a new, enlightened era of ethnic relations, when "race" and "ethnicity" are no longer regulative considerations. The assumption in this respect is that the establishment of parity in the formal sectors of social life is all that is needed for eradicating intergroup conflict and harmonizing intergroup relations. In the same vein, analysts of the interethnic problem may consider the abolition of the formal circumstances of ethnic inequality, as when the latter is expressed in the gross underrepresentation of ethnic minorities in the upper economic, political, and educational strata, to be the most logical and reliable indicator of intergroup progress or retardation across multiethnic societies.

Additionally, it is generally assumed that the structural or institutional assimilation of groups need not be accompanied by society-wide cultural integration. In other words, the latter is not seen as a *conditio sine qua non* for achieving the unification of formerly antagonistic ethnic segments of the society and drastically reducing social inequality between them, because, first of all, its structural counterpart appears to be all that is required for bringing together physically in the public sphere - the workplace, the schools, public establishments - under conditions of apparent equality, groups which had been kept rigidly apart in the past. This type of large-scale institutional alteration in the society is also regarded as providing formal safeguards that will insure the further expansion of this new mode of intergroup relations. Secondly, the former attitudes of mutual aversion and belligerence have mostly dissipated over the last couple of decades of institutional change, having been replaced by those of toleration and civility, when not open cordiality. In connection with this, even though institutional and interpersonal separatism are as a rule drastically reduced with the removal of the framework of legal legitimation, it is possible that the patterns of separatism which formerly governed the symbolic (i.e., cultural and psychosocial) and biological dimensions of intergroup life will persist. This latter form of separatism is tolerated because it is not judged incompatible with the assimilative processes under way in the economic, political, and educational spheres. In fact, it may happen, as in the case of U.S. society, that, as the process of structural assimilation of minority segments advances, systemic tendencies may emerge which promote the coexistence of the opposing elements of structural assimilation and sociocultural separatism, as evidenced in current multiculturalist trends).

Although the extension of civil rights to the entire citizenry is the essential precondition for the construction of a just social order - in the context of ethnic relations it unquestionably represents a necessary level of progress towards that goal - this is not a sufficient condition by itself. In time, the society may come to realize that although this legislative change in very large measure eliminates the formally-sanctioned, overt subjugation of ethnic subcultures, it fails to produce the root-and-branch overhaul of the fundamental patterns of intergroup stratification and conflict. While it is true that civility in intergroup relations has a generally beneficial and reassuring effect, it is scarcely a sufficient measure and guarantee of intergroup concord, stabilization, and unity, let alone equality. The precariousness of this aspect in insuring these outcomes becomes obvious when we consider interethnic developments in American society over the past couple of decades. Specifically, the old divisive ethnic and racial enmities and prejudices, as well as patterns of separation and inequality, so readily associated in the public mind with the arrangements and practices of the Jim Crow period, have begun to resurface, ever more assertively and ubiquitously, in all areas of social life. The formal trappings of this phenomenon are, of course, gone. Nevertheless, it should be plain to all that the fundamental problem persists, and that the transformations wrought by legislative reform have fallen short of a real resolution and/or eradication of interethnic conflict. The specific limitation of the law in this area of social life has long been recognized. In the beginning of this century, James Bryce (1968:246) remarked that in situations where the fusion of different ethnic communities is rendered impossible because of deep-going racial antagonisms, this "presents a problem which no Constitution has solved."

It appears, then, that too much is made of the "quantitative" dimension of ethnic stratification, that is to say, of the actual, measurable degree of formal rectification of structural inequalities pertaining to the economic, educational, and political inclusion of minority-group members. The excesses in this regard have reached the point where this has become the standard of choice for assessing the progress made by multiethnic societies towards interethnic integration and equality. Yet, it seems clear that in dealing with this issue, particularly in comparative context, if one is to

6

judge the modernization of multiethnic societies by the strides made by these societies towards the reduction of formal inequality between the hegemonic and subaltern ethnic components of the population, and this type of progress still does not translate into the disappearance of the "ethnic problem" - that is, if it still fails to weed out deep-rooted interethnic divisions and animosities - then we ought to be searching elsewhere for additional insights into how and why this problem is being perpetuated. It is argued here that reducing the investigation of cultural/intergroup processes and aspects to quantitative cross-sectional studies with time as an index variable (Abbott, 1991:205), or to the discourse of political economy, will substantially limit the understanding of the interethnic dynamics, and that greater heuristic benefits concerning this part of social life may be had if the focus is shifted to the domain of culture, that is to say, to qualitative aspect of the problem.

Culture as analytical frame of reference

The view of culture adopted in the present work is generally compatible with standard treatments, from the earliest conceptions by the 19th century British anthropologists (Tylor, 1871, in particular) to the subsequent formulations by the American anthropologists in the first half of the present century (e.g., Wissler, 1923; Cooley, Angell, and Carr, 1933; Lowie, 1934; Kroeber and Parsons, 1958; Kluckhohn, 1962), among whom the definitions of culture put forward by their British predecessors had gained wide acceptance. All of these conceptions tend to be amply comprehensive in meaning, subsuming under the rubric of "culture" all material and nonmaterial elements of society, "all modes of life," in the words of one writer (Azevedo, 1971:2), "the entire social heritage of man," in the words of another (Malefijt, 1968:3). To cite some examples: Wissler (1923:1-3, 49) saw culture as "... this round of life in its entire sweep of individual activities," including all the objective manifestations such as artifacts and collective forms of behavior, methods of securing the material necessities of life, as well as a core of ideas and beliefs. These "in the aggregate" form the total culture complex of the group, although Wissler did see the ideational aspects of culture as the "unifying element, in the culture-complex." Herskovits's definition (1966:305-6), though maintaining the separation of "culture" from the "raw materials ... from which it derives," treats the concept broadly, as "all the elements in man's mature endowment that he has acquired from his group by conscious learning or by a conditioning process--techniques of various kinds, social and other institutions, beliefs, and patterned modes of conduct."

This study has two parts, a descriptive one, where two models of culture and interethnic relations are ideal-typically contrasted, and an explicative one, where this crossnational difference is accounted for in terms of the influence of the dominant religious ideology. Although the present analysis is generally compatible with the inclusive meaning of culture found in these earlier anthropological viewpoints, there is a twofold intent here, which is, first, to distinguish the elements conventionally understood as "cultural," that is, those which are expressive of, and more directly tied to, social relationships, from those associated with the means and relations of production, or, more broadly, with the material framework of the society and its technology.[4] Secondly, to direct attention to the role of nonmaterial (i.e., symbolic) factors and to explore their heuristic potential. This concern with the explanatory value of the nonmaterial elements of culture is especially pertinent to part II of this work, which deals with historical explanation. The symbolic material involved here has been referred to as "representative culture" (Tenbruck, 1989:22), and comprises beliefs, understandings, images, ideas, and ideologies. Another writer views "the cultural" as pertaining to "issues of ritual and symbol, belief and ideology, [and] meaning and moral order" (Wuthnow, 1987:3). This emphasis on the symbolic, ideational, and representational dimensions of cultural life is also found in Geertz's conception of culture as a symbolic system (1973, 1987), "an ordered system of meaning and symbols in terms of which social interaction takes place" (1973:144, 363). Overall, the ideational view of culture has the advantage, according to Mayntz (1922:219-220), of affording greater flexibility in terms of allowing the concept of culture to be formulated and circumscribed in different ways. In the context of this investigation, this ties in with the analysis of religious ideology and symbolism as the principal cultural force shaping the character of social and individual life as a whole, therefore shaping interethnic practices.

This study also takes into account current debates on the persistently ambiguous nature of the concepts of "society" and "culture," and acknowledges the problematic character of the assumption, common in mainstream social science (sociology, in particular), that society and culture are rigidly separate unitary totalities. Nevertheless, without denying the existence of problems of terminological specification, or treating culture and society as mutually exclusive entities, proper and specific attention to the aspect of culture remains indispensable, a "crucial requisite" (Tenbruck, 1989:16), in social inquiry, if we are to probe the dynamics of social life for its fullest significance. We have only to remind ourselves of the concern and active research involvement of the founders of the sociological discipline - Marx, Weber, Durkheim - and

8

other scholars who have followed in their footsteps, with problems of culture, and their recognition of the relevance of these problems for social investigation (see Wuthnow, 1987:1). The focus on culture has the effect of counteracting the widespread tendency to assess the reality of human collective life exclusively in terms of formal processes and arrangements, or, as one observer (Tenbruck, 1989:16) has stated it, the tendency to equate "social change narrowly with objective alterations."

We may consider at this juncture a distinction between two basic approaches to the study of culture, the "structural" and the "hermeneutical" (Eisenstadt, 1989:5-11). The first is the mode of analysis endorsed by structural anthropologists and structural linguists (e.g., Levi-Strauss, 1963, 1979; Lacan, 1977), who assume that the rules and tendencies which regulate social interaction are derivable from the structure(s) of the human mind. In other words, they assume that the meaning of cultural action is naturalistically grounded. The second approach, which is favored here, is the predominant mode of analysis among symbolic anthropologists (Schneider, 1968; Geertz, 1973) and symbolic interactionists in sociology, whose point of departure is the primacy of meaning in the understanding of social life, and its origin in a context of intersubjectivity in which individuals collectively and actively interpret their world of experience and then "negotiate" so as to make their understandings of this world a property of the community. In this perspective, cultural meaning is not conceived as a set of invariant, decontextualized, interconnected rules from which individuals produce specific behaviors in order to adjust to given social situations, but in terms of its manifestation in the concrete networks of social interests, practices and arrangements (Eisenstadt, 1989).

The focus on meaning in cultural analysis gains further validation from a recent assessment of developments in the sociology of culture (Griswold, 1992). In that account, the events and trends of this subarea of sociological inquiry are examined in reference to the conceptual coordinates of meaning, power, hegemony, and action, which will also be used here as guiding points to develop the analysis. The issue of meaning in particular, we are informed (1992:324), continues to animate the discourse in cultural sociology, as evidenced by its centrality in much of the work done in this area in recent years. Meaning is a key prerequisite for social order, insofar as it is only in a context of intelligibility, that is, of shared understandings, that social actors are able to identify, and then abide by, the requirements of the normative system. In this context, meaning is a crucial consideration regarding the aspects of intelligibility and normativity in social life (Swanson, 1992), as it is directly involved in the regularization and stabilization of social and institutional practices.

I hope to demonstrate this very point in chapters 6 through 8, that is, the vital function of meaning in the creation, stabilization, and maintenance of particular networks of institutional and social practices. The primary intent behind this effort is to show how ways of thinking derived from the dominant religious faith, and deeply internalized in the collective consciousness, have a continuous shaping influence on social conduct, even if this influence is no longer detected as having originated in religious principle. The enduring heuristic value of meaning in social inquiry may be seen in the ascendance of "hermeneutical" approaches in cultural studies (Eisenstadt, 1989:8; Griswold, 1992:324).

The emphasis on the cultural meaning of the various aspects of empirical reality functions as a safeguard against the "naturalistic fallacy," the long-standing and still revered procedure of restricting the assessment of social situations to the tracing of their empirical, more readily apprehendable contours. The results typically obtained from this analytical procedure may be directly disconfirmed by an alternative approach that goes beyond the immediately manifest configuration of social phenomena, and shows keener sensitivity to other, less concrete, less technical aspects that emerge from the meaning-contexts where these phenomena are embedded. By avoiding this common tendency to impart a kind of meta-physical permanence and, shall we say, sacredness, to the empiricity of phenomena, a culturally-informed account that relies on the explanation of the *meaning* of these phenomena comes closer to providing a truer *social* explanation of the problem under study. Thus, as regards ethnic relations, there is much about these relations that may escape the investigation if the latter is restricted solely, as is so often the case, to empirical strategies, or to formal typologies and conceptual schemes; if it lapses, in other words, into the excesses of empiricist and/or rationalistic analysis. I have already drawn attention to the sterility of indiscriminate, unduly formalistic (hence, overgeneralizing) applications of traditional ethnic-racial taxonomic categories (e.g., "minority group," "ethnic minority," "minority identity," "dominant-minority relations", and so on) across different multiethnic contexts. (Instructive in this regard: Frazier's 1944 research on race relations in the multiethnic setting of Brazil, where he discussed the fact that, because of the relative absence of a "consciousness of racial differences" in the country and other related aspects, one could not, "in a certain sense...properly speak of race relations in Brazil" - 1944:255). I have also stressed how the accounts of sociologists and other practitioners in the human sciences have generally been vitiated by this excessive formalism and/or naturalism. Finally, I have pointed to the greater fruitfulness of alternative methodologies, particularly those that focus on the symbolism underlying the manifold aspects of collective behavior. Although methodologies geared to the discovery of the meaning of social things run the risk of being characterized as catering to conservative ideological positions, which would render them unsuitable for illuminating and denouncing the workings of power inequality between dominant and minority social groups, this kind of characterization typically reflects a misconception of the issue because a politically-informed critique of social situations can be accomplished quite effectively, and in some ways more incisively, by reference to the symbolic components of these situations, without necessarily relinquishing the focus on the empirical. The culturalist explanation of the workings of intergroup political life may be justified on the grounds that the political behavior of individuals is deeply rooted in *experience*, and thus not only in *existence* (to use Marx's words), and is therefore suffused with meaning (see Geertz, 1973; also, Alexander, in Munch and Smelser, 1992:293-323). Yet, there are important counterarguments, such as for example, Wuthnow's (1987), whose critique of "neoclassical approaches" problematizes the whole issue of meaning, and in fact advocates the transcendence of "meaning" itself. In that critique, it is argued that when interpretive sociologists emphasize meaning, what is being referred to is not meaning as such, but "discourses about meanings." What then is proposed in lieu of the conventional preoccupation with the "meaning" of phenomena is that the effort be directed towards establishing their "significance" (1987:60). The idea of significance here is meant to denote the intelligibility of the phenomenon under study, which is revealed by placing it in a "clear interpretive framework." This requires the identification of its origin, function, and effect(s) in the larger social, economic, and political context where it appears. The following may be offered in the way of a very brief and preliminary critical review of Wuthnow's position. His rejection of the focus on meaning in cultural analysis, in the context of this semantic distinction between "meaning" and "significance," needs to be qualified in some respects. First of all, it must be noted that his reservations regarding the reliance on "meaning" *do* bring to the fore the issue of *the meaning of meaning*, that is, of how exactly the term is being used. The duality introduced in his discussion (1987:65) between aspects of human life that are collectively shared (i.e., "discourse and behavior") and those which cannot be collectively shared (i.e., meaning) due to being grounded in the individual consciousness, is not entirely tenable, simply because private meanings--at least as I understand them--emanate from shared, collectively "negotiated," understandings; hence, they are social in nature. Weber clearly establishes the social genesis of meaning when he stresses that the meanings individuals rely upon to function in society are not, as

11

one observer (Lindbekk, 1992:289) put it, "isolated pictures in people's minds," but belong instead to meaning-complexes (*sinnzusammenhangen*). It is from the wider context of meaning-complexes that the contents of individual consciousness acquire their subjectively-intended meaning. Furthermore, the analysis of discourse and behavior in isolation from "meaning" seems to push aside the fact that social practices and social discourses are concrete articulations of underlying ways of thinking, and that these ways of thinking are in turn maintained by the corresponding networks of practices and discourses. The idea of a relationship of mutuality between meaning and social structure should discourage the assumption that the focus on meaning is inevitably linked to psychologism, or to a radical subjectivism of the Kantian or Husserlian variety, where the world is construed purely from the point of view of individual consciousness, and where, in the context of research, the researcher embarks on what might be called an endless unveiling of subjectivities. The latter procedure would involve the exploration of the personal understandings and motivations of the main participants in a given social situation--for instance, the attempt to establish the intentionality and motivation of the main figures involved in the *Bauhaus* movement - without taking consideration of the sociohistorical milieu of early 1900s Germany. The present investigation prioritizes the meaning of cultural action as the indispensable analytical framework that makes possible the more effective explication of the interplay of culture and social structure. Thus, the intent is to situate meaning historically and socially, to place it in the context of (to use Geertz's words) "the political, economic, stratificatory realities within which men are everywhere contained" (1973:30). The crucial requirement in this connection, it seems, is not to let the analysis lapse into the reductionist linearity of radically subjectivist, economicist, or formalist explanations. The "trick" is to pursue the more dialectical route of explicating the phenomenon in terms of a part-whole relationship, which involves the constant analytical *va-et-vient* between "subjective" concepts, that is, those drawn from the experience of the social actors, those that pertain to their turn of mind (a kind of "getting into the actors' skin"); and "objective" concepts, that is, those that come from preconceived analytical frameworks, those which the researcher retrieves from her/his conceptual *armamentarium*. In other words, what is at work here is a process, an oscillation, between what Geertz called, in the context of ethnographic description, "the most local of local detail and the most global of global structure" (1987:145). The "objective" type of concept, drawn from pre-established templates, is linked to the researcher's apprehension of the phenomenon within a totality. This is a more synchronic procedure. The "subjective" type of concept reveals the diachronicity or historical particularity of the phenomenon. The effort to proceed along the lines of confluence and tension of these two dimensions protects the analyst from embarking on a purely subjectivist analysis, on the one hand, or a purely formalist one, on the other.

As for power and hegemony, these may be taken up together as interrelated aspects that bear importantly on this analysis with respect to the linkage between the cultural and social factors. It is important to stress here that cultural factors are intimately bound up with the workings of social power, in the specific sense that they exercise a direct influence on patterns of social stratification. This means that cultural processes and aspects are effectively able to create and sustain social distinctions, a viewpoint that counters the notion that culture is basically a reflection of these distinctions. The Foucauldian conception of power (e.g., 1966; also see Sheridan, 1982) as a phenomenon that is neither binarily exercised (i.e., attached to the interests of some dominant class over those of a subordinate class), nor flows from any single, centralized, institutional source, but is, instead, realized as "discursive practices" in a multiplicity of microcontexts throughout the entire network of interpersonal relations, is only of tangential interest here, because the present discussion is aligned with the more conventional view of power as being related to group (though not necessarily group *qua* economic class) interest. Thus, it connects more directly with the issue of whether culture exercises a binding effect on society independently of the latter's material development, and a shaping effect on arrangements of inequality, or whether economic and political interests dictate the contours of the cultural system. The main thesis defended in this study is that "culture" exerts a shaping and sustaining effect on the general framework of social action, hence, on the specific sphere of interethnic relations and stratification. This concerns a process whereby the dominant religious ideology of the society plays a central role in what Weber (1958:91) called the "qualitative formation and quantitative expansion" of a particular worldview, which in turn, as the overarching cultural force of the society, gives rise to broader socio-cultural formations, including particular modes of interethnic life, in the case of pluralist social systems (these interethnic formations will be examined here in terms of their cultural, psychosocial, and biological components). Lastly, since interethnic patterns are everywhere characterized by varying degrees of dominant/minority inequality of power and wealth, cultural factors may be seen here as bearing heavily and directly on this political and economic asymmetry between social groups. This position is in agreement with that of Munch's (1994:34) as pertaining to the point that the effects of social power are limited (hence, directly affected and circumscribed) by "traditional belief prevailing in society."

Another standpoint from which the discourse on culture may be addressed is in terms of its relation to social action, focusing specifically on the problematic of (minority-group) identity formation and its attendant political implications (see Griswold, 1992:325-6). In a later chapter, I shall probe the manner in which the type of cultural identity developed and worn by individuals is not only an indicator of the nature of the society's cultural system, but also a mechanism that is directly related to the maintenance of patterns of intergroup division and inequality. I will be considering, therefore, the ways in which the broader cultural system determines the type of cultural identification exercised by minority-group members, and what implications this has for their standing in the social hierarchy.

Several writers have noted the fact that cultural and material structures interact in a flexible, dynamic, and relational manner (see, e.g., Williams, 1958; Bosi, 1993), and not in terms of unilateral determinisms, as manifested, for instance, in the more orthodox readings of historical materialism, or philosophical idealism. Material arrangements and processes are therefore treated as concrete externalizations of ways of thinking, while, concomitantly, the meaningfulness of cultural or symbolic elements is understood in terms of their materiality. This means specifically that the meaningfulness of these elements is assumed to emerge only in the context of their embodiment in particular historico-material contexts. Bakhtin makes this point in his Marxist, nonsubjectivistic interpretation of ideological meaning. "It is true," he writes (1978:7), "that [cultural-ideological products] are things of a special nature, having significance, meaning, inner value. But the meanings and values are embodied in material things and actions. They cannot be realized outside of some developed material." Bakhtin's analysis underscores the mediative function of what he calls the "ideological environment," referring to "the realized, materialized, externally expressed social consciousness of a given collective" (1978:14) in the relationship between the world of materiality and the world of social action, or, stated differently, between the economic base of society and the practices of the collectivity. This ideological environment comprises written and spoken language, cultural symbols of all kinds, objects of art, networks of beliefs and values. In a parallel vein, Alfredo Bosi (1993) lays stress on the interplay of material and nonmaterial factors as being the main aspect in the phenomenon of colonization. "Colonization," Bosi states (1993:377), "is a process at once material and symbolic: the economic practices of its agents are tied to their ways of surviving, to

14

their [collective] memory, to their modes of self-representation and representation of others, in short, to their aspirations and hopes. Stated differently: there is no colonial condition without the interrelation of [the structures of] work, beliefs, ideologies, and cultures" (my translation).

As for the present study, its acknowledgement of the interrelation of material and nonmaterial factors is not intended to obscure its effort to direct attention to the special role of cultural forces, and to the autonomous way(s) in which they shape the nature and course of collective action. Although rooted in the material framework of society, systems of ideas may also come to insulate themselves against the impact of material forces, and to follow independent lines of development, while at the same time influencing the material context, and giving rise to new social formations. In this sense, the interpretive position defended here is similar to Bakhtin's, in the sense of acknowledging the interrelation of cultural and material factors, and the mediative role of ideology in the production of social behavior. But, the present analysis goes on, and does not stop, as does Bakhtin's, with the attribution of a mediative function to ideological forces (i.e., to the "ideological environment"), in the larger context of the causal relation between existence (i.e., material or economic existence), as manifested in the human involvement with the economic mode of production, and experience (i.e., the patterns of social conduct), while stressing, a la Marx, the role of existence as the principal causal factor in social life (see also Wuthnow, in Munch and Smelser, 1992:158-70). Thus, while not expressing a cruder form of Marxist orthodoxy in his interpretive approach, Bakhtin clearly leans on dialectical materialism as a basis for synthesizing the project of the idealist (neo-Kantian) philosophy of culture, with its universalizing, generalizing thrust, and the project of positivistic social science, with its empirical, atomized cataloging of unconnected facts. As he puts it, "[t]he desired synthesis of philosophical world view and the concrete historical study of specific phenomena of art, science, ethics, religion, etc., is only possible on the basis of the solid principles of dialectical materialism" (1978:6). In this approach, meaning, which is embodied in the elements that make up the ideological environment, is treated as a self-contained totality, with its own internal structure and unity, standing apart from consciousness, and between consciousness and the material world. He says that "... for each given collective in each given epoch of its historical development this environment is a unique and complete concrete whole, uniting science, art, ethics, and other ideologies in a living and immediate synthesis" (1978:14). Fundamentally, then, it is the historically-conditioned and materially-determined ideological environment that has temporal priority over the acts and products of consciousness, and which imposes (an economically conditioned) uniformity on the character of ideational (symbolic) elements. Consciousness, in this perspective, does not apprehend the world of experience directly and/or autonomously, but only mediatively, through the ideological environment. In the final analysis, his Marxist position is asserted, in the sense that despite his recognition of the irreducibility of "ideological material" to economic production (1978:10), economic structures and praxis remain the chief determinant of the character of the cultural world, at which point the collective cultural formations determine individual consciousness and meaning. The investigative mode adopted here is at variance with these ideas, insofar as it does not assign a subordinate status to ideas and meanings vis-a-vis the material base of society, but stresses instead that, although originating in the world of action, culture also restrains and directs the conduct of individuals.

The linkage between ideas of culture and ideas of race

The intent here is to clarify more systematically the rationale for focusing on culture and using this concept epistemologically so as to gain greater insight into the nature of interethnic and interracial relations. We may begin by reiterating a principle that has become quite axiomatic in the social-scientific community, among anthropologists in particular, namely, that race is a notion to be understood not so much in the context of the discourse of biology as in the discourse of culture. Seen in this light, the idea of race loses its fixed and absolute character, and becomes culturally and historically specific. This aspect may be instantiated in the fact that the 19th-century Irish immigrants in the United States were perceived and treated as a separate (and inferior) *racial* community. In fact, they brought this stigma with them, from the British Isles. Certain Southern and Eastern European groups (e.g., Italians, Hungarians) had the same experience. However, by the early decades of the present century, social and political relations between the ruling English-American group and these minorities had changed sufficiently to cause the latter to lose their racial distinctiveness and be absorbed concretely as well as symbolically into the mainstream (i.e., "white") population. Considering this social and cultural (hence, fluid and variable) constitution of race and of the interracial sphere, it is to the cultural framework of this problem, not to the biological, that we ought to be turning our attention, as crossnational comparisons of ethnic/racial relations cogently demonstrate.

At the same time, in societies such as the United States where a pattern of separatism, derived from the racially bipolar organization of social life,

16

has been consistently maintained in custom as well as in the law from the earliest colonial times to about three decades ago, matters are quite different. The opposite principle, in effect, obtains: now it is precisely in reference to biology, *as construed socially*, that the dynamics of culture is to be grasped. In this context, social groups are marginalized and confined to minority status chiefly on the basis of racial factors. A further ramification of this biracially-produced separatism is that the basic conceptual distinction between race and culture breaks down. Whereas, strictly speaking, the one (i.e., race) denotes biological or genetic variations among human groups, and the other (i.e., culture) denotes variations among these groups regarding their way of life (which explains why cultures may take different forms within the same large-scale racial population - consider, for instance, the cultural variations among the Sudanese peoples of Northwest Africa), in actuality these two elements are equated with each other, and therefore treated synonymously. Moreover, culture is subsumed under race, so that cultural traditions and patterns are seen as derived not from the particular experiences, past and present, of human populations, but from their particular racial background as "social races." This means, then, that culture is treated as intrinsic and exclusive to each (socially construed) racial population.

This causal linkage between race and culture has always been taken for granted in the American setting, most strikingly, as one would expect, by those who do not know any better, namely, the general public, who remain mired in endless misconceptions about the relationship between these elements. But those who should know better - say, academics - are not entirely immune to this tendency either, which is not surprising when one considers the profound impact that three centuries of race-based cultural segregation have had on the society's understandings of race, ethnicity, and culture. Gates writes in this regard (1997:194), commenting on the rather common tendency of members of the white and nonwhite communities alike in American society to assume (an assumption directly in keeping with the larger attribution of culture to racial origin) that the dialectal peculiarities of speech exhibited by African-Americans stem directly from their racial background, and that the anatomical features bestowed on them by this racial background (in connection with this, the distinctive shape of lips) impair their ability to speak English in the way that whites do, and vice-versa. This is absurd, of course. There is surely an element of difficulty surrounding the attempt of groups that have been culturally segregated for centuries to reproduce each other's linguistic patterns perfectly, and this difficulty is also physical in nature since it involves the operation of the vocal cords, tongue, lips, and so forth, but this simply reveals the effect of social training, not of some essential,

17

biologically predetermined condition. At birth, the individual's phonetic apparatus is "raw material," ready to be molded and adapted to any set of articulatory challenges presented by the society's language system. The social conditioning of the physical structures of speech is so forceful and systematic as to make it seem that the difficulty experienced by adult members of a group when they attempt to learn the language of another is somehow genetic in nature. At the adult stage, even when that goal is accomplished, in most instances the person will retain an accent. Thus, for example, the characteristic pronunciation of the "r" by speakers of American-English, and of other consonants such as "d" and "t" by speakers of English in general, invariably yields an accented reproduction of these same sounds in Latin languages like Portuguese or Italian. Or, to take another example, the absence of the "z" sound in Spanish necessarily transforming that sound into a sibilant "s" when it rolls off the tongues of native speakers of Spanish.

When structural and cultural separatism is systematically imposed on ethnic-racial minorities over a long period of time, these groups are forced to forge an indigenous culture, which signifies a new set of coherent cultural responses to the social environment where they find themselves, to the particular intercultural and interethnic challenges which they face. These considerations apply most forcefully to the historical experience of African-Americans in the U.S.: on the one hand, their cultural links with the ancestral homeland were suppressed from their earliest years as slaves in this society, and therefore, unlike other African-American communities in the New World (e.g., those of Cuba, Puerto Rico, or Brazil), they were unable to retain direct continuities with the West African cultural matrix. On the other hand, they were also denied full admission into the mainstream ways of life, which accounts for their modifications (e.g., linguistic) of mainstream cultural forms. To the extent that these subcultural patterns remain a consequence of their long-standing social and cultural marginalization, they stand as the hallmark of this marginalization.

In any given pluralist society, the dominant patterns of culture will afford insights into the manner in which that society has handled the incorporation of its formative groups. Thus, these aspects of culture serve as valuable indices of the degree of inclusion or exclusion of ethnic and racial groups. In other words, the formal processes of incorporation of these groups, such as the extension of civil rights to ethnic-racial minorities (i.e., the actualization of these rights and liberties), will be significantly affected by the type of framework of dominant-minority cultural relations enforced by the society. That this is so, as I hope to

demonstrate in this study, gives indication of the fruitfulness of a culturalist focus for the analysis of interethnic/interracial life.

The idea of culture is thematized here specifically in terms of a tripartite
model comprising interrelated aspects, or "moments," of the larger
assimilative process. The first aspect concerns cultural assimilation, or the
cultural interaction between the dominant and the minority ethnic groups,
and more specifically, the degree to which minority cultural strains are
incorporated syncretistically and dialectically into, or kept marginalized
from, the hegemonic cultural system. The second aspect concerns
biological assimilation, or the societal treatment of intermarriage and
amalgamation between the dominant and minority ethnic groups,
specifically when the latter are also racial minorities. The third aspect
concerns psychosocial assimilation, or the degree of subnational
consciousness and identification on the part of ethnic and racial minorities,
that is to say, the nature of the cultural identity that these groups will
assume in relation to the larger society.

The analysis will be based, furthermore, on an ideal-typical contrast of
"integrationist" and "separatist" types of cultural systems, using Brazil and
the United States as selected examples. Intergroup relations will be
examined in reference to the conceptual treatment of the assimilative
process formulated here. From this standpoint, a given multiethnic society
will be categorized as having either an integrationist or a separatist
cultural structure. Regarding the former type, it entails a basic
assimilationist orientation, animated by large-scale syncretism and
interpenetration of the various ethno-cultural streams of the society,
whereas for the latter type the outstanding pattern is the juxtaposition of
the hegemonic cultural tradition and the minority ones, together with a
compartmentalization of these traditions. Cultural separatism mandates that
minority cultural orientations linked to incoming groups deemed
assimilable be quickly and effectively suppressed, and that their remnants
be dissolved into the majority culture. As for the cultural traditions
associated with minority groups deemed non-assimilable - or, at least,
only partially assimilable owing to considerations of race (i.e., these
would be essentially the groups perceived and classified as nonwhite),
these are to be suppressed in the same manner, which does not mean
however that these groups will be necessarily absorbed into the cultural
mainstream. This situation clearly bespeaks a dual pattern of assimilation,
which is consistent with a biracial management of intergroup relations. Be
that as it may, in both cases - that is, of both the groups classified and
treated as white, and those classified and treated as nonwhite - the
minority cultural communities are barred from making a fundamental

contribution to the dominant cultural system in terms of a reciprocal process of exchange (see, e.g., Gordon, 1964:109).

The process of syncretism will be addressed more systematically later, so for the moment a few brief considerations shall suffice. It consists of the intermixture or interfusion of diverse (dominant and minority) cultural elements ("disparate objects", Bastide, 1971:155), a relationship of which the end result is a new "cultural physiognomy" (Valente, 1976:11). Syncretism has a dialectical basis, insofar as the diverse cultural materials or traditions involved have a relation of tension, which makes for the preservation of the uniqueness of the original traits, and concomitantly, a relation of attraction, which brings them together. There is a twofold aspect here, therefore, meaning that these elements coalesce into a new cultural product while their original identities remain identifiable, in a type of coexistence based on the dynamic equilibrium of the parts. This is what Bastide refers to as "mosaic syncretism," citing the Brazilian religious context as an example. The syncretic situation also acts as a deterrent to the more radical impulses (that would normally be a feature of the integrationist model of culture) towards the unilateral annexation of minority cultural communities, and to the requirement that the latter be totally subsumed under the dominant culture. Through syncretism assimilation proceeds on the basis of greater exchange and reciprocity between the dominant and minority cultural groups. Park and Burgess have described this conception of assimilation as "a process of interpenetration and fusion in which persons and groups acquire the memories, sentiments, and attitudes of other persons and groups, and, by sharing their experience and history, are incorporated with them in a common cultural life" (1969:735-6; also, 509-10, 663-5). These points will be taken up more fully in chapter III.

The segmentation or compartmentalization of cultural communities that is promoted by the separatist model of cultural relations, on the other hand, expresses a situation in which the original distinctiveness of the groups is maintained. These cultural communities coexist side by side, with minimal, if any, interfusion of cultural traits. The dominant culture largely exercises tolerance towards the minority communities, unless their cultural expressions are asserted in such a degree or manner as to pose a challenge to the former's hegemonic status. This attitude of tolerance, which is woven into the operation of cultural separatism, is not, however, associated with a willingness to share, accept, or intermix with the minority cultural patterns to any great degree (see Cole and Cole, 1954:148, in this regard). The ideal-typical formulation of the separatist principle may be seen, for instance, in Kallen's model of pluralism (1970), with its emphasis on the idea of a "federation or commonwealth

20

of national culture," whereby the various ethnic-cultural groups function independently, in terms of their ability to maintain a degree of continuity with the ancestral culture, while being commonly united only by a political state and citizenship status. This needs to be understood while taking into account the essential double standard of dominant-minority cultural relations in U.S. society. As already noted, the operation of separatism is related specifically to the relationship between the dominant ethnocultural community and those that are permanently designated as minority cultural groups, on the basis of some ascriptive factor ("race", in this case). The other incoming ethnic contingents that are not designated as such are afforded the possibility of full-range assimilation in the future. In effect, the core culture in this model of assimilation normally achieves its uniformity by imposing itself on these communities, from the earliest stages of contact, in a very draconian, unilateral, and thoroughgoing fashion, aiming at their swift and complete absorption, and greatly inhibiting impulses of syncretistic exchange and interfusion. The cultural model of U.S. society illustrates this pattern, which has been called by some writers the "Anglo-conformity" model of assimilation (Cole and Cole, 1954; Gordon, 1964). The historical evidence suggests, says Gordon (1964:89) that this has been "the most prevalent ideology of assimilation in America throughout the nation's history."

Integrationist cultural systems also exhibit a high level of biological assimilation of ethnic minorities, while separatist systems do not. This means that the former will be historically marked by extensive intermixture and intermarriage between the dominant ethnic population and the various ethnic minorities, while the latter will erect the barriers of the law and social custom against this practice, causing it to appear in markedly lower levels. Finally, in integrationist cultural systems, the psychological assimilation of ethnic minorities is high, which means that their degree of group consciousness is very low. As a rule, these individuals place their national membership (citizenship) before their racial classification. In separatist cultural systems, in contradistinction, the psychological assimilation of minority-group members tends to be low, which means that their ethnic-racial consciousness is very high. They see themselves, first and foremost, in terms of their subcultural membership.

The aims of this investigation may be reiterated as follows:

(a) to demonstrate that the dynamics of intergroup life and inequality extends beyond the strictly formal (economic, political, educational) dimensions of social life, and that, consequently, a fuller understanding of dominant/minority patterns of ethnic relations cannot be attained solely by reference to these aspects.

(b) to explore, alternatively, the element of culture as a conceptual tool for further elucidating the interethnic problematic. The heuristic returns here can be substantial, both in the general sense and as relates to the more specific aspect of interethnic stratification, when we consider that cultural structures not only tend to endure beyond the occurrence of material change, but also to infiltrate the workings of social institutions, with direct consequences for the distribution of resources among social groups. In this regard, the general course of this analysis resonates the Hegelian conception of the dialectical evolution of culture unfolding in accordance with its own laws and exerting a shaping influence on social structure, and the corollary tendency of social arrangements and practices to reflect faithfully the patterns of operation of regulative Reason (i.e., Reason understood as the prevailing norms and values), to move "towards a closer consistency with moral ideas" (Munch, 1994:61).[5]

(c) to formulate ideal-typical models of the processes and tendencies involved in the interaction between dominant and minority ethnic groups in the sphere of culture, and to orient the discussion towards the contrast of selected societies (Brazil and the United States) as examples.

(d) to assess the causal contribution of the dominant religious ideology in the production and reproduction of sociocultural formations. This assessment will not be directly geared to the explicit influence of religion on modern life and on patterns of collective conduct, but to its role as an implicit normative system. In this connection, the analysis re-examines conventional views regarding the secularization or "disenchantment" of the world.

Notes

1   Regarding this trend in the educational sphere, a recent report indicates how "[a] four-decade effort [at integration] is being abandoned as exhausted courts and frustrated blacks dust off the concept of separate but equal." (*Time*, April 29, 1996, pp.39-45).

2   Research in the early 1990s showed a sizable increase, within a three-year period (from 1988 to 1991) in the percentage of people who chose to be called "African-American" instead of "Black" (*Time*, May 20, 1991, p.15).

3   Some critics (e.g., Elkins, 1976:229) have in fact asserted the heuristic sterility of this investigative position, to the effect that, while the focus on the crosscultural distinctions of a given phenomenon

tends to enlarge the researcher's field of vision and understanding, the focus on uniformity leaves things pretty much as they were in the beginning of the investigation. There is an investment of time and effort only to end up in the realization that, in a sense,"there is nothing new under the sun. "

4   On the autonomous and nonderivative conception of culture in the context of a critique of Pierre Bourdieu's homological view of the relationship between culture and social structure, see LiPuma, 1993:14-33; see also Herskovits, 1966:ch.7. Two other examples are also worth considering here. First, the consideration of how "culture" has been seen to resist "social structure" in the urban context. Some sociologists (e.g., Gans, 1962; Suttles, 1968) have observed the remarkable resilience and dynamic quality of the "community" (*gemeinschaft*) way of life in certain neighborhoods of cities like Boston and Chicago, vis-a-vis the larger, relentlessly homogenizing pressures of urbanization. In the same vein, Daniel Bluestone's study of the architectural history of Chicago (1991) cogently demonstrates the dominant role of cultural factors (primarily, the role of a class-related urban conception and aesthetics) in the definition of the pattern of urban development of that city, a process where the forces of capital were, essentially, only a mediating variable.

5   The importance of cultural forces in social evolution is apparently acknowledged even in traditional materialist interpretations of history. At the very least, there appears to be a sensitivity to the complexity and difficulty of determining the exact nature of causal relations in the unfolding of history, as with the delineation of the interaction between economic ("structural") and noneconomic ("superstructural") variables. Marx himself uses language in the Preface to his *Critique of Political Economy* that is somewhat qualifying, in terms of "the mode of production in material life [determining] the *general* character... [of culture]," and "the entire immense superstructure [being] *more or less* rapidly transformed" by change in the economic foundation of society (Marx, as cited in Williams, 1958:266; emphasis added). This awareness of the role of nonmaterial forces in social life, while maintaining the emphasis on the principle of socio-structural development being the "master process" of history, is clearly expressed in a comment by Engels in a correspondence from 1890:

"According to the materialist conception of history, the determining element in history is *ultimately* the production and reproduction in real life. More than this neither Marx nor I have ever asserted. If therefore somebody twists this into the statement that the economic element is the *only* determining one, he transforms it into a meaningless, abstract and absurd phrase. The economic situation is the basis, but the various elements of the superstructure - political forms of the class struggle and its consequences ... and then even the reflexes of all these actual struggles in the brains of the combatants: political,legal, and philosophical theories, religious ideas and their further development into systems of dogma - also exercise their influence upon the course of the historical struggles and in many cases preponderate in determining their *form*. There is an interaction of all these elements, in which, amid all the endless host of accidents (i.e., of things and events whose inner connection is so remote or so impossible to prove that we regard it as absent and can neglect it) the economic element finally asserts itself as necessary" (Engels, letter to J.Bloch, 21 September 1890, in *Marx and Engels, Selected Correspondence*, p.998; emphasis added).

2 Culture and ethnicity: A crossnational contrast

Systems of ethnic stratification in the American hemisphere display certain basic characteristics that lend them a uniform character across different multiethnic societies. Foremost among these is the high concentration of members of the original European settler group, that is, the dominant ethnic group, in the most privileged social, educational, economic, and political statuses, concomitantly with the underrepresentation of the ethnic minorities - primarily individuals of African and Amerindian extraction, but also including those from non-European groups that arrived later - in these more favorable conditions.[1] This pattern of socioeconomic and political inequality translates concretely into the more limited access of ethnic minorities to the basic social resources, that is, to the workplace, housing, health care, education; also, to legal justice, property ownership, and bureaucratic power. Because this material dimension of intergroup inequality is more immediate and readily intelligible, it becomes that which is invariably relied upon as the basis for scholarly as well as lay appraisals and comparisons of the interethnic problem. As noted in the preceding chapter, the prevalent approach in the last couple of decades, as for instance in the "revisionist" literature on slavery and race relations (e.g., Davis, 1966; Degler, 1971; Pescatello, 1975; Conrad, 1983), has been to accept the uniformity of ethnic and racial oppression across different societies as a given, and to make little effort to account for the variance in the degree and manner in which this phenomenon is actually expressed in different cultural systems. The general tenor of conventional comparative analyses of the interethnic problem is that if the outward appearances of the different models of group relations are essentially the same - that is, if ethnic minorities, and people of African descent in particular, are everywhere victimized by the lingering presence of material arrangements of inequality and by ideological disparagement - then, things must be the same everywhere. Which is to say, there are really no differences worth making a big fuss about. This judgement is deplorably myopic and unjustified since it bypasses, or worse, steamrolls, important differences that *do* exist, and may in a sense be even more fundamental than the similarities.

In a well-known essay of some thirty years back, Nogueira (1959:166) warns against this tendency, saying that "[t]he recognition of the existence of prejudice against nonwhites in the Americas since colonial times does not imply ignorance of national and regional difference in various racial situations." These crossnational differences generally form the context which we refer to as "culture," and, because of their greater subtlety vis-a-vis the more concrete aspects of ethnic stratification, may escape the grasp of cursory analysis. However, the fact remains that, despite the systematic character of ethnic/racial discrimination and prejudice in hemispheric perspective, in association with different sets of historico-cultural influences in each society (e.g., the dominant religious tradition, the legal heritage, the racial ethos of the original settling group, the colonial pattern of settlement), these elements come to be expressed in terms of rather dissimilar intergroup configurations. It is necessary, therefore, to identify and explore these distinguishing features so as to establish a basis for effectively differentiating between interethnic models. This task will be undertaken here by means of a comparison of Brazil and the United States, societies which, as already suggested, bear strong resemblance to each other regarding a number of historical and structural circumstances, including their ethnic composition and developmental patterns. In this connection, Marger writes: "Both were originally colonized by Europeans who overwhelmed the indigenous population; both imported vast numbers of Africans who were the mainstays of an institutionalized slave system that lasted until the late nineteenth century, and both were peopled by immigrants from a variety of European societies" (1991:398-399). Regarding the population of African descent, it is true that in both societies generations of blacks have remained hindered in their capacity for social mobility by the legacy of slavery, "trapped in the culture of poverty," as one observer (Toplin, 1981:xxiii) put it, "and without easy access to economic opportunity." Additionally, in both societies they have been made the target of prejudicial evaluations and attitudes.

However, beyond the larger and more fundamental aspect of the existence of an ethnic hierarchy, shared by the two societies, insofar as other highly important interethnic considerations are concerned, Brazil and the United States have handled the diversity of their ethnic panorama in diametrically opposed ways. Indeed, this "administrative" difference is of such a magnitude as to call into question the assumption that the same concepts, definitions, and taxonomic frameworks of race and ethnicity can be automatically applied across different multiethnic milieux. My employment here of the term "ethnic minority" in crossnational context presupposes the need to problematize this practice. In connection with this, it has been stated (van den Berghe, 1978:xxvi) that ethnic minorities in Brazil do not exist in isolation from the sociocultural whole. The population of African descent, for example, has never constituted "a corporate group, with separate institutions." And some analysts have gone so far as to say that in a certain sense "one may not *properly* (my italics) speak of race relations in Brazil"(Frazier, 1944:255), and that "there are no racial groups" in that society (Harris, 1974:61). From this perspective, the terms "white" and "nonwhite" (or "white" and "black") are not really terms of "race," as might readily be assumed by observers from the United States. They relate more directly to *color*; the latter is therefore a more appropriate analytical category, inasmuch as greater emphasis is placed in Brazil on distinctions based on physical appearance than on those of racial origin, with the variety of types between the polar categories of "white" and "black" being accounted for. But, even color categories become problematic in the longer run because they are themselves "amorphous, tentative, and unstable ..."(Pierson, 1967:xxxii). In the final analysis, the criterion of color in turn comes to play less of a role in the determination of social position in Brazil than that of *class*, and the class-related factors of education, wealth, power, and interpersonal associations. Pierson points out that "[a] person may be 'genealogically black' since his ancestors came from Africa, and 'phenotypically black' by reason of his physical appearance, but also 'associationally white' by reason of his achievement of high social position and the predominantly white color of his associates, whose company he keeps by reason of that achievement" (1967:xxxii). More on this aspect later.

Starting with the most characteristic and readily perceivable aspect of ethnic stratification, we can begin to differentiate the two models in reference to the degree of operation of two very important and interrelated aspects, one structural, the other ideological. We have, on the one hand, what might be termed the administrative or bureaucratic management of intergroup life, expressed in the formalization and codification of arrangements and practices of race-based segregation and discrimination, and on the other hand, a national ethos of race-based institutional, cultural, and interpersonal segregation. These interrelated patterns may then be concretely manifested either in terms of a biracial system of intergroup relations, with the corresponding array of supporting structures, namely, the strict enforcement of interracial norms (such as the legal

27

prohibition of intercaste marriage) and the application of formal and informal punishments for their transgression; the operation of additional mechanisms of social control and intimidation of the subordinate group, such as various forms of physical violence, lynching, etc.; and sociostructural and cultural separatism. Or, alternatively, the societal administration of intergroup life may be carried out in terms of a multiracial model of intergroup relations, with greater recognition and tolerance of intercaste unions, the lack of a systematic enforcement of formal and informal processes of control of the subordinate ethnic group(s), and a dominant national tendency toward ethnic-cultural unification.

On the basis of this twofold schema of differentiation of the models of intergroup relations, involving the degree of formalization of action patterns (or legal explicitness of interracial rulings) together with the corresponding ideology, Brazilian society has historically lacked a formally-instituted system of race segregation and discrimination, and the extreme polarization and bitter antagonisms between the dominant and minority ethnic groups, as well as rigid separatism in all spheres of cultural life, in the mold of the codified separatism that remained in effect in the U.S. social system until about three decades ago. One analyst of this problem had this to say, some forty years ago, at the time when the Jim Crow period of legal segregation was drawing to a close in the United States: "It is fairly well known that Brazil has few of the egregious problems and flagrant earmarks of racist discrimination familiar in the United States, primarily in the so-called Deep South. Brazil has no Jim Crow practices - segregated schools, restrooms, or churches - and neither poll taxes, lynchings, nor the Ku Klux Klan, all symptoms of interracial tension and fear that are happily on the wane in the United States, but still linger on in varying forms and degrees" (Christopher, 1953:4). Even during the slavery period in Brazil the pertinent legislation and related mechanisms of surveillance and discipline which maintained the Africans under subordination on the plantation as well as in the larger society do not seem to have had the same draconian severity of their counterpart in the U.S., nor to have been enforced as strictly (Camara, 1983:77-91). The general indication is, in fact, that the legal provisions bearing on slavery life in colonial and Imperial Brazil--once allowance is made for the universally prohibitory nature of slavery statutes--were largely favorable to the slaves.[2] Travelers' reports, from the 19th century in particular, on the whole bear out this fact, such as, for instance, the richly informative account of 1850s Brazilian social life by the Revrs. J.C. Fletcher and D.P.Kidder, where we learn that the larger social climate - the law and custom - was "in favor of freedom" for the enslaved population (1857:133); or the chronicles of Richard Burton (1969; orig. 1869), who was in Brazil during the 1860s, and not only makes hyperbolic reference to "the exceptionally humane treatment of the slave in Brazil" (1969:270), but also, and more relevantly for our purposes, highlights the fact that the bondsman there had "every chance of becoming a free man" (1969:271). Also worth noting here is the illuminating study of the colonization experience in Brazil by the French geographer Eliseé Réclus, who maintains that Brazilian slavery legislation as a whole was "less terrible than the Black Codes of the Confederate States"; it was a body of laws that did not "lock the slave into an insurmountable circle of servitude" (1862:387). This pattern is corroborated, for the 19th century, in Southey's history of colonial Brazil (1970:675, Book II; orig.1822); in fact, we are informed (Boxer, 1964:138) that even during the 18th century, a period generally regarded as one during which slavery in Brazil was particularly arduous for the slave population, the latter "were not entirely without legal means of redress." Finally, we may consider here the report of the Brazilian legal historian Agostinho Marques Perdigão Malheiro, who states that these laws tended to facilitate the process of manumission, something which he contrasted with the essentially restrictive effect that slave legislation had on manumission in the French-American and Anglo-American colonies (1944:110; orig. 1866).[3] This contrasts markedly with the situation of the freed African in the antebellum United States, which was extremely precarious regarding the possibility of re-enslavement because, as Goodell reports (1853:356), "the law *presumes* him to be a slave unless he can prove himself free."

It is not my intention here to suggest that slavery life in Brazilian society, or in any other slavery regime, was anything less than severe. The very nature of slavery as a system of forced labor made it possible for the management of the slaves to range from paternalistic benevolence to extreme inhumanity - and expressions of the latter were by no means wanting in the Brazilian setting. Yet, after all is said about the matter, we must still contend with the fact that in hemispheric perspective there was significant crosscultural variation between these poles, and that instances of extreme inhumanity in the treatment of the Africans were not, in the main, as common in Brazil as in other settings. Moreover - and this should weigh heavily in the comparison - it seems that their occurrence clashed with public sentiment. Southey writes about how it excited "a very general feeling of indignation and abhorrence" (1970:783, orig. 1822) in the population. It is not unreasonable to suppose that this may have been an inhibiting factor on the level of violence perpetrated by the masters against their African slaves (on this point, also see Pierson, 1967:46; Rugendas, 1976:144). Concerning this last aspect - and, again, as

29

indicated by reports from the 19th century - public opinion in the antebellum South does not seem to have had an equally mitigating effect on slavery practices. For, if it had, indeed, influenced the nature of slavery life in this way, could it not be inferred here that in postbellum times it would have continued to function even more intensely as a deterrent to the pattern of generalized violence against blacks, such as lynching for instance, a practice that clearly exemplifies the communal participation in the public punishment of offenders, and not just participation by isolated groups or organizations in the community? I note elsewhere in this chapter that greater insights may be gained into the question of slavery life by differentiating the aspect of slave treatment itself, that is, by breaking it down into its material and social components. Its social dimension is where one would be looking to find more variation across slavery systems. Still, a closer analysis of the material side of plantation life, such as the aspect of slave punishment - though this aspect itself was strongly shaped by the nature of dominant-minority relations-- yields interesting contrasts. We can consider this briefly. For example, the picture that emerges from the descriptions in Freyre (1968:49, 131, 330) of the treatment of runaway slaves in Brazil is that, first of all, the slaves there apparently enjoyed physical mobility in sufficient measure to allow them to escape from one plantation to another, or simply to run to freedom, with a certain degree of regularity - apparently with greater ease and regularity than their counterparts in the Old South, in the United States, owing to the latter country's formidable system of surveillance and control of the physical movements of the slaves, and to the incredible brutality with which runaway slaves were punished when apprehended. Slave punishment in Brazil, as in other slavery regimes, relied commonly on the practice of flogging (see, e.g., Williams, 1930:327), but also on other (somewhat less severe) modalities of punishment for smaller offenses (see, e.g., Marjoribanks, 1853:106, and Burton, 1969:277, on the *palmatória*). Wetherell's report (1860:70) throws into relief another form of legally-mandated punishment, designed for recidivist runaways: "Runaway blacks, when brought back, have, as a punishment, a ring of iron fastened round the neck, and from it a small piece stands upright, four to six inches long, the head of which is shaped like a cross; this *badge* is considered a great disgrace, for when out their acquaintance jeer at them" (see also Spix and Martius, 1824:179; Debret, 1989:167, orig. 1834). We should direct our attention to two additional issues. The first has to do with the apparatus of control of the physical movements of blacks in Brazil during slavery times, on the countryside and on the plantations, which, as Genovese notes (1976:180), was largely "in the hands of men of color." The slave catchers, commonly known as *capitães-*

do-mato, or bush captains, were in some areas of the country, "chiefly mulattoes or other people of color," according to Spix and Martius (1824:120; also see Rugendas, 1976:159; Southey, 1970:786). The second pertains to the fact that the practice of flogging was not something that was indelibly associated, whether in actual practice or in the collective consciousness, with the punishment of the black offender. Rather, it was a punishment of a more general nature, which, until the first quarter of the last century, appears to have been meted out to white and black alike. Reporting from the state of Pernambuco in the early years of the last century, Tollenare writes: "The lash is an ordeal that is imposed here on both whites and blacks" (1956:240). In any event, there is much to encourage the impression that the machinery of control and correction of Africans in Brazilian society was not enforced as systematically as in Anglo-American contexts. Freyre (1968:326) tells us about a petition sent to the Army commission in Rio de Janeiro in the 1820s, denouncing the laxity with which the surveillance and discipline of the slave force were carried out, and stressing the need for more vigorous action in this respect. Overall, the matter of surveillance and control of the physical mobility of the black population during the slavery period becomes especially relevant in comparative context. Reflecting a broader pattern of legal and social consistency or ambiguity in Brazil regarding the management of the black population, public practice did not always accord with legal directives, such as the Salvador ordinance of 1847 forbidding slaves to be in the streets after the ringing of the bell, or those which forbade slave gatherings and dances (1837). Luis dos Santos Vilhena, a professor of Greek in Salvador at the end of the 18th century, confirms this fact as he writes with displeasure about the lax fashion with which the mechanism of control of the black population was adhered to in that city. He mentions the ringing of the curfew bell as a ceremony so discredited as to make one wonder whether in fact it served any real function (1969:142). In this connection, we may also cite the Count da Ponte who in 1807 had this report from Salvador:

> The slaves in this city manifest no subjection whatsoever to the edicts and provisions of the government, they assemble wherever and whenever they please; they dance and play their instruments noisily all over town and at all hours; on religious feast-days they dominate the festivities, drowning all other musical events." (cited in Nina Rodrigues, 1932:236).

Additionally, many legal directives, in particular those of the Imperial period (1822-1889), which were designed to act as a restraining force on black physical mobility, were actually meant as a deterrent to lower-class customs in general (see Freyre, 1968). The law seldom singled out blacks as a separate caste because in Brazil there was no self-contained body of laws in the mold of an Anglo-American "Black Code," a situation that may be better understood in the context of the high degree of racial intermixture which characterized Brazilian society from the earliest phases of colonization. The difficulties surrounding archival searches for specific black legislation in the colonial and Imperial periods of Brazil give significant indication of this. One cannot locate, for instance, direct references to slaves in the municipal ordinances of Salvador in the period from 1650 to 1787. Blacks were normally lumped together with other lower-class elements, frequently by occupation. This is very instructive inasmuch as it affords a glimpse into the overall character of social relations between the dominant and subaltern ethnic groups in the society, pointing to the "class" regulation of these regulations, and suggesting, in a more substantive sense, how legal restraints were probably easier to evade under those circumstances, than if they had been designed to apply invariably and exclusively to blacks as a group.

As for the comparative aspect of intergroup hostility, the following accounts dramatically foreground the crossnational variation. The first comes from the writings of Frederick Law Olmsted who, traveling through the American South in the 1850s, reports on the burning of a slave which had taken place some years before, near Knoxville, Tennessee, an act perpetrated by a crowd of about one thousand people, which a local newspaper had characterized not as "an excited multitude," but as "good citizens ... cool, calm, and deliberate." Olmsted further cites the comments of the editor of a local newspaper, a Methodist preacher, on this incident, to the effect that the punishment had been "unequal to the crime." "Had we been there," the man proceeded, "we should have taken a part, and even suggested the pinching of pieces out of him with red-hot pincers - the cutting off of a limb at a time, and then burning them all in a heap" (1970:446; orig. 1860). However monstrous the suggestion by this man of the cloth may have been, the more shocking aspect is that it should, as it did indeed (as pointed out by Olmsted), express "the uppermost feeling of the ruling mind of his community." Other passages are of like character, and equally disturbing. One is drawn from an essay published in Texas at the turn of the century, penned by one W.C. Brann, who expounds on the fact that the African-American community ought to be presented with the alternative of emigration back to Africa or annihilation: "We have tried the restraining influence of religion and the elevating forces of education upon the negro without avail. We have employed moral suasion and legal penalties; have incarcerated the offenders for life at hard labor, and hanged them by the neck in accordance with statutory law. *We have hunted the black rape-fiend to death with hounds, bored him with buckshot, fricasseed him over slow fires and flayed him alive*, [emphasis added] but the despoilment of white women by these brutal imps of darkness and the devil is still of daily occurrence ... Drive out the "nigger" - young and old, male and female - or drive him into the earth!" (cited in Sickels, 1972:35-36). A turn-of-the-century chronicler of slavery times in the antebellum South (Johnston, 1969) informs us of the extreme cruelty attending the punishment of slaves for virtually any offense, but especially for certain offenses, such as thefts, which were always punished "by the most frightful floggings, often ending in the slave's death," (1969:375) or running away from the plantation. Upon recapturing a runaway slave, the white captors

> delighted in torturing [the captured slave] to death, unrebuked by public opinion. Public opinion indeed had, as likely as not, been evoked to 'see the fun'; and had ridden over on its blood horses or driven with its fast trotters to see a wretched negro or negress ... whipped to death or lunacy by hickory switches; or hung by the thumbs and flogged into a bloody pulp with cowhide thongs dipped into scalding cayenne peppertea before each stroke (1969:377).

The absence of commensurate social and legal reproach regarding the frequency and ease with which dominant-group violence against subordinate-group members was expressed - Southerners, Johnson writes (1969:376) thought no more of killing a "Negro" than of killing "a cow or a mule." [In fact] "they rather liked killing them for fun" - reveals a great deal about the nature of dominant-minority relations in Southern society before the Civil War.

I do not wish at this point to probe into the causal forces behind this type of fierce animosity described in these accounts, on the part of the dominant ethnic group toward members of the subordinate one(s), nor do I wish to elaborate this contrasting analysis on the basis of logical inference, but it should be noted all the same - at least provisionally - that in Brazil the regular expression of these sentiments and the regular occurrence of these practices would not have fit well with the general architecture of dominant-minority interethnic relations there, even during the slavery era, and therefore it is not as likely that this kind of interpersonal violence would have been as common. In contrast, the configuration of interethnic/interracial relations in the U.S. has historically been more compatible with its expression. Again, as with the preceding considerations on slavery, this comparison of levels of intergroup conflict and inequality in the broader context should not be taken to mean that properly racial prejudice and stereotypes, derogatory attitudes, as well as exclusionary practices against people of African extraction, have been entirely absent in Brazil, and that social standing in that society is unaffected by racial factors. This issue has already been acknowledged here, and it has been stressed and elaborated on by several analysts of race/ethnic relations in Brazilian society (e.g., Bastide and van den Berghe, 1957; Davis, 1966; Degler, 1971; Fernandes, 1971; Harris, 1974). Still, when comparisons take into account certain factors related to the particular historical and cultural circumstances of the societies involved, they reveal not only that there was much that intensified or mitigated the "bitter draught" of African bondage in the different American slavery systems, to a degree that allows us to make useful contrasts, but also, as pertains to the overall pattern of intergroup relations, the relative absence of inflexible, large-scale structural and ideological supports of race discrimination and segregation in Brazil has made for substantial dissimilarities: interracial enmities in Brazil have been "relatively mild and equivocal," says one writer (Wagley, 1971:131); "irregular and indistinct," says another (Morse, 1953:303). Race prejudice and discrimination have occurred not only on a smaller scale, but also entwined with class factors (i.e., wealth, education, professional position). A research project of some decades ago in Brazil established that in that society, where the lines of economic stratification were so strongly drawn, and vertical mobility so greatly restricted, "all of the familiar symptoms of racial discrimination tend to be subsumed by the class differentials" (Harris, 1974:63-4; see also Willems, 1949:407; Christopher, 1953; Ribeiro, 1956:98; Wagley, 1963, 1971:ch.3). One analyst of Brazilian slavery, while essentially contributing to the "revisionist" project of rejection of the idea of a comparatively milder Latin American/Brazilian slavery and interracial relations, offers nevertheless this incisive commentary: "While color prejudice certainly existed in Brazil, it was strikingly different from North American racism ... Brazilian racial attitudes allowed friendliness and affection among people who were racially different but of a similar social rank, and Brazilians had less place in their system of values for the kind of discrimination and segregation that were normal in all parts of the United States" (Conrad, 1983:232). This idea is borne out by Nogueira (1959:172), who states: "... the Brazilian ideology of interracial relations, as part of the national ethos, involves an ideal of race egalitarianism and provides a reference point for public condemnation of overt and intentional manifestations of prejudice, as well as for the protest of nonwhites against discrimination."

The Englishman Henry Koster, a longtime resident of the state of Pernambuco in northeastern Brazil in the early 1800s, left us this account, which is quite germane to the issue at hand. After leasing a sugar mill, he invited friends and acquaintances for the occasion of his formal taking possession of the property. At that time, he informs us, "blacks and whites, all down and ate together; the health of Our Lady of the Rosary was drunk first, then that of the chief of the [corresponding religious] brotherhood, and of the new tenant [himself]" (1816:242-43). Koster highlights the social equality which he thought to have permeated their interaction, which makes this incident quite noteworthy because of the symbolic importance normally attached to this type of event, that is, to the collective sharing of a meal. In contrasting perspective, it is difficult to imagine a similar occurrence in the antebellum United States, or in the subsequent period. Myrdal (1972:608-609) comments on how the taking of meals in U.S. society is "almost barren of all the rituals and ceremonial niceties commonly preserved in the older countries," but added that when this event is placed in the context of interracial relations, it took on immense social significance, becoming, in fact, the "main symbol" of black-white inequality. As a Southerner explained to him (in the 1940s): "In the South, the table, simple though its fare may be, possesses the sanctity of an intimate social institution. To break bread together involves, or may involve, everything." Such a declaration suggests how a communal meal involving blacks and whites, right up to the end of the Jim Crow system in the 1960s, would call forth "serious condemnation" in the U.S., particularly in the South.

There are numerous instances of Brazilian social history indicating the greater power of "class" over "race" in social relations in Brazilian society. Koster offers again valuable commentary in this regard, stating that it was surprising, "though extremely pleasing, to see how little difference is made between a white man, a mulatto, a creole Negro, if all are equally poor and if all have been born free" (1966:152; orig.1816). The appointment of mulattoes to civil office or to the positions in the "holy orders," he adds, frequently led to their official classification as white. In this connection, he relates this interesting and enlightening incident: "In conversing on one occasion with a man of color who was in my service, I asked him if a certain *capitao-mor* [captain-major, a prestigious military post in colonial and Imperial Brazil] was not a mulatto-man; he answered, 'he was, but is not now.' I begged him to explain, when he added, [How] 'Can a capitao-mor be a mulatto man?'" On other occasions he observed how people of mixed ancestry regularly entered the holy orders or became magistrates, their official papers declaring them to be white, but with their appearance (as judged by

Koster) "clearly denoting the contrary" (1816:391). More recent accounts are equally instructive. We are informed, for instance (Wagley, 1964:133-4), of how the townspeople of a small community in the Amazon (the northernmost region of Brazil) refused to classify the woman who held the highest-ranking social position in the community for her physical appearance, which was that of a dark-complected mulatto; and the local porter/town drunk, a man "clearly of European descent, having light pigmentation," as white. "How can Oswaldo be white?," exclaimed a town resident, in a clear allusion to the man's low social position. Pierson (1967:xxv) relates another instance, witnessed by a researcher in the Sergipe area (northeast Brazil) some forty years ago: "On the beach at a seaside town a group of persons from the lower class were engaged in a folk dance, accompanied by singing, known as the *cururu*. Although composed largely (but not exclusively) of colored persons, this group was led by a lower-class white. Approaching several other persons nearby, who were spending their vacation at the seaside, and asking if they would like his group to sing and dance where they could be seen and heard more easily, the white leader referred to himself and to the other members of his group as 'Nós pretos' (We blacks)." This element of collective solidarity as arising from common socioeconomic status, without direct regard to color, has been amply documented. Nogueira (cited in Pierson, 1967:xlvii), for example, observed how there was "a more complete fraternization between colored and *brancos* (whites) in the less-favored stratum." Frazier's (1944:266) and Pierson's (1951:190) investigations also reveal how class solidarity is especially noticeable in the lower socioeconomic echelons of the population. This is quite the reverse of the pattern of interethnic and interracial attitudes in the lower classes in U.S. society, where race-based solidarity and antagonism tend to be more intense precisely among people in the less privileged levels of society. Overall, then, the great mass of whites, mixed-bloods, and blacks in Brazil occupying the less favored social strata could be said to be unified far more directly by their collective economic standing in the social hierarchy than by color and/or racial considerations. In Pierson's words (1967:xlvii), "they share very much a common life."

This preponderance of the class aspect in social distinctions is important enough by itself. But, it is equally important to realize that, even though class stratification suggests the greater valuation of the "white" category within the Brazilian social structure - a pattern not at all surprising given that in *any* multiethnic society everything associated with the dominant ethnic group is held to be superior - the admission to the dominant ethnic status (i.e., one's ability to be socially perceived as belonging to the "white" category) is theoretically within the reach of virtually anyone, insofar as this is a process mediated by the experience of socioeconomic betterment. (This situation, that is, the assumption of the possibility of universal inclusion of society's members, by means of which they may be granted the "racial" status of the dominant group, differs radically from a situation where the prevalent assumption is that no amount of change in socioeconomic standing will alter racial classification. This issue will be explored in greater depth in the next section). This aspect, together with the greater overall malleability of the social structure, has prompted observers and visitors since the 19th century to comment on the striking crossnational variation, and on the freedom enjoyed by the population of African ancestry in Brazil from extensive, systematic, and institutionalized racial prejudice and discrimination, and the comparatively easier access of ethnic-racial minorities to the process of national integration.[4] Some random testimonies may be cited, beginning with Southey's historical account of the early phase of colonization in Brazil (the 1600s), a time when circumstances were already of such a character as to promote the "amalgamation of castes and colours ... [whereby] ... [t]he *Mamaluco* [the offspring of a Portuguese father and an Amerindian mother] was as much respected, and as eligible to all offices, as the man of the whole blood, or as the native of the mother country. There were no laws to degrade the Mulatto, or the Free Negro, nor were they degraded by public opinion" (1970:692, Book II; orig. 1822). The 19th century yields a plethora of similar reports, among which that of the famous naturalist Louis Agassiz, a resident of Brazil in the 1860s, who commented that "any enterprising Negro may obtain his freedom, and once obtained, there is no obstacle to his rising in social or political station" (1868:65). Fletcher and Kidder wrote that "[t]he Brazilian [Imperial] Constitution recognizes, neither directly nor indirectly, color as a basis of civil rights; hence, once free, the black man or the mulatto, if he possess energy and talent, can rise to a social position from which his race in North America is debarred" (1867:132). In 1910 another visitor commented: "Blacks and whites mingle freely in the schools. Negro lawyers and doctors appeared to be patronized by whites. Officially, at least, there is not distinction" (Winter, in Eads, 1936:372). At about the same time, another observer remarked that "northern Latin America is tolerant of the Negro and has avoided the tension and repugnance which are so noticeable in Anglo-Saxon America" (Warshaw, in Eads, 1936:372). The testimonies of Réclus and Malheiro, both from the 19th century, are also worth considering:

... protected by the social customs and traditions, [manumitted blacks] cross freely with the superior castes ... The offspring of freed blacks become citizens; they join the Army and the Navy, ... and are able to, in the same manner as their Caucasian comrades-in-arms, defend the cause of their country and the honor of the flag. Some rise through the ranks and become officers over white subordinates; others pursue the liberal professions, and become lawyers, physicians, professors, artists. It is true that the law does not grant the blacks the eligibility, or the actual right, to vote; but the public functionaries who are themselves darker-skinned do not find it difficult to recognize as whites all those who declare themselves as such, and give them the necessary papers to establish legally and incontestably the purity of their origin. This is how the children of former slaves are able to enter administrative careers, and even to sit at congressional assemblies right beside aristocratic planters. In Brazil, the shameful condition is not color, but servitude (Réclus, 1862:388) (my translation).

To be a person of *color*, even a black African, is no reason for not being somebody in our country, to be admitted into societies, into families, into public vehicles, into churches in some places, into employments, etc; moreover, the man of color enjoys as much consideration in the Empire as any person to whom he may be equal; some have even occupied and now occupy the highest offices of the State, in provincial government, in the Council of State, in the Senate, in the Chamber of Deputies, in the Diplomatic Corps, in a word, every kind of position; others have been and are now distinguished doctors, lawyers, illustrious professors in the highest scientific fields; to sum up, every area of human activity is completely open and free to him. It may perhaps be said that there are indications that he has had an exceptional degree of influence" (Malheiro, cited in Conrad, 1983:245).

More recent assessments of race and ethnicity in Brazil continue to give strong indication of the more powerful shaping effect of class over that of race. Hutchinson (1963:46), for example, typically concludes in his study of race relations in a rural community in the state of Bahia, that "there are no social activities closed to the *homem de cor* [man of color] provided he has the money and the education to take advantage of them."

A related aspect that is consistent with this overall picture was the absence of direct pressures and constraints on the activities of the ethnic-racial minorities, as they set out on an independent course following the end of slavery. This may be instantiated by the situation of blacks in Brazil, who, having been emancipated from slavery only in 1888, understandably showed little inclination in the immediately ensuing decades to embrace the life of competitive work relations of the larger society - a society that was beginning to experience industrialization and the bureaucratic organization of the economic sphere - preferring to enjoy the leisure that had for so long been denied them, and working only in the sufficient measure to survive (Eads, 1936:370). Yet, they seem to have been spared any societal retaliation, harsh imposition of controls, or widespread and systematic stigmatization. "[T]he Negro," said the distinguished English publicist Lord Bryce early in this century, in his analysis of the Brazilian interracial situation, "is not accused of insolence ..." (1921:480). This occurred at a time when the U.S. system of legal segregation was two decades old and in full swing, and the black population in American society was constantly subjected to violent punitive sanctions for anything that might be perceived as insolence, excessive autonomy, or any transgression, however slight, of the prevailing interracial etiquette. The Jim Crow system sanctioned the use of violence and physical intimidation as the main strategy for exercising social control in the general sense (i.e., maintaining the subservience of the minority group) and for dealing with violations of the rules governing black-white relations. Lynching can be cited here as the extreme (but disturbingly frequent) form of punishment and social control of the African-American population in the United States in the early phase of Jim Crow. Franklin (1969:439) examines a thirty-year period, starting in 1884 (or, twelve years before the Supreme Court upheld segregation through its Plessy vs. Ferguson ruling) through the outbreak of World War I, when *over 3,600* lynchings occurred, primarily in the South, and involving mostly black victims.

But this pattern had begun much earlier, in fact right after the Civil War, when the Black Codes, which were meant to replace (in form, if not in content) the defunct slave codes, were put into effect. The Ku Klux Klan, an organization formed in Pulaski, Tennessee in 1865, originally as "a group of merry-makers bent on a good time" (Quarles, 1976:139), within a few years had become a highly organized, extremely violent, and singularly successful apparatus of social control of the black population. The significance of this pattern of physical violence against the black population as a whole was that it was, first of all, stimulated by the very legal stringency of the Black Codes. Secondly, it was not limited to the radical and/or marginal element, such as the KKK, but found expression in the actions of the ordinary citizenry as well. The Reverend Charles Stearns, a resident of the postbellum South in the years immediately following the Civil War recounts how "[i]n 1867, three white men in front of my house, boasted of the crimes they had committed against the colored people; one of them laughing heartily while he described the appearance of the woman whom he had beaten, saying 'she was the bloodiest looking beast you ever saw.' Another of them said he made it a point to whip one or more negroes soundly every year as an example to the others. Another owned that he had fired at a negro for disobeying an order, and 'should have shot him, but he dodged behind a tree.' Neither of these men were rowdies in the common acceptation of the term, but well-to-do farmers, living very near my place, and I do not suppose they imagined they had done wrong" (1969:402, orig.1872). He continues, in the same vein: "I cannot begin to recall the instances, of maimed and wounded [black] men, who have come to me with the story of their wrongs. Some with great gashes cut in their heads, some with wounds in their bodies, and others with mangled and shattered arms; ..." (1969:405, orig.1872).

The "whitening of race" concept: Material and symbolic implications

The idea of the progressive lightening of color has historically been treated in Brazil as something that is both feasible and desirable, an aspect that has sometimes lent itself to much criticism and misinterpretation. This aspect is pivotal in its indications of the nature of ethnic relations. In "revisionist" circles, it is invariably seized upon as unmistakable evidence of racial prejudice. But there is simply more than meets the eye here, and the tendency to treat this relationship as a *fait accompli* sidesteps a crucially important level of meaning, and thus limits the process of explanation.

The societal reaction towards the notion of the "whitening of the race" can be highly illuminating as it presents a dimension of intergroup life that serves as a basis for distinguishing between the interethnic models of Brazil and the United States. The U.S. model of race relations and racial status is predicated on the assumption of the essential immutability of difference - human difference, as manifested here in terms of ethnic difference, which in U.S. society is equated with *racial* difference - whereas the Brazilian model is marked by greater conceptual fluidity assigned to the idea of difference, ethnic and/or racial. In the U.S. context, the attitude towards difference converts fundamentally into the collective assumption of the immutability of ethnic/racial difference, an idea that operates as grounds for permanent intergroup separation; and in the Brazilian context, this attitude converts into the collective assumption of the transformability of difference, which then encourages the interweaving and integration of the ways of life of all the different groups.

40

The properties of the U.S. model are consonant with those of classical caste stratification, concerning a number of characteristics. Of interest here is the fact that in classical caste systems the membership and characteristics of subordinate-caste members are not altered by contact with members of the higher castes. This character of unchangeability is rigidly and systematically safeguarded by a complex of legal, social, and ideological provisions which severely circumscribe intercaste contact, restrict social mobility to its horizontal (i.e., *intra*-caste, not vertical or intercaste) manifestation, eliminate the possibility of exogamic marriage, and thus maintain the larger societal pattern of intergroup segregation. One such provision is the symbolic mechanism of "ritual pollution," according to which the contact between higher-caste and lower-caste members always leaves the condition of the former inevitably altered, in terms of having been defiled, or made impure. The condition of the latter, however, is not reciprocally changed by becoming purified. It remains the same. In the interethnic milieu this concerns the anthropological rule of hypodescent (or the "one-drop rule"; see, e.g., Harris, 1974, 1997:320), which establishes the automatic affiliation of the offspring of intercaste unions with the subordinate, rather than the superordinate, group, for the purpose of avoiding the categorial complications and ambiguities of the resulting intermediate identity. The social meaning of this process is well-known: it reveals the ideological roots of the collective assumption of several interrelated aspects, to wit, the inferior constitution of members of the lower castes, the intrinsic and unchangeable nature of this condition of inferiority, the greater civil and moral superiority of the higher castes over the lower ones, and finally, the resulting need to erect rigid boundary lines between the castes, or, to say it differently, the need to create and maintain separate worlds of human existence linked together by their asymmetrical relations of interdependence within the larger social hierarchy - and to keep the lower castes in subordination. In a castelike system of ethnic stratification, the idea of difference, as applied to the interaction between human groups and relied upon as a regulative mechanism of this interaction, is accordingly established as being inherently and ineluctably inferior. Difference cannot aspire to becoming nondifference - a transformation that, in the intergroup sphere, would involve the full-fledged absorption into the social mainstream. Therefore, the regulative principle here is that of *permanent exclusion* of the element of difference from the mainstream - a principle which, when contradicted by structural changes in the society that take the form of the gradual *formal* assimilation of subordinate-group members, endures nevertheless at the symbolic level, and in this capacity continues to inhibit the process of societal integration.[5]

The presumption of the possibility of a "whitening" process is a natural development in multiethnic contexts where ethnic and racial divisions and distinctions are more fluid and unsystematic. The "whitening" transcends the purely racial aspect, that is, it goes beyond the immediate aspect of the lightening of skin color which generally results from mixed parentage, although this is what is ordinarily addressed by analysts, and mostly in terms of its negative repercussions. When attention is drawn to the whitening process, it is to show it as irrefutable evidence of the greater valuation of "whiteness" and the concomitant undervaluation of "nonwhiteness" in the society in question. But, it must be kept in mind here that, in all multiethnic settings, social hierarchization occurs primarily on the basis of ethnic affiliation - that is, on the basis of the economic, political, and cultural dominance of the "white" population - and, therefore, everything that is associated with the dominant ethnic group will be held in higher regard than that which is associated with the minority (i.e., unassimilated) populations. Thus, dominant-group characteristics, such as for example, skin color, inevitably become a symbol of superior social status, and a standard for general emulation. In this connection, what is of greater importance to focus on regarding the Brazilian interethnic model is not so much the preponderance of this tendency, but the fact that the intermingling of the dominant and subordinate groups works as a process of *social inclusion*, a means through which the "nonwhite" can become "white" - and not only in a racial sense, but also and more relevantly, in a *social* one as well. Therefore, the positive aspect of this transformation is not linked to some intrinsic goodness of "whiteness" *qua* racial status. Skin color as an attribute of race, though not inconsequential, becomes a secondary consideration in this particular context. Of course, this assertion is not intended in an absolute sense, since racial considerations (i.e., the general societal favoring of "white" over "nonwhite") may still be found surrounding the process of transformation towards "whiteness" (i.e., the process of miscegenation), as well as the multiple social benefits deriving from the passage to the dominant "white" status. Be that as it may, a cautionary note must be added here regarding the reductionist "reading" of this situation that normally prevails in standard analyses. The goodness of the "whitening" process must be found in its symbolic *as well as material* implications. Beyond the obvious aspect of change in color or race categorization, at a deeper level this process stands for sociocultural mainstream, which is to say, it comes to symbolize the complete integration into the national culture. Above all, it directly and indirectly underscores the collective assumption that the mainstream culture is within the reach of minority ethnic contingents. Thus, it represents a phenomenon of social inclusion and assimilation.

The positivity of the notion of "whitening of the race," therefore, does not lie solely in the change towards the dominant color or race affiliation, but mainly in the change towards incorporation into the dominant mode of life. In this sense, it demonstrates the changeable nature of difference (unlike the case of caste systems of ethnic stratification) because difference is assumed to be transformable into nondifference. Furthermore, this transformation overwhelms the consideration of color, making it peripheral in the long run. In fact, because the "whitening" of the nonwhite element is a gradual process, in its concrete manifestation intermediary shades or gradations will appear allowing for the perception of "nonwhiteness," but this does not matter so much because this progressive movement towards dominant-group physical characteristics is seen as a movement towards eventual full social assimilation. In an interethnic model such as that of the U.S., however, where castelike tendencies may still be said to influence the pattern and developmental course of intergroup relations, this type of progression towards the "white" standard of appearance is rendered inconsequential, in that it is nullified by the rules of biraciality, i.e., intermediary categories are eliminated through their automatic absorption into the subordinate ethnic group. A concept of progressive inclusion, such as denoted by "whitening" in this analysis, is an impossibility. Harris (1974:56) has stated, concerning race and ethnicity in the the United States, that nothing is admitted in between the polar identities of white and black. Biracial classification treats the circumstances of inclusion and exclusion dichotomously, while at the same time steering intermediate identities in the direction of "nonwhiteness," (i.e., exclusion), and not "whiteness," (i.e., inclusion.) The universal assumption is not of the transformability of difference, of its potentiality for "whiteness." Rather, the presumption is, again, of the immutability of difference, of its impossibility of "whiteness" - that is to say, of inclusion.[6] The resistance to inclusion has been historically demonstrated, to begin with, in the enduring formal and informal barriers against miscegenation, which is a factor of vital importance in the consolidation and integration of multiethnic contexts. In this respect, the societal rejection of the principle of inclusion of ethnic and racial difference may be identified in two senses. First, in the operation of the aforementioned principle of hypodescent, through which the children of mixed unions are deemed an anomalous category (i.e., being an intermediary type, they threaten the stability of the boundaries that separate difference from nondifference) and are therefore automatically assigned membership in the category of the subordinate-group parent, the category of difference. Secondly, this rejection is expressed in the systematic pressures issuing from *both* the dominant and minority groups (i.e., the racial dichotomization of the society causes both the ruling and subaltern ethnic segments to internalize separatist values through their socialization experience) on minority-group members to maintain their "authenticity," their "difference," their "nonwhiteness"-which means, to remain culturally distinct and not to try to adopt mainstream (i.e., "white") practices, tastes, tendencies, etc. These are powerful cultural injunctions against intergroup fusion, the implications of which will be addressed more systematically in a later chapter.

"Patrimonial" and "bureaucratic" patterns of ethnic stratification

The crossnational variation in ethnic relations described up to now may call to mind the Weberian distinction between patrimonial and bureaucratic patterns, a distinction corresponding to the difference in the structure of social action in traditional and modern societies. This will be briefly clarified here. The question may be raised as to whether the Brazilian model would not be best characterized as "patrimonial," reflecting the level of modernization of the society, and the larger pattern of social paternalism that has historically regulated social relations there, particularly during the Imperial era (i.e., the 19th century; see, e.g., Freyre, 1970:167-8), while the U.S.model, on the other hand, would be classified as "bureaucratic," with respect to the level of societal modernization, and impersonality in social relations. In the context of intergroup relations, patrimonialism ideal-typically refers to the operation of a patron-client relation of interdependence between dominant and minority groups, involving a complex of legally and/or informally sanctioned mutual rights and obligations, whereby the patron (the dominant group) exercises the right of tutelage or civil parenthood over the client (the subordinate group), but remains bound to the duty to provide the client with protection, legal and otherwise, as well as material sustenance, such as clothes, food, shelter, either directly or through the facilitation of circumstances which guarantee these elements. The client has a claim to these protections, but is bound to the duty of perpetual loyalty and compliance (*services de complaisance*) towards the patron. The all-embracing process of social inclusion of minority groups through the granting of citizenship takes, in this context, the form of a passage to a relation of patronage, within which the ties of subordination effectively maintain the subordinate element in a condition of inequality (La Grande Encyclopédie, vol.VIII, 1886-1902:104-5). In this model, the granting of citizenship to all minority segments, or their absorption and equalization into the larger and undifferentiated social "family," dissolves the boundary lines that make them distinct and visible, without however entailing an equalization in the distribution of social resources and benefits. The breakdown of these boundary lines hinders the formal, or bureaucratic, and informal identification of these groups, a process that is normally linked to (in the sense that it normally precedes) the legal rectification of intergroup inequalities. Ethnic relations of the "bureaucratic" type, on the other hand, are linked to a higher level of formal administration of intergroup relations, by means of legal codification and classification. The relations between individuals and the larger society are mediated by a system of impersonal laws and legal procedures, the logical generalization of which is expected to override considerations of a personal nature, such as those of personal favor. Thus, the bureaucratization of social life, involving its management in an impersonal, routinized, and generalizing fashion, is thought to extend the administration of justice and civil equality to all sectors of the population.

While this traditional Weberian duality is useful for distinguishing and describing the general features of models of social action, it can lead to stereotyping and misleading conceptions when applied in an indiscriminate and decontextualized fashion. This has not deterred revisionist scholars, however, from using it as a basis for assailing academic as well as popular depictions of the Brazilian interethnic situation as an exemplar of intergroup integration and harmony. The main tenor of this criticism is that the presentation of Brazilian life as an ethnic and racial paradise is overly idealized and only serves to obfuscate the reality of a "patrimonial" or paternalistic social system in which ethnic hierarchies and prejudices have not been erased. Concomitantly with the rejection of what is characterized as a patrimonial model of ethnic relations, there is also an implicit and/or explicit legitimation of the "bureaucratic" model as a more advanced stage towards the resolution of the interethnic problem. This position is very problematic, and begs for a number of clarifications.

To begin with, the distinction between "patrimonialism" and "bureaucracy" in Weber's work is a distinction of *social structure*, in that it pertains to categorizations of opposing modes of social action that correspond to different stages of societal modernization. That is, the distinction refers to structural transformations in the institutional network of the society, as the latter moves into ever higher levels of "rationality." In the present analysis, however, while keeping in mind the interplay of structural and cultural forces, the analytical focus is shifted precisely from social structure to *culture*, in the effort to demonstrate, via the example of U.S. society, that the prevalence of the bureaucratic mode of social action and the formal management of intergroup relations, expressing the greater rationalization of the social system, has proved insufficient for eliminating ethnic conflict and inequality. In the case of Brazil, although it was not until World War II that the country entered the phase of full-scale industrialization, the structural assimilation of ethnic minorities had been going on steadily since the 19th century, and even earlier. Thus, despite the fact that an ethnic hierarchy and a pattern of ethnically or racially related discrimination and prejudice may be common to *both* societies, and that the conventional understanding of "patrimoni-alism" in social relations is that it will be necessarily associated with lower levels of structural assimilation of minority groups, while "bureaucracy" will be associated with higher levels, the contrasting analysis of the intergroup situation in Brazil and the United States does not strengthen this distinction, especially when the focus is directed to the structure of the cultural system as a key determinant of the character of dominant-minority interaction. In the Brazilian setting, however "patrimonial" the regulative tendencies in social relations may have been (in this connection, Freyre, 1970:167-8, discusses the social and political paternalism that prevailed in the wider Brazilian society, particularly during the 19th century), they had the effect of facilitating the formal incorporation of ethnic minorities, whereas in the U.S. setting, despite the greater rationalization towards a "bureaucratic" social structure, the operation of cultural separatism has retarded this assimilative process, as evidenced, for instance, in the pervasive lack of identification on the part of members of the African-American "underclass," with institutional and cultural patterns of the larger society (a theme to be developed in a later chapter). This aspect has also been borne out by the resurgence of interethnic antagonism and inequality during the last decade, despite the important legislative reforms of the 1960s and 1970s which dismantled the framework of *de jure* segregation and discrimination. Thus, societal modernization does not appear to be sufficient for decisively establishing the character of intergroup life, which requires therefore that greater attention be paid to the effect of the cultural processes of the society.

When comparing patterns of ethnic relations in the two societies, some observers may note the fact that industrialization in Brazil reached its mature stage only about forty years ago, approximately a half-century after the U.S. economy did the same, and may then proceed to argue that the crossnational difference (in the structure of interethnic life) has mainly to do with contrasting levels of modernization, the implication being that once the Brazilian social structure reaches a higher stage of modernization, it too will exhibit more competitive relations between social groups and, therefore, similar patterns of racism and ethnic antagonism such as those described for the U.S. The basic fallacy with

46

this line of reasoning should already be apparent from the considerations made thus far. The following can be added. First of all, to try to establish a correspondence between stages of socioeconomic development between the two societies is a thorny enterprise, because, for one thing, the lines of socioeconomic evolution of Brazil and the U.S. have been rather divergent. For instance: in the first half of the nineteenth century, when slavery was in full operation in the United States, Brazil, and several other societies in the New World, the American slavery system already had the highest level of economic rationalization brought on by capitalist activity of any other slavery regime in the Americas (see, e.g., Fogel and Engerman, 1974, in this regard). In any event, these points must be noted: in its early phase of industrialization - in the second half of the 1800s - and, naturally, during the century-long period which preceded industrialization, U.S. society could be said to have been still characterized by a *gemeinschaft* quality in social life. Yet, this was not conterminous with significant levels of assimilation of the minority ethnic contingents - at least, those classified as nonwhite - into the social, economic, and political mainstream. The opposite was, in fact, the case. That was precisely the time when these groups were most thoroughly and harshly barred from participation in national life. Focusing on black-white relations, for instance, we find that from the late 1700s to the Civil War, the halcyon days of slavery activity the United States, not only was the manumission of slaves a limited process, laden with all sorts of difficulties, but even emancipated blacks found their social (and physical) mobility curtailed by numerous formal and informal impediments. In a comparative analysis of Ibero-American and British-American slavery systems, Tannenbaum (1946:50-72) stresses how the social and institutional environment in the British-American settings was as hostile to the freeing of slaves as that in Ibero-American settings was favorable; and how in the latter "[a] hundred social devices narrowed the gap between bondage and liberty, encouraged the master to release his slave, and the bondsman to achieve freedom on his own account." In fact, this author views the opposition to manumission and the "denial of opportunities for it" as being the "primary aspect" distinguishing the character of slavery life in British-American contexts from that of Ibero-American ones. In Brazil - as in the Ibero-American colonies as a whole - the legal and social provisions for the liberation of slaves were diverse, and also rich with implications regarding the societal conception and treatment of this ethnic group. In his *History of Brazil*, written in the first quarter of the 19th century, Southey informs us that "... the laws empower a slave to demand his freedom, whenever he can offer to his owner the price which was originally paid for him, or which he is

47

considered to be fairly worth in the market" (1970:781, Book III; orig. 1822). Foreign residents in Brazil left corroborating reports (e.g., Grant,1809:111-2; Wetherell,1860:16-17). And where the law faltered in its function of upholding the right of the slaves to self-purchase and freedom - an occurrence that may not have been altogether infrequent - the overall social climate, that is, custom and public opinion, seems to have provided the strongest and most effective basis of legitimation. It is worth noting, in this regard, that newspaper notices of manumission that had been facilitated or directly brought about through the efforts of white citizens (as, for instance, those reported in Verger for Bahia [northeastern Brazil] in the mid-1800s, 1968:515-18) came under the heading of "Acts Worthy of Praise." White philanthropy towards the freeing of slaves was deemed a "noble enterprise." This phenomenon bespeaks the strength with which public sentiment supported the idea of slave emancipation. Writing in the 1860s, Burton (1969:271; orig.1869) noted how manumission in Brazilian society was generally held to be a "Catholic duty." Koster's report on social life in Brazil some decades earlier (1816), a time of ever-expanding slavery activity, attests to the frequency and relative ease with which manumission was already being attained. It was common for slaves to obtain their freedom via several avenues: at the death of masters; at the baptismal font, upon the presentation of a sum corresponding to the value of the infant slave; when the freedom of a slave *afilhado* (godchild) was purchased by a person of high social rank; in the case of female slaves who were employed as *amas-de-leite* (wet nurses) - this was a very frequent occurrence in Brazil during the slavery era (see, e.g., Freyre, 1956:366) - and were often emancipated as soon as their work was over (Fletcher and Kidder noted in the 1850s how "a faithful nurse is generally rewarded by manumission," 1857:134); or, finally, when the slave purchased his or her own freedom. This last aspect, in turn, appears to have been significantly stimulated by the practice among Brazilian slaves of selling vegetables from their provision grounds, or by their extensive participation, especially in the urban context, in a diversity of occupations, by hiring themselves out and giving back part of their earnings to their owner. The French cotton merchant Louis-François de Tollenare, who lived in the Pernambuco region (northeastern Brazil) from 1816 to 1818, observed that the slaves there managed to become craftsmen - some "very skilled" - of various kinds, such as washerwomen, seamstresses, street vendors, oarsmen, carpenters, cabinetmakers, masons, blacksmiths (1956:145-6). A quarter of a century later, Ewbank saw slaves in Rio working "as carpenters, masons, pavers, printers, sign and ornamental painters, carriage and cabinet makers, fabricators of military ornaments, lamp-makers, silversmiths, jewelers, and lithographers." He went on to note that "sculptures in stone and saintly images in wood are often done admirably by slaves and free blacks. *All* kinds of trades are carried on by black journeymen and boys" (1856:195).[7]

Finally, in Brazil patrimonial tendencies in social relations have been mainly a phenomenon of class, not race. With due regard to the sharp social and economic cleavages that have historically separated the classes in Brazil, and which persist (to a lesser degree) even in the present time, and to the fact that members of ethnic-racial minorities are found predominantly in the lower social strata, these individuals have naturally become the targets of the paternalistic behaviors and attitudes that the elites are inclined to adopt towards those of lower social rank, irrespective of ethnic or racial origin. Aspects of this paternalism are described in Wagley's discussion of key dimensions of Brazilian social organization, such as the *parentela* (1971:ch.5). This Portuguese term refers to a large web of kinship, which extends outward from the nucleus of the patriarchal family, so as to incorporate, in addition to those individuals who are already interconnected by genealogical relations, a good many others. During the colonial and Imperial eras, the latter would have included "slaves and *agregados*, Indians, Negroes, or mixed bloods ... [including] ... the concubines of the [*paterfamilias*] ... and his illegitimate children" (1971:171). Another factor that has further augmented the structural parameters of the *parentela* is the well-known *compadrio* relation. A very important Catholic institution in Latin cultures in general, the *compadrio* is especially influential in Brazil. It involves the sponsorship of a child at baptism by an individual or married couple of prominent social rank, which establishes an asymmetrical relationship of interdependence that unites, through reciprocal rights and obligations, not only the *afilhado/a* (godchild) and the *padrinho* and *madrinha* (godparents), but also the latter and the parents of the child, who then begin to call each other by the reciprocal terms *compadre* and *comadre*. "This relationship," remarked Koster (1816:239), "is accounted very sacred in Brazil ... it is a bond of brotherhood, which permits the poor man to speak to his superior with a kind of endearing familiarity, and unites them in links of union, of which the non-observance would be sacrilegious." These social structures have consistently and forcefully expressed the primacy of kinship relations in Brazilian society, as well as the preservation of social hierarchies in connection with these relations. They have not only shaped the character of social relations in general, such as marriage patterns (which tend to be rather endogamic in accordance with socioeconomic level), but also constituted the nucleus of a great deal of political and economic influence in the wider national context, in a manner, one might say, reminiscent of the clans of preindustrial Scotland (on this aspect, see, e.g., Weber,

1978:250). Given this basic circumstance, the characterization of the Brazilian system of ethnic stratification as being of the "patrimonial" type is not especially viable. The unqualified application of the term is misleading, and dismisses the fact that social paternalism in interethnic relations in that society is exercised mainly as a reflection of variations, not of race, but within the class structure.

Notes

1   Some analysts (e.g., Nogueira, 1959) have traced the origins of this fundamental pattern of ethnic stratification to the implantation of the *latifundium* - the semi-feudal system of large-scale agricultural production, "generally dedicated to a single product for export," and framed in a sharply hierarchized social structure - early on in the colonial history of these societies, and consolidated during the slavery phase.

2   An important distinction must be stressed here concerning the "treatment-of-the-slave" aspect. Genovese (1969) reformulates this concept by breaking it down into three distinct levels of treatment: (a) material conditions of day-to-day existence, involving diet (the quantity and quality of the food supply), clothing, general conditions of labor); (b) conditions of life, involving family structure, physical mobility, "opportunities for an independent social and religious life"; and, (c) access to freedom and citizenship, involving social influences and circumstances linked to the process of sociocultural assimilation of the Africans. Insofar as the strictly material aspect of plantation life was concerned, the U.S. slave population can be considered to have been comparatively better clothed, fed, and cared for in the United States (Phillips, 1909:109-30, vol.I; 1969:chs.xii through xvi). This was primarily due to the more privileged U.S. economy, which made it possible for the material maintenance of the slave force to be accomplished more easily and adequately than in Brazil or other New World slavery systems. As Genovese claims (1969:208), regarding the specific factor of slave diet, "[t]he national economic structure of the United States greatly facilitated the provision of food supplies for the slaves, whereas that of Brazil inhibited it". At the same time, it is useful to keep in mind that, even though the Southern plantation system had a high level of economic rationalization and capitalist organization, this only facilitated but did not necessarily guarantee, in all cases, the proper physical maintenance of the slave force. The

fundamental structure of inequality, arbitrariness, and economic exploitation undergirding the relation between the master and slave classes conspired to interfere with this process. The collection of slave narratives put together in the 1930s in connection with the Federal Writers Project reveals many instances of this. One former slave, from Texas, recalled how in the antebellum South "[w]asn't many massas what allowed dere niggers have patches and some didn't even feed'em enough. Dat's why dey have to get out and hustle at night to get food for dem to eat." Another former slave, from Tennessee, had this to say of the masters: "They didn't half feed us, either. They fed the animals better" (in Yetman, 1970:112, 116).

3   An in-depth comparative analysis of slave legislation in Brazil and the United States is beyond the scope and aim of the present study. However, some points may be addressed. It is certainly a matter of historical record that official corruption, together with the considerable autonomy of the master class vis-a-vis civil powers, served to undermine the enforcement of protective slave legislation in Brazil (see, e.g., Conrad, 1983:235, in this regard), but the lax enforcement of this type of legislation and its frequent and mostly unpunished violation was also a feature of the antebellum American South, as Stampp (1956:217-24) informs us. Economic interest in every slavery society provided a most powerful incentive for masters to bend or simply ignore the legal protections of the slave at every opportunity, and that they did, mostly with impunity. At the same time, arrangements and practices related to the structure of the legal system and its historical antecedents, in each slave society, *did* produce significant crossnational differences in the degree and manner in which slave law was exercised in the two countries (for a fuller treatment of this issue, see Camara, 1983:chapters IV and V); hence, a more fruitful line of investigation and comparison would have to take these aspects under consideration.

4   The position adopted here is aligned with Nogueira's analysis (1959) which, starting from the acknowledgement of the presence of race-based prejudice in the United States as well as in Brazil, proceeds to stress the dissimilar manner in which this phenomenon is expressed in the two societies, not only in terms of the level of intensity, but also in the very nature of race prejudice itself. The typology introduced by Nogueira is based on a distinction which characterizes the type of race prejudice operative in the United States as genotypically regulated, whereas the Brazilian version is

51

phenotypically regulated. This distinction is consistent with the rigidly biracial basis of intergroup relations in the U.S. and the multiracial basis of these relations in Brazil. Nogueira's analysis also addresses the divergent social, institutional, and ideological treatment of the minority element in the two societies.

5   The point defended here is that, after the initial phase of intergroup contact has passed, cultural assimilation, or structural assimilation, does not follow as a matter of course, as the next stage of development. The manner in which the assimilative process is handled and how it will affect the different groups will hinge primarily on the nature of the cultural system of the society. The absence of cultural integration (i.e., the complex of cultural blending, biological blending, and the formation of a national identity that will be prioritized by all the members of society) will be a systematic obstacle to progress in the structural or institutional sectors of social life. Thus, under ideal circumstances, cultural assimilation ought to proceed hand in hand with structural assimilation, so that the complete incorporation of minority segments into the social mainstream can be brought about. Myrdal (1962:929) underscores this aspect, with specific reference to the situation of members of the African-American community in the United States (although his point is applicable to unassimilated groups in general), by remarking that their full-scale absorption into the larger society would chiefly depend on their acquisition of "the traits held in esteem by the dominant white Americans." Regarding the same group, Dubois (1990:14, orig. 1903) suggested that, in addition to economic and educational advancement, cultural integration and interpenetration with the dominant group would be a critical factor behind their incorporation into the mainstream, and a process that would in fact be mutually beneficial for all concerned. The minority community, he recommended, ought not to try to develop in isolation, but "in large conformity to the greater ideals of the American republic, in order that some day on American soil two world-races may give to each the characteristics both so sadly lack."

6   The historical pattern of non-transformability of ethnic difference, as manifested in the exclusion from the social mainstream, may be exemplified by the phenomenon of *plaçage*, in 19th century New Orleans, an institutionalized practice whereby Quadroon women (i.e., the term "quadroon" applied to those of mixed racial ancestry, specifically, with one African-American grandparent) were groomed to become concubines of upper-class white young men. These were

52

young women who not only, by all outward appearances, "passed for white" in most instances, but were also formally educated and socially refined. In spite of this, they were systematically denied social inclusion into the mainstream society. These concubinary liaisons generally lasted until such time as when the young man took a white wife. "Every Quadroon woman," wrote Martineau in the 1830s, "believes that her partner will prove an exception to the rule of desertion" (1962:225; orig. 1837). In some cases, the man would continue the connection after marriage, but this did not remove the aspect of social illegitimacy of the *plaçage*. As Blassingame informs us (1976:18), these relations were not "recognized by the law."

7   By most accounts, city slaves in the American South also hired themselves out in large numbers, in a variety of occupations (e.g., Phillips, 1969:ch.XX; Wade, 1964), in a manner that strongly paralleled the Brazilian case. However, the emphasis here must be placed on the crossnational variation with respect to a number of specific aspects of the hiring-out process, namely, the degree in which the practice occurred, the range of its formal regimentation by the Slave Codes, and the extent to which it functioned as an avenue to manumission. In the U.S., the hiring-out of urban slaves appears to have been subjected to an array of highly restrictive measures, legal and otherwise, to a degree higher than in Brazil. Specific legislation was enacted in all the major Southern cities (e.g., Savannah, Ga., Mobile, Ala., Richmond, Va.) for the purpose of regulating and inhibiting this practice, expressing the larger concern of the Southerners with reducing black physical mobility to a minimum. In this connection, Southern cities had mounted, by the mid-1800s, a formidable apparatus of control of the physical movements of the black population, to the point of one observer (Olmsted, 1970:460) referring to it simply as "the military condition of the South," a condition that comprised such appurtenances as "citadels, sentries, passports, grape-shotted canon, and daily public whippings of the subjects for accidental infractions of police ceremonies" (1970:444). This larger preoccupation with the control of black physical mobility stemmed from a generalized public fear of black insurrections, and it created a generally unfavorable social climate for the hiring-out practice. Additionally, there was the aspect of economic competition with whites, and, finally, the intense Southern discomfort with the fact that, by hiring themselves out, slaves stood a better chance of purchasing their freedom. This was probably the most problematic aspect of all. The very notion of blacks in freedom was aberrational

53

within the social organization of Southern society, inimical to all that the latter stood for. Free blacks, as Stampp (1956:215) reminds us, were perceived as an anomaly, "a living denial 'that nature's God intended the African for the status of slavery.'" "To be a free Negro," declared William Goodell in his magisterial documentary study of the American slave codes, "differs widely ... from being a free man" (1853:357). In time, the emancipation of the Africans came to be seen as a plausible proposition only when "connected with transportation to Africa" (Goodell, p.364). The general sentiment to deport liberated slaves, and Africans in general (the "Back-to-Africa" movement) found material expression in the formation of the American Colonization Society in 1817, under the auspices of which the West African colony of Liberia came into existence in 1822, with assistance from the U.S. government (Quarles, 1976:95-96).

3 The meeting of dominant and minority cultures: Integration vs. separatism

Patterns of interethnic contact

As indicated in the foregoing, the examination of intergroup relations in the cultural realm will be directed to specific aspects of the assimilative process. We begin with the nature of the interaction between the dominant and minority cultural communities. The guiding principle here is that interethnic inequality and conflict can be alleviated or exacerbated on the basis of whether the society enforces a pattern of cultural integration or unification (through syncretism), or cultural segmentalization (through separatism). In his statement on the effect of cultural unity on the larger society, Park (1964:206) supports this general position: "It is probably true ... that like-mindedness of the kind that expresses itself in national types, contributes, indirectly, by facilitating the intermingling of the different elements of the population, to the national solidarity."

In Brazil, ethnic minorities (the term is used here to designate primarily the African and Amerindian populations, but it applies *latu sensu* to the other groups that arrived later, in the 19th century, mainly from Germany, Italy, and Japan) have been affected by a general tendency of the society to amalgamate and assimilate all ethnic minorities (Pierson, 1944; Wagley, 1948, 1971; Freyre, 1956). The cultural contributions of these groups have been fused into the national culture, and are recognized as an integral part of the latter, not as peripheral or subcultural expressions, as "quaint or exotic excrescences," as Frazier (1944:263) aptly put it. Therefore, there is no differentiation between people from the dominant and minority ethnic communities insofar as the basic patterns of language, aesthetics, morality, and social ethos are concerned. Although distinctions regarding these elements can surely be made on the basis of *class*, what prevails is a "general framework of cultural uniformity" (Wagley, 1948:461; this author speaks elsewhere of this societal framework as the "Brazilian Great Tradition," 1971:5). In relation to this, members of ethnic minorities identify first and foremost with the larger or national culture, not with their groups of origin.

To some extent, of course, an awareness of ethnic-racial distinctions, and the implications and effects of this on intergroup life and social structure, forms part of the self-understanding of Brazilians of racially-mixed background. After all, they can see that their racial background must have had something to do with their overrepresentation in the less privileged social echelons. Still, the aspect of race is not paramount in the minds of these individuals, nor should it be understood in abstraction from the larger circumstance of their slavery background and the socioeconomic and political handicap it imposed on them. Race has not directly made for the marginalization of the population of African descent in the sense that Park postulates the notion of "the marginal man," a person "who lives in two worlds, in both of which he is more or less a stranger" (1964:356). This is a situation which Park, arguing along the same lines as the present analysis, attributes largely to the absence of biological assimilation of the ethnic minority in question, which in turn prevents full cultural assimilation from occurring.

But, to return to the question of cultural unity in the Brazilian setting. We may consider, in this regard, a duality which expresses the action of centripetal and centrifugal forces on the formation of Brazilian culture. From the standpoint of centripetal action, we find that the term "Afro-Brazilian" for a Brazilian of African descent is not entirely appropriate because it denotes the permanent subcultural segregation of Brazilians of African descent from the mainstream population, which is not reflective of the dominant pattern there, that being the amalgamation of all ethnic-cultural strains into a national "center." In the area of collective identity, the term would also suggest the primary identification of these individuals with the subcultural community within the larger society, when in fact their primary identity is "Brazilian." (The same consideration would also apply, for instance, to individuals of African extraction in other American and/or Caribbean multiethnic societies, like for instance Cuba or Puerto Rico, where the prevailing pattern is cultural integration, with direct repercussions for processes of cultural identity). From the standpoint of centrifugal action, it must be noted that it would be considered appropriate (or culturally "permissible") in Brazil for individuals of *any* ethnic or racial background to acknowledge and express the African influence as they live out the national modes of life, inasmuch as that influence, though syncretistically preserved in its distinctiveness, has concomitantly formed an integral part - in the arts, music, diet, speech, religion--of the national culture, a culture that is in turn fundamentally accessible to everyone. The ability of all individuals to incorporate and express cultural traits from the diverse heritages that make up the sociocultural system--whether it be dominant-group members appropriating the foreign influences without losing touch with the core culture, or minority-group members experiencing inclusion into the dominant institutional spheres without losing the connection with their ancestral traditions--has been characterized by Bastide (1971:25) as the *principe de coupure*, or principle of dissociation.[1] In this hybrid context, anyone - any educated person, for instance - is able to relate equally and lay claim to such diverse aspects of national life as African-style musical percussion, 18th-century *divertimenti*, or Amerindian folk remedies, simply because these are elements drawn from the three main cultural streams - the African, the European, and the Amerindian - that merged to form the cultural system of the society. They are part of the overall mixture. In this way, it becomes possible for "race" and "ethnicity" to be transcended by "culture." The latter emerges as the general unifying principle, as can be seen in the following incident. During the late 1960s, the Brazilian masses, struggling to bear up under the strain of a very oppressive political regime, eagerly embraced and identified with any cultural manifestations - in the arts, music, literature - perceived as expressing the popular yearning for political liberation. One such manifestation was the very popular song at that time entitled *Zumbi* (by E. Lobo and V. de Moraes), which everyone knew and sang at song festivals, and which became a vehicle of political protest. So far, nothing very extraordinary. This type of collective behavior, whereby different cultural products are appropriated by the masses for political or ideological purposes, may be witnessed everywhere in societies undergoing political authoritarianism. In fact, during that same time in Brazil other popular songs (e.g., *Disparada*, by G. Vandré) were even more clearly symbolic of the popular sentiment against the existing socio-political order. The greater significance of the "Zumbi" song in this regard, however, emerges when we consider what or who Zumbi is or was: the brave leader of a 17th century community of runaway slaves in northeast Brazil, the *Palmares Republic*, which stood for half a century. Brazilian schoolchildren study about Zumbi and the Palmares incident, and people regard him as an icon of resistance and defiance against organized power. That, to this day, the wider society finds no inconsistency in the symbolic appropriation of a 17th century African slave for embodying a universal principle, namely, freedom, as in this song, is the aspect of greatest relevance here, and it becomes all the more relevant when we contrast it with parallel situations

57

drawn from the U.S. context, such as for instance the slave insurrections led by Denmark Vesey (1822) and Nat Turner (1831) in the antebellum South. The question to be raised in this connection is how these slave leaders have fared symbolically in the collective consciousness of U.S. society since that time. (The immediate consequence of slave uprisings in every slave society was, of course, swift and harsh retaliation, with only some variation in the degree of societal resentment and punishment; but this is not the focal point here.) It might also be argued that Martin Luther King is a recent and equivalent example of a minority-group leader whose martyrdom is regarded in the society at large as a symbol of resistance against organized oppression. The problem with this idea of universal (i.e., society-wide) appropriation and "ownership" of subcultural or minority-group symbols is that it simply does not mesh with the workings of a separatist, biracially-organized social system. One is reminded of this fact by events like, for example, the defacing a few years ago of a sculpture of Martin Luther King on the campus of a Midwestern university. This sculpture had to be brought indoors after it was vandalized twice (*Chronicle of Higher Education*, March 17, 1993, p.A4).

At this point it must be stressed that the assimilationist policy and ideology which have yielded in Brazil (and in other societies of the hemisphere, like Cuba or Colombia, for example) a unified national identity for all members of the society, is not a phenomenon to be necessarily understood in terms of the rigid imposition of the neo-European cultural model (neo-Portuguese, in the case of Brazil), under which all other cultural strains would have been forced to submerge and disappear, in the mold of what Gordon (1964) and Cole and Cole (1954) have called the "Anglo-conformity" model of assimilation. As previously stressed, this process has instead been based on the cross-pollination and eventual integration of the various cultural traditions. Herskovits (1937:635) has written regarding the interaction between African religious patterns and the dominant Catholic tradition in Brazilian society, to the effect that "the exchange has been less than one-sided, and the elements ancestral to the present-day organization of [the Afro-Brazilian religious cult] worship have been retained in immediately recognizable form." The reciprocity of this cultural interplay was recorded by Koster (1816:411), when he wrote, regarding the Brazilian slaves, that "[n]o compulsion is resorted to to make them embrace the habits of their masters ... The masters at the same time imbibe some of the customs of these slaves, and thus the superior and his dependent are brought nearer to each other."

In the United States, one finds a sharply dissimilar pattern of dominant-minority cultural relations. U.S. society has historically upheld a cultural framework based on separatism, a pattern that may be evidenced, among other things, in the thematic preponderance of the idea of ethnicity itself, in the public and official discourse of the society. At root, this separatism is linked to the dualistic cultural relation (derived from the racially bipolar administration of social life in general) between the core culture - which is perceived as the exclusive "property" of all those ethnic contingents that have been fully absorbed into the dominant *social race* on the basis of their classification as white - and all other cultural communities that have from the outset been classified as biologically unassimilable. It is true, of course, that the incoming groups categorized as biologically assimilable upon their arrival (the "white ethnics," such as, for instance, the Scandinavians), and which rapidly (i.e., within the first couple of generations) came to form an integral part of the dominant group in the society, were pushed towards as swift and full-range assimilation as possible. And it cannot be denied that this process of "Americanization" reveals the presence of an assimilationist tendency, indeed in extreme form. Nevertheless, even in this case the assimilative process at best rarely took the form of cross-fertilization and mutual contribution of the various cultural strains at the morphological and institutional levels, the form of "true syncretism" (Bastide, 1971:153), at the same time that these strains were preserved, through their coexistence. Rather, as indicated earlier, this model of assimilation, a kind of "pressure-cooking" assimilation (Gordon, 1964:99), has significantly hindered the syncretistic exchange between the core and minority cultures.[2] In this model of intergroup relations, the host culture, in its effort to maintain its own monolithic uniformity, actively incorporates the foreign cultural elements that it defines as compatible and assimilable, while keeping its distance and separation from those which it deems unassimilable. Over time, this process led (in the U.S. setting) to the formation and crystallization of a fundamental dualism on the basis of biology or "race" which has divided the society into a cohesive "American" culture formed from the cultural traits of "white" groups, on the one hand, and a network of minority (i.e., nonwhite") cultural communities, on the other. However, during the initial period of intergroup contact (that is, during the time when the newcomers are entering the society), the *general* relation of appropriation of the host society toward *all* of the various cultural communities is marked by ambiguity. The former hastens to obliterate the presence and the perceived potentially pernicious effect of the "foreign difference" by absorbing it as swiftly and completely as possible, and yet it proceeds with trepidation because of its deep distrust and discomfort regarding this difference. Since colonial times, we are told (Gordon, 1964:89), the Anglo-Saxon core culture has reacted with suspicion towards all that was "foreign," whether that be in reference to religion or national background. In fact, during most of the 1800s, a period when large-scale immigration would have proved most beneficial for the larger U.S. society insofar as labor and demographic considerations were concerned, the same attitude of ambivalence prevailed, practical interests notwithstanding. The concrete consequences of this attitude may be seen in the vehemence with which 19th-century nativist political programs and exclusionary immigration policies were pursued. As for the groups classified as nonwhite (hence, as biologically unassimilable), they have been barred from full-scale acculturation and from significantly contributing to the formation of the national culture. In general terms, the impact of minority-group cultures - the "white ethnics" as well as the groups permanently categorized as racial minorities (principally the latter) - on the core culture has been, as Gordon has noted, only of "modest dimensions" (1964:109).[3] At the present time, minority ethnic communities are legally guaranteed inclusion into the formal or institutional sectors of the society, but continue to experience limited cultural, biological, and psychosocial assimilation.

From the standpoint of this analysis, the overriding pattern that emerges is therefore one of dualism in the treatment of minority-group cultures in U.S. society, and this judgement is particularly applicable to black-white relations. This basic pattern of separatism has not been altered by the eradication of *de jure* segregation involving the dominant and minority ethnic communities since the 1950s. The circumstances that could illustrate cultural separatism are innumerable, but a few examples shall suffice. The case of black dialectal English is classic. It is common knowledge in U.S. society that someone speaking on the radio or on the phone can be readily recognized as a "white" or "black" person. Additionally, regional variations in patterns of speech, which are quickly detected in members of the dominant ethnic group, are generally assumed not to be operative for African-Americans. That people in general should find this normal attests to the high degree of internalization of the separatist consciousness by members of the dominant and minority ethnic communities alike. Evidently, when dialectal versions of the national language, which, as expected, are treated by the larger society as substandard and, therefore, marginal, versions of that language, continue to be cultivated by members of a given ethnic minority, coming to function as a mark of identity for those individuals (as in the case of African-American dialectal English) this will at best slow down, at worst completely prevent, their full structural incorporation into the institutional and social mainstream.

Another example may be cited in the arts - the area of music, specifically. People *outside* the United States may consider jazz music to be the quintessential American cultural form, but not people *in* the United

States. During the entire Jim Crow period and even immediately afterwards, this music was widely shunned and denigrated as "nigger music," particularly in its early phase of development, or the period prior to World War II (Leonard, 1970). Peretti (1997:92) writes about, during World War II, the renowned white jazz musician Gil Evans "brought V-disks of his favorite players, especially Louis Armstrong, with him in Europe, and white GIs almost assaulted him for carrying 'colored music.'"

These attitudes of hostility towards jazz music derived simply from the fact that the majority population did not quite see this music as a *general* American phenomenon, but as something intimately connected with the African-American community. In the early decades of the century, in particular, jazz was also widely perceived as being associated with liquor and unbridled sexuality, which further intensified its rejection by white folks, and its characterization as "an abomination" (Collier, 1978:127). It was clear that the presumably pernicious social effects of jazz were cast in racial terms, that is, in terms of the racial contamination and degeneracy of white society. As one observer describes it:

Traditionalist notions about the origins of jazz provided fuel for ... racial fears. Whereas some traditionalists believed that jazz was born in the Negro brothel, others traced the origins of the music to the jungle and believed that the African roots of *jazz* explained its association with violence ... Such notions helped spread fears that Negroes under the influence of *jazz* would become violent ... Many traditionalists found that the African origins of *jazz* held even more frightening implications ... Dr. Florence Richards, medical director of a Philadelphia high school for girls [wrote that] 'its influence is as harmful and degrading to civilized races as it always has been among savages from whom we borrowed it.' She warned that continued exposure to this evil influence 'may tear to pieces our whole social fabric.' Others believed that *jazz*, the music of the jungle, was a form of retrogression that was returning American society to an age of barbarism" (Leonard, 1970:39).

The cultural marginality of this music, and of black music as a whole, has, therefore, been well documented (see also de Lerma, 1970).[4] It is true, of course, that jazz music has experienced greater acceptance into the musical mainstream in the U.S., thereby enlarging and enriching the musical vocabulary significantly over the past half century. Norman Mailer wrote some decades ago of jazz's "knife-like entrance into the culture; its subtle but so penetrating influence on the avant-garde

61

generation" (in Hentoff, 1975:138). However, in a fundamental way, its image and existence as a subcultural phenomenon linger on. Additionally, within jazz itself some distinctions should be noted concerning the kind of jazz played by black and white musicians. Though the latter have been drawing much more freely on black rhythms and melodies, at the more funda-mental level the separatist cultural framework of the society has prevailed, meaning that the larger pattern of biracial management of social relations, and the resulting differential avenues of cultural conditioning for blacks and whites have, in the longer run, caused black and white musicians to produce distinctively different versions of jazz music. Case in point: the musical tendencies associated with the "West Coast" jazz movement of the 1950s, a movement spearheaded primarily by white musicians and composers. In its attempt to unite elements of classical music with jazz, this movement stood in sharp contrast with the general directions emphasized by black jazz musicians of the same period, and, of course, in even sharper contrast with New Orleans-style "hot jazz," a primarily black phenomenon, heavily geared towards musical and rhythmic improvisation.

But, if a common ground is to be found for jazz musicians as a group, it would have to be in the technical area. As might be gathered, the bulk of what has been absorbed from the culture of jazz by white musicians consists of technical material, that is, it has to do with musical craftsmanship. Given that jazz is a product of the African-American assimilative experience in the United States and, as such, an important existential vehicle for the black community, it is culturally specific and not general, in terms of symbolizing that which is quintessential to this subcultural group: its joys, sorrows, aspirations, failures, and achievements. Considering this factor against the background of cultural separatism in the larger social system, one can see how jazz cannot possibly symbolize American life as a whole, American life in its mainstream sense. It is an artistic medium that translates the creative energy and the specific existential impulses of African-Americans as a group. Having been born in the last years of the 19th century, and developing through the Jim Crow period of legally-santioned segregation and discrimination, during that period in particular it gave musical expression to the psychological turmoil, collective anger and frustration, of blacks over their subjugation - it externalized "the angry bitterness," which, as Hentoff (1975:140) argues, is "at the base of much jazz." The jazz that has been played by black musicians and white musicians may, therefore, exhibit technical and stylistic commonalities and continuities, but these afinities do not extend into the existential space because the life circumstances of these two groups in American society have been radically divergent (this gap has narrowed considerably since the end of legal segregation). Hence, what flows from their art is not a sense of oneness, the same collective spirit and direction.

Undoubtedly, white jazz musicians, as they worked out from the outset their own jazz idiom, as they adopted the stylistic and technical influences of the leading figures in black jazz, were eventually able to exert their own influence over their sources of inspiration, and over the developing jazz movement as a whole. Such was the case, for instance, of Bix Beiderbecke's impact in the early 1920s over the entire spectrum of jazz music (Williams, 1983: chapter III). This was clearly an instance of syncretic exchange of musical tendencies. Still, taken as a whole, the distinctions and qualifications I have made here warrant closer attention.

This pattern of cultural compartmentalization may also be identified in reference to the recent growth of Hispanic or "Latino" musical influences in the U.S. entertainment market. These are mainly rhythms such as Cuban and Puerto Rican *salsa* music and other musical hybrids. Though these influences have sometimes been perceived as seeping into the musical mainstream since the late 1970s-early 1980s, according to the manager of a NYC radio station back in the late 1980s they were still being characterized by the public at large as Spanish music (*Time*, July 11, 1988, p.52).

There are many other black/white cultural differences in American society that represent the larger pattern of cultural separatism, some easily noticeable, others more subtle. One that has developed and solidified over the years, and which, like so many other cultural traits, is perceived by many as "natural," that is, as genetically inherited, a peculiarly "racial thing," is a certain style of gait and arm-and-hand movements that has become associated in this society with African-American males. In connection with this, white "rappers" (i.e., the musician-singer-dancers who play Black "rap music") in the early 1990s were generally regarded by African-Americans as being inherently incapable - because of their "white" background - of duplicating these movements correctly, so as to use them in their dance routines. Obviously, that was not the case - that is to say, those white performers were not *inherently* incapable of duplicating the dancing style of the black groups - and what was involved in that situation was simply another instance of the all too common attribution of cultural traits to "racial" origin. The trait in question here - the dancing style of U.S. black entertainers - is evidently a reflection of cultural training within the African-American community in the United States, and as such a pattern that is peculiar to this specific cultural (or subcultural) milieu, and not something that one would find among blacks-as-a-group in any other part of the world, so far as I am aware. But this is not the crucial aspect here. It is not unusual for an ethnic community to display these kinds of cultural peculiarities. What is unusual is for this to occur as a variation *within the same national group*, as is the case here. It draws attention to the failure of the society to integrate the entire population culturally. Thus, in the United States this type of situation, which takes a number of different forms, stems from the enduring presence of sociocultural separatism as the regulative criterion of intergroup life.

Further notes on syncretism

Bateson (1935:179) has conceived of cultural contact in terms of three possible outcomes: "the complete fusion of the originally different groups; the elimination of one or both groups, [and] the persistence of both groups in dynamic equilibrium within one major community." We should stress here that these distinctions are only formal and ideal-typical. In reality, the syncretic process, because it is dialectical and not linear, encompasses all three aspects. The integrationist model of culture introduced here, for instance, exhibits associations between the various cultural streams of the society which reveal all three outcomes simultaneously. In other words, these streams fuse together into a new, coherent cultural whole, which involves an alteration of their original constitutions, and, in this sense, their elimination in "pure" form. At the same time, as already discussed, these formative elements retain enough of their original identity to be thus recognized, and in this "moment" of the dialectic, they coexist with one another in "dynamic equilibrium," as Bateson put it.

This problem deserves closer scrutiny. Where intergroup relations express a dominant-minority pattern of differentiation, as is always the case in any context where minority ethnic communities interact with a dominant ethnic group, cultural relations between these groups will necessarily reflect their structural (i.e., related to power and wealth) asymmetry. It may be said that in national contexts where syncretism is the chief property of the cultural system, cultural relations will exhibit greater overall symmetry and reciprocity than in contexts where cultural separatism is enforced. Moreover, the greater symmetry or asymmetry in intergroup cultural relations will affect the broader aspect of material inequality in the social system, in terms of attenuating or aggravating it. Thus, one may reasonably speak of a situation of (relative) equality in the cultural sphere, mediated and facilitated by syncretism, even though this may still operate within the larger framework of economic and political stratification. This may be pursued in reference to the idea of cultural

64

reciprocity and symmetry. This implies that, insofar as interethnic cultural relations are concerned, though they normally take place contiguously with dominant-minority material inequality and social distance, it is possible for the modes of behavior and thought of the groups involved to be exchanged and combined interchangeably, in a complex and wide-ranging process, provided these behavioral and thinking modes are functionally correspondent. Cultural reciprocity and symmetry are enhanced when accomodation, instability, and plasticity prevail in the societal treatment of the identity of cultural objects - which then affects the society's stance towards the "difference" of minority communities. Essentially, this society-wide interchangeability in the treament of diverse (dominant and minority) cultural objects amounts to (for lack of a better phrase) the "undifferentiation of difference." This is what imparts greater equality to intergroup relations in the cultural sphere, that is, the superordinate and subordinate cultural traditions come to interact on a fairly egalitarian basis.

Additionally, the interchangeability (made possible by structural-functioal equivalences and complementarities) of cultural objects is the basis of the centripetal and centrifugal properties of the syncretic process, mentioned earlier, which in turn account for the pliable cultural identity that individuals are able to have in this type of cultural system. In other words, the absence of rigid cultural definitions and categorizations enables the individual to identify with, and move back and forth between, the different formative cultural streams of the society without experiencing cultural disorientation. (It is in this sense, for example, that a person of African descent in Brazil can see him/herself as a Latin, and display the modes of thought and behavior associated with being *Latin*-American, because of his/her complete symbolic and material access to, and participation in, the Ibero-American cultural heritage of the country; and, conversely, a white Brazilian, of more direct European ancestry, may feel completely at home in relation to the African influences in the wider culture (e.g., in music, the *cuisine*, religion) - and neither individual feels that this in any way contradicts and/or compromises their national identity as Brazilians. In fact, they may feel reassured that this truly expresses the syncretic nature of that identity. The entire process is stabilized and made coherent syncretically, whereby neither the merging of the various cultural traditions (the centripetality aspect), nor the independent operation of each tradition as a distinctive cultural structure, its separateness from the other formative strains of the larger culture (the centrifugality aspect), reaches the point of completion. The structural coherence obtains from the dialectical interrelation of these cultural traditions, by a constant coming-together and coming-apart, which produces neither the obliteration of the individuality of each tradition, nor the latter's permanent withdrawal into self-sufficient isolation, but maintains instead everything in equilibrium. To illustrate: among the various functional correspondences found in Luso-Brazilian folk religion between Catholic saints and West African nature gods, we find the equivalence between *Omolu*, the Yoruba god of smallpox, and St. Sebastian. The latter, who is lithographically represented in the Catholic tradition as a martyr shot through with arrows, has his body covered with wounds which also suggest the pustules produced by smallpox (see, e.g., Bastide, 1971:157). Thus, both the Christian and non-Christian motifs are represented simultaneously in the Catholic saint. Notwithstanding the integration of these two elements in the cultural object (i.e., the divinity) of the hegemonic religious tradition, they remain juxtaposed, and therefore discernible, in their original aspect.

The mechanisms of cultural reciprocity and complementarity, manifested in the constant cross-fertilization of cultural items, lend a quality of overall fluidity, rather than stable compartmentalization, to the cultural system. The latter assumes an ever-changing conformation, much like the patterns in a kaleidoscope. The driving force here is the constant syncretic incorporation of difference, and the possibility of reciprocal interaction between dominant and minority modes of life, which is what gives substance to the idea of cultural equality in the social system.[5] The prevalence of an amalgamationist orientation in the larger society generally results in the greater valuation of assimilated and recombined (i.e., syncretized) minority difference, over the "pure" type, that is, over the type associated exclusively with the dominant ethnic group. This may be detected, for instance, in the case of Brazil, in the widespread popular attraction for the hybrid physical type, such as the *morena* woman, with implications of standards of aesthetic and sexual desirability (see Freyre, 1956:14; also, Pierson, 1967:136-37, who describes the *morena* as follows: "Typically, she has dark-brown eyes and dark hair, quite wavy, perhaps even curly, and Caucasian features; her color is *café-com-leite* [literally, 'coffee-with-milk'] like that of one 'heavily tanned.'"

In contradistinction, the interaction of the ruling and subaltern cultural communities in nonsyncretistic social systems, in particular those systems where cultural separatism has been officially and unofficially enforced, is clearly asymmetrical or inegalitarian. As indicated earlier, the maintenance of precise and rigid boundary lines between the dominant and minority cultures first of all inhibits the establishment of syncretic relations between them. Even where the acculturation of the minority element is actively pursued by the host society (as in the case of the "white ethnics" in the United States, in particular during the peak of the "Americanization" crusade, in the early 1900s), this generally takes place in terms of the unyielding preponderance of the core culture over this element. Thus, there is no basis of reversibility and mutuality of influence, as manifested in the large-scale intertwining of behavior and belief patterns. An illustration of this is the nature of the cultural relationship between the Southern masters and their West African slaves, which displayed such features as the fact that the slaves absorbed the Protestantism and the English of their masters - up to a point, of course, and with modification - but the dominant religion and language were, in the main, efficiently shielded from any significant degree of African religious and linguistic influence. Genovese (1976-431-41), for example, addresses the fact that there was virtually no absorption whatever of African linguistic patterns into the English of the Southern slaveholding class, and the decades of contact of U.S. slaves with the English of their masters were characterized by a separatism which eventually led to the emergence of a "plantation dialect," the latter forming the basis for the distinctive pattern of speech of blacks in U.S. society. The mutual shaping of linguistic patterns between the slaveholding and slave classes is simply not registered. Granted, Genovese does make a general reference to the cultural convergence of groups under long-term and close contact with each other, but in this particular case of dominant-minority relations in the Old South, the cultural separateness of the nascent African-American dialect is clearly emphasized. More importantly, the enforcement of cultural separatism may be detected in the fact that white masters in the South often punished slaves for using "good English," rather than their own developing dialect (see Freyre,1956, *inter alia*, for contrasting examples of linguistic exchange on the Brazilian plantation; also, Camara, 1988).

It happens that even in separatist cultural systems minority-group cultural traits will be incorporated into the core culture in varying degrees, as the earlier discussion of jazz should have indicated, but the provisos must be retained. To begin with, in separatist systems regulated by racial bipolarity, the degree of absorption of minority-group traditions is generally much higher when the minority cultural communities in question are classified as white. Secondly, owing to the segregationist policy governing the cultural relations between the groups classified as white and those classified as nonwhite, the absorption of cultural aspects from the nonwhite groups by the white tends to be much more limited. In any case, it bears stressing again that in nonsyncretistic sociocultural systems the process of absorption of minority-group traits *in general* lacks the basis of exchange between interchangeable cultural objects, which have the capacity for mutually influencing one another. The cultural traits judged assimilable are not ordinarily related to on their own terms, but rather assimilated and "processed" in a way that renders them almost unrecognizable (i.e., in the sense of becoming qualitatively different) in reference to their original condition. One could point to numerous instances of this phenomenon. A particularly good example, I believe, is found in what might be termed the "Americanization of soccer." Football-association (soccer), as developed by the English in the last century and practiced in virtually every corner of the globe down to the present time, remains fundamentally a game of which the most thrilling aspect is its very unfolding on the field, the playing itself, and the final outcome becomes, in this sense at least, an almost irrelevant part of the whole spectacle. It is thus a sporting event that is best grasped and appreciated as *process*, not as *product*. This is why final scores and other empirical dimensions become secondary to the form in which the playing has taken place. This is probably the most fundamental idea to emphasize in trying to depict this game, and the most salient feature to bring into focus here regarding the way it has been played over the past century. When soccer was introduced to American society in formal, systematic, and large-scale fashion in the 1970s, it was quickly ascertained that a formidable barrier in the way of public acceptance would be precisely the matter of "outcomes," that is, game scores are generally not high enough to satisfy the American taste. In relation with this, there has been a concern and effort in some quarters to alter the rules and structure of the game sufficiently so as to facilitate the production of higher scores. (This has, in fact, already been done in the American version of indoor soccer. Lately [1996], this tendency has gathered momentum with the organization of a nation-wide professional soccer league). As for the assimilative situation involving the cultural expressions of the nonwhite groups, the absence of cross-fertilization between the dominant and minority cultures, and of explicit society-wide acknowledgement of the operation of the minority-group influence, is naturally even more pronounced, as already emphasized.

This brief clarification of syncretism and the cultural processes linked to it should serve to show that intergroup cultural relations are not the same across different cultural systems, and that while some measure of syncretism between the dominant and minority ethnic communities may be obtained in the separatist model of culture, inquiries into this subject must ascertain the extent and generality of the syncretic processes, as well as the nature of the interaction between the majority and minority cultures (concerning this last aspect, see Herskovits's idea of *reinterpretation*, 1972).

Points of agglutination

Structurally, the polar types of culture discussed here reveal their cardinal importance in the degree that they have a totalizing effect on the society, that is to say, in the degree that they directly mold the life circumstances and consciousness of the groups that make up the body social. This occurs either in terms of bringing about the cultural consolidation of intergroup life, or, alternatively, the latter's cultural fragmentation. In the integrationist model of culture, the consolidation process, as I have insisted, is effected dialectically, by means of syncretic processes that render the larger assimilative process less one of authoritarian erasure of minority-group difference, and more one of coexistence *cum* interfusion of majority and minority traits. In this way, all members of the society experience a centralization of their cultural identity and, indeed, existence in the more general sense, in particular patterns which are emblematic of their cultural world. These aspects therefore generate a high level of synchronicity in the cultural sphere, which expresses the condition of cultural integration. They may be called "points of agglutination,"[6] and pertain either (1) to predominant cultural orientations of national groups - such as, for instance, for American culture, the pragmatic impulse (and related aspects, like, e.g., the cult of the present, the instrumental conception of reality); the anti-urban ethos (see, e.g., Flanagan, 1995:ch.II); the values of self-reliance and informality; the tendency to demystify and reduce everything to the level of the commonplace or ordinary; interpersonal egalitarianism; attitudes towards work generated by the Puritan work ethic; and, for Brazilian culture, the collectivist impulse; the "marked ascendancy of sensibility over reason," and the tendency to emphasize ideas over things (Lima, 1956:119), of the aesthetic over the functional; the urban ethos, the propensity for improvisation and combination, rather than calculation and division; and so forth; or, (b) to concrete cultural items, such as the sports culture, hamburgers and soft drinks, the love of pets, and colloquiallisms, for the U.S.; and the soccer culture, the annual *Carnaval* celebration, popular music, and social and family gatherings, for Brazil. These elements act as Archimedean points of reference, centripetally pulling together all segments of the population into a cultural "center." As such, they tend to override all other criteria of social differentiation (e.g., class, gender, race, age, etc.), affording individuals from all backgrounds the ability to transcend other categorial memberships and to group around these central axes of the national culture.

It is important to note that these points of agglutination must be considered in their universal validity and applicability *within the society as a whole*, not just for a "majority" segment of the population. In other words, they must serve as frames of reference for everyone in the society. Through them, the national culture and the identity of individuals in relation to it, as well as various other aspects of people's lives, are implicitly and explicitly symbolized and reaffirmed. This phenomenon may be demonstrated in the discourse of popular music in Brazil, regarding the strong identification of individuals there with the national musical/dance form, the *samba*. The functional properties of the *samba* as a major point of agglutination are suggested in (composer) Chico Buarque's hugely popular *Tem Mais Samba* (There is More Samba). In this composition, the *samba* comes across as a panacea, a context within which all of the tensions and conflicts of interindividual life are harmonized and resolved, all hardships are alleviated:

> There is more *samba* in the meeting than in the wait
> " in ill will than in injury
> " in the port than in the sail
> " in the forgiveness than in the farewell
> " in the hands than in the eyes
> " on the ground than in the street
> " in the man who works
> " in the sounds that come from the street
> " in the heart of those who cry
> " in the tears of those who see
> That the true *samba* can occur anytime
> And the heart beats a *samba* rhythm
> Without quite meaning to ...
>
> ... If everybody danced the *samba*
> Life would be so much easier ...

In relation to this, the *samba* also functions as a vehicle for the expression of the sorrows of the everyday life, as illustrated, for instance, in *Danca da Solidão* (Dance of Loneliness, by Paulinho da Viola). In this song, human discontent is externalized in a *samba* that becomes a "dance of loneliness," in a way that invokes the oftentimes transitory and precarious nature of the human connection:

> Disillusionment, disillusionment ...
> I dance, you dance,
> The dance of loneliness ...
> Camelia became a widow

Joana fell in love
Maria tried to end her life
On account of a love affair ...

But, dialectically, the samba equilibrates and reconciles joy and sorrow, as in these verses, from *Desde que o Samba é Samba* (Since the *Samba* is *Samba*), by Caetano Veloso:

The samba is the source of pleasure
And the product of sorrow
The great transforming power.

The applicability of the *samba* for conveying the range of human emotion includes its being a medium for spiritual expression, a medium through which personal supplications - to the Divine or to the loved one - can be sent forth effectively. In this sense, it becomes a form of prayer, as indicated in B. Powell and V. de Moraes' *Samba da Bênção* (The Blessing Samba):

... the true *samba* is a form of prayer
because the *samba* is the melancholy that swings ...

This thematization continues in a similar vein in the verses below, from *Feitio de Oração* (Like a Prayer, by Vadico and Noel Rosa):

To dance/sing the *samba* is to cry for joy
To smile nostalgically
Inside the melody

The *samba* in fact
Does not come from the hillsides
Nor from the city
And anyone who has been through
An ardent love affair
Knows that the *samba*
Is born in the heart.

The message here is that, with the passage of time, the geographic, ethnic, and socioeconomic origins of the *samba* have receded into the background, as this musical form has become increasingly universalized within the larger culture, and the medium of popular expression *par excellence,* the *[A] Voz do Povo* (The Voice of the People, by Ivan Lins).

The central notion of the grounding of identity in the sphere of culture, that is, in the active and full-blown participation of individuals in the national culture, is directly underscored in the song *Tereza Sabe Sambar* (Tereza is a Good *Samba* Dancer, by Francis Hime and Vinicius de Moraes):

Hail, hail Tereza
She will go to heaven some day
Because she has that regal bearing
That (the 19th-century Brazilian Imperial Princess)Isabel
Used to have
There cannot possibly be
A *branquinha*[7] like this one

Tereza is white in color
But that's all right
Because she knows how to dance the *samba*
Tereza knows how the dance the *samba*.

It seems clear here that culture prevails over physical appearance and racial considerations. Tereza is white, but this is irrelevant because she is an expert *samba* dancer. This cultural skill, though rooted in the African background, became a skill that is potentially accessible to all members of the society (through socialization), independently of ethnic, racial, gender, or socioeconomic affiliation. The mastery of this skill imparts to Tereza an air of nobility, it aggrandizes and grants social legitimacy to her existence.[8]

In separatist cultural systems, by contrast, the integrationist effect of the points of agglutination does not exactly apply in the *national* sense, that is, it does not fully reach the entire population. As a rule, it is manifested locally, presiding over the majority population, but not necessarily over the culturally-marginalized communities. In this way, certain cultural traits, products, or tendencies, which may be thought to pertain to the culture as a whole, are not necessarily claimed by the groups that have historically been barred from full assimilation. To illustrate: the tenacity of the Puritan influence in American culture has the effect of encouraging individuals to cultivate emotional restraint, a trait that could reasonably be said to apply to the mainstream population, to the point of being one of its dominant values and distinguishing features. In other words, a point of agglutination. Yet, it hardly functions in that capacity for incompletely assimilated groups, like those still slotted today as ethnic-racial minorities. Members of the African-American community in the U.S. provide a good example of this, insofar as their cultural marginalization and resulting patterns of socialization have rendered them far more expressive emotionally as a group than the general population. In this societal model of society, therefore, each of the ethnic-racial subcultures, though *generally* aligned with the cluster of dominant cultural tendencies of the larger society, has nevertheless its own points of agglutination, towards which its members exhibit *primary* identification.

Crossnational variations in minority-group assimilation: The case of the Africans

Regarding the assimilation of the African element in Brazil, Pierson (1967:337) calls our attention to the steady cultural and biological mixture of the African and the European into "one race and one common culture." The pervasiveness of this process has prompted another observer (van den Berghe, 1970:541) to call Brazil a "Luso-African country rather than a Luso-American one."

Shortly after the Africans began to arrive as slaves in Brazil in the 1500s, they began to influence several areas of the dominant culture, and in turn had their own traditions modified as well as sustained thorugh the syncretic process. This phenomenon has been richly documented in the literature (e.g., Herskovits and Herskovits, 1942; Ramos, 1951; Freyre, 1956; Bastide, 1959; Rodrigues, 1962; Pierson, 1967; Valente, 1976; Nina Rodrigues, 1977). Manchester (1965:32) writes:

As cooks in the Big House and in the slave quarters they followed their own traditional practices, thereby in the course of time Africanizing the Brazilian diet. They introduced palm oil, chilies, okra, the Guinea fowl, the Sudan cola-nut, and countless dishes which long since have been accepted as Brazilian specialties. Their influence on dress is evidenced by the kerchiefs, the silver buckles with amulets, the bodices, robes, and skirts which are still worn by the lower classes in Bahia. Their impact on language was even more pervasive. They effected no basic structural change but their simplification of verb forms and inflections became common practice. They enriched the vocabulary by the addition of an endless variety of words and under their influence the language lost the hardness characteristic of Portuguese spoken in Portugal and acquired the soft, melodious quality of Brazil.

73

Under ideal circumstances the syncretic process in Brazil involved direct structural correspondences or equivalences between the different cultural traditions, which means that these traditions were assigned beforehand the property of reversibility, dealt with earlier in the discussion of syncretism. This process may be elucidated here by examining the specifically religious acculturation of the Africans, which comprised the syncretic interplay of traditional West African religious forms and Luso-Brazilian Catholicism. We may begin by listing the chief characteristics of traditional West African religion:

(a) elaborate ritual and sacramental structures (see Landes, 1940: Herskovits and Herskovits, 1942; Mbiti, 1970:chapter 7).

(b) magic and divination (Evans-Pritchard, 1937; Davidson, 1966:170; Mbiti, 1970:chs.15, 16).

(c) the cult of the dead. According to Bastide, this religious aspect is "deeply rooted in the moral code and civilization of all the peoples of black Africa" (1978:128). Herskovits adds that the ancestral cult in Africa "is the most important single sanctioning force for the social system and the codes of behavior that underlie it" (1964:300), becoming a length "one of the most important cults ... in all of West Africa" (1966:85).

(d) polytheism. West African religion emphasizes the notion of a High God or Supreme Being, creator of all things (Mbiti, 1970:37). The exalted status of this supreme deity, however, precludes a direct involvement in the ordinary daily affairs of human beings. This becomes the sphere of responsibility of a pantheon or group of lesser divinities and ancestor-spirits. Through these spiritual beings God manifests Himself and controls "major objects or phenomena of nature" (Mbiti, 1970:98).

(e) sacrifices and offerings. The sacrificial element stands among "the commonest acts of worship among African peoples" (Mbiti, 1970:75). It is an integral part of Afro-Brazilian cult ritual.

(f) direct deity-devotee relationship. An essential function of the African nature gods is that of mediation between individuals and God. This is so because one cannot approach the High God directly or personally, as already mentioned. Mediation occurs in various forms, such as sacrifice, divination, and spirit possession (Raboteau, 1980:11). In addition to the mediating aspect, ancestor spirits and specific deities become personal gods and the source of selfhood and identification, as well as protection, for each member of the group. This can be exemplified in the Yoruba cult ritual, when the various deities (*orixás*) "arrive" and "take possession" of their human intermediaries. Mbiti adds that ancestor spirits

74

act as "guardians of the family affairs, tradition, ethics, and activities" (1970:108).

(g) hierarchy of power. African deities are differentiated on the basis of their ontological attributes; jurisdiction over natural phenomena, such as rain and thunder, and social activities and experiences, such as war and diseases; and their male/female personification (Mbiti, 1970:98).

(h) no formal separation between the sacred and the profane, between the spiritual and the material. Mbiti states that in African societies religion "permeates into all departments of life so fully that it is not easy or always possible to isolate it" (1970:1). It must be added that traditional African religious expression is generally inseparable from musical expression (singing and dancing).

(i) pragmatic orientation. On the whole, African religions are geared to the resolution of earthly problems and to the achievement of earthly objectives. Accordingly, patterns of worship are characterized by instrumentality and magical manipulation, such as exemplified in the offering of foods to the nature gods.

(j) collectivism. Traditional African religion is a not a matter of personal ethics, a private spiritual affair, but rather, a communal or collective experience. As a rule, in African social systems the individual cannot dissociate himself/herself from the religion of the group, any more than from his/her "... roots ... foundation ... context of security ... kinship ... and the entire group of those who make him aware of his own existence" (Mbiti, 1970:3).

These religious features found direct counterparts in the variety of Catholic Christianity transplanted to Brazil by the Portuguese settlers. This was not the rigid Catholicism of the Tridentine reforms, with its strong emphasis on dogmas, the sacraments, and orthodoxy of beliefs and practices. Rather, it was a late-medieval religious model, which had been deeply affected by centuries under Moorish influence; a religion, as Bastide tells us (1951:334), "softened by North African sensuality and Moslem voluptuousness, but that made place for the saints of the Reconquest, knights caparisoned in iron and with lace in hand." Additionally, it exercised a greater cultural, rather than spiritual, impact over Brazilian society, shaping social life as a whole far more decisively than it did individual life (Coutinho, 1943:190). It is not surprising then that one should also find a carnal, paganistic quality in this Catholicism. As Freyre (1956:30) describes it, this was

... a soft, lyric Christianity with many phallic and animistic reminiscences of the Pagan cults. The only thing that was lacking was for the saints and angels to take on fleshly form and step down from the altars on feast-days and disport themselves with the populace. As it was, one might have seen oxen entering the churches to be blessed by the priests; mothers lulling their little ones with the same hymns of praise that were addressed to the infant Jesus; sterile women with upraised petticoats rubbing themselves against the legs of St. Goncalo D'Amarante.

This same writer reports that in the 19th century women of patriarchal families of planters who had settled in the city would often buy articles from itinerant merchants, including "rosy-cheeked" images of St. Anthony which became "objects of fervent devotion and, in certain cases, of practices of sexual fetishism" (1963:32). And the cult of St. John had a basis that was "essentially aphrodisiac, and sexual songs and practices are bound up with is rites" (1956:254). This element of paganism is part of the larger characteristic of all folk religion to combine religious and secular aspects. This was quite evident in the Portuguese tradition of including masked dances and profane singing in festivals of the Church, a custom which remained in vogue as late as 1855 (Bastide, 1978:124). Boxer writes about the "gaily and richly decorated religious processions, with their masqueraders, musicians, and dances" in colonial Bahia, and stresses that Portuguese Catholicism tended to "blend the sacred and the profane together in the most intriguing ways" (1964:134). The books and diaries left by nineteenth century travelers in Brazil yield a wealth of information about the religious life of the period, and reveal how this particular feature of Luso-Brazilian Catholicism was very widespread from the colonial to the early Imperial period (i.e., up to the first quarter of the 19th century). The French traveler Le Gentil de la Barbinais must have been much scandalized by the Christmas festivities and the feast of St. Gonçalo d'Amarante which he witnessed in the churches and convents of colonial Bahia; veritable pagan festivals, with much dancing and revelry, in which clerics, noblemen, top government officials, blacks and prostitutes enthusiastically participated (cited in Verger, 1981:80; Boxer, 1964:134). There is also the report by Tollenare (1956:135) who in the early 19th century saw young men and women dancing nightly at the St. Gonçalo Church in Olinda (state of Pernambuco), not without some objection from the clergymen, who sensed that European visitors would surely see in that custom something much too indecent to be witnessed in the house of God. With the advent of the imperial era in Brazil in 1808, this phenomenon showed no apparent signs of decline, judging from the continuing reports of observers. John Mawe noticed in the southern province of São Paulo in 1809 that religious festivals usually ended with "tea, card games, and dances" (1978:72). At that same time, Andrew Grant wrote in his *History of Brazil* that in Rio de Janeiro "[a]ll classes of society ... display an unbounded propensity to mirth and pleasure, nor does their religion, which is chiefly ceremonial, impart anything like gloom or austerity to their manners" (1809:146), and added that "[s]carcely a day passes without the celebration of some festivals, in which the extremes of devotion and pleasure are united" (1809:231). While traveling through the province of Pará in the 1840s Kidder also lamented that religious festivities had to be carried out amidst "amusements and follies" (1845:297). The Rev. Walsh, in residence at Rio de Janeiro in the 1820s, was appalled to see that even many of the religious celebrations and services were attended "with the levity of a puppet-show, and without the slightest regard to solemnity or decorum" (1830:387). And as late as the 1880s, as another account goes (Dent, 1886:147), the Feast of the Purification was followed by "a great ball [which] ... was kept till midnight."

It should be added in this regard that the treatment of the sacred and the secular as undifferentiated spaces of social life is one of the most important structural features to throw into relief in attempting to sketch the homological relationship between Luso-Brazilian Catholicism and West African religious systems. As in traditional African societies, Brazilians did not centralize their religion in the temple and in the sacraments, to the exclusion of the world outside this formal sphere. Instead, religion permeated the daily round of life and was not allowed to take precedence, in the ethical-normative sense, over the exigencies of everyday existence. In the rural setting, as Freyre (1956) has described it, the formal structures of the Church and the familial aspects of the domestic religion of the Big House became intertwined in a dynamic relation of mutual opposition and complementarity: on the one hand, the formalism of religious dogma, on the other, the contextuality of familial life. But, in the end, the patriarchal universe of the plantation was victorious over Christian orthodoxy, such as, for instance, in breaking down the sharp distinctions between the sacred and the profane (see e.g. Azevedo, 1958:69). Bastide (1951:336) has pointed out how "[t]he Catholic saints who were adored received that worship only to the extent that they also integrated themselves in the domestic life and took on the character of protectors of the family." In the particular case of Brazil, this phenomenon is also relevant with reference to the integration of the affairs of the State and those of institutional religion. Since an all-powerful state dictated the norms for social and institutional life in Brazilian society, and since it also upheld vigorously the model of a Catholic existence for all the citizens, there was no need, strictly speaking, for religious ethics.

One simply had to be integrated into the mainstream of Brazilian cultural life to display the behaviors and attitudes associated with Catholicism. Hence, the frequent observations by foreign visitors in colonial and Imperial Brazil regarding the stress laid by the population on the external manifestations of the cult, while religious worship as such was ordinarily characterized by a lack of solemnity and seriousness (e.g. Walsh, 1830:387; also see Bruneau, 1982: chapter 1).

This specific facet of Luso-Brazilian Catholicism, that is, the tendency towards pageantry and festivity, was yet another area of convergence with the West African religious tradition, to the extent that the latter also enforced the observance of sacred days and festivals, and a concern for ceremonial elaboration. The emphasis on pageantry was also a carry-over from the Portuguese heritage which favored, as Boxer informs us (1964:134), "the external manifestations of the Christian cult." In Brazil this reached such proportions as to cause Fletcher to affirm in the mid-1800s that Catholicism there "in pomp and display ...is unsurpassed even in Italy" (1879:140). He gives a very detailed account of the religious processions and festivals which he saw in Rio de Janeiro, with the multitudes of the faithful, the pyrotechnic displays, the ringing of bells, the gown-clad dignitaries of the Church and government, the ornamentation of the churches and the images of saints, the bands (1979:ch IX). Caldcleugh (1825:71-72) confirms this: "If the quantum of religion existing in a country," he states, "were to be measured by its external signs, no country could possibly possess more than Brazil" (see also the chronicles of Rugendas, 1976:126; Mawe, 1978:69-72; Debret, 1989:31-45).

Luso-Brazilian Catholicism also contained the pervasive Portuguese belief in, and practice of, witchcraft and sorcery. The settlers had brought with them a religious mentality as intensely receptive to magic as that of their African slaves. The reports of foreign visitors, especially those of the Protestant clergymen, repeatedly underline this fact. Rev. James Fletcher was offended in his Calvinist sensibilities by what he described as "the marriage between heathenism and Christianity," in Rio de Janeiro in the mid-1800s. He saw people in that city offering votive tablets at the altar of their favorite divinity or saint for a recovery from various ailments, just as the ancient pagans had done centuries before. They also offered representations in painting and sculpture of various portions of the afflicted body. "In the Gloria Church," he writes, "may be seen any quantity of wax models of arms, feet, eyes, noses, breasts, etc." (1867:95). The same phenomenon was witnessed by Kidder in a convent in the northern province of Maranhão in the 1840s (1845:244). Fletcher describes another practice that was equally widespread during religious festivals:

> ... the faithful (and others for that matter) can obtain any amount of pious merchandise, in the shape of *medidas* and *bentinhos* - pictures, images and medals of saints and of the Pope, etc. These are "exchanged" - never sold -in the church, and fetch round prices. A medida is a ribbon cut to the exact height of the presiding Lady or saint of the place of worship. These, worn next to the skin, cure all manner of diseases, and gratify the various desires of the happy purchasers ... *Bentinhos* are two little silken pads with painted figures of Our Lady, etc. upon them. These are worn next to the skin, in pairs, being attached by ribbons, one bentinho resting upon the bosom and the other upon the back. These are most efficacious for protecting the wearer from invisible foes both before and behind (1867:98-99).

Kidder (1945:292) saw a great many of these *bentinhos* as well as beads, crosses, and miniature images for sale, hanging on the door of the Santa Anna Church, in the Para province, after having been properly blessed, or sprinkled with holy water. Ecclesiastical wares were often peddled through the newspapers, in connection with a forthcoming feast of the Church.

Another salient characteristic of this religion was the cult of the dead, as suggested by this passage from Abel du Petit-Thouars, who saw the following scene in the province of Santa Catarina in 1825:

> ... I saw at the rear of the room a platform on which an infant was arranged on an altar, surrounded by lilies and vases of flowers; its face was uncovered and it was richly dressed, with a crown of forget-me-nots on its head and a cluster of them in its hand.

Around the altar on which this dead child rested, women were kneeling on mats, singing, after which "there were gay dances" (cited in Freyre, 1963:58). At about the same period, Walsh witnessed the practice in Rio churches of keeping the bones of departed ones in cases or boxes, which were then encased into receptacles in the walls of the cloisters. Underneath these boxes, gaudily ornamented shrines were erected, where people prayed (1830:336-337).

Ancestor worship stood out as a feature of the Catholicism of the plantation which, as Bastide reports, became a sort of household religion, based on "the worship of the patriarch's guardian saints and of the family

79

dead, who were buried in the same chapel and surrounded by the same reverence" (1978:41). But it also prevailed in the urban context, in institutions such as the *confrarias* or *irmandades* (confraternities or brotherhoods), where much of the syncretic process took place. In Brazil (as in Cuba; see Klein, 1969), these agencies, as we shall see later in more detail, came to play a vital role in the social and cultural life of blacks, whether slaves or freedmen. As early as 1589 the Jesuits in Brazil founded religious organizations for the slaves, among which stood out the *Confraria das Almas* (Confraternity of the Souls), based on the characteristic Portuguese devotion to the souls in Purgatory (Leite, 1938).

A further dimension that brought together the Catholic and West African religious traditions was the emphasis on sacrifices and offerings. This may be considered by looking at the specific aspect of communion. There is a certain point in the AfroBahian cult ceremony when those in attendance may be able to participate in the communion rites. The ceremonial dancers, who are the structural mainstay of the entire ceremony, sit on the floor and eat a little from the sacred dishes offered to the *orixás*. Some of this food is then placed on pieces of banana-tree leaves, and passed around among those attending the service, so that they can also join in this sacramental procedure, by means of which some of the mystical powers of particular deities can also be passed on to them (Bastide, 1959:72). Similarly, in the Catholic Mass, the rite of consecration involves the transformation of the sacred bread and wine into the body and blood of Christ (transubstantiation), at which point the priest-celebrant consumes this consecrated bread and wine, and then makes it available to those congregants who may wish to partake of the sacramental communion.

As for the specific correspondences between the Catholic saints and the deities of the West African pantheon, they were direct and wide-ranging. We may first consider certain key structural features of this syncretic association, such as the fact that full membership in the AfroBrazilian cult requires membership in the Catholic Church as well, and the fact that the *peji* (i.e., the African [Yoruba] term for sanctuary) of the African cult-houses, such as those found in Salvador (capital city of the state of Bahia), with their sacred stones bathed in the sacrificial blood of animals and in the food offerings to the deities, generally stands right beside a Catholic shrine decorated with statues of the Catholic saints (Bastide, 1959:66). The following aspects are also germane:

(a) both the Catholic saints and the African *orixás* have anthropomorphic attributes;
(b) in the Portuguese religious folklore certain saints, like their West African counterparts, have been associated with the control of natural

forces, such as Santa Barbara, thought to be a protector against lightning. Thus, an immediate equivalence was established with *Xangô* deity of the thunderbolts (see Pierson, 1967:307). The same parallel relation is observed between the *Stella Maris* (Star of the Seas) Madonna in Catholic worship, identified in Salvador as Our Lady of Conception at the Beach (the reference to the beach refers to the location of the church consecrated to this iamge of Our Lady), patroness of all seafarers, and *Yemanjá* Yoruba goddess of the sea;

(c) Catholic saints also exert their influence in accordance with a hierarchy of power, in similar fashion to the West African *orixás*. In Bahia, for example, our Lord of Bonfim is considered the most powerful and important Catholic saint by the lower classes, thus becoming identified with *Oxalá*, the greatest of the Yoruba deities (Pierson, 1967:306). A merging of ritual procedures is often encountered in the worship of these deities. For instance, a central aspect of the Yoruba religious tradition is the washing of the sacred stone of *Oxalá*. In Brazil religious syncretism gave rise to a parallel ceremony in which female devotees of the AfroBahian religious cults, dressed in the traditional African garb of the service, carry on their heads large vases with flowers and perfumed water with which they wash the steps of Our Lord of Bonfim Church;

(d) the worship of the saints in Brazil had a strongly pragmatic basis, and was linked to the attainment of material goals, just as in Africa;

(e) the faithful in Brazil developed a strong bond and identification with a personal deity, and the latter could be not only their guardian angel but also a particular saint to whom they might have been consecrated in infancy. This deity would provide protection as well as help in the solution of earthly problems. This was homologous to the individual-deity relationship in Africa;

(f) also, the profusion of saints venerated in colonial Brazil may be seen as a parallel phenomenon to West African polytheism (this type of parallelism between formally monotheistic religions and polytheistic ones is also underscored by Weber [1978:518], when he states that "...in practice, the Roman Catholic cult of masses and saints actually comes fairly close to polytheism").

Finally, as much as this was a religion "impregnated with mysticism" (Azevedo, 1971:148), Luso-Brazilian Catholicism was not mystical in the contemplative or illuminative sense (Weber, 1978:544-545), nor was it, for the most part, particularly as practiced in the sugar cane and cotton producing regions of the Northeast, and the coffee regions of the South, brutally or tragically mystical, like the Catholicism of Spain and the Spanish colonies in the New World. It was, instead, a softer and more malleable system, possessing, "neither inflexibility of dogma nor puritanism of conduct" (Bastide, 1951:336). As such, it also mirrored the West African example of pragmatically-disposed religion, by emphasizing experience over abstract principle, by adapting to political and economic circumstance, by subordinating the ethical impact over individual or collective action to practical requirements. This utilitarian quality was couched in a cost-benefit approach to religion, whereby the satisfaction of immediate needs was attained via magical instrumentality. The mechanism of indulgences, the buying of masses for the departed, and so forth, stood for economic transactions through which special favors from the Church could be granted. "The iniquity of indulgences still obtains," deplored Dent (1886:278), during a period of residence in Brazil in the 1880s. Koster (1966:115) tells us about the cult of our Lady of the O, in the Recife (state of Pernambuco) area in the early 1800s, "an avaricious personage, whose powerful intercession is not to be obtained unless she is in return well paid for her trouble." Similarly, in the African religious context, as befitting the model of "primitive religion," the offering of entreaties and gifts to the various deities aimed not at ethical reparation or an increased awareness of sin; instead it constituted a form of practical exchange, of "calculated trading," to use Weber's term (1978). Herskovits (1944) has noted how devotees in the African cults in Bahia may seek to gain special favors from the cult priest by offering him a new ceremonial drum.

Shifting now to the more general or secular level of cultural interplay between Luso-Brazilian and West African culture (though it must be borne in mind again here that the religious/secular distinction does not really hold here, strictly speaking, since, as will be recalled, there is no real separation between the sacred and profane realms in traditional African societies), we find that the Bantu influence has been especially prominent in relation to Brazilian popular festivals. It was manifested, for example, in the *congada*, a Congolese festival from colonial and Imperial times, consisting of the symbolic coronation of the Congo King. This festival was incorporated into the worship of Our Lady of the Rosary, that became a patroness of the blacks. The *maracatus* and *reizados*, African-derived organizations which became part of the street *Carnaval* associations, can still be seen nowadays, particularly in the state of Pernambuco, which imported large numbers of Bantu slaves. The Englishman Henry Koster, a resident of the state of Pernambuco in the early 1800s, wrote in reference to the *congada* festival that

the Brazilian Kings of Congo worship Our Lady of the Rosary, and are dressed in the dress of white men; they and their subjects dance, it is

82

true, after the manner of their country, but to those festivals are admitted African Negroes of other nations, creole blacks, and mulattoes, all of whom dance after the same manner; *and these dances are now as much the national dances of Brazil as they are of Africa* (1816:411) (emphasis added).

The accounts of travelers in colonial and 19th century Brazil corroborate the large-scale participation of the blacks in the celebrations which took place on the feast-days of the Church.[9] The variegated nature of the Catholic ceremonial structure provided a fertile terrain for the symbolic reconstruction of African cultural patterns, especially in terms of theatrical dances and representations associated with national kingships and tribal chiefhoods, as exemplified by the *congada* (see, e.g., Koster, 1816; also, Burton, 1969:238, and Tollenare, 1956:136). Wetherell recounts how in the 1840s the blacks in the state of Bahia used to congregate around important churches of the city on feast days, while dancing "their national dances, whilst thousands looked on and these orgies would be incessantly continued" (1860: 122). Ewbanks (1856) reported from Rio de Janeiro on the pervasive black presence in festivals like the Holy Ghost, Good Friday, Palm Sunday, and Ash Wednesday. Freyre (1968:40), writing on the blacks in the Ouro Preto (Minas Gerais state) region, tells of how "on the Feast of the Magi, they celebrated with great merrymaking their festival, more African than Catholic, presided over by the old leader dressed as a king. To be sure, there was a high mass; but the main feature was the dancing to the sound of African instruments. Dances in the street in front of the church, Negro dances."
In addition to the religious holidays and festivals, Brazilian blacks also actively syncretized their aboriginal traditions with several nationally-observed public celebrations of the more secular type, such as the *bumba-meu-boi*, *autos*, *pastoris*, and *cheganças*, all very popular in certain parts of the country during colonial times and persisting to the present day. The *bumba-meu-boi* is a kind of folk drama; *autos*, *pastoris* (called *ternos* and *ranchos* in Bahia), and *cheganças* are types of theatrical representations and dances. Nina Rodrigues (in Ramos, 1951:73) detected several Sudanese totemic influences in the *ranchos*. These festivities, secular though they might be in their outward appearance, also had their origin in medieval Portuguese Catholicism and, as such, typically combined religious and profane motifs. In Bahia they were an integral part of the entire cycle of religious feasts which started in December and ran through January (Verger, 1981:73-5), but in that region, as well as in several other parts of the country, they were also a conspicuous feature of the nationwide four-day pre-Lenten celebration called *Carnaval*. The *Carnaval*

was infiltrated shortly after 1800 by African customs and dances, and presently continues to show unmistakable signs of this influence. At about the end of the last century, Nina Rodrigues (1977:180-1) commented on how this feast in Salvador had become a vehicle for the presentation of the various African clubs, and the entire street scene reminded him of a "colossal *candomblé*[10] traversing the streets of the city." Various African Carnaval clubs were represented in the procession, among which the most prominent were *A Embaixada Africana* (The African Legation) and *Os Pândegos da Africa* (The African Clowns). Of lesser importance were *A Chegada Africana* (The Arrival of the Africans), *Os Filhos da Africa* (The Children of Africa), and others. Some of these clubs, Ramos informs us (1954: 85), were survivals of cyclical celebrations from the African Slave Coast. As pointed out, they constituted a medium through which the Africans were able to resurrect annually (albeit in syncretized fashion) many of their aboriginal institutional forms.[11]

As for the *congada*, by the mid-1800s this festival underwent a structural transformation and developed into a Congolese-derived *auto*, shifting from its former hierarchical-administrative relation to a cultural pattern consisting principally of theatrical representations sustained by dance and music, incorporating various elements of Bantu animal totemism. In time, this typical African cultural carry-over came to be known as the *maracatu*, already mentioned, and became a major fixture of the *Carnaval* festivities in the Recife area. The members paraded the streets in elaborate and richly-decorated costumes while the orchestra played several African percussion instruments, including different kinds of drums (Maranhão, 1960:17-21; Guerra-Peixe, 1980:19020; Bastide, 1971:182-84).

Public festivals of the kind represented by the *Carnaval* serve to foreground the operation of dominant-minority cultural reciprocity in the secular sphere of activity. Originally an European pre-Lenten festivity reaching back to antiquity, *Carnaval* (of which the earlier Portuguese version implanted in Brazil in the 1800s was called the *Entrudo*, and later took on the present name), developed over the centuries as a vehicle for individual expression. In its late 19th-century version in Brazil, however, the *Carnaval* was altered structurally towards greater collectivism, by virtue of its massive incorporation of African culture. The main feature of the festivities progressively became the parade of independent clubs and associations - such as, for instance, the *maracatus* in the Pernambuco carnaval, the *afoxés* in the Bahia carnaval, the *samba schools* in the Rio de Janeiro carnaval, and so on. It was, and still is, largely through these organizations that individual participation in the street celebrations is mediated. By introducing a collectivist framework of participation to the *Carnaval*, the African influence facilitated the transformation of the latter

84

from a medium for personal expression (as was characteristic of the merrymaking of the *entrudo*) to one where this emotional exuberance was externalized in collective fashion.

Also worthy of notice here is the African contribution in the area of music. The frequency of aboriginal dances and the use of native instruments among Brazilian slaves was witnessed by many foreign visitors. Maria Graham watched slave dances in a Rio de Janeiro plantation in the 1820s in which "crude African instruments" were used (1969: 198-199). Koster left us a similar report (1816:241).[12] Some of these dances, such as the *coco*, the *batuque*, the *jongo*, and the *lundu*, were of Bantu origin, and predominated among rural slaves (Bastide, 1978:49). The German scientists Spix and Martius describe a slave celebration which they saw in a southern province: "The numerous slaves of the *fazenda* [plantation] were celebrating a festival, which continued from sunset until late in the night, with dancing, singing and noisy music." They also comment on the "din of the *atabaque*, a kind of drum, and the *canzá*, a thick tube with iron bars across, on which they produce a jarring sound, by passing over it backwards and forwards with a stick ..." (1824: 228). Similar phenomena were witnessed in the urban context.

Regarding African instruments, their use was widespread in the secular and religious functions of blacks in Brazil from the earliest phases of slavery. These instruments remained particularly noticeable in Salvador, mainly in connection with their employment in the Afro-Catholic cult ritual, but also in public places and circumstances, such as the public market, which James Wetherell, the British consul in that city in the 1840s, found to have a "thoroughly African appearance" (1860:29).[13] During the present century, these carry-overs of the West African musical heritage came to form an integral part of the Brazilian musical culture, and many of these instruments are now essential for setting the rhythmic and percussive foundation for mainstream popular music, specifically, samba music, in the traditional style or variations.

The cultural interfusion may be seen in other related areas. The West African art of wood carving has flourished along with the rituals of the AfroBrazilian religious cults, especially those of Yoruban and Dahomean extraction. The bulk of this art form is geared toward the representation of religious symbols, images, etc. African dishes, still used in the cult ceremonies as offerings to the various deities, have become a central feature of cuisine of the northeastern regions. Linguistic Africanisms have not only been a critical component of the ritual of the AfroBahian cult centers, down to the present time, but the adaptations of Portuguese by the slaves and their descendants have exercised a significant impact on the national language (see, e.g., Freyre, 1956:342-49). As late as the 1930s, when Pierson was doing his research on ethnic relations in Salvador, he noticed that *Nagô*, as was called in the Bahia area the language of the Yoruba slave, could still be heard in the streets of the city (1967:72-3).

Finally, the intensity of Luso-African cultural interpenetration is also shown in the fact that the plantations in Brazil frequently had African names (Freyre, 1956:457). There is an irony in this, given the plantation's position as the very nucleus of the subjugation of the Africans. In the degree that the name of somebody or something encapsulates the "essential nature" of that person or thing to which it is attached, it seems ironic that this symbolic dimension should be conveyed, as in the case of the Brazilian plantation, through the appropriation of a cultural trait (i.e., language) from the subaltern community. Yet, the irony vanishes when we consider the larger social and cultural context. The fact that the Brazilian plantation had African names could be seen as an all too predictable tendency of a slavery system which, in reproducing on a smaller scale the nature of the larger social system, exhibited a conciliatory and fraternizing stance towards minority groups at the level of culture, through the process of cultural syncretism, notwithstanding the extreme inequality prevailing in the sphere of economic and political relations.

U.S. culture yields a markedly contrasting picture regarding the assimilative pattern of the Africans (and minority segments, in general). By and large, African-Americans, because of their special circumstance, have not historically been able to maintain a dynamic and meaningful connection with their native heritage, over the course of their acculturation into the Anglo-American Protestant core culture, and their only recourse has been forced submersion under the latter, though that process itself has been, as already noted, significantly limited by the larger societal circumstances of institutional and informal separatism. Where patterns of syncretistic association can be detected, these tend to be localized, rather than generalized, and thus do not constitute a typical feature of the broader cultural system. The historical record reveals how from the very beginning the suppression of African cultural traits was systematic and all-encompassing. As structural segregation continued to be imposed on the black community, it perpetuated the patterns of cultural separatism. This externally imposed isolation, however, did not automatically lead to the preservation of the original African modes of life. Had this been the case, it might have been a source of existential comfort and security for the Africans and their descendants, offsetting the harshness of life under slavery and in the subsequent period. But, if African-Americans were to enjoy this comfort and security, it would have to come from an indigenous cultural world, created *de novo*, as it were (though, strictly speaking, no cultural complex is born in a sociohistorical vacuum, but always from prevailing structural configurations), from the very circumstances that denied them, on the one hand, full admission to the ways of the host culture, and on the other hand, the ability to re-knot, on a meaningful level, the threads of their ancestral heritage. This would be an independent culture - a subculture -with its own separate impulses and orientations. The patterns of intergroup segregation, first legitimized by law in 1896 (through the Plessy vs. Ferguson Supreme Court decision), and remaining in effect until the 1960s, being sustained after that by the force of custom and ideology, meant that the social inclusion of the black population would remain incomplete. The prevailing pattern, therefore, has been one of double estrangement, entailing forced separation from the African cultural matrix, on the one hand, and incomplete acculturation into the dominant mode of life of the society, on the other (see Dubois's remarks on this phenomenon, 1990:10). The collective effort to cope with the incongruities and strains of this situation has produced a subcultural community of the kind Bastide (1971:ch.IX) characterized as a "Negro" community, which is "neither European nor African."

Even when one acknowledges the argument of writers like Blassingame, who writes on black musical acculturation in the United States, and argues that despite all restrictions U.S. slaves were "able to draw upon their African heritage to build a strong musical tradition" (1979: 36), the differences are still notable in crosscultural perspective. Slave dancing in the United States met with multiple legal, social, and ecclesiastical restrictions (Phillips, 1981: 314; Jackson, 1930: 110; also see the travel accounts of Lyell, 1950:353, and Bremer, 1968:117, volume II). In any case, wherever and whenever these restrictions did not exist, or could be bypassed, the pattern of slave dancing tended to lean toward the European end of the acculturation continuum. Whereas in Brazil (and other New World settings such as Haiti, Cuba, Guiana) the African character of black dances was at once apparent to anyone familiar with West African dance forms, it has been said that in the United States "pure African dancing is almost entirely lacking except in certain subtleties of motor behavior," and that, in the overall sense, the U.S. remains the New World setting where "departure from African modes of life was greatest" (Herskovits, 1972:270, 122). Black entertainment in the Southern cities often represented an attempt to duplicate the model of the white society. In the mid-19th century, Olmsted saw slave balls ("assemblies") in Montgomery, Alabama, which in elegance and formality paralleled similar events in upper-class white society. These balls, he says, were held in "very grand style." Furthermore, "all the fashionable dances were executed; no one is admitted, except in full dress. There are the regular masters of ceremonies, floor committees, etc; and a grand supper always forms a part of the entertainment" (1968: 554). In Louisiana he witnessed creole balls which were "conducted with the greatest propriety" and the ladies were all very "becomingly dressed" (1968: 646). In the latter part of the 19th century black dances were very popular in New Orleans. The dances favored were "the quadrilles, waltzes, continentals, Prince Imperials, varieties, New Yorks, pinafore lancers, polkas, mazourkas, valses, cotillions, grand marches, and schottisches" (Blassingame, 1976: 146).

To be sure, the African influence may have held over in the music and dances of American blacks in certain areas of the South, particularly Louisiana (see Blassingame, 1979: chapter I). Cable (1886) reports on African dances being performed in New Orleans in the early 1800s. Most of these dances were probably related to voodoo, something that may be attributed to the fact that in the 1790s a large number of French planters from Saint Domingue (Haiti) fled that island to escape the bloody insurrection that led to its independence, and went to Louisiana taking their slaves along with them. The latter, in turn, brought with them their voodoo beliefs and practices. However, following the increasing American occupation of the Louisiana territory from 1803 onwards, these dances disappeared quickly. As has been stated: "Recognizable African dances in their full context are probably entirely lacking in the United States, except perhaps for the special area constituted by Louisiana; and they all seem to have been absent for generations" (Herskovits, 1972: 271).

Some of the instruments used by antebellum blacks in the U.S. resembled African ones. Cable (1886: 521) comments on some that were used in the New Orleans area. There are also references in the narratives of ex-slaves from Georgia and South Carolina to musical instruments that apparently had an African origin, such as for instance the "blowing quills" (Rawick, 1974, 1977). Blassingame (1979: 39) and Escott (1979: 101) maintain that, because most slaves generally had to make their own instruments, they would draw upon their African background for inspiration. This is evidenced in the nature of some of the instruments used, such as gourd rattles and drums. Again, as we place this discussion in hemispheric perspective, the African influence in U.S. society does not come across as pervasive as it could have been, nor did it reach the same degree of institutional integration and purity that it did in other New World contexts. The presence of these instruments, like that of the New Orleans dances, was limited and short-lived. By and large, the instruments used by U.S. blacks, whether slaves or freedmen, were of European extraction, the most common being the banjo and the fiddle. Genovese (1976:571:2) confirms this, stating that instruments on the U.S. plantation were generally hard to come by, particularly insofar as the blacks were concerned, and the latter sometimes "got a fiddle or banjo from a solicitous master ... [but, more often] they had to improvise ... [by making, in addition to a number of stringed and percussion instruments] many of the fiddles and banjos so often in evidence at their parties." The preponderance of the latter type of instrument is referred to in numerous reports. Olmsted, asking a Mississippi planter in the 1850s about what kinds of instruments his slaves used to accompany their dances, was told: "Banjos and violins; some of'em has got violins" (1972: 146). *The Slave Narrative Collection*, a group of autobiographical accounts of former slaves collected during the 1930s, attests to the dominance of European-derived instruments in slave amusements. Some of the more representative passages may be cited here. An ex-slave from South Carolina, George Fleming, informs us that at the plantation dances "de music was mostly made by fiddles ...'" (cited in Rawick, 1977: 128). Another ex-slave, C.B. Burton, remembers that "fiddles was de most used musical instrument" (in Rawick, 1977:95). An ex-slave from Mississipi gave the information that "[u]s have small dances Saturday nights ... and banjo and fiddle playing...There was fiddles made from gourds and banjoes made from sheep hides" (in Yetman, 1970:337). Also from Mississipi was an informant who said: "Some Saturday nights us had dances. De same old fiddler played for us dat played for de white folks" (in Yetman, 1970:190). Another informant, a former slave from Texas, said: "When we went to a party the nigger fiddlers would play a tune dat went like this ..." (in Yetman, 1970:253). In postbellum Louisiana, blacks are considered to have been particularly fond of violins, banjos, and drums (Blassingame, 1976: 139-140). The several brass bands of the period that were seen in that area, New Orleans in particular, played a kind of music that later came to be known as jazz.

Notes

1   The contrast marked here is with the people of African descent in U.S. society, who have in recent years emphasized their collective identity as "African-Americans" which in addition to indicating their ethnic origins in the African continent, suggests the idea of cultural continuity with Africa (in the manner of the "white ethnics," who are able to juxtapose varying degrees of attachment to their ancestral customs - the case of the Irish and the annual celebrations of the St. Patrick's Day Parade springs to mind - to their primary membership in the national culture, without compromising the latter). Yet, this development needs to be problematized, inasmuch as the comparison of the U.S. African-American community with other such

communities in New World societies reveals that the former has had the lowest degree of cultural continuity with the African cultural complex. It is a community where the break with African modes of life has been most complete.

2   Novak (1971:44-50) passionately addresses the plight of "white ethnics" and the psychological turmoil and ambiguity they experience over the process of identity formation in American culture, in connection with the "other side" of the cultural separatism pattern, namely, the monolithically unilateral imposition of the dominant Anglo-Protestant model on incoming groups classified as white, a process which received its fullest expression in the so-called Americanization movement of the early 20th century (Gordon, 1964:98), and which has amounted to a cultural "disinheritance" for these groups, insofar as they are - were, in particular during their earlier phases of acculturation - denied the chance to re-establish stabilizing ties with their native cultures.

3   Freyre's account of an aspect of colonial life in Brazil (1951:958) offers an enlightening contrast. It makes apparent that a pattern of mutual influence between the dominant and minority cultural communities in that society was operative as early as the 1700s. Upper-class young men, returning from extended periods of education in Europe, deplored the fact that the cultural ways of the masses, particularly of the African slaves and freedmen, were blending with those of the dominant society. One of these individuals expressed this sentiment in verse, referring to the fact that the *batuque* (an African dance) was no longer being danced only by the blacks, but in upper-class settings as well: "You used to belong to the humblest huts, where the lowly black and mulatto women ... and the rogues and country hicks honored you, stomping the ground with their bare feet. Now, you are admitted into the palaces and honest homes" (my translation). (The *batuque*, along with other similar 18th and 19th-century musical forms of African [i.e.,Bantu] derivation, such as the *lundu*, the *coco*, the *maxixe*, the *jongo*, etc., were early prototypes of the Brazilian national dance, the *samba* (Andrade, 1989).

4   A jazz writer (cited in DeLerma, 1970:44) informs us that in the early 1920s mainstream record shops in downtown Manhattan did not stock "Negro jazz." Bessie Smith, who is considered by most analysts to have been the greatest of all the classic blues singers, became highly

successful in the 1920s with her recordings, but her records "were never sold in white stores."

5   The wide-ranging formation of new hybrid musical styles in recent years in the Bahia area also exemplify this aspect.

6   A parallel conceptualization may be seen in Da Matta's notion of "national rituals" (1983:36), which concerns "rites grounded in the possibility of dramatizing the global, critical, and all-embracing values of the society."

7   *Branquinha* is the diminutive and affective form for the feminine *branca* (white); literally: little white one.

8   The negative side to this idea of "points of agglutination" and what it symbolizes and entails, is, of course, the difficulty experienced by members of the society in adopting alternative courses of action (i.e., vis-a-vis the dominant patterns). In other words, the methodical fashion in which cultural integration shapes and validates individual existence through the various points of agglutination is matched by the strong sense of marginalization that the individual may be gripped with, should he/she fail to become aligned with these key aspects of the national culture. From this standpoint, it might be said that these aspects come to acquire ontological significance for every one, in that they become an inherent property of Being. As such, they cannot be easily objectified, questioned, or dismissed in favor of alternative modes of life. This suggests an authoritarian tendency, built into the apparent monoculturalism of cultural integration. Yet, I think it useful to return here to the point that the aspect of authoritarianism is more appropriately linked to the monoculturalism of models of assimilation which, in the main, prevent dominant-minority cultural reciprocity from occurring (e.g., Gordon's Anglo-conformity model, already discussed), rather than to the (sort of) monoculturalism achieved through syncretistic cultural integration, where the elements in the mixture more or less interact interchangeably, and not in terms of the automatic and complete submersion of the minority traits under the minority ones. In other words, the syncretic incorporation of minority "difference" does not translate into ruthlessly ferreting out this difference, but rather juxtaposing it to the dominant pattern in dialectical equilibrium. Thus, it may be said, at the same that a syncretistically-oriented integrationist system encourages amalgamation - hence, the emergence of distinct points of

agglutination for the population as a whole - it also encourages variety - hence, the existence of "differences." The two are not mutually exclusive, but are instead coexisting, it seems to me, in this model. To illustrate: That one be a Catholic - culturally so - in Brazil is the general expectation. You may even be Protestant or whatever else, provided that one is *also* a Catholic. So, this requirement does not necessarily preclude simultaneous affiliation with other religious, or quasi-religious orientations (e.g., Kardecist spiritualism, the Rosicrucian system). Female heads of Afro-Brazilian cult centers are quick to proclaim their good standing as Catholics - but this, after all, should be expected; it is the very essence of syncretism.

In any event, the chief aim of this work in contrasting models of culture is to highlight the disadvantages of systems which are structurally set up to block the access of minority segments of the population to the mainstream mode of life, on the basis of ascriptive factors, such as race; and to point to the advantages - cultural and otherwise - of allowing and promoting universal access to the sociocultural mainstream.

9   These national religious holidays must be considered as a distinct factor and vehicle of cultural exchange. Koster lists them at over thirty a year, for the period (the early 1800s). Tannenbaum states that, all together, Sundays and holidays amounted to eighty-four days a year, throughout the nineteenth century (1946:61).

10   The *candomblé* is the name given in Bahia to the AfroBrazilian syncretic cult.

11   It should be instructive to contrast this celebration with its version on U.S. soil, namely, Mardi Gras. Blassingame (1976:145) reports that large numbers of New Orleans blacks "viewed the annual parade in the 1860s and began to join in the processions in significant numbers, and to hold balls during the season in the 1870s." He adds that the Mardi Gras season opened with "a series of masked balls late in January," in connection with which the costumed participants at one such ball, in the 1880s, exhibited names like: "Italian Peasant," "America," "Butter Cup," "Folly," "German Maid," "Scotch Queen," "Duke of Wellington," and "Charles II." It is amply clear here that it was the European model of culture that the New Orleans black were attempting to emulate and incorporate, not the African one. The twofold implication here is, first, that it points to the suppression of the African cultural connection among the blacks, and secondly, it

92

suggests that the cultural model of the host society was the only truly viable alternative for African(-American) collective expression, and even that, as has been demonstrated, was not made fully accessible to them.

12 One particular instrument is described by Koster (1816:241) as "a large bow with one string, having half of a coconut shell or of a small gourd strung upon it. This is placed against the abdomen and the string is struck with one finger, or with a small piece of wood." To anyone familiar with Brazilian music and musical instruments Koster is obviously describing the *berimbau*, an instrument still used in AfroBrazilian religious cult dances, in popular music in general, and for accompanying demonstrations of *capoeira*, a dance-like foot fighting technique developed by runaway slaves in colonial and 19th-century Brazil, as protection against their pursuers.

13 Pierson (1967:251-52) lists the following instruments as being used in the *candomblé* ceremonies: the *atabaques* (wooden drums), the *agogô* (two hollow iron cones joined together, which are struck with a metal stick), the *agé* (a large calabash containing pebbles and covered with a small cotton net in whose meshes cowries imported rom Africa are firmly secured), the *xaque-xaque* (a hollow metal instrument shaped like a dumbbell, each of whose enlarged extremities contains small pebbles), the *caxixi* (a tiny reed or straw basket containing cowries or small pebbles, to be shaken in the hand), the *cuíca* (a type of drumlike instrument, open at one end. Sound is produced by drawing the hand along a resined stick appended to the center of the drumhead), and the *berimbau* (see endnote above. This is not strictly part of the group of sacred instruments, but it is probably one of the most familiar instruments of African derivation to practically everyone in Brazil. It consists of a wire strung upon a stick to form a bow, with a dried gourd open at the top attached at the lower extremity. The instrument is beaten, to produce numerous complex rhythms, with a wooden stick held, together with a *caxixi*, in the right hand, while with the left a copper coin is alternately pressed against the wire and released).

4 Miscegenation and intermarriage in the formation of society

The nature of biracialism

The story is told, in the 1920s musical *Showboat*, of a young couple in love, in a Mississipi town - he is white, she is black -and the young man is confronted by the local sheriff, who charges him with violation of the state's anti-miscegenation law. The fast-thinking young man quickly pricks his beloved's finger with a knife, swallows a drop of her blood and then resists arrest on the grounds that now he is no longer a white man, since he has got "Negro" blood in him. The poor sheriff, caught by surprise by the novelty of the situation, is befuddled for a moment, but finally succumbs to the logic of racial classification prevalent in Mississipi (according to which the young man's act radically restructured the situation, and therefore created a need for a different interpretation of it), and lets the young man off.

   This incident is at once humorous and serious. Regardless of how it may be taken, however, it is richly instructive and revealing of the nature of interethnic and interracial life in U.S. society. Its humorous side is self-evident, in the interpretation and observance of a cultural norm taken *ad absurdum*. Its serious side is seen in the firmness with which the principle of biraciality is adhered to as the primary governing and organizing principle of intergroup relations in American society, and in the thoroughgoing fashion in which it orients social practice and thought, to the point where this story is rendered credible. That is, it makes it reasonable for one to assume that this incident could have actually taken place, since it is not entirely out of keeping with the norms, definitions, and expectations that govern interethnic and interracial relations in this society. The behavior of the sheriff, however irrational it may appear at first glance, becomes reasonable enough upon closer scrutiny, and in the context of the societal enforcement of racial bipolarity. The anti-miscegenation law that forbade the biological fusion between members of the dominant and the minority ethnic groups, and the zeal with which the sheriff sought to uphold it, rested first of all on the premise that races exist as clearly-demarcated, biologically-pure, distinct communities, and, secondly, on the idea of the indisputable supremacy of the "white" race. The superior racial status of the dominant group would be irretrievably defiled by the intermarriage of the young couple, but now, in a strictly technical sense, it was no longer under the threat of contamination because the racially-pure partner in the relationship had altered his condition forever through direct contact with the blood of the racially-inferior partner. Given how biracialist ideology imparts a special relevance to the operation of "blood" in the racial constitution of groups, what is involved here is nothing less than an ontological transformation, a transformation of the condition of Being (of the young man), insofar as the larger societal community understands this condition to be biologically grounded, and thus subject to alteration through biological processes. Therefore, in adopting a new stance towards this fundamental shift in the situation, the sheriff, blindly uncritical though he may have been towards the incongruities arising from the rigid enforcement of patterns of racial bipolarity, and towards the particular problem that developed at that moment; and unable as he was to grasp its historicality and relative nature, and then to transcend it (as someone with greater critical insight might perhaps have been able to do), in fact gave evidence of having properly internalized the laws and expectations of biraciality, and acted in strict accordance with them, regarding the aspect of innovation presented by the young man's behavior.

The norm of biraciality may be said to influence U.S. social life as deeply and as pervasively as economic status once influenced early-industrial society in the 19th century or developing industrial societies in the present century. Race remains the Great Divide, the all-powerful levelling, homogenizing, and categorizing principle of individuals and groups in American society. Its effect on institutional relations and processes remains quite evident, as does its subtle, though very effective, orchestration of the minuet of verbal and nonverbal interaction. Imperiously, it admits of no challenge by any other criterion of social differentiation. All persons of whatever cultural, economic, or ideological background and walk of life are ultimately grouped together as equals on the basis of their "white" or "nonwhite" classification. It does not matter a great deal in this connection - that is to say, it does not matter in an absolutely determining way - that one's name be typically Anglo-Saxon, orthographically and phonetically, or very different in this regard; that one's lifestyle be very conventional or unconventional; that one's physical features conform, or fail to conform, to the mainstream Anglo-Saxon aesthetic standards; that one be highly successful economically or fail to reach the higher rungs of the socioeconomic ladder; that one's values and norms express, or fail to express, the hegemonic cultural model - in the final analysis, what is really and truly going to matter, explicitly and implicitly, is whether one is perceived and classified as white or nonwhite. National origin, ethnic and cultural difference, all manner of distinction, eventually dissipate under the power of the white/nonwhite dualism. Furthermore, the dissolution of ethnic and national distinctions brought about by the norms of racial bipolarity, and by the fact that the biracial framework of classification and understanding makes the "white" category the context of universality and the "nonwhite" category the context of marginality or difference (i.e., in relation to the universal standard), leads to a generalized conflation of race and ethnicity in U.S. society, in reference to which members of the larger, undifferentiated "Anglo-Saxon" population consider ethnicity a property of the "nonwhite" groups only, and do not see themselves as having any kind of ethnicity, but simply as being "white." Racial identity emerges as the all-embracing unifying ground. This situation calls to mind the declarations of a young woman in Little Rock, Arkansas, at the time of the upheaval in that city over school desegregation (1957). She was shown being interviewed in one of the episodes of the Civil Rights documentary *Eyes on the Prize*, and trying to justify the fierce resistance on the part of whites against integrating the school system. She stated that if this movement involved integrating "the Mexicans or the Chinese" into the educational system, that would not be so bad, but the blacks were just too different! That was truly an astounding assertion, for, who could have been any more similar to the Southern whites than the Southern blacks? For all of the cultural separatism enforced in that region, and the extreme social distance as well as economic and political inequality that kept these two groups apart from colonial times to the time of the desegregation movement, they had evolved together, sharing (in however imperfect form) the same cultural system. As a result, blacks acted and thought much like Southerners in general. If any group were to be perceived as different from the white people of Little Rock, Mexican-Americans and Chinese-Americans should have been, with their maintenance of a subcultural lifestyle within the enclosure of American society. But, their greater *cultural* difference - according to the young woman's statement - would be overridden by the fact that racially they came somewhat closer to the white population. (Let us not even bother to imagine here the radical instance of cultural difference of, say, a person from Finland, who, from a cultural

96

standpoint, might as well be from Mars, yet this cultural strangeness would not stand in the way of this person's racial status prevailing over everything else, causing him/her to be perceived by the Southerners as "one of us," a known quantity, as readily identifiable and familiar as one's next-door neighbor). Obviously, the difference, the alien quality, of the Southern blacks did not lie in their subcultural distinctiveness, but in the criterion that weighed most heavily in the determination of what constituted intergroup difference: their racial status. And that, to say it with Frost, made all the difference.

In this regard, individuals in this society are rendered quite powerless to ignore or resist the authoritarian imposition of this form of classificatory management of the interpersonal sphere. There is no such thing, in other words, as being left alone to tend to other kinds of concerns. The awareness of race and the self-identification and self-management on the basis of this biracial blueprint become inescapable, a matter of absolute priority, a non-negotiable requirement. This seems especially applicable to the black-white dualism, primarily because members of the subordinate (i.e., nonwhite) racial category have themselves been enculturated into the biracialist-separatist model of racial and cultural identity of the society, and consequently, like the majority population, engage in the common practice of homogenizing individuals on the basis of their "white" or "black" classification. For them, racial status and identity are totalizing circumstances, which yield a sense of racial obligation, and therefore allow no variation regarding the conduct of those who have been categorized as nonwhite. In other words, these individuals are expected to express racial kinship and loyalty, above all other considerations (see, e.g., Kennedy, 1997, for a pertinent commentary). A television documentary on children from African-American fathers and Japanese mothers (1995) bore out this aspect, in that some of these children had grown in Japan and were thus entirely Japanese from a cultural standpoint, but in the African-American community in the U.S. they were defined as "black," and expected to assume a "black" identity and to identify readily with "black" culture.

From a procedural standpoint, biracial social organization requires that the intermediary racial categories obtaining from the intermixture of white and black be neutralized and disregarded, conceptually and empirically. Since these categories are not acknowledged, individuals are forced to find their existential and cultural moorings in either one of the racial poles, which means, they have to form an identity as either "white" or "black." This model of social organization, whereby social relations and social consciousness remain bound by the ascriptive consideration of race and ethnicity, is a carry-over from the dominant model of social organization of earlier (i.e., preindustrial) times, which was anchored, first and foremost, to race and ethnicity.

The ideological principles that support biraciality are anchored to the premise of the essential purity of one category (i.e., the category "white"), and the essential non-purity of the other (i.e., the category "nonwhite"). The perfect purity of the former demands that it be protected at all costs from any degree of contamination by the non-purity of the latter. The condition of non-purity allows for greater flexibility, in the sense that, while the white element is considered potentially besmirchable by all manner of contact and intermixture with the nonwhite, the latter is bound to its condition of impurity forever, therefore it is free to engage in processes of fusion within the nonwhite category; and if association between these people and those that form the white category should ever occur, this will not matter, insofar as altering the essential ontological condition of the nonwhite element is concerned. The biracialist concern with keeping these two categories rigidly separate and distinct is geared, therefore, towards the preservation of the condition of the dominant element. This may be witnessed in the zeal and consistency with which anti-miscegenation law and attitude were enforced at one time in American society, and in the continuing cultural injunctions against the practice. Myrdal (1972:58) observed in the 1940s that the anti-miscegenation forces in U.S. society set up a boundary "between Negro and white [which] is not simply a class line which can be successfully crossed by education, integration into the national culture, and individual economic advancement. The boundary is fixed. It is not a temporary expediency during an apprenticeship in the national culture. It is a bar erected with the intention of permanency." An integral part of this separatist framework was naturally the force of ideology. In his study Myrdal goes over a list of popular beliefs in American society designed to discourage miscegenation and to keep up "biological distance even in regard to cross-breeds" (1972:108).

The societal treatment of intermarriage and miscegenation

We shall turn next to the question of the social treatment of intermarriage and miscegenation, and race classification. At the outset, it must be acknowledged that the early phase of colonization of New World societies was typically characterized by sharp asymmetry of power and wealth between the colonizing and colonized groups, and by the sexual exploitation of members of subjugated group, specifically, in terms of the sexual exploitation of the female members of the colonized group(s) by

98

male members of the colonizing group. This aspect figures consistently in the history of these societies, giving rise to the steady growth of a distinct proportion in the population made up of the offspring of these unions.

In looking at interethnic and interracial relations from the standpoint of miscegenation, it is necessary to go beyond the sexual exploitation of the oppressed group within the broader context of intergroup power inequality, in order to assess first of all not only whether the society in question shows higher/lower levels of miscegenation in comparison with another, but also how it has addressed, through its cultural-ideological and legal framework, the problems of intergroup relations, the national role of the subordinate ethnic element, and the idea of interracial fusion itself. Secondly, whether the practice of miscegenation has been formally regulated (i.e., via legislation). Thirdly, whether this pattern will, as a result of legal and informal influences, be manifested merely as a sexual relationship, or as intermarriage, with the implication , in the latter case, of the constitution of a family unit. Finally, whether the offspring from these interracial sexual unions will inherit the permanently marginal status of the female parent (should the female parent be that which represents the subordinate ethnic group in the union) - the case of separatist multiethnic systems, where castelike segregation and rigid biracialism preclude the possibility of viable intermediary, assimilable racial categories - or whether they will have access to social mobility on a larger scale than the members of the group to which the female parent belongs, which is the case of nonseparatist multiethnic systems, where multiraciality is the prevalent mode, and personal identity does not follow dichotomic rules of classification.

In Brazil the practice of miscegenation was strongly stimulated by both official policy and "local attitudes and customs" (Lowrie, 1942:416). One commentator insists that "[i]n few places in the world, perhaps, has the interpenetration of peoples of divergent racial stocks proceeded so continuously and on so extensive a scale" (Pierson, 1967:119). The travel literature of the 18th and 19th centuries systematically confirms this point. In the U.S., by contrast, the record of social and legal obstruction to interracial unions has been significant. In the 1940s, Myrdal witnessed "intense resistance on the part of the white majority group to biological amalgamation" (1962:928). The following incident, from an even earlier time, reveals the intensity of this social opposition. Writing in the late 1800s about social life in the United States, the Cuban patriot José Martí refers to a case in Oak Ridge, Tennessee, where several blacks were lynched in retaliation for the fact that one black was known to have been living with a white woman (Martí, 1975:212). From the legal standpoint, anti-miscegenation laws prevailed throughout the colonial and antebellum periods (see, e.g., Jordan, 1968 and Ruchamés, 1969, for the colonial period) and were still standing only a quarter of a century ago, in some states. Back in the mid-1700s, the Swedish visitor Peter Kalm reported from New England to the effect that a law had been passed "prohibiting the whites of both sexes to marry negroes, under pain of almost capital punishment, with deprivation and other severer penalties for the clergyman who married them." Of much more recent date is Tischler's account: "As late as 1966, nineteen states sought to ban interracial marriage through legislation. The laws varied widely. In Arizona before 1967 it was illegal for a white person to marry a black, Hindu, Malay, or Asian. The same thing was true in Wyoming, and residents of that state were also prohibited from marrying mulattoes" (1993:248). The accounts of foreign visitors in the 19th century also attest to the maintenance of this legal posture, as shown in the account of (the famous English publicist and sociologist) Harriet Martineau, who traveled through the United States in the 1830s, and remarked that in the South there could be "no legal marriage between whites and persons of any degree of colour" (in Nevins, 1928:211). By the 1870s, Southerners had enacted specific legislation against black-white intermarriage "in every Southern state" (Franklin, 1969:342). Yet, for all the official and unofficial injunctions against intermixture in U.S. society, miscegenation is said to have been extensive, from the earliest phases of the colonial period, on through the antebellum period in the nineteenth century (see, e.g., Jordan, 1981:70-71). "The record is replete with the occurrence," says Tannenbaum (1946:123), "in spite of law, doctrine, and belief."

The high frequency of interracial mixture in the United States by itself should not, however, be construed as the all-determining factor. This practice will occur, in varying degrees, the stringency of legal and/or cultural controls against it notwithstanding. What is more critical to consider here, however, is that the cultural and ideological framework of the society was such that it produced a national ethos of intergroup separatism, a generalized and profound sense of aversion to processes of fusion between the dominant ethnic group and minority one - in particular, sexual fusion. This was concretely expressed in the law as well as in the maximal enforcement of castelike segregation in all spheres of social life. It also caused intermixture, whenever it occurred, to take mainly the form of sexual mating as such, and not of formally-legitimized unions, and it was also always attended with a sense of guilt, conflict, and cognitive dissonance (see, e.g., Jordan, 1981:70, on this second point). The misgivings surrounding interracial mixtures under the particular circumstances of U.S. society constitute a rather understandable process of collective psychology, but for our purposes here their greater heuristic value is found in what they disclose about the nature of social organization and intergroup relations.

In multiethnic settings where the material and symbolic injuries perpetrated on the subordinate ethnic group(s) are not exacerbated by the predominance of castelike separatism, miscegenation is likely to proceed on a larger scale, legal intermarriage (and not just sexual relations) becomes a more viable proposition, and the offspring of these unions become potentially eligible for eventual absorption into the mainstream (see Freyre, 1951:ch.12).[1] In Brazilian society the extensive pattern of miscegenation often took the form of legal intermarriage because, as the record indicates, neither the Church nor the State erected barriers to the union between the Portuguese settlers and the Amerindian and the African groups. In fact, these institutions appear to have expressly encouraged ethnic fusion at all levels. Pierson (1964:313) writes about how the governmental and ecclesiastical sanction led gradually to a tradition of legal intermarriage that became firmly entrenched in the mores of colonial Brazil and has gone on uninterruptedly right down to the present day. The ubiquitous character of intermarriage in nineteenth-century Brazil, and the preponderance of "class" over "race," in the regulation of this practice, is addressed in the chronicles of Rugendas, written in the first quarter of the 1800s. He says:

The marriages between white males and women of color are very common in the middle and lower classes, and are in no way shocking; one may in fact observe this, to some extent, even in the more privileged classes. Generally [these marriages] are formalized when a white woman from a well-to-do and distinguished family marries a very dark-skinned man; but these unions provoke more surprise than they do social condemnation. It cannot be denied that in Brazil the general public is far more tolerant towards these mixed marriages than in Europe in general, in the same social echelons. It is, of course, common for a white male from a traditional family to choose to marry a white woman, for women of this color, and with European blood, always constitute an advantage and form a kind of aristocracy; *but this preference prevails only in this sense* [emphasis added]. All things being equal, dark color and African blood are passed up [in favor of white], but a white man from the higher classes would be *equally reluctant* [emphasis added] to marry a lower-class white woman. Thus, with reference to the woman of color, the obstacle in this case would be equivalent" (1976:77; my translation).

In his voluminous report on life in Imperial Brazil, penned at about the same time as Rugendas's observations, Jean-Baptiste Debret writes about manumitted African women in the cities, and informs us that some of these women managed to become small-scale proprietors of grocery stores that sold fruits, vegetables, and various African-derived pastries and delicacies, and they frequently became "wives to white workers, who generally never leave them" (1989:131, vol.II). From Koster (1816:393) comes yet another report, in the same vein:

> Marriages between white men and women of color are by no means rare, though they are sufficiently so to cause the circumstance to be mentioned when speaking of an individual who has connected himself in this manner; but this is not said with the intent of lowering him in the estimation of others. Indeed, the remark is only made if the person is a planter of any importance, and the woman is decidedly of dark colour, for even a considerable tinge will pass for white; if the white man belongs to the lower orders, the woman is not accounted as being unequal to him in rank, unless she is nearly black.

Half a century after these chroniclers published their observations on Brazilian colonial life, the French scientist Eliseé Réclus, after a period of residence in Brazil, recounts how "protected by custom [the manumitted blacks] mingle freely with the superior castes, and the mixed population increases incessantly in very large proportion ..." (1862:388; my translation). These reports bear witness to the widespread nature of miscegenation in Brazilian society. That individuals of mixed racial ancestry in Brazil have generally been deemed qualified for social opportunities open to members of the majority population is likewise corroborated by Raymundo José de Souza Gayoso, in a treatise from the early 1800s titled *Compendio Histórico-Político dos Princípios da Lavoura no Maranhão* (Historico-Political Treatise on the Beginning of Agriculture in Maranhão), in which he analyzed patterns of miscegenation and ethnic incorporation in his home state of Maranhão (northern Brazil). He wrote that racial intermixture in that region was proceeding apace, to the point where it had brought the intermediary categories ever closer in appearance to the dominant white population, and that the former "enjoyed all the privileges" of the latter (cited in Freyre, 1951:1043). These privileges concerned not only the access to economic, political, and educational opportunity, but also to the sphere of kinship and friendship relations; in other words, to the social life of the community. In this century, Pierson's Cruz das Almas research on village life in Brazil (1948) may be presented here, as it addresses this issue in detail:

Persons of color will be invited, just like anyone else, to the house of a white. They will eat at the white's table. They will participate with whites in religious, as well as secular, *festas* (celebrations). They will in no way be discriminated against in friendship, in employment, in voting, or in treatment by local officials. In the groups of conversation which form spontaneously at the *vendas* (general stores) and elsewhere in the village are to be seen men representing the entire range of color variation in the community. All converse together in terms of intimacy. There is no segregation of any kind. Similarly, blacks, mulattoes, *cafusos* (individuals of African and Amerindian descent) and *mamelucos* (individuals of European and African descent) regularly drink and joke together at the *botequins* (bars), play cards with one another or otherwise share activities, without any restraint being laid upon their conduct by reason of color. Of special significance here is the highly ritualized practice of the *virada* (the "taking-of-turns"), in which everyone present partakes of a "common cup" (of a strong alcoholic beverage, like sugarcane rum) on equal terms (1948:190-1).

Intimate relations among the different racial categories in the community presented no exception in this regard. At a local dance, Pierson observed, "the white girls danced with blacks and mixed-bloods, without there being apparent the slightest indication, on either part, of strangeness, or opposition." There is also a reference to a case of *namoro* (courtship), which was going on at the time of the research, involving a white boy and a mulatto girl. This case brought "[n]o word of reproach or disapproval of any kind on either racial or color grounds" (1948:191).

In American society, although the legal prohibitions of intermixture have been taken off the books by the legislative reforms that outlawed and finally dismantled the Jim Crow system through the 1960s and 1970s; and although over the past three decades the changes in the institutional sectors of society, in its "secondary" institutions, such as the workplace, the educational system, the armed forces, and so on, have also altered the pattern of ethnic relations significantly, the cultural pressures (i.e., collective attitudes and sentiments, not the least of which are beliefs and feelings justified on religious grounds) against the practice remain strong, and as a result, the number of couples in interracial marriages has risen only minimally from 0.7% of all married couples in 1970 to 1.6% in 1986, not a sizable increase when one realizes that these unions constitute less than 2 of every 100 married couples (Tischler, 1993:248-9). There is no question that, as the present decade rolls on, societal attitudes in the U.S. towards the biological assimilation of "nonwhites" have become rather more liberal than they were years ago. One even finds specialized

103

publications on interracial dating(!), movies in recent years have been made on this subject, and the popular press of late (Spring 1997) has devoted increasing attention to the spread and larger implications of interracial marriage. Still, by and large, individuals continue to be strongly socialized, either directly or indirectly, into endogamic relations. There are many ways in which this socialization pattern is enforced and can be detected, such as, for instance, in the fact that interracial couples continue to be virtually nonexistent on television programs, and story lines in drama or comedy shows consistently steer characters away from emotional entanglements with members of another "race," unless it is done for the express purpose of presenting a controversial situation so as to stimulate debate about it. This pattern is also significantly indicated, for example, in department-store catalogs: a quick examination of these catalogs covering, say, the last ten years, shows that when models are shown as couples they are invariably paired off by "race." These examples illustrate the remarkable consistency with which the unwritten laws of biracial existence are enforced in all aspects of social life in U.S. society, and the way in which this has directly impeded the growth of miscegenation. On the official side, the matter of interracial adoption is pertinent here. It is generally perceived as a highly inflammatory issue, and state adoption agencies have been oriented, as a rule, to matching the racial and ethnic backgrounds of children to that of their adoptive parents (Brophy, 1989:73-4; *Utne Reader*, Nov/Dec 1991:59). In 1972 the National Association of Black Social Workers took a firm stand against transnational adoptions, and in 1978 Native-American groups forced the passage of laws mandating that Native-American children be placed with Native American families. As long as ideological forces continue to discourage the racial intermixture, this will inevitably be reflected in the operation of bureaucratic structures, such as the adoption agencies mentioned above, and the latter in turn will function as safeguards and reinforcing devices of the national ideology of race and ethnic relations, thus establishing a vicious circle of segregation which is very difficult to overcome. The latter would require the revamping of the pattern of enculturation of individuals regarding interethnic and interracial life, with corresponding alterations in social behavior and in the bureaucratic treatment of interethnic and interracial affairs in the society, such as expressed in the official system of classification of social groups. These changes can hardly be accomplished on a short-term basis.

Concerning the system of race classification, many analysts (e.g., Frazier, 1944; Bastide and van den Berghe, 1957; Wagley, 1971; Harris, 1974; Marger, 1991) have noted how the designations "white" and "nonwhite," as employed in the United States, find no precise equivalents in Brazil. In the latter society interethnic relations are organized and regulated via a multiracial system of classification, whereby racial status is assigned phenotypically, or on the basis of appearance, at both the official and informal levels. This system allows for the identification and inclusion of a wide variety of physical types. The racial categories, and consequently racial identity, are more arbitrary, imprecise, unstable, and susceptible to change by means of the impact of other social variables, especially class. This means that the racial status of individuals may vary in their lifetime, provided their social and economic circumstances change in sufficient measure to warrant a change in the social perception of their racial condition. This quality of arbitrariness of the system may, in this case, be said to impart greater fluidity to it. Racial distinctions are mainly drawn on the basis of "sociological" (i.e., phenotypical) criteria, rather than "anthropological" (i.e., genotypical) ones, which means that this is done in terms of the social perception and classification of physical traits or appearance, such as skin color or hair texture, as opposed to being done on the basis of biological criteria (i.e., ancestry). In any case, as stressed earlier in this analysis, color itself is not an objective, systematic, or uniform category, but a highly subjective phenomenon. "In this society," says Pierson in reference to Brazil, "a person is white if [she/he] looks predominantly like a white, and if his friends and associates so consider him" (1948:24). Bureaucratic classification as well was oriented to appearance, rather than to ancestry, as this author continues: "If a given individual appears to the registrar to look more like a white than a black or *pardo* (of mixed parentage), he is listed as white, even though to persons sensitized to racial distinctions, and especially to the trained specialist, physical traits of non-European origin are clearly observable" (1948:190).

Interethnic relations in the United States differ strikingly in this regard. As has been said, they are governed in accordance with the rules of racial bipolarity, whereby racial status is assigned genotypically, that is, on the basis of ancestry, making physical appearance an irrelevant consideration. This system operates dichotomously, with all of the diverse physical types being lumped together into either of the two possible and mutually-exclusive categories, to wit, white and nonwhite. The elimination of intermediary categories is effected through the operation of the law of hypodescent, or "one-drop rule," previously mentioned. There is more organizational precision to this type of racial taxonomy - notwithstanding the enormous inconsistency of its application regarding the laws of genetics - because of the greater clarity and stability of the racial categories, which makes them more suitable for administrative manipulation, as in the case, for example, of bureaucratic identification of underprivileged groups, be it for the purpose of granting them civil rights and protections, or for establishing their social exclusion. Classification systems that are couched in racial bipolarity also take on a monolithic rigidity that impinges directly on the life of minority-group individuals, at all formal and informal levels.

In chapter II, the material and symbolic implications of race classification patterns were examined, in the context of the aspect of "whitening of race." We may bring this issue to the fore again, by reiterating that systems of racial taxonomy which are grounded in the rule of hypodescent represent the maximum of exclusion for those who are not categorized as white, since all that falls outside the white frame of reference is, by definition, nonwhite, hence, burdened with exclusion or marginalization. In the contrasting model of race classification of Brazilian society, the variations resulting from racial intermixture are accounted for on the basis of phenotypical distinctions (which are themselves unstable, imprecise, and arbitrary, as noted earlier). At any rate, I think that it is particularly important in this regard to draw attention to the historically common saying in Brazilian culture *Quem escapa de preto branco é* (literally: "One who escapes the [category of] black is white"). This belief clearly issues from the collective assumption that the social inclusion of all individuals situated outside the white category, towards the eventual ethnic-racial consolidation of the society, is well within the realm of possibility. In the early years of this century, James Bryce noticed that in Brazil not only "no colour line is sharply drawn" (1921:414), but also all avenues were open to individuals of mixed racial origin and their descendants to gain eventual admission into the dominant white population through socioeconomic betterment (1921:408-9; 414-15).

This is quite the opposite of what obtains in biracial contexts of race classification, where the categories are formed genotypically. The end result is a castelike duality supported by the rule of hypodescent. We have seen how this rule establishes, first of all, the biologically homogeneity and purity of the dominant racial segment of the population, and the need to protect this condition from any degree of fusion, hence, contamination, with the condition of the subordinate racial segment. Secondly, it establishes that the union between members of the dominant and nondominant racial segments of the population produces offspring whose racial status is necessarily already compromised, causing these individuals to be automatically assigned membership in the minority racial community of the "nonwhite" parent. As Park (1964:112) remarked in this connection, "[e]very person with a tincture of the African in him is classed as a Negro." Finally, the condition of all individuals classified as being outside the dominant racial grouping is deemed irreparable, or a *natural* condition, that is, a condition made permanent by a natural determinism that lends an ontological fixedness to it. Thus, these people cannot ever alter their racial status and classification towards blending into, and adopting the ethnic/racial identity of the population. (This process is generally feasible in multiethnic societies that enforce a multiracial system of classification being mediated, as a rule, by the factor of socioeconomic or "class" betterment.) This betrays a treatment of "race" that is fundamentally static and deterministic, and which flies in the face of the fact that race, even when considered strictly in its biological (i.e., as opposed to socially-constructed) aspects, is a *dynamic* concept. More important still, it is dynamic by virtue of its existence and expression in the social context, its manifestations being primarily manifestations *of the social*, not of biology (see Freyre, 1951:1080-81).

Further insight into the enormous importance of interethnic and interracial fusion for the overall framework of social organization in integrationist cultural systems (as exemplified by the Brazilian model) may be gained by considering the interweaving of intergroup biological relations and cultural relations, focusing on the interrelation of "race" and "culture." This may be demonstrated in a particular aspect of religious syncretism - something which speaks to process of *cultural* fusion - taking the form of an extra-religious aspect, in the sense that the syncretic fusion of West African and European religious practice and belief often occurred in terms of the corresponding or parallel process of fusion going on in the interethnic and interracial spheres. Specifically, the saints of the dominant religion, while being associated in the religious behavior and practices of the people with their functional counterparts in Amerindian and West African religious systems, also frequently took on the physical characteristics of the subaltern ethnic populations. We see then in the phenomenon of cultural syncretism the symbolic reproduction of the pattern of ethnic and racial interpenetration. The Catholicism transplanted to Brazil, already heavily hybridized by virtue of the particular historical experience of the Portuguese settler, underwent in Brazil an intensification of this trait. Thus it was that, as Freyre informs us,

> the glass doors of the shrines opened wide to let in the African *orixás* disguised as St. Cosme and St. Damião, coal-black St. Benedicts and St. Efigenias, dark-hued Madonnas of the Rosary. Colored saints who took their place beside rosy-cheeked St. Anthonys and golden-locked cherubs, in a fraternization that imitated reality. Saints and angels, traditionally blond, were forced here to be like the people - not all white, also some blacks, many mulattoes - becoming, like them, the relatives of blacks, browns, and mulattoes. Even Our Lady took on

mulatto characteristics: in the hands of our sculptors of religious images, she became corpulent and acquired the breasts of a 'Negro mammy' (1951:1072-73; my translation).

Materialist interpretation and the miscegenation-race consciousness nexus

The ongoing amalgamation of ethnic and racial strains, as characteristic of integrationist-type cultural systems, acts as a deterrent to the emergence and development of independent ethnic and racial movements, and of a separatist racial consciousness among "people of color." The concerns of "race"- racial origin, classification, and identity - generally cease to be a matter of concern for individuals and groups, in the degree that these individuals and groups have undergone biological incorporation into the dominant population. Their energies will be channeled instead towards advancement in the socioeconomic hierarchy. Conversely, the absence of systematic, continuous interethnic and interracial fusion engendered and guaranteed by the biracialist administration of the society leads inevitably to a concern on the part of individuals with who they are racially, and with how they stand in relation to the larger racial context of their society (this issue is taken up in greater depth in the next chapter). In Brazil, as discussed in more detail below, there have been overtures towards the formalization of ethnic movements, but these have been sporadic and unsystematic, hence, hardly representative of the most fundamental impulses of the "AfroBrazilian community," primarily because this community has never existed as a segregated ethnic-racial community over the entire span of Brazilian history. At the time when Frazier was conducting his research on race relations in Brazil in the 1940s, he surmised that such separatist movements were unlikely to take root under the prevailing structural circumstances of Brazilian society, "unless outside influences affect present tendencies." (1944:268). This last remark, on the infiltration of interference of foreign influences in the interethnic/interracial sphere in Brazil, was made in reference to the way in which prominent English and American visitors (e.g., business consultants, technical advisors), up to the time of World War II, ordinarily pressured the management of the hotels they were staying in to eject even distinguished black guests, an imposition that, when complied with (it was not always complied with) could only have had the effect of accentuating color-based distinctions and antagonisms in a societal context where these distinctions and antagonisms were deemed fundamentally unimportant. Another example, of more recent date, that also demonstrates the possibility that certain situations may be interpreted as evidence of the operation of a separatist racial consciousness, when in fact this is not quite what is involved, may be seen in the following. Some years ago, in the late 1980s, the practice of letting one's hair grow out and braiding it in (what came to be known locally as) the *Ras Tafari* style of Jamaican blacks became quite common among the population of African descent in Salvador (Bahia). Along with other patterns of collective behavior, this was widely perceived as a sign of the greater valorization imparted to African culture by Salvador blacks at that time. Yet, this perception is shortsighted in that it fails to recognize other vitally important factors in the situation. Essentially, this phenomenon was not *primarily* the expression of an emergent group solidarity and consciousness of color among a particular segment of the population, but rather, the expression of a larger foreign (West Indian, and more precisely, Jamaican) cultural influence, which endured into the 1990s in the artistic landscape of that city, especially in the area of music. Of even greater relevance for the analysis of ethnic-racial relations is the fact that this was not a manifestation limited to the population of mixed descent, but trend - a general fashion fad, really - that affected the Salvador population as a whole. According to one of the several reports in the popular press on this event,[2] during that period hairdressers who specialized in the *rastafari* hairdos were in great demand. One of them remarked: "Every Saturday about thirty people come to our salon to get this hairstyle, men and women, *whites* and blacks" (emphasis added). There is also mention of a birthday party where about fifty young *white* and black children sported African-style braids and dreadlocks in their hair. Finally, the report stresses that the new celebration of African cultural influences in the Salvador area was something endorsed and shared by the white population as well, citing the particular case of a white professional who not only wore his hair in the *rastafari* style , but also had a "veritable passion" for Jamaican music (see note #2, p.66, of the report). These aspects are perfectly consistent with my view here that in integrationist contexts the culture moves as a whole, its movements are not normally subcultural expressions of particular segments of the population, but general expressions of the population as an integrated unit.

I laid stress earlier on the untenability of a *lingua franca* for the race and ethnicity discourse, a universally applicable metalanguage that would yield high heuristic and explanatory returns irrespective of the multiethnic context being analyzed. In societies where a society-wide pattern of miscegenation has prevailed from the beginning, thus resulting in a largely hybrid population, the application of traditional conceptual and classificatory schemes to the study of ethnic and racial relations in that society has little utility, particularly when these analytical schemes are derived from special cases of multiethnic systems which, like the U.S. model, stand out for their historically inflexible enforcement of castelike racial dichotomization of the population, and where collective understandings of ethnic and racial matters tend to be more linear, and oriented to binary distinctions. In light of this, when patterns of interethnic and interracial life in different pluralist societies are discussed without allowing for the appropriate conceptual and classificatory modifications, the analysis is already somewhat suspect, and may in effect obfuscate more than it will clarify. This tendency is rather pronounced in the Marxist literature (though it is found in "materialist" analytical approaches in general) on race and ethnicity, such as manifested in the accounts of Marxist-oriented writers who customarily employ the traditional ideas and categories of the race-and-ethnicity discourse (e.g., "whites," "blacks," "racial groups," "racial minorities," "people of color," "Black social movements," "the Black community," and so on) to cover *any* situation of interethnic or interracial life. This is done, one might suppose, because a conceptual equivalence between the dominant and subordinate ethnic-racial categories and their economic counterparts (i.e., the ownership and working classes) must, first of all, be assumed and deemed necessary, before a class or political-economy analysis of dominant-minority ethnic relations can be effectively elaborated. This means that the dominant (i.e., "white") ethnic group and the minority (i.e., "nonwhite") groups must remain neatly set apart conceptually so as to correspond to the mutual exclusiveness that separates their counterpart economic categories, namely, the dominant and subordinate economic classes of society, or the owners and the workers.

Marxist analyses, because they concentrate their energies on the elucidation of the workings of economic and political power between dominant and minority social groups, tend to assign secondary importance to, when not completely leave aside, crucial aspects of institutional and interpersonal life, which at length come to exert a decisive impact on overall social organization (e.g., problems of group identity, kinship formation, interethnic cultural relations, and so forth). Even less attention is devoted to the symbolic and representational dimensions of interethnic and interracial life. These, as is known, are generally treated as offshoots of the material circumstances of intergroup life.

An important work of some three decades ago may be examined in this regard. This is *The Negro in Brazilian Society* (1971), by Florestan Fernandes, where a contrasting argument is presented. In this work, the discussion of race and ethnicity in Brazil reveals, first of all, its embeddedness in the language of historical materialism, judging from its references to "the return of the Negro and mulatto to the historical stage of action," their integration into the industrial-capitalist "competitive social order," and so on. Also, the analysis appears to be vitiated by this overgeneralizing or "homogenizing" tendency indicated above, in terms of its unproblematized reliance on the standard conceptual repertoire of race and ethnicity, an approach that implicitly dispenses with crossnational distinctions (in this connection, a review commentary of Fernandes's work says that it "suggests dozens of thoughtful analogies to the life of the U.S. Negro"), thus sidestepping the particular character of the interracial and interethnic context under scrutiny, in this case, that of Brazilian society. Additionally, the economic and political reductionism built into this type of analysis, though only moderately manifested in Fernandes's work, appears nevertheless with sufficient force to thwart the focus on the properly racial aspect of the marginalization of people of African descent in Brazil. The analysis does not fully succeed in doing so, that is, in keeping this racial dimension from being subsumed under the larger discourse of political economy.

Fernandes states categorically, in a chapter on *Social Movements in the Negro Milieu*, that during the early decades of the present century in Brazil "there developed spontaneously several movements representing the Negro's growing awareness of his situation and his criticism and rejection of the difficult destiny to which black men were relegated" (1971:187). The most salient of these movements was the *Frente Negra Brasileira* (Brazilian Black Front), founded in 1931, which is presented as emblematic of the emergence of a specifically racial consciousness among the "black" masses of Brazil. Not to question the historical accuracy of this report, nor the specific aspect of the receptivity displayed by the so-called people of color towards these movements (Fernandes talks about this in terms of "the influx of enthusiastic supporters *en masse*," p.196), I wish nevertheless to make some qualifying and cautionary remarks, to the effect that these reactions, at root, do not appear to have been so much the expression of the frustrations and aspirations of Brazilian "blacks" as a distinct, segregated *racial* underclass, but as a *politically and socio-economically*-disenfranchised underclass. So, the question is not reallly whether the "AfroBrazilian" community gained an awareness of its historical marginalization from the social, economic, and political mainstream. Their limited access to vertical mobility was, as late as the period immediately following World War II, tangible and undeniable, and it was primarily a manifestation of the legacy of slavery, of its crippling effect on the succeeding generations of Brazilians of African ancestry. That this subset of the population should collectively have come to the realization that their racial (i.e., in the phenotypical sense) background

111

had something to do with their continuing underrepresentation in the institutional life of the society is entirely plausible, but it should not be automatically inferred from this that it expressed racial consciousness and racial protest in the separatist mold of multiethnic societies like the U.S., South Africa, etc. Fundamentally, the greater indication is that this was a case of group mobilization against structured socioeconomic inequality as such, in other words, a collective protest framed in the larger context of opposition between the "haves" and the "have nots," a *class* movement aiming at socio-economic and political reform.

With regard to the opposite situation, that of the racially-oriented polarization of the majority and minority ethnic-racial communities, a classical example is the situation of Asians in the first half of the present century - a historical period which is in fact concurrent with that discussed by Fernandes with respect to Brazilian blacks. The dissimilarity between the two societies clearly emerges here, inasmuch as the U.S. social system, ostensibly founded upon the democratic principles of full extension of civil rights and privileges to all segments of the citizenry, irrespective of their ascriptive statuses, was still upholding at the time of World War I,[3] the 1790 Naturalization Act which restricted citizenship status to all but the "free *white* person," (Gulick, 1918:55) and on the basis of which particular segments of the population (i.e., the "nonwhite" segments), such as Asians and African-Americans, were denied citizenship rights like the suffrage, and were kept marginalized and segregated as self-contained minority racial communities. Brazil, on the other hand, despite sharing with the U.S. the experience of slavery and the related presence of millions of Africans and their descendants, did not erect formal barriers to the gradual sociostructural incorporation of this element on account of their ethnic and/or racial background. This was true even during the slavery era, when free blacks in Brazil appear to have had access to a higher level of physical and social mobility than that registered for the U.S. free black population during the same period, and this contrast was even more striking in the postslavery period. In a study of the biracialist organization of intergroup relations in American society, Landes (1955:1256) refers to this historical comparison between Brazil and the United States, pointing to the common feature of these two societies of having depended on "vast numbers of African slaves" - in the case of Brazil, from the 1500s to the late 1800s, in the United for about a century less - but that the similarities end there; as she remarked, "it is the difference that uncovers the Americanism." She constructs ideal types of "humanism" and "chattelism" to classify and explain the models of slavery in Brazil and the U.S. South, arguing that the tendencies of the one made for easier absorption of the former African slaves into the larger society, as regular members of the larger citizenry, "according to general criteria of family, accomplishment, and the relative handicap of color," while the tendencies of the other (i.e., the out-and-out economic rationalization of the African as commercial property) locked the freed Africans into a "segregated class of serfs" after 1863. This pattern of formally-upheld subordination endured and, indeed, gained momentum, through the remainder of the 19th century, finally crystallizing in the form of the Jim Crow system. Thus, these background aspects demonstrate the generalized - that is, class-related - aspect of minority-group subordination in one society (Brazil) , and the specifically racial basis of this subordination in the other (the U.S.). The same analyst echoes the assessment offered here of the basis of interethnic stratification in Brazilian society, by asserting that blacks in Brazil suffer more from "the general inequities of an aristocratic class organization" (Landes, 1955:1257).

Fernandes states that these movements on the part of the AfroBrazilian segment of the population "had a clearly and expressly integrationist stamp." The blacks and mulattoes of Brazil did not seek to subvert or revamp the social order ushered in "by the Abolition [of slavery, 1888) and the Republic [1889] because they never questioned the material and psychological bases on which it rested" (p.189). What they sought most of all was to gain access to greater socioeconomic and political equality and integration than that which had already in principle been made accessible to them, even during the Imperial time. This aspect, it seems to me, also distinguishes the Brazilian version of minority-group action from that which was in effect in American society, that is, from black protest movements in the United States. It is true that African-Americans in the U.S., as they began to give full impetus to their liberationist movement during the 1950s, were also seeking to gain admission into the institutional and social spaces of social life, since this had been denied to them for half a century, legally and extra-legally, through Jim Crow arrangements and practices, but they also clearly understood that the structural framework of the society, in other words, its very social and institutional make-up, its "material and psychological bases," (as Fernandes put it) had to be overhauled from the ground up, if their aspirations of becoming integral members of the society were ever to materialize. To this day, these individuals have yet to enjoy full participation in U.S. national life, on equal footing with everyone else in the dominant ethnic population, precisely because of the fact that this reorganization of the society, at the structural as well as interpersonal and symbolic levels, has not come to pass. In Brazil, Fernandes informs, "[t]he economic, juridical, and political ideology of the ruling circles of the dominant race were acknowledged and accepted" (1971:189-90), they were not perceived by the minority ethnic segments as fundamental obstacles in the way of their assimilation. In the United States, on the other hand, despite the official codification of the ideals of liberty and equality for everyone under the Constitution, insofar as certain groups were concerned, the juridical, educational, economic, and political institutions of the society functioned right up to the 1960s in flagrant violation of these democratic principles and ideals, with the definition and extension of full citizenship being contingent, up to the time in the 1960s when Jim Crow arrangements began to crumble, mainly on racial considerations. (For African-Americans, this applied throughout the seven decades of Jim Crow. As for the specific reference to the issue of citizenship made above, it was related to the naturalization of Asians in American society during the first part of this century). Therefore, African-Americans in the U.S. could not possibly have simply pushed for their progressive incorporation into national life without also calling for significant alteration of the institutional framework of the society as a whole.

Fernandes points to the primary aim of these movements as being to attack and remove "the contradictions existing between the legal substratum and the social reality implanted through abolitionism and experience with the republican form of government," and in this way to accomplish the full social integration of the people of African descent - supposedly in parallel fashion to the chief impulses and objectives of the Civil Rights Movement of the 1950s and 1960s in the United States. The accomplishment of this program would represent, for Fernandes, the "modernization of the system of race relations in Brazil." (1971:188). This point warrants closer attention. If the meaning intended here was the eventual full-scale social and institutional inclusion of a particular segment of the population, whose advancement had been retarded by a severely crippling experience in the past, as slavery certainly was for the Brazilian blacks, then the idea of modernization is fitting, insofar as it is being equated with the overcoming of the old social order, a social order whose origins and basic configuration were anchored to the old, neofeudal ("seigneurial," in Genovese's terminology, 1971) rural aristocracy and slavery-based economy, with its castelike model of stratification based on race. After the abolition of Brazilian slavery in 1888, the basic asymmetry of dominant-minority relations of slavery times persisted tenaciously, even as the society slowly embarked on the course of industrialization and modernization. But the latter turned out to be a very slow process, hampered precisely by the remarkable durability of traditional social and political structures. Burns (1993:312) remarks, for instance, on how "the

114

new political institutions [in effect during the first quarter-century of the present century] proved to be as exclusive as their predecessors, marginalizing nearly all Brazilians from power ... [and] even the small but significant middle class grumbled with discontent." More importantly, the continuing pattern of extreme social stratification between the upper and lower classes expressed itself fundamentally in *economic*, not racial, terms, whereby these classes remained rigidly separated by socioeconomic status, but not by racial status, something that may be easily inferred from the tangible signs of centuries of racial intermixture across the economic class lines. From this perspective, modernization would be conceived as the social, economic, and political integration of the minority contingent, the integration of a disadvantaged stratum of the population, which happened to be made up mostly of "people of color." This is the conceptualization that seems to fit the Brazilian case the best, in terms of involving a minority group which, hindered though they may have been in their vertical mobility by virtue of their ethnic-racial background - the social ascent of lower-class persons "of color" in Brazil may generally be said to have been more complicated than that of lower-class individuals with more direct European ancestry - their difficulties did not rest *primarily* with this background, because the latter never functioned as a distinct, self-contained, readily identifiable circumstance, standing in a relation of strict separation from, and opposition to, the ethnic-racial background of the dominant classes. The historical crisscrossing of the two backgrounds, as emphasized throughout this study, has prevented this kind of interethnic dualism, while making concomitantly for the large-scale hybridization of the population, particularly in (but not restricted to) the lower socioeconomic strata. The greater obstacle to their mobility, as indicated, lay in the social impairment bequeathed to them by the experience of slavery. In the final analysis, the picture that emerges for Brazilian society is *fundamentally* one of class, not race, stratification.

Moreover, regarding the idea of modernization of the pattern of ethnic relations in multiethnic systems which, like the U.S., enforce a racially-based politics of difference, with the concomitant compartmentalization of the various formative ethnic communities, this notion tends to be defined and understood mainly in terms of increased levels of minority representation in the formal sectors of society, even if this goal is accomplished concomitantly with the structural and cultural segregation of the dominant and minority parts of the population. For the right to participate in greater and greater numbers in the economic, political, and educational spheres, this model of formal (i.e., structural) assimilation strips minority-group members of the ability to become fully integrated into the mainstream mode of cultural life, being forced to exist (from the standpoint of culture) as separate nations within the larger nation. I do not see how this can really be considered progress in interethnic relations. It is only a form of "civilized" separatism, a separatism which, no longer being sustained by the force of the law as in times past, now draws its sustenance from the racial essentialism of the politics of difference mentioned above, which insures the perpetuation of cultural dualism in the society, on the basis of racial bipolarity. The very process of inclusion of minorities into national life, as I have maintained throughout this analysis, is significantly hampered by this cultural dualism: minority-group members (the "nonwhites"), permanently locked into the minority status, into a reified *minority difference*, face an array of social difficulties and exclusionary forces as they seek to merge with the core culture. The official rationale offered for this preservation of minority life and identity is that it affords greater visibility to the groups involved, and thus facilitates their recognition by the various bureaucratic structures, which in turn enables the latter to better address minority-group needs and interests. I have already delved into this issue, stressing that this is justified only on a provisional basis, not indefinitely, which defeats the whole purpose of minority assimilation. Therefore, to present, first of all, this model of interethnic life - namely, civic integration *sans* sociocultural integration - as a yardstick for gauging the progress of dominant-minority relations in pluralist societies everywhere; and, furthermore, to characterize lower levels of *formal* assimilation of minority groups in a given society (of the type I have called integrationist here) as a sign that the society is behind the times, without considering the fact that this same society may have, nonetheless, succeeded in fully integrating these minority segments at the level of culture (as the term is used in this study), is, as I see it, entirely unjustifiable. In fact, I believe the opposite to be true, that is, the integrationist social system to be ahead of the other (i.e., separatist) model in this regard.[4]

We can further clarify the issue of miscegenation and its shaping effect on the character of interethnic relations and stratification by considering here a historical incident from the Imperial phase of Brazilian history (1822-1889), described in Freyre (1968:ch.8). With the advent of the Imperial era in Brazil came the growing disdain of the aristocracy towards the cultural idiosyncrasies of the lower classes, as well as their concern with ridding the society of all vestiges of cultural retardation (meaning: attachment to non-European cultural models) and with following the civilized, modernistic influences set by Europe. The lower classes were mostly composed of blacks and mixed-bloods, especially in the urban setting, but also included the rustic population of the hinterland, composed of African-Amerindian and Amerindian-European mixed bloods, *as well as whites.* This upper-class reaction against aboriginal ways of life as cultivated by the common folk (e.g., particular religious and secular practices of the African slaves and freedmen) was given concrete expression in a number of municipal ordinances geared to their suppression. This type of cultural repression, again, does not represent the opposition of racially-dichotomized dominant/minority social groupings (this unveils here a contrasting example to the same phenomenon of repression of African cultural manifestations in the antebellum U.S. South; see, e.g., Camara, 1983), but rather, a wider and generalized crusade on the part of the aristocracy to suppress the *modus vivendi* of the masses--an all too typical tendency of societies still living under the political, economic, and cultural influence of the colonial "mother country," and understandably, showing concerns with living up to the standards of civilization set by the latter. In this respect, it may be noted here that there was a widespread tendency in Brazilian society, throughout the nineteenth century under the full auspices of the Imperial Court, right up to World War II, to follow the cultural example of Europe. Expectedly, the European society whose mode of cultural life was most influential in this respect was Portugal, given the institutional continuities of Brazilian society with its European colonizing nation. However, the French cultural model also figured very prominently in this process until about the middle of the present century. Freyre (1968:208) remarks that the importation of European customs reached such a high level in the second half of the 19th century that, although many of these cultural imports, such as the wearing of heavy, dark-colored attire ("the heavy frock coat of London or Paris") were clearly inappropriate for the tropics, what really mattered for those who adopted them was to look English or French; the physical discomfort would be disregarded in favor of looking fashionable in accordance with the European model. In this connection, the cultural ways of the lower classes of society were antithetical to this concern. They represented a cultural barbarism which, in the eyes of upper crust, was increasingly incompatible with the impulses of modernity beginning to make themselves felt in Brazilian society. Thus, all manner of cultural expression associated with the lowest social echelons - however these echelons may have been formed ethnically and racially - was treated with disdain and fiercely repudiated by the ruling classes. The latter sought to bring about the full-scale implantation of the European cultural model on the society as a whole, a campaign which surely had a suppressing effect on the ways of the ethnic-racial minorities. Still, this phenomenon was not rooted in the racial status of these minorities, but in the official and extra-official intent to have the society appear in the most favorable light to foreign eyes. This meant that it had to reflect the European cultural

117

influence as faithfully as possible. The expression *Para inglês ver* (For English eyes; literally: For the English to see), still common in Brazil today, reaches back to the early Imperial period (the early 1800s), and is clearly symptomatic of this tendency. It is customarily used to refer to a situation where appearances are emphasized, so that the best possible impression can be made on outsiders, especially outsiders of distinction.[5]

In offering this caveat regarding the idea of "modernization of the system of race relations in Brazil," my intent is to underline the very important point that, in the degree that this idea is put forward to suggest the greater democratization and egalitarianism of the social structure, manifested in the formal and informal integration of the citizenry (i.e., of all of the ethnic and racial streams which constitute it), then it surely deserves to be held up as the ideal for multiethnic societies to strive for. If, however, this notion was meant to refer to the evolution of the "minority ethnic segments"[6] into separate ethnic-racial enclaves, with a separatist racial consciousness and identity, and with the assumption of permanent withdrawal into a subnational mode of life, then I see no reason for upholding this as the criterion to rely on in assessing the degree of modernization of the society's interethnic sphere, even if this is accompanied by comparatively higher levels of minority representation in institutional life. Instead, what I see it representing is a retrogression to the 19th century stage of nation-building, when nations lacked ethnic and cultural - hence, legal and institutional - integration, and existed mainly as conglomerates of warring ethnic factions.[7] Although a full discussion of this specific question is not part of the plan of this work, the examples of ethnic and cultural separatism in U.S. history, and, more recently, that of Yugoslavia, may be cited as lending considerable importance to this factor in the attainment of national consolidation. A hundred years ago W.E.B.Dubois fulminated against the premises and proceedings of the Atlanta Compromise, where, under the exhortations of Booker T. Washington, the educational advancement and overall social progress for the African-American community was being conceived in separatist (and strictly technical) terms. Washington's was a programme, his critics (like Dubois) argued, designed primarily for the appeasement of Southern whites and other conservative factions in the wider society, who would have resisted any idea of black progress through full-range integration into American institutional and social life. In exchange for the chance for blacks to pursue economic opportunity, Washington exhorted them to surrender their civil rights and liberties (such as, for instance, the vote), an agenda that "practically accept[ed] the alleged inferiority of the Negro races" (Dubois, 1990:44; orig.1903).

A final ramification of large-scale miscegenation in the society, and one which appears to exert an additional integrating effect at the symbolic level, is the explicit acknowledgement, by members of the community-at-large, of the distinctiveness and social significance of the various hybrid physical types produced by the smelting of the ethnic-racial strains, as well as their awareness of the depth in which centuries of racial intermixture have shaped the character of the land and of the people. This collective recognition is conspicuously expressed in the scholarly (arts, literature) and popular discourse, such as in the popular song *Aquarela do Brasil* (Brazilian Watercolors), by the celebrated composer Ary Barroso. This song, a veritable paean to the hybrid constitution of Brazilian society, familiar to virtually every Brazilian, articulates this idea in the opening verses: "Brazil ... my roguish mulatto ... this beautiful and *trigueiro* Brazil ..." (*trigueiro* refers to the color of *trigo*, or wheat, a light brownish color). Also representative in this connection is Freyre's well-known statement to the effect that "[e]very Brazilian, even the light-skinned and fair-haired one, carries about with him on his soul, when not on soul and body alike...the shadow, or at least the birthmark, of the aborigine or the Negro." (1956:278). Of even greater significance here is the symbolic value generally assigned by people in Brazil to the hybrid type as an icon of the national identity, as conspicously manifested, for example, in the way the *morena* woman is construed in the public imaginary. She has been described as typically having "dark brown eyes and dark hair, quite wavy, perhaps even curly, and Caucasian features; her color is *café-com-leite* ..." (Pierson, 1967:136). In general terms, she may be identified in a range that goes from a dark brunette to even a very brown mulatto. This physical type has been idealized nationally as congregating all that has been defined in the society as most desirable, aesthetically, sexually, psychologically, and affectively (see Bastide, 1959:62-3, on the high popular valuation of the morena regarding aspects of affectivity and emotion). In an important research project of the 1950s on race relations in Brazil, Wagley (1963:123) noted how people leaned towards the *moreno* (male) and *morena* (female) types "in their ideal of beauty and physical attractiveness." Pierson (1967:136) has noted, regarding the *morena* woman, how "[p]oets, both professional and amateur, pour out passionate stanzas in her honor, songs are sung to her, romances written."

This phenomenon points to the profound subjective impact that concrete processes of racial fusion come to exert on the collective consciousness, and on the nature of the social construction of the hybrid element. There are a number of implications here, at the more abstract level (in addition to the material ones), which I have already addressed. The mixed racial category is not construed as *difference*, in the dichotomous sense of a division between "difference" (i.e., the nonwhite status) and "non-difference" (i.e., the white status, and universal standard). It is not perceived as the mark of non-assimilability, an aberration with regard to the dominant pattern of life, in the sense, for instance, that the manumitted slave in the U.S. South was perceived as a contradiction of his/her (socially-constructed) *natural existence* as slave.[8] The hybrid type in this context is recognized in its distinctiveness as a self-contained and viable social type, one of the manifold possibilities obtaining from the intermixture of the ethnic and racial streams, inasmuch as the social system acknowledges and accomodates these phenotypical varieties within the population. Of all the ethnic-racial categories in Brazilian society, that of "whiteness" expectedly ranks the highest, chiefly because this is the category associated with the dominant group, and therefore, with the greatest access to social power, wealth, and prestige. Nonetheless, as pointed out previously, the idea of "whiteness" is linked to societal impulses towards universal inclusion, not exclusion, of the citizenry.

The foregoing considerations underscore the important contribution of this biological component of culture (culture as treated conceptually here), which is to say, of biological assimilation, in paving the way for interethnic solidarity and cohesion. Although processes of biological fusion normally occur simultaneously with the formation of an integrated cultural system, and an integrated cultural identity for society's members, and dominant-minority biological separatism, in like manner, occurs together with cultural and psychosocial separatism, to a considerable extent it seems that assimilation at the biological level is a necessary precondition for assimilation at the cultural and psychosocial levels. We may consider in this respect, for example, the enduring divisiveness that has historically marked the U.S. population on account of the biracial organization of the society, which has insured that minority ethnic-racial groups remain not only biologically segregated, but also, more broadly, imcompletely assimilated at the cultural and psychosocial levels as well. The biological absorption of all citizens into the mainstream population rounds out the process of national and sociocultural consolidation in a most crucial way, and thus becomes, in this respect, the very cement of social unity. This claim may be substantiated through even a cursory examination of the structure of the plantation system, to take one example. In Brazil, the material harshness and the enormous social distance that this sytem established between the slaveholding and slave classes were mitigated (though certainly not eliminated) by the fact that the population as a whole was becoming ever more deeply marked by the fusion of the dominant and minority ethnic and racial streams, a phenomenon observed

120

even (if to a lesser extent) in the upper social echelons. Likewise, in the degree that miscigenation was inhibited in other slavery regimes, the profound disparity of social condition between the masters and the slaves, as well as the overall physical harshness of plantation life, were, in the main, greatly exacerbated. In Brazil, the large-scale amalgamation of the ethnic strains created a large intermediary population, made up of a variety of hybrid types, a situation that contradicted the tendencies of polarization stimulated, on the one hand, by the slavery regime, and on the other, by the larger social conservatism of the Imperial era. Concomitantly, this consolidated and democratized the social system as a whole, disentangling it progressively from its roots in the highly hierarchized, rurally-based, semifeudal social world of the early period of colonization.

Notes

1   On the social ascendance of the "mixed-blood" (mulatto) in Brazil, we are told (Pierson, 1967:159) that "[e]arly in the colonial period race mixture resulted in an intermediate population group in more favorable position for social advancement." This is borne out by the remarks of foreign visitors, like J.M. Rugendas, the German painter who traveled through Brazil in the 1820s, and noticed that "men of color were found in all the branches of public administration, in the clergy, in the army, and many are of excellent family background" (1976:76). Or M.P.A. de Lisboa, who wrote about the presence of "men of colour ... in the highest circles (*la meilleure societé*)" of Rio de Janeiro in the middle of the nineteenth century (1847:66). Rugendas notes, in fact, (and, in so doing, gives testimony of the national policy of ethnic/racial integration, vs. the opposite pattern of ethnic segregation required by biracial social systems) that "it was very rare, and one may even say that it never occurs, for [his/her] (the mulatto's) color or the mixture of [his/her] blood to become an obstacle [to social mobility]. Even when the mulatto is very dark-skinned, the official classification is that of "white," and in this capacity [he/she] is eligible for any job." This brings to mind Koster's comment along the same lines. In this century, the measure of social recognition and integration of this intermediary class was seen by one observer (Pierson, 1967:173) to be "constantly increasing." In contradistinction, the mulatto element in the U.S., because of the biracial organization of the society, remained first and foremost a black person, throughout the slavery period and

afterwards, and as such, subject to the same kind of social treatment accorded all blacks. Genovese stresses how "[t]ypically, the mulatto, especially the mulatto slave, was 'just another nigger' to the whites" (1976:429).

2 See "Um Templo Africano", in *Veja*, April 20, 1988, p. 65.

3 See Gulick (1918) for a discussion of how in the first quarter-century of the present century the nation was still grappling with the matter of race, at the bureaucratic level of definition, classification, and governmental action, towards the process of shaping its naturalization policy, and its determination of to which national groups to extend the access to full citizenship.

4 Gates's account of the nature of the presence of "people of color" in British life (1997) is quite suggestive and elucidating in this respect.

5 When the Portuguese monarch D. João VI arrived in Brazil in January of 1808 arrived in Brazil with his court, fleeing Napoleon's invasion of Portugal, he immediately ordered the city lighted up, "to show the English." Freyre (1968:203) comments on how this phrase became "highly characteristic of that attitude of simulation or pretense the Brazilian assumes, as does the Portuguese, before foreigners. Especially the Englishman, who by 1808 was no longer the heretic nor the 'animal' who had to be sprinkled with holy water before being received in one's home, but, on the contrary, a person looked upon as superior in many respects."

6 These designations must always be accompanied here by quotation marks, to underline the fact that they are not really applicable in the Brazilian situation. Subnational communities do not exist in the conventional sense of their existence in societies where separatism has prevailed, thus preserving their clear-cut demarcation and distinction from the mainstream society. The "minority ethnic segments" in Brazil, despite their incomplete institutional assimilation, have nonetheless experienced complete cultural and psychosocial assimilation, in terms of not being distinguishable at the level of cultural action, nor at the psychosocial level of identity.

7 Park (1964:205) writes: "The growth of modern states exhibits the progressive merging of smaller, mutually-exclusive, into larger and more inclusive social groups. This result has been achieved in various

ways, but it has usually been followed, or accompanied, by a more or less complete adoption, by the members of the smaller groups, of the language, technique, and mores of the larger and more inclusive ones. The immigrant readily takes over the language, manners, the social ritual, and outward forms of his adopted country."

8   Jordan (1968:134) remarks in this connection that "[t]he free Negro was a walking contradiction in terms, a social anomaly, a third party in a system built for two."

5 The psychosocial aspect: Group consciousness and cultural identity

The meaning of race consciousness

The final dimension of culture to be assessed in comparative perspective here, that of psychological assimilation, pertains to the nature of the collective identity developed and worn by minority-group members. This is linked directly to the way and degree in which individuals formally and informally identify with the hegemonic mode of life of the society, that is, with its action and thought patterns, institutions, traditions, worldview. This aspect, as stressed earlier, is vitally important in the degree that it influences the level of social assimilation of individuals. In U.S. society, collective identity, anchored as it is to the racially dichotomic administration of social life and to the workings of subnational racial arrangements and classifications, is the chief regulatory mechanism of social relations, thus having, in the longer run, a greater generalizing impact over individuals than any other identity, including that which is tied to nationality.

The issue of identity is part of the larger aspect of consciousness, since identity is a dimension of the social consciousness of the group. The focus here will be on the interaction between the dominant social consciousness, namely, that of the dominant ethnic group or the majority population, and the minority consciousness, or that of groups permanently marginalized as minorities. In societal contexts where unassimilated ethnic minorities are defined as ethnic-racial groups, their collective consciousness is marked by a high degree of race consciousness. Park (1964:ch.7) has in fact made race consciousness - i.e., its existence or absence - the main indicator as well as determinant of the nature of intergroup relations. As regards crossnational variations, the focus here must be on whether members of minority ethnic groups see themselves in terms of an integrated national identity, or in terms of a segmented, subcultural identity. The preceding discussion of the nature of dominant-minority cultural relations, and of the societal treatment of racial intermixture, has indicated that the integrationist and separatist tendencies which respectively represent the cultural models of Brazil and the United States will necessarily be manifested in the area of identity as well. In the Brazilian cultural model, individuals of all ethnic backgrounds rely first and foremost on their national (citizenship) identity, the identity that comes before all others. Also, from the standpoint of the society, every citizen is regarded first of all, as a Brazilian, and "every Brazilian takes pride in all other nationals, irrespective of racial origin" (Pierson, 1967:218). There are scores of examples (as cited, e.g., in Wagley, 1971:121) of individuals of "nonwhite" ancestry, from the time of the Empire (the 1800s) to the present, who have distinguished themselves in the arts, liberal professions, sciences, etc., and are claimed as *national*, not subnational, figures.[1] The hyphenated identity that so characteristically stands for members of ethnic minorities in the United States is not a feature of the Brazilian interethnic complex. The fashioning of a cohesive national identity is effected through the distillation of all the cultural and ethnic strains of the society, and insofar as this identity functions as the primary frame of reference for everyone in Brazilian society, it leaves no room for marginal or peripheral, or subcultural, identities. Therefore, the traditional analytical approach of distinguishing ethnic minorities from the majority population by reference to the hyphenated identity is, as suggested earlier, basically misleading when applied to the analysis of the Brazilian situation.

The dominance of the consciousness of national membership is inversely correlated with the consciousness of racial membership. In Brazil, racial consciousness has been virtually absent, historically, from the social landscape. When manifested, it has been mainly in an irregular and intermittent fashion.[2] In the United States, on the other hand, the consciousness of racial identification among ethnic-racial minorities has been "permanent, pervasive, and obsessive" (Nogueira, 1959:173), and continues to function as the central orienting principle of intergroup relations, notwithstanding the eradication in the 1960s of institutionalized racial segregation, as practiced in the context of the Jim Crow system. The strength of the minority ethnic identity in the United States (e.g., African-American, Mexican-American, Filipino-American) derives from the *racial*, and not simply ethnic (i.e., pertaining to a national-cultural group) meaning assigned to this identity by the larger society, and from the social subordination of these groups on the basis of "race." As a rule, only those groups that are racially classified as nonwhite remain identifiable, officially and unofficially, in terms of the aforementioned hyphenated identity. From its earliest phase, the socialization of individuals classified as nonwhite in U.S. society steers them into internalizing the racial bifurcation of personal identity (i.e., either white or nonwhite) as a perfectly normal thing, whereby the unqualified adoption of "American" as the primary identity becomes, in the main, a practice of members of the majority (or "white") population, those who have been fully assimilated.[3] The separatism barring members of racial minorities from this process causes them to rely principally on the subnational identity (i.e., that which denotes the particular minority racial community to which they belong) as their primary frame of reference, and secondarily on the national identity (i.e., that which denotes citizenship). Consequently, these individuals are steered into cultural attitudes, behaviors, and ways of thinking that are considered to be expressive of their identity as nonwhite. A case in point: a department-store catalog (1992) selling toy amplifiers for "young rappers," with a black child as a model. White children would not be used as models in this situation because rap music is perceived and treated as black music and part of black culture, hence, as something that is distinct from, and not to be mixed with, aspects of the core (i.e., "white") culture. Also, in connection with the larger pattern of biracial regulation of the society, which requires that individuals of mixed (i.e., particularly, black-white) racial origin be genotypically classified, at both formal and informal levels, as members of the subordinate racial community, the problems of identity that may arise for individuals in this situation are always resolved in terms of their eventual recognition that they are indeed black (e.g., cover story of *Parade* magazine, *Chicago Tribune*, July 10, 1994) - though it is obvious that, from a cultural standpoint, these individuals tend, in a good many cases, to be "white," and from a biological standpoint, to be in all cases neither white nor black, but an intermediate and hybrid category, since half of their genetic material comes from one parent and half from the other. The following account is very instructive regarding this type of societal treatment of identity on the basis of racial dichotomy, and how it contrasts bluntly with other multiethnic models. The renowned African-American writer Alice Walker, on a visit to Cuba, tried to assess the patterns of social relations of Cuban society by relying on the familiar racial definitions and categorizations of U.S. society. She soon realized the untenability of this project. The Cubans, she stated, "did not see themselves as I saw them at all. They were, like their music, well blended into their culture and did not need to separate on the basis of color, or to present any definition of themselves at all" (1983:212). This incident illustrates a major aspect emphasized earlier, which is that of the societal specificity of traditional analytical categories, frameworks of understanding, and informal expectations related to race and ethnicity in the United States, and the unfeasibility of their universal application.

The dominant social consciousness

This section examines the posture of the dominant social consciousness towards minority difference, which concerns the manner in which minority difference is construed, experienced, and related to at the symbolic level by the dominant group, in integrationist vs. separatist social systems. In traversing this terrain, we will rely on the language of phenomenology, for more efficient terminological handling of the issues and aspects encountered along the way, and also because this language captures the dynamics of intergroup and intersubjective life in ways that escape more conventional discourses.

In the separatist context of intergroup relations, the dominant social consciousness has essentially reacted in twofold fashion towards the difference of alien cultural communities: it engages in total absorption or total rejection of this difference, and therefore neither approach represents an experiential or cognitive "openness" (i.e., a receptiveness to interchange) towards minority difference. We will analyze this problem ideal-typically, by presenting the dominant social consciousness as being centrally distinguished by the authoritarian impulse to control and absorb the world of experience. More technically put, this impulse involves the conceptual appropriation, demarcation, and classification of external objects, without a deliberate attempt to exercise reciprocity and reversibility towards them. In basic terms, this consciousness appropriates in a predatory fashion all that which is outside itself, or *not-itself*. When this pattern of response is concretely identified in the social world, it takes the form of a distinct model of assimilation, in which intergroup relations are marked by the rigid imposition of regulatory and classificatory schemes, as well as exclusionary practices. Minority cultural communities are straitjacketed into conceptual ghettoes, which become emblematic of their inferior social standing, and are prevented from breaking through the lines that separate them from the mainstream population, and from entering processes of large-scale interchange and fusion with this population.

Under these circumstances, the presence of the *Other* - that is, the presence of the alien cultural group - as difference is construed as contradiction. "Whatever differs in quality," Adorno maintains (1979:5), "comes to be designated as contradiction." As such, the Other's difference is apprehended as "dissonant," "negative," unfit for interchangeability. A dominant-minority relation will, of course, be established, but on the basis of inequality. These tendencies are most clearly evidenced in settings of castelike social organization and stratification, where the segregation of groups is strictly enforced by law and by custom. This type of social domination evolves from the construction of the subjectivity of subaltern ethnic populations by the dominant population, whereby the former are permanently maintained in the category of the Other, an alien element, an element that deviates from the hegemonic standard, being therefore judged as permanently inferior and unassimilable. This dominant-minority pattern of contact is established early on, becoming the basis for a separatism that will reach across the entire spectrum of intergroup life: informal relations, kinship formation, institutional practices and arrangements, the arts, language, and so forth.

The dualistic posture of the dominant social consciousness towards minority ethnic-cultural difference may be restated as follows. There is, on the one hand, the imperialistic appropriation and transformation of this difference when the latter is perceived to be *only cultural* (but not physical). In the context of interethnic relations, this relates to the case of the cultural difference of groups designated in the United States as "white ethnics," and to the Anglo-conformity model of assimilation. The idyosyncratic nature of the otherness of the minority group is simply cast aside here, while the group's swift and uncompromising adoption of the dominant cultural model is assumed and enforced as the *desideratum*. There is no stimulation of syncretic processes here, but only unilateral appropriation of the minority-group traits judged assimilable, hence there is little chance for these traits to survive on their own terms. The Americanization crusade of the early 1900s represents the culmination of this tendency, and it was manifested in several ways. One was the practice, common among entertainment figures in the United States at one time, particularly among those of Eastern-European extraction, of modifying their original names, or simply replacing them with names that sounded more Anglo-Saxon, a procedure they relied upon as a technique of cultural survival.

The other side of the dominant social consciousness's voracious consumption of minority difference deemed assimilable is the emphatic repudiation and exclusion of difference deemed unassimilable. This occurs when the group remains categorized as a minority group on the basis of *race*. The dominant social consciousness then establishes and maintains an unbridgeable gap betwen itself and the minority difference. This phenomenon may be identified in the castelike separatism regulating black-white relations in American society especially during the Jim Crow period. This separatism, as already indicated, is also the chief force behind the emergence of an indigenous cultural lifestyle among the subaltern ethnic communities, this resulting from their having been denied full admission to the mode of life of the host society, while at the same time being methodically stripped of their cultural and social heritage. This twofold process of oppression of the minority group represents the negation of its very existential condition, a form of ontological domination expressed in the hierarchization of the ontological domains of the dominant and minority populations, respectively. This effect obtains both in terms of the negation of the original status of the minority-group members (i.e., that of "alien," of newcomers) at the initial stage of intergroup contact, through the suppression of their aboriginal cultural ways and identity; and in terms of the negation of their present circumstance as, one might say, cultural apprentices; in other words, in terms of the negation of their potential as equal participants in the formation of the larger sociocultural system. This creates an existential dilemma for the members of the minority group, a deep sense of inferiority, anomie, and alienation, which results in their dual pattern of response, already addressed, entailing tendencies of overidentification with the dominant mode of life, on the one hand, and rejection of the same, on the other.

By contrast, in the integrationist context of intergroup relations the dominant social consciousness exhibits an opposing set of tendencies, manifested in the higher level of reciprocity and interchangeability between the dominant and minority cultural traditions. These dominant-minority patterns of interaction might be viewed in the context of what Adorno, in a discussion of the operation of Consciousness as ruled by the principle of Identity, referred to as nestling or adhering as closely as possible to Otherness (i.e., in this case, to cultural difference) without, however, absorbing it in predatory fashion (1979:13, 191). In other words, the dominant social consciousness does not seal itself from minority-group difference in complete self-enclosure, but resists at the same time the impulse towards parasitic annexation of it. It acknowledges the original character of this difference by allowing itself to coexist with it dialectically, now in tension and equilibrium, now exercising a non-possessive openness and attraction towards it, in a manner that eventually brings about the "reconciled condition." Thus, it is not governed by a concern for preserving what it sees as its own conceptual unity, nor for rejecting and isolating itself from everything that it sees as a threat to this unity. In the realm of interethnic relations, this concern would be attached to the situation of non-syncretistic cultural systems, where intergroup arrangements and relations are strictly governed by ascriptive (i.e., racial) considerations, and where the dominant group would endeavor to protect and preserve its perceived cultural and/or racial purity, and to keep at a distance all elements regarded as potentially threatening to this purity. In contradistinction, the integrationist version of dominant consciousness operates in a complex and dynamic process of cross-fertilization, which reveals the workings of cultural syncretism. Bastide discusses this matter in reference to the phenomenon of dual identity for individuals, something he accounts for by means of his principle of dissociation, already discussed. Another illuminating example in this connection may be drawn from early Brazilian colonial history. Early chroniclers inform us that when the Jesuits there embarked on the educational and religious assimilation of the young *Tupinambá* Indians (the *culumins*), they began by first learning and adopting their language, songs, and dances--the *culumins* were, in this respect, at once "the disciples and masters" (Freyre, 1956:168) - thus setting in motion an intense and long-term process of cultural reciprocity that was to endure over the ensuing centuries, down to present times, and which may be witnessed especially in the Northern regions of the country, where the Amerindian cultural impact on religious and secular life has been significant. This impact has been felt in terms of a syncretized Luso-Brazilian Catholicism, but also in the national language, in the poetry and music, in children's games and pastimes, in the diet (see Freyre, 1956:chapter II). On the basis of the foregoing, this analysis might be summed up, ideal-typically, by saying that in the integrative model of sociocultural organization, the interaction between the dominant social consciousness and the difference of the minority element is informed by intersubjective egalitarianism, which, in the context of intergroup life, is experienced as relations of cultural exchange and syncretism, whereas in the separatist model of sociocultural organization this interaction is informed by intersubjective inequality, experienced concretely as relations of cultural separatism and compartmentalization.

The foreignness of the minority identity

Rather than signifying a fundamental change in the pattern of intergroup relations, the exaltation and, indeed, hypostatization, of the minority identity for particular groups, such as encouraged by the multiculturalist movement, simply adds paradox and ambiguity to a situation which, though of long standing, was not ambiguous in former times. To clarify this further: the situation in question here is that of the structural inequality between the dominant and minority ethnic communities that characterized the Jim Crow system of castelike segregation and discrimination. Within this system, the permanently inferior status of minority groups was legitimized and enforced by law and by custom, these sources of legitimation in turn being maintained by a full-blown popular ideology of racism that raised the sanction of these arrangements of inequality to the level of sanctification. Thus, the *foreignness*, the inferior otherness, of the minority group(s) was a foregone conclusion and an article of faith for the mainstream population. There was no ambiguity or discomfort in the legal system or in the public mind at that time regarding the reality of a racially-divided society. Now, however, with the destruction of the legal supports of ethnic-racial inequality, together with the more recent societal shift towards affirming and maintaining the minority presence-as-difference for its own sake, on the basis of continuing racial bipolarity, what has emerged is a paradoxical situation whereby the minority consciousness gains renewed awareness of itself as *otherness* in relation to the dominant cultural model, which then leads it to show itself as such to the public at large, and even to flaunt this difference, hoping by this to achieve what I see as essentially incompatible outcomes: on the one hand, the recognition of its individuality and distinctiveness in terms of permanent differentiation from the national mode of existence; and, on the other hand, the disappearance of this difference, through its gradual absorption into the mass of undifferentiated humanity that makes up national life. This premise rests on a fundamental misconception. It is possible, to be sure, for all nondominant groups *classified as white* to draw the society's attention to whatever cultural distinctiveness they may have retained (this cultural distinctiveness is naturally more pronounced during the early acculturative phase, but oftentimes some aspects of it still linger on after full assimilation has taken place, as, for instance, in the case of the Irish-Americans), and for this to impact favorably upon their standing in the wider society. The tendency of these groups to maintain a degree of continuity with their ancestral cultural heritage may generally delay the assimilative process, but it also helps this process along insofar as it affords members of these groups the psychological comfort and stamina necessary to get them through the worst spots along their journey to full social incorporation. This represents a dynamic conception of being, the condition of *being-as-becoming*, which is grounded in the promise of change to occur in a future time. Members of these groups assume the identity of "foreigner" upon arrival, but this is an identity in flux, in that it lasts for the initial period (usually, the first generation of the immigrant group in question) as a source of existential and psychological support, then gradually recedes into the background, and the void is proportionately filled by ever increasing identification with the way of the life of the host society, and by an increasingly automatic adoption of the national identity. Thus, the outstanding characteristic of the "difference" of all the groups categorized as white is its temporary nature, or the fact that it is only a "moment" in their broader acculturative experience.

But, where the permanently distinct ethnic-racial communities are concerned, matters are quite different indeed. Their simultaneous attachment to two different cultural traditions is a fundamentally different circumstance from when it is experienced by the "white ethnics." In the latter case it is a more dynamic situation because it does not preclude the possibility of change in the future: members of the "white-ethnic" communities participate simultaneously in two cultural worlds, that which they left behind and that of the host society, but mainly as a temporary condition, which, typical though it may be of the experience of immigrant groups in general, comes eventually to an end as the assimilative process is completed. In the case of the permanent ethnic-racial minorities, the continuing straddling of two cultures is not so much a product of free choice - that is, the members of these groups did not start out with the collective decision to remain a permanent subcultural presence in the larger society - as it is the only option available to them. This represents a more static state of affairs. It rules out the possibility of the freedom that is found in the anonymity, undifferentiation, and interchangeability afforded individuals as they undergo full inclusion into the mainstream. The minority identity is thus doomed to perpetual visibility and operation as otherness, to the perpetual need to call attention to its difference, and what is most important, to function exclusively in a way that has been established as the "minority way" (of acting and thinking). This rigidly-imposed social duty effectively and necessarily impedes its dissociation from "otherness" and its absorption into "non-otherness," that is, into the sameness of the mainstream. The glorification of its foreignness by a social system that is, concomitantly, the context of its genesis, development, and current existence, only serves to harden the biracial lines of ethnic division, and to reinforce ideas in the public mind about the presumed inherent difference and inferiority of minority ethnic-racial groups. As such, an outcome that was once guaranteed through formal mechanisms is now being facilitated through cultural ones. Seen in this light, the preservation *ad infinitum* of the minority status becomes the very source of imprisonment for the minority community, an aspect emphasized in the following statement by Franklin (1997:18): "The ethnic grouping that was a way-station, a temporary resting place for Europeans as they became American, proved to be a terminal point for blacks who found it virtually impossible to become Americans in any real sense."

Material and symbolic consequences of the separatist consciousness

The impact that the dominant social consciousness has on the existence of minority ethnic-racial groups that are permanently preserved as *minorities* is that, as noted, their difference or otherness is not construed as being merely a transitional stage, as is that of the "white ethnics," the latter lasting only until these groups blend completely into the majority population and thus become indistinguishable from it. The otherness of the groups classified as nonwhite takes on a quality of eternity, so to speak, in the sense that it is deemed nontransformable, hence unassimilable, or at least it is judged to be only partially assimilable. Accordingly, the assimilation of these minority individuals occurs at the formal level only, such as in the workplace, the educational system, the political system, and so on. The negative ramifications flowing from this are many. As a result of their being perceived and treated in this way by the dominant society, members of these groups learn to see their difference with respect to the mainstream standard not in a neutral sense of simply being different, that is to say, not as simply standing for a different modality of existence, but as *inappropriate*, *inferior* difference. They see it as "contradiction," to use Adorno's term (1979:5). This phenomenon is demonstrated in studies that reach back to the 1940s and 1950s, on self-perception in black children in the United States, as expressed in their play activity and choice of dolls (Clark and Clark, 1939, 1950; Clark, 1955). These studies have been replicated more recently (see *Time*, Sept. 14, 1987, p. 74), confirming the earlier findings. Being segregated and essentialized in this way, the minority difference remains a source of insecurity, stigmatization, and alienation for these individuals.

It is worth repeating here that the minority consciousness, forged under society-wide circumstances of separatism, functions in a twofold fashion. Given the historical absence of large-scale syncretic interfusion of the dominant and minority ways of life, the minority group's knowledge of its inalterable difference in relation to the dominant model causes group members to move *both* towards overidentification with the latter - it absorbs and expresses dominant-group traits, one might say, "with a vengeance" - and towards deviation from, and rejection of, these same traits. In the first instance, that of overidentification with the hegemonic cultural model, members of these culturally-marginalized groups strive all the harder to compensate for their exclusion by acting out dominant patterns of behavior and thought in a manner that amounts to exaggerated reproductions of these patterns. This phenomenon is addressed in the sociopsychological literature as *role overimmersion*. The prominent scholar Gunnar Myrdal asserted, in relation to this, that despite the separation of blacks and whites in all areas of U.S. social life - a circumstance he was able to witness first hand, at a time (the 1940s) when it was being enforced by law and tradition - black institutions and ways of life "[were] ... similar to those of the white man." Furthermore, black institutional and social patterns were seen by Myrdal to show "little similarity to African institutions. In his cultural traits, the Negro is akin to other Americans. Some peculiarities are even to be characterized as 'exaggerations of American traits'" (1962:928). This was especially true of the time of Myrdal's analysis, when the concern with integration was foremost on the minds of African Americans. We draw another instantiation of this phenomenon from Clark's research (1957:59), carried out in the 1950s (allowance will be made here for the prevailing racial and otherwise social mores of the time) on the behavioral patterns of middle-class and upper-class African-American young women. He found that, not only did these young women generally observe the same social demands, restraints, and conventions of the dominant society regarding speech, clothes, and general etiquette that they presumed to be important for social advancement, but also "reacted against the stereotyped concept of the Negro by rigidly controlling their own behavior, and at times maintaining almost unrealistically high standards of personal and sexual conduct." This aspect of overstriving to reproduce dominant attitudes and patterns of behavior, in my view, has basically continued down to the present time. That is, minority-group members who now consider themselves to be well on their way to absorption into the mainstream ("middle-class") society appear to be reluctant to show any level of receptivity or affinity toward any "foreign" traits or elements, those they perceive not to be part of the dominant Anglo-Saxon cultural complex. A contrasting reaction to these same cultural traits or elements is seen in people who are fully integrated into the majority population (i.e., those defined as white), and who, having gained the sense of security and confidence that flows from full membership in and identification with the core culture, feel that they can afford to explore terrains beyond their own cultural borders.

In the second "moment" of this dialectic, that of separation and rejection, the minority consciousness shuns dissolution into the national culture and national identity. Its internalization of the separatist principle and its concrete and non-concrete consequences (i.e., separatist arrangements, values, expectations) leads to the unwavering affirmation of its otherness, followed by the search for alternative, independent ways of collective expression and identity, in the attempt to preserve this otherness, this distinctive character. A number of interrelated trends that characterize certain segments of the African-American community in the United States may be considered here as illustration of this pattern of collective action, starting with (a) the neologistic production and use of personal names that noticeably depart from mainstream models; (b) the pursuit of alternative religious models, some non-Christian, like the Black Muslims; some being hybrid variations on Protestant themes, like the Holy Trinity Ethiopian Orthodox Church or the Ethiopian Hebrew Church (*The New York Times Magazine*, April 19, 1992, pp.14-21); still some, cultic strains such as the House of Judah Cult (*Kalamazoo Gazette*, July 10, 1983, p.A-3); (c) finally, this separatist impulse must also be examined in light of the fact that a segment of the African-American teenage population, as a report of a few years back[4] informs us, has come "to equate black identity with alienation and indifference" and academic industriousness and commitment with "acting white."

The immediate consequences of this pattern, both for the society at large and for the individuals involved, seem clear. Leaving aside the obvious implications regarding the fact that the framework of liberal democracy upon which U.S. sociopolitical life has been built is seriously compromised and damaged by the permanent (once *de jure*, now *de facto*) marginalization of certain segments of the population, we may direct our attention to the identification of the adverse effects of this intergroup pattern from a functionalist standpoint. It is widely acknowledged that in the degree that society's members are impaired in their ability to develop and utilize potential talents and skills to the fullest, the larger system will suffer by depriving itself of these contributions. It is a lamentable waste of human resources. While it is true that members of culturally marginalized groups in the U.S. have been substantially incorporated into the formal spheres of the society in recent decades, their less than full-scale assimilation into, and identification with, the dominant mode of sociocultural life results in varying degrees and forms of functional impairment regarding the standards and requirements of the wider society, particularly with respect to their performance in the workplace. The less educated, lower-skilled strata of this population are naturally going to be affected more seriously by this problem. The likelihood is greater that they will discharge various duties and deliver an array of institutional services in a manner that is bureaucratically inappropriate and inefficient, with direct repercussions for the welfare of the general population. This may be seen in one of the most common ramifications of institutionalized cultural separatism, namely, the development and cultivation of dialectal forms of speech by minority-group members, as observed, for instance, in the African-American community in the U.S. These dialectal speech patterns are so pervasive and deeply-ingrained in this particular ethnic subculture as to show up, in varying degrees, even in individuals who have obtained higher education. In the context of social performance being focused on here, this may, in the long run, become a problematic situation, in the degree that it compromises the proper delivery of public services to the population. An illustration may be offered in reference to communication services that involve the delivery of various types of information to people, over a public-address system. The use of dialectal speech in this case is likely to limit the access of many people to the information and, therefore, their ability to utilize the service productively. (Regional variations in speech are another matter, in that the inflectional and intonational peculiarities in this case will at least be intelligible to the natives of the region in question). Taken as a whole, the limited internalization of, and compliance with, the norms of mainstream contexts of service, by those placed in charge of the delivery of these services, may in some cases be attended with dire consequences for the client population, such as when matters of life and death are involved. Also, going back to the already mentioned effect that this process has on the minority individuals involved, the continuing partial social inclusion of these people and their lack of identification with the mainstream culture perpetuate their lower social standing and social alienation, which may then result - and often does - in various forms of dysfunctional social behavior on their part, and the eventual aggravation of large-scale social problems, such as poverty, crime, mental illness, and substance abuse.

From the standpoint of the minority-group members, we may initially consider the positive implications of the enforcement of the minority identity in the larger context of civil society, and of the bureaucratic management of intergroup affairs in a liberal democratic context. It may be stated that the demarcation and maintenance of minority-group identities facilitate the official recognition, identification, and classification of the disadvantaged groups involved, and, at least in principle, the redressing of past injustice through the full extension of civil rights and privileges to these groups. Therein lies the social utility of the minority identity. It must ideally be, as previously stressed, a transitional phase, a "moment" in the historical evolution of the minority group towards full citizenship. In this capacity, it imparts greater visibility to ethnic minorities, thus enhancing their ability to benefit from the application of an array of bureaucratic procedures and compensatory measures (e.g., Affirmative Action) designed to speed up their civil inclusion. Minority status and identity should not, however, be reified and treated as an end in itself, as has historically been the case in U.S. society (as noted earlier), a function of the essentialism of biracial social organization. Rather, it must necessarily disappear as the minority group becomes fully absorbed into the majority population and way of life. The need for overcoming minority-group difference and status equates with the extirpation of the particularist condition of otherness, of being outside the universal standard, the existential standard of those who have been granted full citizenship, involving all levels of assimilation. It hardly needs repeating here that the indefinite preservation and widespread fetishization of minority status and difference of groups maintained as ethnic-racial minorities, such as currently fueled by the racially-oriented multiculturalist politics of difference in the United States, stand in the way of the full integration of the citizenry, perpetuate the cultural fragmentation of the social system, and generally remain a powerful deterrent to intergroup harmony and equality.

The pernicious effects of the separatist identity may be examined at the material and psychosocial levels. The article mentioned above, on the widespread attitudes of apathy and rejection of the mainstream way of life among a segment of the African-American teenage population, stresses how the cultivation of such an anti-achievement ethic is liable to function as a major impediment to their social incorporation. This countercultural stance towards the larger society brings multiple adverse effects to this group, permanently hindering their civic participation and their ability to benefit fully from the resources and services of the system. As illustration of the latter aspect, we may consider a 1991 CBS report to the effect that many blacks, afflicted with AIDS, would not seek to be tested and treated at an early stage (which would then have afforded them access to the anti-AIDS drugs available at the time, such as AZT) because they did not want to have anything to do with the white establishment.

These outcomes are concrete manifestations of a set of interrelated psychosocial effects. I have already pointed out how the sense of permanent foreignness imparted by the society to the minority identity is a major element behind the problem of social anomie and dislocation that besets at different levels members of racially-marginalized ethnic populations. This may now be examined more closely in reference to the aspect of meaning and intersubjectivity. The present analysis consistently stresses the need for the peripheral (i.e., minority) identity to remain in effect on a provisional basis only, and to be phased out in the degree that the minority group is absorbed into the general population, at which time the national identity takes over as the primary identity for members of the group, and as the mainstay of society-wide consolidation. The national identity emerges and develops from the embeddedness of individuals in the larger intersubjective world of meanings, expressed in ideas and conceptions we have about the world of experience, as embodied in language. Taylor (1977:119; 1987:117) has stressed the fact that intersubjective meanings are "constitutive of the social matrix," the background of social action, which means that collective practices are structured and guided by the meanings which are shared and relied upon not only at the conscious level, but also non-reflectively, to the extent that they are the constitutive material of modes of thinking. That is, they are expressed not only in the content but also in the form of collective thought. Though coming from a different perspective, Habermas indicates how the "moral norms that regulate possible interactions between speaking and acting subjects in general" are contained, indeed embodied, in the linguistic universe (1994:124). This means that the wider formative, normative, and integrative effect of the meaning (i.e., cultural) system on collective action, and the embeddedness of social actors in this system, are anchored fundamentally to linguistic practice, at two levels. First, the level of technical competence, involving phonetic, syntactic, and semantic components. Secondly, the level of performative competence, involving extralinguistic properties and requirements, tied to social meaning, such as those involved in the ability of social actors to establish the connections between spoken language and the external world, the world of events (Habermas, 1979:1-68; Taylor, 1977:117). Language unifies the social collectivity as the repository of ideas through which societal members get to know their world of experience, establish a cognitive correspondence with it, both explicitly and implicitly, and thus gain control over it. If there are problems in meaning, if social actors are not coordinated as a group in terms of their frameworks of understanding, the social universe will become a veritable Tower of Babel, where not only will communicative confusion reign, but also those who are not full participants in the hegemonic frameworks of meaning will be significantly impaired in their social functioning, in the degree that their schemes of signification will not be always suitable for apprehending and responding to the exigencies of daily life in the society at large. Their ideas will not "match the real ... [and these individuals will indeed only] ... be building castles of illusion, or composing absurdities." (Taylor, 1987:112). The existence of peripheral systems of meaning in the larger society, produced by intrasystemic separatism and exemplified by the operation of dialectal forms of speech, may, admittedly, establish meaningfulness, coherence, and integration for minority-group members, but this obtains only within the parameters of the subcultural community itself. When considered in terms of the larger society, the effect is quite the opposite: it maintains the symbolic and material exclusion of the minority element.

As a reflection of syncretistically-obtained cultural integration, the national identity not only facilitates structural or institutional incorporation, but is also the source of self-respect, psychosocial equilibrium, and existential situatedness for all of society's members. It is the critical aspect of full membership and participation in a collective cultural pattern, which, as Schutz points out, functions for the members/participants as "an unquestioned frame of reference," that is, as a "scheme of interpretation," and more important still, a scheme of orientation to the larger social system. Schutz's analysis (1944) explores the cognitive, phenomenological, and interpersonal processes involved in the adaptation experience of the newcomer (to a new culture), and clearly indicates how full integration into the hegemonic cultural system is the very basis and determinant of the social functioning of individuals. Outside the dominant scheme of sociocultural orientation, the *stranger* - in this case, the culturally-marginalized segments of a population, the groups categorized and maintained as minority groups, which have been transformed into the alien element by means of intrasystemic cultural separatism - is at best able to secure limited orientation (and thus function only marginally) within the wider cultural milieu. In Schutz's words, the limited admission of these individuals into the dominant cultural code transforms them into a "border case outside the territory covered by the scheme of orientation current within the group" (1944:504). They become limited in their ability to incorporate and utilize the meanings and rules of guidance of the larger society, as part of their "thinking as usual" (1944:505). To a lesser degree than the typical stranger described by Schutz, these individuals come to experience their society as an alien society, their cultural system as a "labyrinth in which [they have] lost all sense of [their] bearings" (1944:507), something which is all the more lamentable, considering that, unlike the true stranger, they are in a society which is their own.

The ascriptively-engendered subcultural identity is therefore not only a distinguishing feature of this kind of social and cultural disenfranchisement, but also a major maintaining mechanism. The imposition of permanent minority status on particular ethnic segments of the population tends to have the effect of self-fulfilling prophecy. In view of the implications of social inferiority attached to the minority designation, and the fact that minority individuals will internalize the whole array of negative images and lowered expectations built into that status, they will come to develop a negative self-concept, built on feelings of inferiority, self-rejection, resentment, frustration, and helplessness, which will push them further into alienation from the majority mode of life. This will then lead to greater impairment in the areas of social performance - instrumental, linguistic, educational, interpersonal - deemed important for social mobility (as already stressed), and that in turn will be perceived as continuing evidence of their innate collective difference and inferiority, reinforcing the original negative evaluation by the society, leading to more substandard performance on their part, and so on, until the vicious circle of social disparagement is completed. The end result is the maintenance of the larger pattern of interethnic inequality.

The biracially-regulated castelike segregation of dominant and minority ethnic communities, along with the myriad forms of prejudice and discrimination against the latter, gives rise to a series of personality conflicts for the minority individuals involved. These aspects were registered by Clark (1957:ch.3), in research done at a time when Jim Crow arrangements were still in effect. They had to do with general feelings of inferiority, self-hatred, frustration, and humiliation - in other words, with unecessary psychological burdens and turmoil over the recognition of having the inferior social identity. When the minority group is no longer burdened by formally-sanctioned segregation and discrimination, but remains culturally segregated, the sense of social dislocation and estrangement of its members does not entirely disappear, even when these individuals experience significant advancement in formal (e.g., occupational) sectors. That is, this effect may persist independently of the political, economic, and educational placement of these individuals in the social hierarchy.[5] In societies like the United States, where social relations are still essentially organized in accordance with the principle of racial bipolarity, it is quite one thing for members of ethnic groups that have, in the course of their assimilative experience on American soil, become fully absorbed into the sociocultural mainstream, to seek, at various times, identification and continuity with aspects of their ancestral cultural background. The awareness that these individuals have of exercising full membership in the society affords them a deep sense of security and confidence, which in turn allows them to maintain an attachment to cultural ways from their ancestral homelands without any fear of stigmatization, without thinking that this will detract in any way or degree from their full citizenship status, or cause others to see it as the product of incomplete incorporation into the larger society. In fact, they may even see this as something that enhances their citizenship status, that enriches their sense of cultural belonging and self-esteem. This would be the case, for instance, of people of Irish descent or German descent in the U.S., and their periodic re-enactment of such traditions as the Saint Patrick's Day Parade or Oktoberfest, respectively. It is quite another matter for members of permanent ethnic-racial minorities to be pushed, by the workings of ascriptively-mandated separatism, into dissociation from mainstream modes of life and insulation into subcultural ones. Rather than complementing, diversifying, and otherwise enriching the sense of cultural identity for these minority ethnic segments, this situation insures their perpetual marginalization, inasmuch as it reifies their intent to remain a viable presence in the wider societal milieu as *a peripheral mode of life*. A relevant aspect in this connection is the "search for Africa," a noticeable trend in the African-American community in the U.S. over the past decade, and one which has been strongly animated by the multiculturalist movement. When it is considered that the Africans and their descendants in the United States were systematically forced to separate themselves from the traditions of their land of origin, throughout the slavery period and beyond, and that, as some writers have suggested (e.g., Herskovits, 1972), what has remained of this aboriginal African heritage has been in "reinterpreted" form, the Africa that is now being rescued through this search for an alternative cultural identity is an imagined, mythical Africa, a *mélange* of ethnically-diverse, frequently disparate, aspects of the broader African cultural complex.[6] A suitable example of this phenomenon is the Kwanzaa festival, observed with ever greater regularity by many African-Americans around Christmas time. This festival incorporates elements from *East* Africa (for instance, it is linguistically anchored to Swahili, a language of southeastern Africa, specifically, Zanzibar and the adjacent coast), a part of Africa that furnished only a negligible proportion of the slaves that came to the Americas, being therefore only minimally influential on the cultural patterns of African-American communities in the New World. Scholars (e.g., Phillips, 1969; Bastide, 1971; Herskovits, 1972:ch.II) are unanimous in considering U.S. slaves to have come almost exclusively from the coastal area of West Africa. Under more favorable circumstances of acculturation (i.e., in the case where relations of dominant-minority cultural syncretism are encouraged, thus allowing the linkages between the cultural patterns of the minority group and those of its specific culture of origin to remain discernible), a process of ethnocultural continuity would have been feasible: the present effort of African-Americans to reknot the threads of their cultural life with the African background would be more directly geared to the *specific area* of cultural convergence in Africa, namely, the larger West African culture-area, which is generally recognized as the main context of origin of African civilizations in the New World. As it stands, "African-Americans," one writer has remarked (White, 1992:52), "have tried to adopt the [African] continent as a whole as a place of origin." This recapitulates the situation that I have drawn attention to all along, regarding the cultivation of a minority existence and identity within the larger social milieu. This is something that has existential and political utility during the initial phase of assimilation of the minority group, but, as a permanent circumstance, it chiefly symbolizes and sustains the group's exclusion from the main axis of social life. Unencumbered by formal mechanisms of control (as operative during earlier times), these individuals now actively seek to rescue their cultural origins, and to build and preserve their subnational identity on the basis of a patchwork of cultural patterns from their ancestral homeland. The upshot of this, however, has been their straddling of two civilizations, the one associated with the land to which they transplanted themselves, the other with the land where their ancestors came from, without, alas, being full participants in either one.

W.E.B Dubois, the incandescent African-American scholar whose incisive writings on black-white relations in the United States and on the malaise of racial prejudice and discrimination span some seventy years, was already articulating at the turn of this century a cohesive defense of integration in direct opposition to the segregationist arrangements and mood of his time. He spoke eloquently and passionately of "the veil," his metaphor for the nature and effect of the polarization of the "white" and "nonwhite" worlds that formed American society. With the same subtlety yet utter impenetrability of the veil, the great dividing line of race in U.S. society was sufficiently transparent to afford a view of the world beyond the veil, but also impermeable enough to bar its access to outsiders. Dubois's family circumstances had placed him, from childhood, in association with white children, such as at school and at play, and this afforded him early on an opportunity to become aware of and familiar with the "veil." At first, he reacted to it with typical childish, and later, adolescent, indifference, then with a "fine contempt" towards those on the other side, most of whom were demonstrably less gifted than he. As time passed, however, he became increasingly aware of the futility and defeatism of this withdrawal into social "otherness," of how that was simply a natural defense mechanism on the part of those who had been denied access to what they in fact desired most ardently. The fact was, he came to realize, that those on the other side of the veil, and their mode of life, were the standard of reality, of validity, of excellence, towards which everyone else should strive. Hence, the only defensible course of action, it seemed to him, was that of struggling to break through the veil, however Sisyphean an enterprise that might prove. Any other reaction would have been inappropriate and unacceptable, for he came to understand that the riches yielded by the world beyond the veil were - or at least ought to be - the property of everyone on *both* sides of the veil. "The worlds I longed for," Dubois remarks, "and all their dazzling opportunities were theirs, not mine. But they should not keep these prizes ...; some, all, I would wrest from them." These revelations bespeak a nascent aversion for separatism on Dubois's part, and for being faced with no option but to cultivate the "otherness" imposed on nonwhites by the larger society. He was chagrined to see, all around him, how sociocultural separatism forced his peers to shrink "into tasteless sycophancy, or into silent hatred of the pale world about them and mocking distrust of everything white; or [to have one's youth] ... wasted itself in a bitter cry, Why did God make me an outcast and a stranger in mine own house?" (1990:8). He understood only too well how this set in motion the vicious circle of marginalization, meaninglessness, self-doubt, and despair, and how it quickly developed into a situation where those who were trapped in otherness straddled two worlds but were fully a part of neither. Experiencing the world beyond the veil through the interposing presence of the veil (such as, in a concrete sense, the "experiencing" of the larger society by minorities through the limitations forced upon them by the framework of legal separatism), meant that they could never reach a sense of existential completeness, in that they were neither full-fledged members of the larger society, nor fully outcasts. This was the dilemma Dubois referred to as "the contradiction of double aims," a dilemma linked to the most profound sense of estrangement and disorientation for those afflicted with it. "It is a peculiar sensation," remarks Dubois, "this double consciousness, this sense of always looking at one's self through the eyes of others, of measuring one's soul by the tape of a world that looks on in amused contempt and pity. One ever feels his two-ness--an American, a Negro; two souls, two thoughts, two unreconciled strivings; two warring ideals in one dark body, whose dogged strength alone keeps it from being torn asunder" (1990:8-9). This split identity of members of groups that are excluded - or only partially included - through ascriptively-decreed social differentiation sent them often "wooing false gods and invoking false means of salvation" (1990:9-10). This may be observed in the several ways in which culturally marginalized populations may venture forth into identity-building projects that may prove inappropriate insofar as they perpetuate the social disenfranchisement of these individuals. Dubois's commentary is uncannily timely today, in terms of unequivocally exposing the problematic nature of a situation which has now been radically redefined, in connection with the current preponderance in the U.S. of a race-based politics of difference. The pursuit by ethnic-racial minorities of alternative cultural affiliations and projects, a phenomenon mentioned earlier in this chapter, is not only being construed without the negative ramifications pointed out by Dubois, but is also being sanctioned and hailed by the majority population as a natural phenomenon, and passionately defended by the minority groups involved as the rightful expression of long-suppressed native impulses and traditions.

143

The totalizing power of racial identity

The bifurcation of identity in U.S. society has been shown to be a function of the racial dichotomization of intergroup life. The latter, as might be gathered, has a distinctly totalizing effect on how individuals apprehend social reality. In this connection, it should be important to consider here that, at the most fundamental level - the level, shall we say, of phenomenological apprehension, the non-reflective, non-theoretical, emotional level of understanding - people in American society resist the idea that the essence of "American life" could (or ought to) be expressed through something like Walt Whitman's suggestive image of a "teeming Nation of nations," a collection of many diverse and intertwining ethnic, racial, and cultural strains that have melded to produce this cohesive and unique model of collective existence, however much this image may have been inculcated in them through their formal socialization experience. The majority population in the U.S. has historically reacted with considerable ambiguity towards the international hordes streaming into the country from various regions, over the past couple of centuries. By and large, people have not always known, do not always know, what to make of this constantly increasing ethnic diversity in their midst. Despite declarations in more formal vehicles, such as in the following excerpt from the popular press, hailing America as "the endless and fascinating profusion of peoples, cultures, languages, and attitudes that make up the great national pool," (*Time*, Special Issue, Fall 1993, p.3), in their heart of hearts a majority of Americans may still find it difficult to imagine the idea of authentic Americanhood as flowing from, and being represented by, such a hybridizing intermixture, particularly when the implications of "nonwhite" cultures forming an integral part of this mixture are taken into account. Naturally, it has been widely understood, for a long time, that the national population includes a number of different ethnic groups that stand out for their nonwhiteness and cultural diversity, but these people are "the other America," they are not the *real* America. For all the new influx of "nonwhite" contingents (Asians, Middle-Easterners, Hispanics) into the society over the past decade, individuals from these groups still have varying degrees of difficulty in truly fitting in, and, even after having been here for two or three generations, they are still regarded (though no longer formally so) by the majority population as "quasi-Americans." For example, a second- or third-generation American of Asian descent, who has become thoroughly acculturated into the dominant mode of life, linguistically and otherwise, and far removed from his/her ancestral cultural tradition other than through the memories of older relatives, but who still bears distinguishing physical characteristics associated with "Orientals," may reasonably expect questions about whether or not she/he has an interest in her/his Asian heritage, or about where she/he is from ("Los Angeles," "No, really?", or "Yes, but where are you *from*?, as in "What is *really* your country of origin?"), whereas an American citizen of Swedish or German descent will not get such a query. A more dramatic illustration of the denial of full citizenship status to racial minorities, at both the formal and symbolic levels, was the internment of some 110,000 Japanese-Americans during World War II, a measure defended by the U.S. government on the basis of ensuring national security. That incident reveals, first of all, the enormous discrepancy between democratic ideal and social practice that prevailed until the 1960s in U.S. society, as manifested in the enforcement of Jim Crow arrangements and norms. The flagrant violation of the democratic rights and privileges of Japanese-American citizens suggests how the society had failed until that time to reconcile its conception of full citizenship and social egalitarianism with the "nonwhite" segment of the citizenry. The Japanese were an easy target for discrimination during that time, given their high visibility as a group, which was precisely a function of the workings of the Jim Crow system, through which they were categorically barred from intermarriage with members of the majority population, which in turn preserved their physical distinction as an ethnic-racial minority. As it turned out, not one single case of espionage or sabotage against the United States on the part of Japanese-American citizens was ever recorded. In the meantime, discriminatory institutional measures were never taken against German-Americans and Italian-Americans, despite the fact that the United States was also at war against Germany and Italy, a fact that is rather consistent with, and mirrors, the intense ideological racism undergirding governmental policy and public sentiment at that time.

It might be said in this respect that the socially-prescribed minority racial identity exercises a tyrannizing influence over the individuals on whom it is imposed, in that these individuals are unable to escape its relentless grip, and to assert the primacy of their national identity by simply stating it. By the same token, as discussed earlier, members of the majority population who may have full or partial ancestry in some "nonwhite" group, but have, by virtue of their physical appearance and socialization experience, managed to escape the minority classification, are discouraged [not formally, but by cultural forces] from publicly claiming, flaunting, or even just referring to, their minority status.

The reason for this pattern is that the acceptance of full interchangeability or reversibility as a condition applicable to all citizens of the republic, irrespective of their ethnic or racial background - a

145

condition which would in effect be the hallmark of social equality - is something that runs directly counter to the more deeply-internalized conception of the American social order as one that is, first and foremost, biracially structured and administered. In other words, to express, and therefore implicitly endorse, the idea of ethnic, racial, and cultural diversity as the foundation and true expression of American social life amounts to compromising the basic dualistic split of the population assumed in the principle of racial bipolarity, and the racial determinism and reductionism built into this principle, which function as organizing categories of the collective consciousness. Thus it happens that, when people in American society are confronted, for example, with the need to recognize the general similarity between the United States and other multiethnic societies, in terms of the fact that the U.S. and these societies exhibit varying degrees of ethnic and cultural variation as well as mixture and fusion, they may fail to grasp this similarity right away, and may even experience some cognitive dissonance, particularly regarding the aspect of *mixture* and *fusion* of the various ethnic and cultural strains. This is because, for people in general, the image of mainstream America that springs most readily to mind is not so much one that conforms to the melting-pot imagery, but one that flows from the principle of biraciality: a society that is essentially homogeneous from a racial and cultural standpoint, but which happens to have some peripheral segments in its its population, which are racially and culturally unassimilable (at least, not in the fullest sense), and which must, therefore, retain this quality of "outsidedness." The biological integration of the "white ethnics" into U.S. society would not have marred the (presumed) racial purity of the majority population, nor would their cultural assimilation have compromised, to any appreciable extent, the society's Anglo-Saxon cultural make-up, because of the thoroughness with which these groups have been culturally "Americanized." This homogeneous mainstream America thus stands distinguished from the other, equally homogeneous, non-mainstream America, composed of a variety of "nonwhite" minority communities, which, for all their cultural and physical diversity, have been rendered uniform in the public mind through the generalizing, reductionist effect of the nonwhite condition. These two segments of the society coexist side by side, but do not, or are ever expected to, fully interpenetrate. This matter was put succintly and unambiguously by the racist sheriff of the small town in Mississipi, in the 1989 film *Mississipi Burning*, as he truculently attempted to tell the Northern FBI agent to leave them alone to run their own internal (i.e., interracial) affairs: "We have two cultures here, a white one and a black one!," alluding to the laws of biraciality undergirding the handling of social affairs, and intimating that that was the

146

natural order of things, something not to be tampered with. He could just as well have been articulating the viewpoint of most of the population about the nation as a whole, especially during the historical period in question - the 1960s - a time when Jim Crow was still in operation (though nearing its end).

Leaving aside for the moment the fact that full racial uniformity is only an analytical construct, a theoretical possibility, and never an empirical feature of world societies, we could still say that people in the United States would have had greater justification in asserting the pronounced racial uniformity of their society back in the late 18th century, because at that time (1790) the "white" groups still constituted as much as 92.4% of the total population (Feagin, 1993:65). The ratio of white to nonwhite in the population, however, has declined drastically over the past two centuries. That fact notwithstanding, official and unofficial classification, being fundamentally governed by the law of hypodescent or "one-drop rule," dismisses the ethnic variability injected into the general population by the major wave of immigration of the 1800s, and the ongoing influx of different strains through the present century, and continues to enforce the dichotomic (i.e., white/nonwhite) framework of classification. Ethnic and cultural diversity is misconstrued as racial difference, that is, as racially-determined group difference. An example of how this is done may be found in the way in which the ethnic and cultural differences that set apart immigrants from Central and South America (minus Brazil and the Guianas) are disregarded and forcibly dissolved, at both the bureaucratic and informal levels, by lumping these individuals together under the rubric "Hispanic." The latter has come to mean, for the U.S. public at large, not simply a designation for groups whose cultural heritage is traced to Spain, but also a totalizing minority category, formed on the basis of the presumed *racial* uniformity of the group(s) involved, thus representing one among several other "nonwhite" ethnic segments. It has come to be understood, therefore, principally as a racial classification, although in reality it is an *ethnic* label, which should not be taken to be denotative of racial uniformity, but, in fact, embraces a striking genotypical and phenotypical variety (i.e., of racial background and physical appearance), across the different world societies colonized by Spain. However, because the label was originally used in reference to the first two major Hispanic groups in U.S. society, namely, the Mexicans and the Puerto Ricans, groups that are largely mixed in their "racial" background, and secondly, because the operation of the hypodescent rule in the United States precludes the recognition and admission of any intermediary racial categories,[7] the word "Hispanic" has become a catch-all term that forces all groups of Hispanic origin (in addition to the Mexicans and the Puerto

147

Ricans, the Hispanic population in the United States has recently included people from Cuba, El Salvador, the Dominican Republic, Colombia, and Venezuela), regardless of their ethnic and racial background, under the racial designation of "nonwhite."

The dominant effect of the ascriptively (i.e., racially)-generated minority identity in the society, as the chief cognitive and existential frame of reference, causes it to muddle up and transform the meaning of other, unrelated conceptual categories. The following may be considered. It seems, for instance, that the meaning of the concepts "middle class" and "Western," the one denoting a particular socioeconomic echelon in the stratification system, the other, a geographical and/or cultural condition (i.e., the use of "Western" to refer to a cultural aspect concerns the broader cultural complex conventionally understood as Occidental civilization), has been recast in racial terms, particularly under the auspices of the multiculturalist movement in the United States, to the effect that these concepts may be used, at least implicitly, as designations pertaining to the "white" population. Similarly, the concept "European," which is indicative of a general sociocultural pattern of living (on the basis of which it can be distinguished from other similarly general conceptual models, such as the "African" or the "Asian"), is used to a large extent in American society as a *racial* badge, a badge of undifferentiated "whiteness," which members of the majority population rely on as a representation of their background. Yet another instance of this trend may be seen in terms like "the poor" or "the people," clearly notions of political economy, the one referring generally to the "have nots," the other, to the masses, with the latter concept usually connoting asymmetry of wealth and power in relation to the upper echelons of the population. It turns out that (the more disadvantaged layers of) the U.S. African-American population have appropriated these economic concepts and use them as *racial* categories, to refer exclusively to themselves.

The reductionism and inevitable distortion of meaning associated with this tendency are such that one may run, for instance, into references in the popular press drawing a contrast between Latin American cultures (e.g., Mexico, Colombia) and the Western way of life; or even between the cultural mode of life of an ethnic-racial subculture in American society like, for instance, the African-American community, and the *Western* lifestyle of the majority population (!). If Latin-American societies are not Western, that is, neo-European, in their ethos and cultural orientation, what else can they possibly be? And, as far as the African-American group in the U.S. is concerned, despite the fact that the larger situation of sociocultural separatism, formal and informal, prevented their full acculturation into the majority way of life, and led to their development of, and adherence to, subnational forms of behavior and thought, they must still be seen as participants in a neo-European cultural complex, as people who have fashioned their basic cultural orientation and identity in the historical context of absorption of English-American ways of life. Therefore, it seems ludicrous to characterize their cultural expressions as anything other than "Western" - unless, of course, there are other considerations and assumptions lurking behind the use of this designation. It is true that their African ancestors, upon arriving on American soil as slaves, did bring with them a non-Western cultural background. However, succeeding generations of African-Americans, notwithstanding their less than full inclusion into the sociocultural mainstream, have not been anything but Western from a cultural standpoint - that is, "American," in the sense of being the product of a combination of many European and non-European cultural forms into a distinctive, cohesive type of EuroAmerican civilization.

As for the placement of Latin-American social systems in the non-Western category, this classificatory tendency appears to result from the widespread perception of Central and South American societies as being racially and culturally mixed, constitutionally mongrelized, hence, "nonwhite" and, as such, ineligible for the "Western" classification. In this connection, the "Latin" designation, which is in actuality an ethnic-cultural referent, has been reconstructed in the U.S. over the last couple of decades, so as to signify nonwhite status, as linked specifically to the minority Spanish-American groups. The idea of Latin America, therefore, that springs to mind (to the minds of a great number of people, at least; to the "person in the street") is not a cultural one, denoting a group of nations which, like American societies in general, have an European background, but differ from their Northern neighbors in terms of their common Iberian cultural heritage. Rather, it is a *racial* idea, this undifferentiated land of "Latins" (i.e., Spanish-speaking nonwhites), a totalizing category that does not leave out *any* national group south of the Rio Grande, including Brazil. The greatest irony with regard to the Latin classification is that the Italians and the French are not *really* thought of as Latins, mainly because they happen to be classified as white, an irony which fairly jumps out at the observer with respect to the Italians, the ethnic group that should have the strongest and most legitimate claim to the Latin identity. It does not take much for one to see that these classificatory judgements are not at all being oriented by cultural criteria, but by racial ones, and that what is really at work here, even if implicitly, is the greater organizing and regulative influence of the principle of biracialism, cutting across and overriding all other forms of social differentiation.

Notes

1 A list of the most salient examples in this regard would have to begin with (Joaquim Maria) Machado de Assis, a 19th century novelist whose Portuguese and African ancestry has not stood in the way of his being generally perceived as the greatest writer--not AfroBrazilian writer--the country has ever produced. Also included would be, among others, the great 18th-century sculptor of churches in the state of Minas Gerais, Antonio Francisco Lisboa, better known as "Aleijadinho" (The Little Cripple);   Antonio Gonçalves Dias, the poet; Tobias Barreto, the poet and jurist; Andre Reboucas, the engineer (the last three from the 19th century). In the present century, one must consider Edson Arantes do Nascimento ("Pelé"), the soccer star;   Grande Otelo, the actor;   Alfredo da Rocha Viana ("Pixinguinha"), the widely revered early-20th century popular composer of some 600 tunes, and arguably the most famous of the founding fathers of the *samba*; Milton Nascimento, the composer-performer; Mario de Andrade, the poet-essayist of the 1920s Modernist movement, and so on.

2 Accounts of the nascent impulses of race consciousness among individuals of African ancestry in Brazil, in the academic and popular press (see. e.g., *Isto É*, April 20, 1988, pp. 34-41) may be understood in the context of what Freyre, writing in a similar vein, referred to as "the reflection of influences coming from abroad" (1956:13), referring, in other words, to the phenomenon addressed in the political-economy literature as cultural colonialism. Specifically, the patterns of interethnic relations and discourse, schemes of race classification, patterns of minority-group race consciousness, etc., of U.S. society, have in recent decades come to exert a considerable impact over other multiethnic societies (particularly those of the economic "third world," as part of the larger cultural influence exercised abroad by the United States). This has resulted in certain incipient impulses in these societies, on the part of the "people of color," to appeal to the U.S. model of ethnic relations as a more progressive standard to emulate. This is being done without any direct regard for the historical pattern of evolution of intergroup relations in these "third-world" countries, which may differ radically from that of the United States, and for the fact that the patterns and categories that regulate ethnic relations in a particular society will not automatically transfer to others, and even if they did, this would not necessarily eventuate in the greater harmonization and consolidation of intergroup

life. The problem underlying these recent separatist tendencies towards the delineation of a minority identity, for members of Brazilian society who have an African ethnic background, is that they seem to stem from deep misunderstanding of the nature of assimilation, and of the specific circumstances and patterns of assimilation of the African element in Brazil (and, for that matter, in other multiracial societies like Cuba, Puerto Rico, Colombia, etc.), as opposed to how these circumstances and patterns have taken place in biracial social systems like the United States (or South Africa). Essentially, the focus tends to be kept solely on the aspect of formal relations, and on the degree of mobility exercised by minority-group members in U.S. society in the economic, political, and educational spheres. In the meantime, the complex nature and relevance of dominant-minority cultural interaction, and its meaning for, and concrete effect on, the larger aspect of life of individuals in society, are missed.

3   The current separatist drive in U.S. society towards educational segregation has given new impetus to the operation of all-black schools, and to the implementation of an Afrocentric education for members of the black community. The following exchange between the teacher and the students in one of these segregated schools (see *Time*, April 29, 1996, p.45) clearly confirms this tendency to treat the U.S. national identity as the primary or core identity of whites only:

> "Who can name an African-American comedian?" inquires [the teacher].
> "Eddie Murphy!" "Bill Cosby!"
> "And some American comedians?"
> "Whoopi Goldberg!"
> "No, an *American* comedian," [the teacher] corrects them.
> "Roseanne!" a boy calls out.
> "Good," says [the teacher.]

4   "The Hidden Hurdle," *Time*, March 18, 1992.

5   Feagin and Feagin (1993:214) give the dramatic example of a distinguished young black journalist, winner of several awards, who took her own life in 1984, apparently as a result of mounting despondency and anguish over what we can term the continuing cultural dislocation of African-Americans in the United States - the sense of a split existence that Dubois wrote so poignantly about

(1990:8-9, orig. 1903), in a separatist society where formal social standing does not normally dissolve the boundary lines of ascription - race, in this case.

6   The absence of direct continuities, and corresponding identification, among African-Americans in the U.S., with specific cultural systems in Africa (or even with larger African culture-areas, such as the Bantu or the Sudanese), may be evidenced in the following account. In a recent (Fall 1995) episode of a popular television series, in which the story unfolds in New Orleans and in connection with the influence of voodoo in that city, one of the characters, a black woman dressed in full African garb, asks the (white) protagonist regarding voodoo and its presumed ability to influence the course of events in a person's life: "You don't believe in that stuff, do you?" This question is quite consistent with the present analysis, and instructive on a number of levels. First of all, it restates the dissociation of U.S. blacks from African modes of life, generally understood, and from African religious patterns, more specifically. Their overwhelming adherence to evangelical Protestantism, particularly of the Baptist and Methodist variety, admits of no syncretistic mixtures with, or even sympathies towards, non-Protestant, least of all non-Christian, religious patterns. Also, it bears witness to the fact that the African attire of the woman is not symbolic of a continuing cultural connection with the ancestral homeland - this relationship, as indicated throughout this work, was suppressed early on in the historical experience of the Africans in the U.S. - but rather, signifies the present search for cultural origins in an overgeneralizing (hence, in a way, decontextualized) fashion. In the TV story the character implicitly asserted her skepticism and suspicion of voodoo, a cultural carryover of the West African religious tradition, as forcefully as any member of the white community might. This type of cultural behavior on her part has already been dwelled on. Members of the U.S. African-American community who have attained high rank in that community, and who feel, furthermore, that they are making progress towards blending formally and informally (minus the biological aspect) within the larger national life, to the extent that they engage in the practice of superimposing African cultural aspects on their life (such as, for instance, the woman wearing an African costume), this does not really reach below the surface level - that is, it is not allowed to interfere with (certainly, not transform) their cultural behavior and identity as Americans. In other words, they try to avoid any significant alteration of their cultural status as Americans, resulting from syncretistic

contacts and fusions with other cultural influences and aspects, even if the latter happen to be linked to their ancestral homeland. Since the larger society has been historically regulated by separatist norms and expectations, it is to be expected that its members will internalize these norms and expectations through their socialization experience, and minority individuals are no exception in this regard, in particular those who see themselves becoming significantly assimilated at the institutional and interpersonal levels of social life. In fact, these individuals, as we have seen, are even likely to overidentify with dominant-group traits.

7   This phenomenon is manifested by the ruling and minority communities alike, because members of the latter (the "nonwhites"), in having internalized the separatist ethos of the larger society and the normative validity of its corresponding arrangements and practices, become fully invested in the cultivation of their minority ethnic-racial identity. On account of this, they would be quite incapable of relating to the presence of an intermediary racial category (e.g., a mulatto community), wedging itself in between the whites and the nonwhites, blurring the dividing line between them, and thus dissolving the separateness which, for nonwhites, is the very basis of self-affirmation *as difference* in the society, their very source of collective identity, the mainspring of their political mobilization. They would therefore perceive this category as disorienting, alienated (i.e., it would be seen as ontologically "illegal" in the larger context of U.S. intergroup life), and a threat to their existence. As such, they would resent it and seek to negate it.

Much of the present work in one way or another addresses this very aspect, that is, the fact that any individual not classified as white in the U.S. social system is immediately claimed by the nonwhites as one of their own.

153

6 Revisiting secularization: Religion as implicit normative system

In this chapter, the focus is shifted from the ideal-typical description and comparison of modalities of culture and intergroup relations to the examination of the genesis and evolution of cultural systems. The full-scale examination of the process by which cultural systems emerge and develop would require a considerable study, which would exceed the purview of this work. Still, the following discussion pays particular attention to the way in which dominant ideological systems - with direct focus on the dominant religion of the society - come to function as the predominant conditioning influence in the formation of culture. The main focus in this regard is on how the dominant religion of the society structures the worldview of its members, and consequently, their patterns of social relations.[1] The task at hand thus consists, in its broader aspect, of showing the importance of belief for the functioning of social and intergroup life.

Regarding this aspect of functional adaptability, the worldview of a social collectivity not only provides individuals with definitions of what constitutes social reality and of the nature of these constitutive elements, thus providing a basis upon which group action may be planned and executed, but it also promotes the psychological health of members of the community (Murphey, 1979:154).

We may begin by stating that this investigation rests on the premise that empirical reality is not self-evident or self-explainable, something to be taken as a given, but must instead be explained in terms of *meaning*, or, in terms of the sphere of significance and symbolism within which social phenomena and events are located, interpreted, and reacted to by social actors. This point becomes especially relevant when it is linked to the study of social problems which have a wide range of cultural meanings, such as the one addressed here, namely, the development of crossnational

154

variations of culture and interethnic patterns. The full understanding of such a problem may not be reached if the focus is kept solely on its immediately observable dimensions, that is, if the problem is apprehended purely on the basis of "the data of the empirical sciences" (Weber, 1949:56), as tends to be the case in traditional single-case or comparative studies of intergroup relations. Secondly, this analysis seeks to advance the explication of the linkage between ideal factors and social structure, and more specifically, as indicated, of the role of religious ideas in the constitution of social arrangements and practices. Systems of ideas and symbolism are treated here as having an existence *sui generis* and as exerting an autonomous effect on social organization, rather than being simply an epiphenomenal expression of the latter. In this respect, they are shown to impinge directly on the conduct and attitudes of the dominant ethnic community towards ethnic and cultural difference, which then converts into an impact on the overall organization of interethnic life. Mainstream empirical studies normally bypass, or at best tangentially address, this process by which social structure expresses underlying systems of thought. At issue, then, is their failure to explore the dynamics of the relationship between material and nonmaterial elements. They tend, as one writer (Comaroff, 1994:311) has put it, "to separate reality from its representations." This analysis, on the other hand, stresses precisely the way in which religious thought correlates with social practices and attitudes that bear on interethnic life. More to the point, how the dominant religion supplies the "essential ideas" (Durkheim, 1965:21), or the key presuppositions, that form the basis of collective thought. Collingwood (1972:41) has referred to these as "absolute presuppositions"; Turner (1974:64, 36), as "root paradigms"; Haskell (1979:141), as "controlling presuppositions". These basic ways of perceiving and understanding derived from religion have a normative or regulative effect on the emergence of social arrangements and practices. One analyst (Murphey, 1979:154) has pointed to how they orient the community to such problems of interpersonal life as "[w]ho may be loved and who must be hated, what one may be proud of and what one must be ashamed of, who is a friend and who is an enemy...".

In relation to this, the *locus* of meaning here is the relationship between the dominant and minority ethnic communities: their ideas, attitudes and practices towards each other. The intergroup patterns that result from this represent the unintended consequences of the behavior and attitudes of the dominant group towards the minority ones. In the Weberian model of causality the element of meaning is not expressed in terms of a simple "idealist" linearity, whereby A, or the idea or value system, causes B, or social structure. The transmission of meaning to empirical reality and its

155

conversion into contexts of action is significantly more intrincate than that. It is set in motion by social actors, congregated in collectivities and intentionally assigning meaning to aspects of their world of experience, which leads progressively to the formation of complexes of meaning (ideological systems). The latter in turn become cognitive frameworks that tend towards autonomous lines of development, at which point they are "reprocessed" by individuals, in a double-hermeneutical exercise (The various aspects of social reality - Durkheim's "social facts" - are, in actuality, for social actors, "interpreted facts," to use Schutz's idea [1974]). The second-order interpretations of meaning that emerge at this point, saturating the social milieu with new meaning, will then influence the patterns of attitudes and behavior of the group, resulting in entire complexes of sociocultural action. These cultural formations are unintended, insofar as social actors do not deliberately set out to make their subjective interpretations the basis for the emergence of social change. They are fundamentally unaware of how their deep-lying assumptions, values, and intentions shape their conduct. It is true that the meaning they assign to the objects of experience orients them in the formulation and execution of their existential projects. That is, individuals may consciously apply their systems of meaning normatively, towards the execution of particular plans of action, towards meeting daily challenges and carrying out daily tasks. But, over the longer term, and in the larger sense of collective conduct, social practices and ways of thinking do not spring from the direct deliberation or intention of individuals.

Secularization theory reconsidered

It is fitting, at this juncture, to reconsider in brief survey the issue of secularization. In the Weberian lexicon the concept of secularization or "disenchantment of the world" (*Entzauberung der Welt*) refers to the overarching, multifaceted process of societal modernization, itself originally spurred (according to Weber) by innerworldly, ascetic religion. This modernization process fundamentally involves greater human control over the physical and social environment, or, as Schutz (in Emmet and MacIntyre, 1970:96) has stated it, "the transformation of an uncontrollable and unintelligible world into an organization which we can understand and therefore master, and in the framework of which prediction becomes possible." In this respect, the modernization of social life has meant its overall regulation in accordance with principles of efficiency and calculability. It comprises a complex of interrelated factors, to wit, the dynamic of modern capitalism, the development of science and technology, bureaucracy, and the rise of rationalist thought. The secularization aspect particularly concerns the ever-declining influence of religious institutions and symbols over the various spheres of social life. This phenomenon has been variously addressed in terms of a dispersal of the theological and the liberation of the modern individual from religious tutelage, the turning away from religious to secular explanations of life, the cessation of the religious production of social behavior, and so forth. In this connection, whereas in traditional societies (e.g., the Amish communities in North America) the link between collective behavior and the religious mandate is explicitly manifested, and therefore readily perceived, in modern industrialized societies the conduct of individuals is no longer seen as regulated by religion, but, instead, by the organizational or bureaucratic needs of the system. Moreover, the structures, processes, and impulses of modern life, which, according to Weber, were originally facilitated and animated by religious thought, are now considered to have become antithetical to the latter. Mainstream social science has traditionally upheld the Weberian interpretation of social change as a basic unilinear pattern of cumulative technological rationalization, and Weber's conception of the relationship between scientific and technological reasoning in modern society as one expressing ever-increasing antagonism between these two forms of reasoning. Weber himself may have been partially responsible for this, as he spoke of the "irreconcilable tension" between the scientific and theological worldviews, in relation to which the movement of scientific rationalization of society spurned any "intellectual approach which in any way asks for a 'meaning' of innerworldly occurrences" (1967:351). He also showed that pure market relationships - as an expression of formal rationalization in the economic sphere - are fundamentally irreconcilable with "the sacred" (along with "status, and merely traditional bonds"). These latter elements have "come to be eliminated" (1978:639). Conversely, from the standpoint of ethically-based religion, the world constitutes a *massa perditionis*, a context of perdition, a natural vessel of sin and eternal damnation; as such, a structure that must be avoided because of its pernicious effect on the moral and spiritual welfare of the believers (Weber, 1978:543). Several analysts (e.g., Berger, 1969:109, Giddens, 1991:589) have noted that secularization has occurred both at the objective level of social life, involving the continuous loss of religious influence in institutional processes and structures, and at the level of consciousness. In the latter context, secularization relates to the growing tension, in the conscience of the believer, between divine mandate and human interest. As the original meaning assigned to phenomena is converted and externalized into patterns of social behavior, and this behavior becomes institutionalized over time, the original

157

meaning eventually becomes objectified into *general* guidelines or principles of cultural action. At the "moment" of mediation between meaning and sociocultural structure (the mediative element being the actions of individuals in groups), the meaning undergoes an unintended detachment from its original context - in Weber's Protestant Ethic thesis this context is the Calvinist interpretation of the appropriate methodology for attaining salvation--and is turned to general use. It is in terms of the eventual detachment of regulative meaning from its original religious source that the idea of secularization has been conventionally understood. As has been stated (Kasler, 1988:93) the original character of this meaning evolves "into general norms of social action, which from then on [can] detach [itself] from their original [religious] context." Thus, patterns of action which were formerly influenced (and recognized as being influenced) by specifically religious injunctions, are thought to lose this religious connection over time, as the society becomes secularized. In this respect, the relationship between religion and society is further conceptualized in antagonistic terms, with an ever-widening gulf between them. Religion recedes into the background, while the enterprises of reason and science establish themselves ever more assertively. This traditional explanation creates dualisms which sharply alienate the categorial features of "traditional" society from those of "modern" society, and imply the impossibility of their coexistence. This matter will be rethought here in a way that makes it possible to throw the religious constitution of sociocultural life into relief, without necessarily invalidating the basic Weberian principle of institutional differentiation as a product of societal modernization. Institutional practices and attitudes will therefore be assessed in terms of their continuing connection with the original religious meaning-context, even though these practices and attitudes ostensibly present themselves as completely "secularized," or divested of their religious significance. In order to rethink this problematic and recognize the continuing linkage between religious meaning and social action, it is necessary to shift the focus from the content of the action pattern to structural homologies related to underlying premises and categories of thought. The forces of religious thought, now suppressed by the normative injunctions issuing from modern life, "go underground," so to speak - that is, they fade from the scene in the sense that their religious identity is no longer recognized - but *continue to exercise a molding influence on social conduct*, via the frameworks of understanding implanted earlier in the collective consciousness through direct religious socialization. These frameworks necessarily structure the manner in which social actors experience the world and conduct themselves in it. It becomes apparent that the contribution of phenomenological factors to this overall process of consciousness building and social action cannot be overestimated. From this viewpoint, the ethical impact of religion, though appearing now only in social action of the secular type, since the action of the sacred type is untenable, continues to operate in the capacity of what Weber termed "psychological sanctions," which originate in religious belief and practice, and "impart a direction to practical conduct and [hold] the individual to it." (1958:97). Thus, although the specifically religious character of these injunctions has been converted into the generality of the larger normative system, this does not necessarily mean that it has dissipated, ceased to exist. It has only been rendered invisible by the overtly secular or non-religious appearance that social behavior acquires once the society has undergone modernization and secularization, thus concealing the continuing, *albeit* implicit, appropriation of religious principle as regulative force.

Because social rationalization or modernization has been associated with the hegemony of the tendencies of efficiency, calculability, and standardization, as well as with formal processes and relations of the "secondary" (or bureaucratic) type, it is assumed that the forces of culture are progressively neutralized and standardized in the degree that scientific and technological advances occur. The universality of this principle is taken for granted since one does not have to look very far to see that industrialization and bureaucratization together have operated in a pervasive and homogenizing fashion on the cultural architecture of developing and developed societies everywhere. At the same time, the preponderance of the material transformation of the world ought not to obscure the fact that cultural structures endure significantly in terms of their own developmental logic, as stressed in the first chapter. Referring to the resilience of cultural elements vis-a-vis the economic structure, Schumpeter (1976:12-13) insists that, over time, "... we almost always find that the actual group and national behavior more or less departs from what we should expect it to be if we tried to infer it from the dominant forms of the productive process." Thus, in this sense, certain patterns of religiosity that still persist in a society like the United States are clearly dissonant in relation to the high level of social rationalization of the system.

In addition to this, the very structural concomitants (to cultural structures) of economic and technological development may be shaped by cultural forces. That is, a society's cultural system, in acting upon the course of social events, may in many cases "preponderate in determining their form" (to use Engels' words) expressing a relational nexus already mentioned, namely, the fact that material arrangements of society stand essentially for the concrete consequences of underlying presuppositions and modes of thinking, and the latter in turn are reinforced by the maintenance of the material structures and corresponding social practices. The relationship between these two sets of influences, therefore, is neither one of mutual exclusiveness (although there is dialectical tension) nor linear causality. From this point of view, whether or not the society has become "disenchanted" or "desacralized" - or, to put it differently, whether or not religion has maintained its institutional tutelage on social arrangements and practices despite the relentless encroachment of the forces of modernity - the main concern here is to show that secularization does not automatically translate into the end of religious influence in social life.[2] Apart from the weakening effect that secularization exerts on the more tangible aspects of the dominant religion (such as levels of membership, economic and political power, the hold of formal teachings, and so forth), the function of the latter as the principal organizing and structuring force of the collective mind, and by implication, of the network of social action, must still be recognized. Regarding this last point one observer (Williams, 1987:249) argues that "[t]he behavior of human beings is largely programmed by the thoughts that are in their heads." Furthermore, it has been paradigmatic, at least in the context of a Durkheimian sociology of religion, that the group mind is constituted on the basis of collective representations produced via the systematic and regular practice by the group in religious rituals (Durkheim, 1965/orig.1915; see also Geertz's Weberian treatment of religion as a cultural system, 1973). In order for this phenomenon to be grasped more clearly, the dominant religious ideology must be explored in reference to its operation as a *subtext*, rather than strictly as an institutional (i.e., ecclesiastical, juridical) force by means of which the religious effect on the social system is concretely achieved. From the earliest stages of colonization of a society, the hegemonic religious system plays a preponderant role in the development of the cosmological vision of the people, and by extension, of their ways of acting, interacting, and interpreting their world of experience. In the language of phenomenology, it establishes the *pre-understandings* that promote the entire structuration of the lifeworld.

In spite of Weber's reference to the "universal diffusion" of properties originating in religious thought (in Gerth and Mills, 1967:309), and his judicious limiting of the causal impact of religion (on capitalist culture) to a "general direction" (1958:91) - that is to say, religion acts in concert with a number of other "interdependent influences between the material basis, the forms of social and political organization, and the ideas current in the time of the Reformation"--he also stresses that if causal continuity is to be found between religious ideology and social structure, this would be in the "purely religious characteristics" of the old Protestant spirit; otherwise, the possible connections between religious thought and particular sociostructural formations will, at best, be "vaguely perceived." Weber recognizes that if the attention is turned - as indeed it is, for the most part - to the outward characteristics of the variables involved, "precious little" will be found that directly and explicitly connects these elements (1958:45). The linkage must be established on the basis of the purely religious aspects of the causal variable. I interpret that to mean the underlying presuppositions and categories of understanding of religious thought, which over time become deeply-set structures of understanding in the collective consciousness, or better yet, the collective *un*-consciousness, inasmuch as we are dealing here with the nonreflective aspect of action. As these structures of understanding are internalized through socialization, they operate as nonreflective motivational mechanisms, Archimedean points that guide the development of a methodical lifestyle and relation to the world. It was noted earlier how in modern, secularized society patterns of collective behavior are perceived as being divested of any religious significance, a perception defended on the basis of the outwardly nonreligious configuration of this behavior. However, the perspective adopted here portrays this behavior as remaining grounded in the original religious meaning-context, which means that religion continues to exercise an ethical and normative claim on social behavior, independently of whether it is formally exercising control over social institutions and behavior, and of the actual formal religious commitment on the part of the community, and of the specific nature and degree of this religious commitment.

In view of these considerations, the present argument may be regarded as a "genetic" argument, insofar as it underscores the generative dimension of religion, with respect to its history and evolution. This contrasts with a more "configurational" approach, in which social situations are interpreted as a sort of topological space wherein the various elements (social arrangements, social rituals) are atemporally grasped on the basis of their immediate spatial interrelations, and the meaning of these elements is understood on the basis of their overt aims. I stress instead what might be loosely termed a collective depth (social) psychology - a depth hermeneutics - whereby the original structures of understanding and cognition (in this case, drawn from religion), once solidly embedded in the collective (un)consciousness, continue to exert a molding effect on action patterns, notwithstanding their metamorphosis into *general* rules of behavior. This is a more dynamic procedure, relying neither on the external form and sensory meanings of the cultural behavior as symbolic gesture, nor on the "conscious, verbalized, indigenous interpretations of [the] symbols" (Turner, in Emmet and MacIntyre, 1970:167), but on the evolutionary career of the original frameworks of meaning provided early on in the formative period of the social community, by the dominant religion. Though stated only in basic form here, these ideas aim at the conceptual articulation of religion as a normative subtext.

In the way of illustration, we may look at the example of American society, and at social behaviors which, on casual inspection, are not seen as related to religion, but in fact could be shown to derive ultimately from injunctions laid down by the dominant religion. These are behaviors and tendencies which represent, to use Weber's phrase (1958:41), "the exact opposite of the joy of living," the reference here being to their roots in Puritanism. They are manifested, to begin with, in attitudes toward work, that is, towards the pursuit of work as an end in itself. It may be that the specific Puritan consciousness and justification of work activity as an act of glorification of God and a measure of the state of grace is not expressed openly and explicitly today (due to the secularization process), but the sense of ethical and moral necessity behind this cultural pattern remains. A case in point is the well-known operational principle of the restaurant and fast-food industry in the U.S., "If you have time to lean, you have time to clean." This is generally thought to reflect the degree of economic rationalization of that industry, along with the attending requirement of efficient utilization of time, and it may indeed have much to do with that. At a deeper level, however, it points to the operation of a religious mandate (as expressed in traditional sayings like, for instance, "The devil finds work for idle hands"), thus calling to mind a higher (i.e.,non-economic) morality according to which *working* is a *priori* preferrable to *not-working*, and to opt for the latter is, in fact, to relinquish the certainty of salvation. Another aspect that instantiates the underlying influence of religion is the tension, discomfort, and guilt marking the relationship of individuals in U.S. society to the principle of sensorial pleasure, that is to say, how people react to the unregulated stimulation and/or manifestation of the senses, such as for instance in their reaction to strong tastes and smells, to the enjoyment of food and drink, to the handling of leisure time; their attitudes and practices in the sphere of sexuality, and towards the body and bodily processes (interesting in regard to this last aspect: a magazine ad for a substance guaranteed to "Stop Sweat for 6 Weeks"). Of relevance here also is the cultural inhibition or suppression of emotional exuberance through norms and expectations that stress decorum, stoicism, and the control of such behaviors as hearty or boisterous laughing, expressions of anger, and even the pursuit of aesthetic interests. We may also interpret the generalized

162

penchant among the lower socioeconomic echelons of society (precisely those classes that exhibit the deepest levels of internalization of ascetic Protestant values and beliefs) for violence and mayhem ("blood-and-guts") in entertainment as a process of collective psychological compensation for the rigid constraints imposed on emotional expression by norms derived from religious thought. Finally, there remains to be considered the deeplying suspicion of formal education ("book learning") and erudition, and academically-related intelligence, among the general public in the United States. One can be "too smart for one's own good," except perhaps when this trait is manifested in utilitarian and instrumental terms - the case of the predominance of "practical reason" over "theoretical reason" - such as, for instance, when one shows considerable problem-solving skill, or instrumental cleverness, ingenuity, or cunning, in a variety of situations, like outsmarting an opponent in a battle of wits. The latter would seem to be virtually the only context in which "having a lot of smarts" would count and be admired. Putting aside for the moment the contribution of the dominant philosophical pragmatism of the society in shaping this aspect, the latter appears to be clearly Puritan in its origins and basic character. Hays and Steely (1963:162) remind us of the fact that the larger Baptist fellowship in the U.S., though less directly aligned today with the Puritan Calvinism of its early (i.e., 18th and 19th centuries) adherents, remains suficiently influenced by this theological perspective to show "a rather widespread suspicion of education and of educated men" (1963:162). It seems reasonable to say, in this regard, that the Baptist community as a whole, and more broadly, the population at large (insofar as its worldview basically expresses underlying Protestant values and ideas) are, as these authors have said it, "still the frontier folk to whom a high degree of education spells death to evangelistic zeal, and accomplishments in scholarship are incompatible with heartfelt religion and deep spiritual insight" (1963:163-64). Hence, the persisting distrust of academic interpretations of religious aspects, and of formal education as such.

All of these aspects (save for the last example, regarding education) may reasonably be seen as ramifications of the Puritan rejection of pleasure. Novak (cited in Burkey, 1978:296) addresses this aspect and identifies a number of specific traits of the American national character, which he contrasts with those of "Catholic ethnics": "... suffering alone, clean with a disgust and fear of germs, reserved, controlled ... inexpressive, considering pain as impersonal and mechanic ...".

The religious etiology of culture

I have advanced the thesis that the dominant religion of the society, in generating the fundamental categories of thinking, understanding, and judging of the collectivity, comes to exercise an organizing, prescriptive, and circumscriptive effect upon social behavior, that amounts to forming the very structure of the social and cultural world (encompassing, naturally, the sphere of ethnic and racial relations, if the society happens to be multiethnic). As Geertz (1973:123) has indicated, referring to ideas in general, the latter act as "templates for the organization of social and psychological [we should include psychosocial here] processes." With reference to religious concepts in particular, this author has argued that they "spread beyond their specifically metaphysical contexts to provide a framework of general ideas in terms of which a wide range of experience - intellectual, emotional, moral - can be given meaningful form." This interpretive position is directly aligned with the central argument of this study. It also has clear implications for secularization or disenchantment theory, as conventionally formulated. As indicated earlier, secularization is normally treated as a process by which religion progressively declines and is ultimately neutralized in its power over the various spheres of social life. This process has been variously put as one by which "religious institutions and symbols cease to legitimate, support, and justify various aspects of society and culture" (Kammeyer, Ritzer, and Yetman, 1990:526); or, by which the dominant or most successful religious organizations in a society "become more worldly and offer a less vivid and less active conception of the supernatural" (Stark, 1992:431). However, these standard treatments fail to clarify the way in which the dominant religious system, though gradually losing its grip on social life in terms of the diminishing impact of its ecclesiastical and doctrinal structures, continues to give form and coherence to the social world by means of its "ethical" presuppositions. Once the dominance of a particular religious system in a society has become secured, its effect on collective thought and behavior will continue, despite the visible manifestations of decline of its *institutional* power. This is accomplished through the previously mentioned psychological sanctions (Weber) which, in being implicit, shape the character of practical life in a way that is not immediately recognized, and that escapes the conscious apprehension of the social actors involved. This process, as one writer has suggested, "seems to derive its authority from outside the will of those [involved in the production of the behavior]" (Comaroff, 1994:313). In his analysis of modern capitalism, Weber sought to locate in ascetic (i.e., Calvinistic) Protestantism the fundamental "ethic" leading to an economic rationalism, that served in turn as the basis for the development of capitalist activity. This line of reasoning suggests that it is to the ethic of religion, not to its formal organizational and doctrinal structure, that we ought to be turning our attention as the primary source of motivation of collective conduct. Weber's contention was that the early (Protestant) reformers did not consciously intend for their ideas to constitute the basis of economic change or social reform--which is to say, that they were unaware of and/or unconcerned with the *cultural* consequences of the Reformation (1958:89). This indicates that the impact of Protestant religion on the development of capitalist activity is to be grasped primarily in reference to the ethical premises of this religion, not in reference to its specific doctrinal principles, which would have been relied upon at the *conscious* level.

Accordingly, the analysis of the influence of Luso-Brazilian Catholicism and ascetic Protestantism on the cultural systems of Brazil and the United States, respectively, will stress the identification of the major religious premises and values, from which stemmed the legitimating and motivating impulses behind the networks of sociocultural action of each society. These religions will be contrasted ideal-typically in reference to these basic premises. In the case of Brazil, the tendencies discussed as being constitutive of cultural integration will be traced to the universalism of the dominant Catholic faith. In the case of the United States, the tendencies discussed as being constitutive of cultural separatism will be traced to the particularism of Protestantism. The brand of Catholicism which evolved in Brazilian society, and that of Protestantism which evolved in the United States, were strongly marked by universalistic and particularist tendencies, respectively. These tendencies may be used as conceptual coordinates orienting the explanation and understanding of the correlative processes of syncretism and accomodation, on the one hand, and separatism and exclusion, on the other.

The centrality of the Catholic religion in the cultural life of Brazil, and of the Protestant religion in that of the United States, is a phenomenon that has been amply documented (e.g., Freyre, 1945, 1956; Wagley, 1971; Siegfried, 1927, 1955; Anderson, 1970), and it is a striking feature of Portuguese colonization in one country, and of English colonization in the other. Indeed, this religious influence was manifested on a level that makes it dificult to set it apart from the process of colonization as a whole. Freyre reports that in the early colonial period in Brazil the national culture was already dominated by Christianity, "not only by Christian ideals, but also especially by the practices, the rituals, the social values of the Church and by the superstitions regarding herbs and animals associated with the Christian symbology and theology" (1945:659). He speaks of how Catholicism became "the cement of our unity" (1956:41). Wagley notes similarly that, at the formal and organizational level, the Church, along with the State, provided Brazil "with national unity" (1971:212). However, the religious impact reached beyond this formal aspect, in terms of Catholicism coming to function "not so much as an active religious system but ... a way of life--a fundamental national institution" (1971:229). Azevedo (1950:139) trenchantly articulates this viewpoint:

> Religion had an influence in the colonial period that was without doubt preponderant and practically exclusive in the organization of the system of culture, which, as much in its content as in its forms and institutions, shows vividly those relations of close dependence between culture and religion. It is not only points of contact that were established between them, zones of influence and interpenetration, but true bonds which tied them together from their beginning, interweaving their roots and obliging us to relate our cultural history to events, institutions, and influences in the field of religion.
>
> Tributary to religion, on whose sap it was nourished for a long time, culture only later, especially in the nineteenth century, became detached from the Church, without ceasing to be Christian in its spirit and in its manifestations, in order to tie itself up with professional life and institutions designed for the preparation for the liberal professions. Thus, of ecclesiastical initiative and religious content at the beginning, growing up in the shade of convents, seminaries, and the colleges of the priests, and later of a utilitarian character, promoted in higher schools for professional training, culture cannot be explained or understood in its evolution, if we neglect to set forth first of all the religious and professional activities to which it was tied, and above all those of the Catholic religion which with its beliefs, its morals, and its rites rocked the cradle and sealed the tomb of succeeding generations.

Freyre (1970:290) also noted the array of ostensibly secular aspects of Brazilian social life in the 19th century, ordinarily seen, at first glance, as devoid of any religious meaning, but which were in fact related to the operation of Catholicism in the broader sphere of practical activity, and to the interpenetration between the sacred and profane realms. These cultural aspects were part of the *patriarchal* social system of the country[3] during its colonial and Imperial phases, a system in which "the very choice of clothing, houses, and furniture ... followed *a religious order and system* (emphasis added) that governed virtually the entire existence of the individual ... [a system whose influence was felt on] ... academic

166

dress, and particularly the academic rings, of the different schools and disciplines ...". Freyre also stresses how the collectivistic and pragmatic orientation of Luso-Brazilian Catholicism reinforced the structure of family life in a way that makes it emblematic of the historical development of Brazil. This Christian tradition, according to Montenegro (in Freyre, Introduction, 1947:32), "maintains to this day a greater power of penetration in the spirit of our people than any other tradition bequeathed by the Portuguese ancestors."

In the United States, too, the predominance of religion in social life, its role as (to use Siegfried's words) "the guiding factor of the community" (1927:40), has been one of the country's most strongly distinguishing features. "From the earliest European settlements", it has been said, "religious factors have been uniquely prominent in this society ..." (Kammeyer, Ritzer, and Yetman, 1990:525). The intense religious character of American society persists to the present time, as indicated by the high official levels of church membership and participation in religious rituals (in 1991 these stood at about 70% of the population), and in the fact that the overwhelming majority of the people (in the order of 95%) claims to subscribe to religious beliefs of one type or another. A major survey (cited in Giddens, 1991:581) shows U.S. society to have a higher level of stated religious commitment "than any country save India."[4]

In this connection, it is useful to examine the colonial beginnings of the two societies to confirm the dominance of the European settling group and its ability to impose its cultural traditions, in particular its religion, on the colonized society. The steady addition of other ethnic streams to the national population does not appear to have seriously disrupted this process of cultural dominance, especially in the aspect that is most critical for this study, namely the formation of the collective consciousness, because the newcomers were in every case required to adopt the mode of life of the host society. Thus, as they transformed the society's institutional and cultural life over the course of several generations, by that time they had already internalized the key ethical principles and values provided by the dominant religious culture, to the point where these principles and values were now their primary ideological resource and inspiration. This means that in spite of the successive waves of immigrants into both societies over the 19th and early 20th centuries, which introduced new cultural influences and thus greatly diversified the sociocultural landscape; and in spite of the ever-expanding process of modernization occurring in both societies since the latter part of the last century, the dominant religious culture, as an all-embracing symbolic template for human existence, remained the principal framework of orientation for members of the society. This continuous effect of the

167

religious idea is suggested in Ludwig (1996:6), when he says that religion "upholds deep-seated attitudes and motivations," and in this capacity makes available "a complete system of values for human life."

In Brazil, throughout its long colonial period and the Imperial era in the 1800s, the population was made up of the ruling Portuguese and their descendants, many aboriginal groups, and the African slaves. It was not until the mid-1800s that non-Portuguese Europeans began to enter the country in significant numbers, which became even larger in the latter part of the century. This massive influx of Europeans, as Poppino points out (1973:160), "continued during the years preceding World War I ...". However, the exposure to different Amerindian and European civilizations failed to bring a radical alteration to the customs and institutions implanted by the Portuguese. As Holanda (1973:11) states it: "Neither the contact nor mixture with indigenous or migrant populations made us as different from our [Portuguese] forefathers as we would sometimes like to be. In our case, the truth ... is that a long and vivid tradition still links us to the Iberian Peninsula, to Portugal, a tradition as forceful and dynamic as to sustain a common soul, right up to present day" (my translation). In the early part of this century, Bryce made a similar observation which, though marked by the typical stereotypes of the time, still gave vivid testimony of this fact. "The Brazilian," he said, "is still more of a Portuguese than he is of any other type. His ideas and tastes, his ways of life, his alternations of listlessness and activity, his kindly good nature, his susceptibility to emotions and to a rhetoric that can rouse emotion, belong to the country whence he came" (1921:409-10).

A similar pattern applied to the United States during its formative period. One can definitely speak of an "Anglo-Saxon core culture" (Feagin and Feagin, 1993) that remained predominant from the earliest phases of colonization. As one writer put it, even when "the lopsided English numerical advantage was reduced in the heavy immigration of the nineteenth century ... English social privileges were sustained" (Anderson, 1970:3). Throughout the pre-Revolutionary era and the first half of the 19th century, the ruling segment of the population was fundamentally made up of people of English extraction, including Scotch-Irish and Welsh, as well as German, Dutch, and Scandinavian. People with their roots in the British Isles made up as much as 78% of this dominant ethnic amalgam in the late 1700s; additionally, a full "ninety-nine percent of all these groups were Protestant" (Burkey, 1978:153). As Marger (1994:156) informs us: "Except for the Native and slave populations ... the vast majority of Americans in the early nineteenth century were of British and Protestant background. Other groups were mainly northwestern Europeans such as the Germans and Dutch, who were culturally and physically not distant from the numerically dominant British. It was this group, therefore, that set the tone of the society and established its major economic, political, and social institutions." Another author adds that, not only was Protestantism the outstanding religious and cultural force in the land during the colonial period, "but by the middle of the nineteenth century it had established undisputed sway over almost all aspects of the national life" (Hudson, quoted in Anderson, 1970:2). More recent observers (e.g., Siegfried, 1955:91, 101) have noted how fundamentalist Protestant values and tendencies are still emblematic of the very national outlook in the U.S.

Finally, inasmuch as the American South is the region of greatest pertinence here - because it was there in the colonial and antebellum periods that the overwhelming majority of blacks lived, and that patterns of racial/ethnic relations were worked out and consolidated under slavery - it is fitting to stress that the Southern region as a whole reflected even more strongly and uniformly the demographic and cultural dominance of people of English and Scotch-Irish, and Protestant, background. The region had been populated early on by the English (who had dispersed fairly evenly across the states), and a bit later, starting in the early 1700s, by the Scotch-Irish, who poured in great numbers into Virginia, the Carolinas, Kentucky, and Tennessee (Anderson, chs. II and III).

The agricultural slave order of the Old South was the foundation upon which rested every aspect of Southern life, and not just the specific aspect of intergroup relations. Genovese (1967:7-8) categorically states this point: Southern slavery was more than just "a system of extra-economic compulsion designed to sweat a surplus out of black labor." It was such a system, certainly, but it was much more: "It supported a plantation community that must be understood as an integrated social system, and it made this community the center of Southern life." As in other New World societies where slavery existed, the Southern version was also, in its main features and day-to-day operation, significantly affected by the cultural framework of the society. Cultural forces, among which religion played a central role, exercised a powerful shaping effect on race relations that endured well beyond the abolition of slavery and down to present day. Some authors (e.g., Phillips, 1969) have argued that Southern slavery entered a phase of decline starting in the late 1700s, while others (e.g., Fogel and Engerman, 1974) have challenged this viewpoint. The counterargument stresses the continuing vitality and economic profitability of the slavery regime, and its central importance for Southern life, for the entire antebellum period. This institution, according to this view, was immensely stimulated by the development of spinning and weaving machinery in England during that period (which immediately established a relationship of interdependence with the cotton-growing industry in the South), and even more directly by the invention of the cotton gin in the U.S. in the 1790s. For several decades thereafter the Southern slavery economy maintained a pattern of steady growth, up to "the eve of the Civil War" (Fogel and Engerman, 1974:5). The following passage of Franklin's (1969:154) is apposite here: "The Industrial Revolution in England, the invention of the cotton gin, the extension of slavery into the new territories, and the persistence of the slave trade into the nineteenth century all had the effect of establishing slavery in the United States on a more permanent basis than ever before. As the nineteenth century opened, there seemed to be little prospect that slavery would ever cease to exist in the United States."

Similarly, in Brazil the importance of the slavery regime (which lasted some three centuries, ending in 1888) in the overall architecture of the society cannot be overstated. Freyre's main thesis (1956) is that it was around the total social complex represented by the Big House of the plantation that Brazil developed as a nation. As he writes it, "[t]he Big House, completed by the slave shed (*senzala*) represents an entire economic, social, and political system: a system of production (a latifundiary monoculture); a system of labor (slavery); a system of transport (the ox-cart, the *banguê*,[5] the hammock, the horse); a system of religion (a family Catholicism, with the chaplain subordinated to the paterfamilias, with a cult of the dead, etc.); a system of sexual and family life (polygamous patriarchalism); a system of bodily and household hygiene (the *tigre*[6], the banana stalk, the river bath, the tub bath, the sitting-bath, the foot bath); and a system of politics (*compadrismo*[7]). The Big House was thus at one and the same time a fortress, a bank, a cemetery, a hospital, a school, a house of charity giving shelter to the aged, the widow, and the orphan." (1956:xxxiii). In this connection, he continues, "slavery of a patriarchal type ... more than any other institution or social process ... left a mark on Brazilian people" (1963:193). As with the Southern slavery regime as a *total system* and its close association with the dominant evangelical Protestant culture, slavery in Brazil, and the patterns of intergroup relations that developed within it, were directly influenced by the dominant Catholic culture (Tannenbaum, 1946).

Religion and cultural genesis: Universalism vs. particularism

The categories of universalism and particularism have been introduced as conceptual poles that illuminate the dualism of Catholicism and Protestantism. They can be elucidated in reference to Weber's discussion of the ethical foundation of Calvinistic Protestantism vs. that of Catholicism (1958). It must be pointed out at the outset that while universalism and particularism address opposing religious attitudes, they cannot be treated in strictly dichotomous terms, however individual religious experience may be conceptualized, because its institutional development requires that the individual religious experience be manifested in the context of a *social* activity. Nevertheless, a fundamental distinction must be established concerning the appropriate relationship between the individual and the divine. In religious universalism the individual project of salvation is carried out in the context of *community*, in a parallel sense to the Durkheimian conception of religion as a phenomenon that is grounded socially, in the collective mind of society, and not inherently in the isolated minds of individuals. That is, the personal religious experience is not construed in purely atomistic terms, but as developing in the framework of collective religious thought and practice. The latter is the source and legitimation of individual religious expression. In his/her participation in the dominant religious belief system and its corresponding ritual life the individual not only becomes an effective member of the religious (and, more broadly, social) community, but also gains assurance of his/her approach to the divine (Durkheim, 1965). Salvation thus becomes a goal that is attainable in the individual's attachment to a creed that expresses the basic beliefs of the larger community.

Universalism, therefore, suggests a connection with what Weber (1978:557) termed "salvation from outside," the conception of salvation as something attainable through institutional grace, that is, through the dispensation of grace by an institutional or organizational structure. The contrary nature of this position vis-a-vis the individualism of particularist religion is evident in the fact that here the individual's own labors are deemed "completely inadequate for the purpose of salvation," and salvation is available to the individual only by recourse to an organization (*ecclesia*), which distributes grace continuously via sacramental devices. In contrast, the individual's own labors are the *conditio sine qua non* of salvation in the particularist position.

The immediate implication from this model of dispensation of grace is that the *status gratiae* - which means, the plenitude of holiness that is gained by full membership in the religious community-becomes in principle available to all human beings, and not just to the religious *virtuosi* (i.e., the elect). This shows the prevalence of structural flexibility and relativism towards the "difference" of outsiders,[8] as well of the idea of the potential universal inclusion of all individuals, regardless of their circumstances or background. Through the ritual and sacramental structure of the Church these individuals can be incorporated, equalized, made interchangeable with everyone else within the mainstream community.

The particularist attitude, in contradistinction, reduces the process of salvation to a "wholly individual affair" (Weber, 1958:107). It does not depend on the association of the believer with the community - that is, with the world of experience - but must be pursued in a strictly personal and interiorized, as opposed to Catholicism, which pursues it in a public and exteriorized fashion. This notion is closely related to and supported by the foundational principle of predestination, operative at the formal level in all Calvinist Protestantism, and at the level of a general "ethic" in ascetic Protestantism as a whole. The collectivism inherent in universalist religion is not believed to insure personal salvation. In fact, we are informed (Weber, 1958:106) that there is explicit admonition, as in the English Puritan literature, "against any trust in the aid of the friendship of men." For the Calvinist, salvation is to be obtained only through direct intercourse with the deity, "carried on in deep spiritual isolation" (1958:107). Hence, no manner of mediation by external sources and mechanisms (e.g., the sacraments) between the individual and God is admissible. This attitude of distrust towards and separation from the world expresses the religious category of "world-rejecting asceticism" to which, according to Weber, belong all ascetic, bibliographic branches of Protestantism.

It seems fitting now to examine in greater detail the manner in which the universalist and particularist positions differentially determine the ways and means of obtaining salvation, to understand more fully how these aspects have a practical effect on the domain of social relations. The Weberian explanation of this aspect stresses that the quest for salvation, whatever form it takes in religious cultures, is of central importance insofar as it produces "certain consequences for practical behavior in the world. It is most likely to acquire such a positive orientation to mundane affairs as the result of a conduct of life which is distinctively determined by religion and given coherence by some central meaning or positive goal" (Weber, 1978:528).

In Catholicism there is a sacramentally-mediated process involved - "a cycle of sin, repentance, atonement, release, followed by renewed sin" (Weber, 1958:117) - through which the state of grace or spiritual plenitude is always within the reach of the believers. This cyclical process is grounded in the pragmatic acknowledgment of universal human fallibility, which means that all of humanity shares in the circumstance of imperfection. This being the case, this conceptualization is contrary to the dualistic viewpoint of ascetic Protestantism (discussed below). It portrays

172

human imperfection as being attended with the possibility of transformation into perfection, by recourse to the sacraments (specifically, the sacrament of absolution). "The important symbolism of the sacraments," explains Ludwig (1996:432), "is that God's power and presence are connected with ordinary activities, like working, eating, and drinking, and so forth. In participating in the sacrament people dedicate their total being to God and *receive divine forgiveness* [emphasis added] and power, sanctifying all of life." This entails a process of purification, a washing away of past imperfection. The analogy to be applied here is with reference to how a background in a non-Christian culture (which, by definition, would constitute imperfection) would be "washed away," and the individual(s) involved would be purified or sanctified, and thus made eligible for induction into the body of the saved, that is to say, into the Catholic fold, and by implication, into the larger Catholic cultural milieu. From this point of view, it should be apparent how the condition of unworthiness - or marginalization - is always deemed a provisional one, and the marginalized individual is, in reference to this, able to exercise greater control over it because he/she can appeal to the power of Providence to change it through the sacraments, and in this way restore his/her full membership in the community of the elect. The starting point is the original condition of sin (i.e., human imperfection), which affects us all. This is followed by repentance and atonement. The individual acknowledges this imperfection and seeks to transcend it by making amends, by undergoing a process of expiation. After that, he/she is released from the state of imperfection, and elevated to that of perfection- that is to say, to the state of grace, which then provides the certainty of salvation (*certitudo salutis*). However, the intrinsic frailty of human spirit throws the individual back into a sinful condition, and the process of purification starts over.

The universalist position, therefore, is not essentially anchored to a conception of salvation as a state contingent on the "rationalization of the world," involving the rational systematization of the ethical conduct of individuals. Furthermore, it is not achieved through the privatization of the religious experience, but rather, through its public and collective expression in a structure of ritual, administered by functionaries that act as mystagogues (i.e., experts in the administration of the sacraments, or "magical actions that contain the boons of salvation," Weber, 1978:447). While good works are still important, they are manifested as a string of rather loosely connected acts, not as "a life of good works combined into a unified system." Thus, the strict regimentation and rationalization of religious life and, more generally, of the larger sphere of practical life, is not an absolute requirement.

This aspect of regeneration of the spiritual condition of the believers implies the operation of an underlying "ethic" - a set of categories of understanding, a general worldview, that bears directly on social organization and has a regulative effect on the domain of social relations, by emphasizing the principle of universal *inclusion*. To begin with, the assumption of universal human fallibility, coupled with the possibility of transformation through structures of ritual, produces an attitude of pragmatic accommodation to, and harmonization of, human diversity. The dominant cultural group will tend to exercise relativism and malleability towards minority segments, insofar as these are perceived as potentially capable of being "released" or liberated from their state of imperfection, which in this case pertains to their *minority* condition (racial, ethnic, etc.), and elevated towards spiritual plenitude, which translates into full incorporation into the society. This then gives the newly-incorporated elements the certainty of salvation, or the assurance of effective membership in the mainstream community, establishing their identity as full-fledged members of the latter. No one is forever marked by sin - which amounts to saying that no individual or group is perpetually hindered by the minority circumstance, but, on the contrary, is always able to experience the *status gratiae* through sacramental or "magical" means, which corresponds to the ability to undergo full-range social inclusion through assimilative mechanisms such as socialization, cultural syncretism syncretism, and intermarriage.[9]

In Protestantism as a whole, the principal tenet is that salvation must be predicated on the personal, socially-unmediated relationship of the believer with God. Moreover, as pointed out earlier, the attainment of the state of grace is not something that can occur through instrumental or technical means, that is to say, through a set of objective and external procedures, like sacramental devices, or maintained through "the gradual accumulation of individual good works" (Weber, 1958:115). Rather, it is a more complex enterprise, fraught with uncertainty and indeterminacy, and requiring that the individual, above all, have a thoroughly rationalized existence built upon good works so as to form a unified system, from which he/she will draw assurance of being one of the chosen, and not one of the damned. There seems to be an element of totalization undergirding this religious conception, establishing human life in absolutist terms as a perfectly cohesive, self-contained whole, which is either good in the measure required for salvation, or it is not. There are no in-between states. The condition of eligibility for salvation is not measured on a continuum, that is, in terms of varying degrees of eligibility. And, the line that separates eligibility from non-eligibility is inflexibly set. These premises stem from the doctrine of predestination, reflecting the impact

174

of Calvinist dogma on ascetic Protestantism. The religious believer, not being able to rely, as in Catholicism, on "a succession of individual acts" - isolated good works - which are further reinforced by the purifying effect of the sacraments, is left with the only option of maintaining complete systematicity and consistency in personal conduct, causing the latter to become "dominated entirely by the aim to add to the glory of God on earth" (Weber, 1958:118). This produces a self-fulfilling effect: the more powerfully the individual struggles to construct this life of righteousness, the more deeply he/she is convinced of the righteous nature of his/her actions, and the more uncompromising he/she becomes in the definition of the "good" and the "bad," and in keeping these two realms rigidly polarized. The unrelenting tenacity with which the faithful attempt to maintain this intensely-rationalized "system of life," aiming to "increase the glory of God," produces an ethical outlook through which things and individuals are seen and judged in strictly dichotomous terms. The human condition is deemed unchanging: one is either a member of the elect, or of the non-elect - as opposed to having the ability to change one's status through ritual manipulation. Human existence is differentiated into two basic forms, one which adds to the glory of God, and one which does not. There is no possibility of integration, reconciliation, overlapping of these categories. The blurring and crossing of the boundary lines, and the fusion of dissimilar categories, is deemed abhorrent, a most serious violation of moral law.

These ideas are reiterated in Hays and Steely's discussion of the Calvinist orientation of the early English (Particular) Baptists, an orientation brought to the U.S. by the Puritan settlers of the early 1600s, and continuing in the religious outlook of their descendants over the next couple of centuries:

> It was fundamental to their theological system that Christ had died only for the sake of the elect (hence, his atoning work was *particular* rather than *general*). God's predestinating grace is extended only to those who are chosen by his immutable will. That will is not thwarted, *no matter what efforts man may employ or what resistance he may exert to the contrary* [emphasis added]. Missionary work when addressed to the elect is unecessary; when directed to the nonelect, unavailing. It is from this perspective that William Carey [distinguished 18th century English Baptist pastor] was answered when he arose to ask, "Is nothing then to be done?" The answer, if brusque, was theologically consistent: "Sit down, young man. When God gets ready to convert the heathen, He will do it without your help or mine" (1963:142).

All of these tendencies, as indicated earlier, are grounded in world-rejecting asceticism, and their main practical consequence in the realm of social relations is the preponderance of a general principle of exclusion. Individuals whose personal lives are perceived as reflecting the condition of non-eligibility, as not "proving religious merit" or giving "active certification" of these individuals' own state of grace (Weber, 1978:543-44), are viewed as unassimilable into the community of the elect. Regeneration is not something that can be accomplished "through good works" (Siegfried, 1955:82); rather, it is something that is fundamentally unavailable, at least in its full measure, for those who have had the misfortune of being cast by Providence among the non-elect. The concrete social implications of this are clear: the community of the elect is the structural analogue of the dominant cultural community, the complete incorporation or membership into which remains unattainable for specific segments of the population. These segments are, metaphorically speaking, forever marked by sin, that is to say, they cannot transcend their imperfection as (what is *de facto* treated as) inferior difference, and be elevated toward the status of full-fledged membership in the mainstream society. Put differently, the non-whiteness of the minority ethnic-racial segments cannot ever be fully *regenerated* into the whiteness of the hegemonic group. Instead, it remains locked in rigidly demarcated social compartments, perpetually trapped in the hard-and-fast dualisms imposed on social life: good vs. evil, rich vs. poor, white vs. black, man vs. woman, etc. Furthermore, the violation of these boundaries is, in every instance, attended with social recrimination and negative sanctions, just as it is in the religious sphere. This means that the stigma of "sinfulness" (i.e., social illegality) is brought to bear on the process and those involved in it. The fervor with which this tendency of social differentiation and separation is pursued in ascetic Protestantism is dramatized in Weber's statement (1958:122) to the effect that the Calvinist's "consciousness of divine grace of the elect and holy was accompanied by an attitude toward the sin of one's neighbor, not of sympathetic understanding based on the consciousness of one's own weakness, but of hatred and contempt for him as an enemy of God bearing the signs of eternal damnation." This idea is illustrated in the account by Bailey (1964:6) of the strong reaction of the Southern Methodist bishops in the late 1800s against the racial integration of their congregations. In the *Journal* for the 1886 General Conference of the Methodist Episcopal Church, the bishops deplored all the "sentimental extravagance in the direction of the discolored current of social equality, through the agency of the schoolroom, the congregation, or the Conference; for there is no conceivable result that would compensate for the *crime against nature* that this theory deliberately contemplates" (emphasis added). Bailey also cites another statement from the 1891 Proceedings of the Mississipi State Baptist Convention, where this segregationist position is expressed just as strongly: "We must insist that they [the black population] are distinct, for their good and ours. To do otherwise is to inflict an evil on them and to raise an insurmountable barrier to success."

Religion and cultural physiognomy: "Roundedness" vs. "angularity"

Religious universalism, as expressed in the tendencies of inclusiveness and accomodation, was a central feature of the Luso-Brazilian Catholicism throughout the colonial era in Brazil and beyond it, a religion which, as already noted, exhibited much flexibility and a penchant for cross-fertilization with other religious traditions.[10]

The cultural system of the society reflected these tendencies of plasticity and adaptation, as evidenced in its multifarious processes of syncretism in areas such as religion, music, language, art, cookery, and so forth. To this must be added the concomitant fusion of the various groups at the biological level, and the fundamental integration of the population around the national identity, which further strengthened the process of societal consolidation.

This model of culture may be said to have been characterized by what has been construed as cultural "roundedness" (Freyre, 1945:420-23). This concept should suggest a number of interrelated tendencies, such as a disposition towards association and compromise, a fluidity of form, an intolerance of rigid boundaries and compartmentalizations, the absence of "jagged edges" opposing cultural difference, a general receptivity to fusion with this difference. The derivation of these tendencies from religious universalism may be examined, first of all, in relation to the universalist stance on salvation. As we have seen, in this viewpoint salvation cannot be obtained apart from membership in the community of the faithful, that is, in an institutional structure that is "vested with the control of grace" (Weber, 1978:560). Salvation, or to state it in a homological sense, full social membership, depends primarily on the collective association of individuals, as they partake in a common system of beliefs and practices. This is deemed to be within the reach of everyone, since humanity is not, as in Christian Calvinist asceticism, divided *a priori* into the saved and the damned. The emphasis here is more pragmatic, linked to the recognition that we all share in the circumstance of imperfection. However, this recognition is not followed by the assumption that there is a need - or even a possibility - of strict rationalization of personal life,

177

so as to make it wholly and uncompromisingly virtuous towards the glory of God on earth. There is no requirement of perfect consistency in the human condition. Individuals can be released from their unworthiness through membership in the *ecclesia* made possible by its sacramental structure. Again, in a parallel sense, the implication is that social rituals and processes are perceived as all that is required for transforming individuals and structures in order to make them eligible for incorporation into the mainstream social order.

This cultural orientation is generally absent in sociocultural systems influenced by particularist ascetic religion, in connection with which ascetic Protestantism of the Calvinist type has been introduced here as the archetype. What one finds instead is its conceptual opposite, namely, something that might be called a cultural "angularity," which fundamentally expresses the Puritan emphasis on the rationalization of life (Weber, 1958:117-118; 1978:534-541) and the organization of the entire pattern of experience into discrete (and often antagonistic) categories, as well as a deep aversion for "sensuous culture of all kinds" (Weber, 1958:105). The pertinent religious principles here are predestination and its related aspect of the absolute transcendentality of God. Predestination establishes that salvation is not accessible to everyone, but only to the *electi*. The idea of the absolute transcendentality of the deity suggests the absolute differentiation and separation of the divine condition from the human condition, which compels the religious believer to deposit his/her energy and trust exclusively in God, while at the same time shunning association with, and exercising distrust toward, the human community. This is the "pessimistically inclined individualism" that Weber comments on, and which is the basis of particularism in all ascetic Protestantism. It shapes the "national character and institutions of peoples with a Puritan past," giving rise to a widespread suspicion of and distaste for an array of interrelated aspects, such as the elimination of categorial boundaries, the integration of social and cultural diversity, collectivist or "tribalist" tendencies in religious worship, aspects of sensuousness and/or sexuality, emotional expressiveness.

One may find numerous instantiations of these ideas in the social life of the societies under analysis. I shall examine three manifestations of culture in this regard, and explore their hermeneutical and phenomenological aspects. The first is the famous American painting *American Gothic*, by Grant Wood. It dramatically encompasses all the qualities I have identified here as being indicative of cultural angularity. The rural couple depicted are unmistakably Puritan archetypes. Their stern countenances suggest the Puritan reservedness and individualistic framework of existence; the sense of confidence and self-righteousness; the utter rigidity of viewpoint; the lack of "openness" or receptivity towards the things of the world, of the flesh - towards all mundane pleasures and activities. The pitchfork held by the man may be said to symbolize what the primary focus of one's existence must be from the standpoint of the Puritan, namely, the relentless pursuit of sanctification and assurance of salvation through a life of purposeful and unremitting toil (the work ethic). This existential stance admits of no deviation from ethical principle, no crossing of categorical boundaries. People and things are thrust into dichotomous categories, where they are treated as fundamentally and unalterably good or bad, sinful or holy, and no intermediary states are admissible that might "smooth out" the rough edges of socially unmediated ethical judgement. There is, additionally, a suggestion that the bodily movements - the actual physical movements - of the Puritan (and, by implication, of Puritan society) will be "angular," that is, harsh, stiff, decisive, goal-oriented, mechanical-like, forged out of a life of strict discipline and rationalization into a particular mode of being. These movements are highly suitable for work and other instrumental activities, which are integral part of the economic, or work-related, project of personal salvation. They are unsuited, however, for the pursuit of artistic or aesthetic pleasures, as, for instance, dancing, or affecting an expression of unrestrained sensuous enjoyment of some aspect of reality, such as a sound, a smell, a taste. The latter situation requires movements of greater malleability and adaptability - greater "roundedness," as we might put it - lyrical or Dyonisian movements, as Freyre has described them (1945:422-23), "inimical to Apollinean formalism and friendly to variations ...," movements which indicate less systematicity and more spontaneity of conduct, less fixity and more flexibility.

Another cultural phenomenon that may be examined here is the "mulatto" category in Brazilian society. I will address its broader conceptual or symbolic implications, rather that the more purely ethnic and racial dimension, since the latter has already been covered. The mulatto and "mulatto-ism" - to force a translation of a term that is more viable in Portuguese (*mulatismo*) - are archetypal categories, thus embodying what is generally thought to be most characteristically Brazilian. As such, their use here is appropriate because of the factor of representativeness, and also in terms of facilitating an effective contrast with the preceding example of *American Gothic*. The mulatto and mulatto-ism convey the idea of cultural roundedness on two interrelated levels: the material level of biological amalgamation, built upon the harmonization and integration of diverse ethnic strains, culminating in a new type; and the nonmaterial level, in which mulatto-ism functions as a basic trait of the national psyche. In the latter capacity, it expresses such tendencies as accommodation to and coexistence of diverse influences, the overlapping of social categories, the equilibrium of antagonisms. In a discussion of the Brazilian style of soccer playing, Freyre (1945:420-423) comments on how the British-born sport underwent in the Brazilian context what may be termed a process of "tropicalization," in the direction of greater emphasis on its aesthetic, rather than instrumental, possibilities. Hence, its dance-like quality, its artistic embellishments, its cunning, its sly and deceiving maneuvers, its penchant for spontaneity and improvisation, its element of surprise--traits which are thought to represent the mulatto basis of Brazilian society.[11] Freyre's comments to the effect that this is a "mulatto" football underscores its expression of a larger process of cultural syncretization, the expression of the outstanding aspect of the national character. "From a psychological standpoint," he adds, "to be Brazilian is to be mulatto." The reference here is precisely to this larger dimension, that is, not to something strictly or exclusively linked to the concrete operations of miscegenation - though it certainly includes that - but more importantly, to the very foundation of the society. Thus, the reference is to the aversion for "excessive internal or external regimentations; to excessive uniformization, geometrization, standardization; to totalitarianisms that lead to the disappearance of individual variation or personal spontaneity" (1945:423).

These considerations are also related to the other dimension of the mulatto-qua-cultural category, namely, the symbolization of the sensuous. This point is consistently underscored in the literature and the arts (e.g., popular music) of Brazil. One of the major characters in Aluizio de Azevedo's celebrated 19th-century naturalist novel *O Cortiço* (*The Tenement*, 1890) is Rita Baiana, a very attractive and sexually alluring woman, who becomes involved with Jeronimo, the recently arrived Portuguese immigrant. Their union may be interpreted as a metaphor for the fusion of European civilization with the native cultural materials of the New World; the integration of what Azevedo saw as European restraint, order, thrift, with the abandon, exuberance, and love of excess of the tropics. This narrative portrays in exuberant and often hyperbolic language the character of Rita Baiana, with all the attendant qualities which have traditionally been assigned to the mulatto type in Brazil, particularly that of sensuality. One of the more restrained passages in the text reads as follows: "The exiled, after the first exchange of glances with the woman from Bahia ... saw in her the sum of all the torrid mysteries that ensnared him voluptuously in this land of concupiscence." Like other works by Azevedo, *The Tenement* upholds the idea of miscegenation and, as Wagley (1971:255) points out, "reflects an attitude that the climate, both physical and moral, of Brazil leads to sensuality." The association of the mulatto basis of Brazilian culture with the expression of sensuality is (as already mentioned) of long standing and widely evidenced in vehicles of popular culture, such as, for instance, songs. But, this is no less relevant connotatively than it is denotatively. That is, the implication of sensuality need not be taken in its strictly literal meaning, but in terms of what has been discussed here as "roundedness," or a cultural inclination that privileges syncretizations and continuity, rather than ruptures, when it comes to the relation between diverse social categories. In this cultural mode, social relations exhibit flexibility and undifferentiation, as opposed to rigidity and separatism. It is in this broader symbolic sense that this aspect is considered here.

Finally, the third illustrative "item" to be examined is an interesting photo taken by the famous photographer E.L. Singley, showing four little boys standing together at the edge of the water, on a beach in Puerto Rico in 1900 (in Stark, 1992:68). The boys are all facing away from the camera.   They did not pose for the picture, but were apparently photographed without being aware of it. They seem to be 6-7 years of age. Conventional racial classifications would have one of them as white, the other three as black. And they are all in the nude. The photo conveys a sense of normality, suggesting a situation that would have been perfectly acceptable in the Puerto Rican society of the turn of the century. The naturalness with which the boys are standing together, looking at the water, supports this idea. They seem to be perfectly at ease with their nudity. It is not apparent that they thought they were engaging in a behavior that was outside mainstream norms and expectations.   The incorporation of public nudity - at least, involving very young males - into the realm of normal behavior points to the absence of laws and social taboos against this behavior(or to the lack of enforcement of such laws, should they have been in effect). The larger society apparently erected no barriers and antagonisms separating public morality from the element of sensuousness, the expression of spirituality (i.e., social morality as quasi-religious morality, in the Durkheimian sense) from the expression of physicality, reason from nature - dualisms which, in contradistinction, deeply mark the constitution of societies guided by the ascetic, particularistic religious principle. The absence of hard-and-fast boundary lines between these two spheres - the spiritual and the sensuous - establishes the possibility of considerable exchange between them, and reveals the operation of cultural roundedness, insofar as "sacred" and "profane" cultural elements, instead of clashing violently against one another, coexist in a pattern of overlap and exchange. The other major aspect here is the fact that we are dealing with different "racial" categories.   Again, the air of naturalness and spontaneity that comes through seems to suggest the absence of formal and informal societal divisions along racial lines - at least regarding social intercourse. The same considerations can be made here with respect to cultural roundedness, in that the apparent absence of racial/ethnic separatisms may have been the expression of the larger, societal trend of cultural plasticity and integration, which would have promoted the wide-ranging interplay between members of diverse ethnic and racial communities.

A note on Calvinism in the United States

In this analysis, the Calvinist system of ideas and values is examined from the perspective of having played a key role in the operation of virtually all forms of ascetic Protestantism, such as those identified by Weber, including "the sects growing out of the Baptist movement" (1958:95). Weber speaks of the "Calvinist asceticism which [during the first two centuries of development of the Reformation] surrounded the Baptist sects in England and the Netherlands (1958:142). This influence appears to have permeated the broadest reaches of Protestantism, being felt even in Methodism, normally seen historically as the classic opponent of Calvinism. The antagonism between these two religious philosophies was clearly evident in 19th-century U.S. society, in the relationship between the Methodist Church and those that were more directly anchored to the Calvinist ethic (Sweet, 1952).

It is true that Calvinism is considered to be the formal doctrinal basis of the Presbyterian and Reformed churches, and also that much theological divisiveness prevailed among the Protestant churches in the United States (in the last century, for example) over central tenets of the Calvinist philosophy. Yet, as Bailey points out, these interdenominational disputes, which at times took on the character of a "fierce sectarian debate," may mislead observers into assuming the existence of insurmountable theological differences, and into overlooking the fact that the latter "often obscured a consensus on fundamentals" (1964:2-3). Doctrinally as well as in the suprareligious sense, the effect of Calvinism was deeper and more widespread than is normally realized, beginning with the arrival of Christianity on American soil, in the 1600s. Williams (1987:32) informs us that "[t]he English Reformation that eventually washed over the Atlantic and onto the shores of New England [was largely animated by] the arguments of Calvins's *Institutes*," and the ideas governing the religious life of people in the 17th-century New England colonies "were substantially restatements of positions already defined in Geneva." In the subsequent period of colonization, up to the end of the eighteenth century and the time of The Great Awakening, the Protestant churches that enjoyed the largest membership and exercised the most widespread influence throughout the colonies were the Congregationalists and Presbyterians, groups formally grounded in the Calvinist doctrine (Sweet, 1952:3). In broader perspective, therefore, for the first two centuries of English colonization the impact of Calvinism apparently remained considerable across the wider context of evangelical Protestantism, "throughout the colonies of British North America" (Williams, 1987:111).

In the nineteenth century, U.S. Protestantism underwent a major change, one which is generally acknowledged by historians of religion in U.S. society, consisting of a gradual departure from the ascetic, pessimistic outlook of Puritan Calvinism, with its belief in and emphasis on the idea of original sin and divine election, to the more positive idea of "acceptance of the good things of this world," and the faith in the natural goodness and perfectibility of the individual. Human beings were still thought to be born with the mark of sin, but were now thought to be endowed with the potential to overcome this condition, to become regenerated from the original deficiency and to become "essentially good" (Siegfried, 1955:84). Yet, despite this fundamental shift in religious orientation, Calvinism continued to exercise a considerable influence in social life in the country, both in terms of its doctrinal connections with evangelical Protestant groups, and of the more fundamental level of penetration of daily affairs and the worldview of the people. This was particularly true for the Southern region in the antebellum period. First, even when the focus is directed to the formal doctrinal correspondences between Calvinism and other strains of the Protestant faith, we are told (Jordan, 1981:94) that virtually all of the religious sects of the region "shared in common a low-church English Protestantism strongly tinged by Calvinism; many of the qualities of mind and temperament which are usually described as Puritan were shared by Anglicans and Baptists and Quakers as well. The similarities among the Protestant sects were fully as important as the differences." That this was so becomes especially pertinent with respect to the Methodist and the Baptist churches, which were predominant in the antebellum South. The Baptist doctrine is said to have come into being as an offshoot of English Congregationalism in the early 17th century (Hudson, 1982:209, vol. III). Yet, it soon split into separate factions, the General Baptists and the Particular Baptists, which followed a moderate (Arminian), and a more orthodox version of Calvinism, respectively. It has been asserted that the history of the Baptist church "has been characterized by an emphasis that has varied from a strong to a moderate Calvinism" (Hudson, 1982:210). These Calvinist tendencies lingered well into the 1800s, and were certainly manifest in the

Protestantism of the so-called frontier churches, in the operation of such staunchly Calvinist groups as the Primitive ("Hard Shell") Baptists (Hays and Steely, 1963:117; Hudson, 1982:212). During the 18th and 19th centuries the Particular Baptists prevailed over all other Baptist branches, both in size and in influence, as a result of which both in England and in the United States the dominant Baptist theology was "strongly Calvinistic" (Hays and Steely, 1973:160). Genovese (1976:243) adds, in the same vein: "The Baptist Church in the South ran the gamut from Calvinism to Arminianism, but the powerful tendency...took extreme predestinarian ground."

In any event, the overall impact of Calvinist Christianity on American culture is the pivotally important aspect to be considered, ranging from the explicit adherence of individuals to formal Calvinist principles, to (and more importantly) their reliance on an underlying set of presuppositions and values that guided them in making judgements and constructing their conceptions of individual and collective life, the nature of salvation, their proper relationship to the world, and how they ought to conduct their social, interpersonal, and intergroup affairs. This is, indeed, the issue to throw into relief here, namely, that of the operation of religion as an implicit source of normative and value guidance. It appears to have been especially in this capacity, as some have argued (see, e.g., Williams, 1987), that Calvinist thought retained its ideological predominance in U.S. social life, even if explicitly non-Calvinist religious ideas, couched in evangelical Arminianism, gradually asserted themselves over the old Calvinist beliefs as the 19th century rolled on. As Williams points out (on the basis of textual analysis of representative works of 19th-century American literature, such as those of Dickinson, Melville, and Hawthorne), non-Calvinist ideas amounted essentially to superimpositions on the "old assumptions." The new creeds "were on men's lips, but the ancient beliefs remained buried in their hearts." The tension-filled, apocalyptic, mystical imagery of Calvinism, with its binary oppositions deriving from the conceptual poles of salvation and damnation, seems to have endured as an ideological substratum and motivational force in the American collective consciousness, notwithstanding the cultural shifts in the last century towards religious ideologies that stressed a more optimistic faith in the human potential (1987:180).

From this viewpoint, it may be asserted that U.S. culture imparts to all its members ideological tendencies and conceptions whose origins may be ultimately traced to Calvinistically-oriented Protestantism. These ways of thinking, understanding, and judging are likely to prevail in the consciousness of the individual whether or not he/she is formally affiliated with a Calvinist variety of Protestantism, or even *whether or not he/she is a Protestant* at all. Siegfried (1955:101) lays stress on this fact, asserting that "[e]ven Catholics share this outlook," and that Americans in general are "essentially Protestant and Calvinist" (1955:83). A case of *cultural* Calvinism, therefore, rather than (formally) doctrinal Calvinism.

The dominant religion and the problem of difference

Having indicated how various key institutional and cultural structures reflect the operation of deep-lying assumptions and values, most strikingly those embodied in the dominant religious ideology, we can now direct our attention to the manner in which the essential ideas of Catholicism and Protestantism in the two societies under study, respectively, shaped the basic response of the dominant ethnic group towards the presence of *difference*. This difference is treated here as *ethnic-racial* difference, as manifested in pluralist settings. In multiethnic societies, the first stage of contact between the dominant ethnic group and minority ones is marked by the *perception* of the latter by the former as "difference," a perception normally geared to both the cultural and physical traits of the minority group, that is, to both its customs and physical appearance. The second stage of this process is even more crucial because it involves the dominant group's *reaction* to the presence of difference. Thus, it is at this stage that patterns of intergroup relations begin to develop and crystallize.

It is contended here that this attitude toward difference is, at the most fundamental level, a product of the type of approach to the problem of salvation that animates the dominant religious culture: its conception of the state of grace, the nature of its relationship to the world, its corresponding prescriptions for the conduct of life. It is the product, therefore, of a broader philosophical framework, to the extent that the dominant religion functions as the backbone of the society's cultural system. One may appeal, in connection with this, to Azevedo's claim (1950:139) that the central part of cultural life evolves essentially out of "religious aims, forms, and essentials." We have seen how Protestantism in the United States, because of its intimate association with the Calvinist ethic since the beginnings of English colonization in the country, addressed the problem of salvation largely in connection with the belief in predestination. This in turn made it essential that there be "maintenance of ethical integrity in the affairs of everyday life," as well as the rejection of "all magical, sacramental, and institutional distributions of grace" (Weber, 1978:574). Therefore, even if the specific Calvinist idea of election or predestination was not formally a part of the doctrinal system of all ascetic Protestant churches, the underlying premises and values of Calvinism exerted an enormous organizing and regulative influence on the broader complex of behavior and attitudes of the people.

We may now explore in greater detail the manifestation of the idea of election in the realm of social relations, and then contrast its exclusionary and separatist effects in the Protestant context with the more inclusionary and accomodating effects produced by the Catholic approach to salvation, as exemplified by the Luso-Brazilian context. The belief in election yields in individuals an indomitable feeling of certainty in their eligibility for salvation and in the absolute finality of their fate, as established by divine decree. The logical corollary of this belief is the irreversibility of the structure of the human condition. If a theological determinism becomes the basis of the condition of election, it functions likewise for opposite condition, that is, for non-election, and therefore neither the elect nor the non-elect can hope to alter their respective circumstances by external means. From a strictly religious standpoint, the condition of non-election or damnation applies to those who will not be saved from eternal suffering. In the context of life in society, its meaning extends beyond religious disenfranchisement to encompass disenfranchisement on the different levels of social existence. Based on this premise, the present analysis treats this spiritual duality as a structural counterpart of the social marginalization of all those who exist as "difference". In pluralist settings this difference is expressed as cultural difference - religious, political, economic, aesthetic, and so on - but in U.S. society these modalities of minority-group difference become secondary to the all-important *racial* difference.

The irrevocability (*character indelebilis*) of human differentiation conveyed by the doctrine of predestination is presumed to find its symbolic representation in the scriptural texts, such as for instance in the reference to the early determinations by God regarding the destiny of human groups, as indicated in the different fates assigned to the sons of Noah - Shem, Ham, and Japheth. The African ethnic groups that had been enslaved in the Old South were thought to be descendants of Ham and, as such, forever marked with disaffection from God, estrangement from holiness, identification with non-election. White preachers, we are told, boldly asserted that "blacks suffered from the sin of Ham ..." (Genovese, 1976:246), for which perennial submission and forced service to the whites, who were thought to descend from Japheth, was a matter of moral necessity. This was the means established by Divine Providence through which the biblical curse on Ham would be fulfilled, and the forces of sin would be kept under control. The equation of this condition of human imperfection with sinfulness is, in fact, frequently found in the scriptural arguments for slavery, both implicitly and explicitly. The Reverend

Thornton Stringfellow, for example, contended that the descendants of Ham would have "sunk down to eternal ruin," had it not been for their being rescued from this perpetual state of spiritual, moral, and civil degeneration by the regenerating experience of slavery (in Faust, 1981:166).

This regeneration, it must be understood, never really reaches the point where the former condition of imperfection is fully erased, and the rehabilitated element is thus elevated to the level of parity with everyone else. Antebellum Southern society acted in concert with this religious idea, by fiercely opposing any proposal or effort geared toward the extinction of human group differences. Attempts on the part of institutions to interfere, legally or otherwise, with the established order of things were deemed futile at best, and at worst, highly detrimental to the social body. The proslavery statement on this issue by Thomas Dew is typical: "The deep and solid foundations of society cannot be broken by the vain fiat of the legislator" (cited in McKittrick, 1963:32).

The fissions among the Protestant churches over the issue of predestination did not keep this doctrinal tenet from exercising a broader ideological and social impact, as already explained. In the words of Weber, it "penetrated all social relations with its sharp brutality." I have already referred to Weber's contention that the Calvinist attitude towards the condition of non-election was not simply one of indifference and withdrawal, but of active contempt and hostility. Essentially, the resoluteness with which the socially "elect" separated themselves from the "nonelect" in U.S. society, reproduced in the sphere of practical activity the pattern of religious separation between the divinely elect and nonelect. In the Old South the difference - the physical and cultural (but principally the physical) difference - of the population of African descent may be said to have symbolized for the dominant group the circumstance of non-election. Therefore, no matter how much members of this (or other) racial minority(ies) were elevated through social training, economic and political advancement, or intermarriage with members of the dominant ethnic group, they could never hope to enter the membership of the elect, which means in the social sense, to abolish their servile status altogether, their mark of intrinsic inferiority, and become fully integrated socially. Their fate as difference, and moreover, as inferior and unassimilable difference, was seen to be perpetually sealed by injunctions originating in Divine Providence. In the final analysis, what this phenomenon points to is the societal impulse towards permanent differentiation and exclusion of specific segments of the population on the basis of race, and suggests the degree in which religious ideas animated this impulse by erecting a permanent symbolic barrier to the full social inclusion of ethnic-racial minorities.

The Catholic context, in contrast, upheld a conception of ritualistic salvation, attained through the mediation of "the confessional, the dispensation of grace by a human being, [and] magico-sacramental grace" (Weber, 1978:562). This ritualistic salvation, whereby the inner grace, or sanctification, of the individual, is produced by the external forms of worshipping the deity, becomes accessible to all initiates. That is, everyone is a potential recipient of salvation through the sacraments - and insofar as spiritual salvation is being treated here as a parallel process to social induction - a potential recipient of social membership. This conception of salvation gave rise to an universalistic orientation predicated on the idea of community, the totality of individuals, and non-differentiation and interchangeability in the application of normative principle. This naturally resulted in a very different treatment of the aspect of difference, starting with the arrival of the foreigner on Brazilian soil. "During the entire colonial period," says Azevedo (1944:142), "what barred the immigrant from entering our ports [entailing, fundamentally, that which barred this immigrant from becoming a full member of the society] was [not racial status, but religious] heterodoxy." This process basically expressed the ability of the dominant religious community to convert the variegated cultural and ethnic presence in the wider society into an integrated and cohesive whole, under the all-embracing aegis of Catholic belief and practice. Thus, in the interethnic sphere the difference of minority groups-- cultural, ethnic, racial - was deemed, in principle, transformable and assimilable into the social mainstream through sacramental induction. In this way, the cultural ritual overrode all other criteria influencing the assimilation process, particularly at the initial stages of contact between the majority and minority groups. The overall liturgical framework of the Catholic Church stood as a formal system by means of which minority-group assimilation was mediated and greatly stimulated. The newcomers were initiated into the community of the faithful through the ceremony of baptism, and, over their life cycle went through a number of sacramental *rites of passage*, such as confirmation, confession, communion, and the last anointing. Their participation in these rituals gives evidence of their full-scale membership not only in the Church, but also in Brazilian social life. The sacramental aspect of Catholicism, therefore, had immense integrative and normative importance for the population as a whole. Prior to their transformation through sacramental induction, the foreigners were clearly the outsiders, a different variety of humanity in a sense. Following this experience, they moved out of the category of *otherness*, and joined that of *sameness*, the one to which belonged those who formed the ranks of the majority social community. At the very least, the sacraments established the *conditions of possibility* for full their social membership. The Church's sanctioning of unrestricted universal administration of the sacraments translated into the universal incorporation of the newcomers. In mediating the admission of the various ethnic and racial streams to the various institutional processes and structures, and facilitating their adjustment to their new status, the dominant religion was the symbolic as well as concrete "opening of the doors," a mechanism that greatly aided their social incorporation.

The sacramental legitimation of the universal assimilation of the outsiders imparted a sacredness to the whole process - thus solidifying and expanding its validity - inasmuch as religious practices originate in the realm of the holy, and express the workings of divine authority (Streng, 1995:772). This power was in turn transposed to the secular sphere, specifically, in terms of being converted into social power. This concerns the fact that the ritual practice (e.g., the baptizing of the Africans upon their arrival on Brazilian shores) established the linkage between the realm of the sacred, of divine authority, and the world of experience, of concrete social relations. In this sense, the connection between the systematic, large-scale religious ritualization of admission of the aliens into the hegemonic culture, on the one hand, and the emerging model of interethnic and interracial relations, on the other hand, should be readily recognized. The unqualified administration of the Catholic sacraments acted in this way as one of the most effective sources of symbolic legitimation of social practice, the latter involving, in this case, ethnic inclusion and amalgamation. Bastide (1959:182) provides pertinent information in this regard, when he reports, in reference to the German immigrants in Brazil in the late 1800s, that German Catholics, much more than German Lutherans, were amenable to the prevalent trends and patterns of the larger society, such as those that had to do with ethnic fusion. By the same token, in societal contexts where religious principle and practice were adhered to more strictly as a means of keeping the universal assimilation of all the minority ethnic and racial streams from taking place, this too would have resulted in a direct and profound shaping effect on the character of intergroup relations.

In summing up, minority-group difference, whether cultural or racial, was not assigned a quality of permanence in Brazilian society, nor was it seen as a circumstance of permanent social inferiority, but only as one of *temporary* inferiority, potentially changeable into the general social pattern. As such, it had the potential for becoming exchangeable with the elements of the host society, towards their eventual overall integration, since, if integration was to be the final outcome, exchangeability among all the cultural and ethnic streams of the society would have been the logical prerequisite. Contrary to the separatist thrust of ascetic Protestant forces in U.S. society towards the aspect of difference, and the long-term societal investment in maintaining intergroup differentiation, Luso-Brazilian Catholicism as a rule spawned integrationist impulses, reaching out to difference in order to absorb it syncretistically.[12] The ensuing syncretism benefitted the integration of dominant and minority traits, without completely erasing the distinctiveness of the minority traits, as already explained in the discussion of syncretism.

This chapter has attempted to illuminate the central role of the dominant religion in the constitution and maintenance of social life. I shall now look more specifically at its contrasting effect on the cultural systems of Brazil and the United States.

Notes

1   This study does not purport to pursue a full inquiry into the reasons why religion - "the idea of the holy" (see Otto, 1958) - exercises such a profound and pervasive influence on human beings, structuring their social consciousness and, by implication, their social world (see Durkheim, 1965/orig.1915, for an in-depth discussion of the religious origins of collective thought, and of the broader socially-integrative functions of religion). However, this ought in no way to belittle the critical importance of such an inquiry for a deeper grasp of the problem.

2   This viewpoint, which underlines the resilience of religious (and, more broadly, cultural) elements in the context of "the modern," is supported in Tiryakian's essay on American religion as a "religion of survivals" (1995:367-82). This author talks about how life in U.S. society is characterized by the "sacralization" of activities normally regarded as being of the "profane" (secular) type, which in fact amounts to a reversal of the secularization trend. In a similar vein, Comaroff (1944:311-14) analyzes "the persistent role of ritual" in modern society, and challenges traditional conceptions of secularization, by pointing out that societies normally classified as "modern" (i.e., in terms of their high level of development of industrial-capitalist production, scientific technology, and institutional bureaucratization) exhibit a concomitant dynamism in the religious sphere that defies the conventional idea of "disenchantment." This,

190

she argues, is expressed in myriad contexts of ritualized, "symbolically-saturated" collective activities and movements.

3   When Freyre and other analysts of Brazilian history use the designation "patriarchal society," the reference is intended in the broader meaning of this concept, to indicate a *seigneurial* type of preindustrial social formation, in the case of Brazil, a slavery-based, semi-feudal model of male-dominated society. Weber describes this societal model (1946:296):

> Patriarchalism is by far the most important type of domination the legitimacy of which rests upon tradition. Patriarchalism means the authority of the father, the husband, the senior of the house, the sib elder over the members of the household and sib; the rule of the master and patron over bondsmen, serfs, freed men; of the lord over the domestic servants and household officials; of the prince over the house- and court-officials, nobles of office, clients, vassals; of the patrimonial lord and sovereign prince over the 'subjects.'"

4   This feature of U.S. society is strongly suggested in Tiryakian's characterization of this society as "a land of religious revivals" (1995:369). This is the focal aspect of his analysis, but he also refers to the fact that "religious activism" has been, and will likely remain, an integral part of the country's history (1995:380).

5   The *banguê* was a form of transport common in the slavery society of northeastern Brazil in the 1800s, consisting of a type of litter with leather top and curtains.

6   In the plantation Big House, the *tigre* was a container or vessel for depositing fecal matter, which was then carried away for disposal by the slaves.

7   *Compadrismo* refers to a particular model of patron-client interdependence, a "system of oligarchic nepotism and patronage" (see Freyre, 1956:xxxiii).

8   Weber (1978:560) in fact speaks of the personal ethical accomplishment which, in the context of institutionally mediated salvation "must...be made compatible with average human qualifications, and this in practice means that it will be set quite low."

9   The effects of religious universalism on the realm of culture and interpersonal relations are strongly suggested in Pierson's account (1948:149) of religious life in Cruz das Almas. This was manifested especially in relation to the aspect of identity. In this country village the people, upon being asked by the researcher, declared their faith in a variety of Catholic saints. The image of some of these saints, such as Our Lady of Aparecida and Saint Benedict, were black. No distinction was made by these people regarding their preference among the saints to whom they regularly prayed. In fact, *Nossa Senhora da Aparecida* and *São Benedito* were among the most popular saints of the community. Some of the informants made the following comments: "I pray to all the *santos*, but especially to São Benedito and Santo Antonio"; "We in our family like Nossa Senhora da Aparecida very much. She is the best worker of miracles"; "I have faith in all the saints; but I go especially to São Benedito for help." Regarding this latter saint, Pierson observed his image (along with that of other saints) in virtually every local church and shrine. All of these saints are endowed by the people with an array of human characteristics.

This example serves to show how the "black" saints cannot be properly designated as such, insofar as they, like the other saints, are made to signify the universal. Their existence is universalized in the collective consciousness, thus allowing *any* member of the community, regardless of his/her ethnic affiliation, to identify with them.

10 This phenomenon may be illustrated in the Jesuit treatment of Amerindian culture, early on in the Brazilian colonial era (this religious order is known to exercise a "liberal utilitarian compromise with the world" - Weber, 1958:81), which emphasized syncretic accomodation to, and incorporation of, Amerindian cultural patterns, as a strategy for better accomplishing the task of catechization (see, e.g., Freyre, 1956:163-72).

11 Freyre was writing in the 1940s, some thirty years before Brazilian soccer (as well as the version of this sport as played in other countries) had to surrender to the technical impositions of World Cup competition, and to the standardization of playing approaches worldwide, towards greater technical or instrumental efficiency regarding such aspects as, for instance, the emphasis on high scores, the achievement of superior physical fitness for the players, and so forth.

12 Maritain (1968, orig. 1936) presents Catholicism's historical conception of the relation between the elements of grace and freedom as a directly contributing factor to Catholic universalism - that is, to the Church's unrestricted acceptance and absorption of believers.

7 The church in Brazil: Folk Catholicism and ethnic assimilation

We now turn to the social manifestations of the religious ideas and tendencies discussed in the preceding chapter, with particular interest in the aspects that have the sharpest bearing on the problem as envisaged, namely, the forms or levels of assimilation selected in this study as being constitutive of "culture." These, as will be recalled, concern the type of cultural interaction between the dominant and subordinate ethnic groups (cultural assimilation), the societal treatment of racial/ethnic intermixture and intermarriage (biological assimilation), and the process of identity formation of society's members (psychosocial assimilation). The patterns of historical evolution of Catholic Christianity in Brazil and Protestant Christianity in the United States reveal that these religions respectively influenced the belief system, social institutions, and social relations very differently in each society, stimulating cultural integration in one, cultural separatism in the other. By examining these institutional arrangements and practices, informal customs and interpersonal patterns, and social ideology (as manifested, for instance, in formal writings) the type of ideological dynamics moving the society - specifically, the type of underlying religious ethic, whether universalist or particularist - may be inferred. This chapter will turn precisely to the ways in which Catholic universalism, manifested through the ideological and organizational-ritual structure of the Church, promoted the social and cultural integration of the population in the religious sphere proper, and, over the longer term, in the wider society. This interpretation is in accordance with the idea that institutional structures and practices represent complexes of action, which are specified by rules, and these rules in turn actualize or lend substance to general principles. The general principle involved here is religious universalism. .

The integrative effect of Catholic universalism will be investigated in reference to ideological and structural features of the Church, such as the treatment of *the sacred* and *the profane*; the lay brotherhoods; the administration and symbology of the sacraments; and the observance of religious holy days. The model of Catholic practice thrown into relief here is the popular or folk version, already introduced, of which the religion of the plantation may be seen as representative. The distinctions between this religion and the orthodox version of Rome are normally emphasized in the literature, but the emphasis here should be shifted to the overarching influence of this cultural Catholicism on Brazilian society, and to the fact that its incorporative tendencies apply to Catholic Christianity as a whole. The testimony of John Turnbull (cited in Elkins, 1976:233), a visitor in Bahia in the year 1800, underscores both the religiosity of the masses and the social absorbency of the religious environment: "We found ... that there was one country in the world in which religion was fashionable, the churches being crowded with all ranks of people, from the meanest slave to his Excellency the Governor himself."

It should, moreover, be worthwhile to examine this phenomenon in the context of slavery, since this institution spans the larger part of Brazilian and U.S. history, thus representing a common and enormously relevant historical experience for both countries. By bringing together the Euro-American and African populations in a master-slave relationship, slavery defined the *general* patterns of interaction of these two groups for that period and beyond. These patterns may be seen as prototypes of contemporary dominant-minority ethnic relations. (Though specific to black-white relations, the commentary offered here is applicable to the broader context of dominant-minority ethnic relations.) Catholic Christianity had acommodated itself early on, in the sixteenth century, to the economic-political realities of New World slavery. Nonetheless, it was able to offset, directly and indirectly, the worst excesses of this institution through a combination of policies and practices geared to universal inclusion; to use Elkins's phrase, through its "extraordinary impulse to absorb" (1976:239). Ribeiro notes, in this regard, that the structural and ideological features of Catholicism in Brazil favored the liberation of slaves as well as inhibited the operation of color prejudice (1956:94). Bastide concurs with this view, stating that instead of providing for the religious education of souls, the mystical task of creating the "vertical liaison of souls with God" (a project befitting a more ethically oriented religion), Catholicism in Brazil devoted itself to the task of "uniting men horizontally," (1951:344), that is, it stimulated social solidarity and integration. It is necessary to show, then, how the universalistic orientation of Catholicism and the particularistic orientation of

Protestantism differentially conditioned the interaction between the dominant and minority ethnic-cultural communities in each society, both during the initial period of contact between these communities - which would be the slavery period, insofar as "black-white" relations are concerned - and in the subsequent era. The incorporative impact of the Church was felt structurally, that is, in terms of facilitating inclusion into formal spheres of society, such as the workplace, political life, and so forth; as well as culturally, that is, in terms of cultural, biological, and psychosocial assimilation. In this analysis we are more directly interested in the cultural aspect. The period of greatest importations of African slaves into Brazil was the 18th century, during which some 1.9 million Africans were brought into the country, and the early part of the 19th. In earlier colonial times, however, the African presence in the country was already quite considerable. Prado (1971:116) sets their numbers for that period at "not less than five or six million." Therefore, this group appears to have contributed considerably to the composition of the population from the very beginning of the Portuguese colonization, and thus formed an integral, indeed the major, part of the interethnic mixture. At the same time, Catholicism exerted a sovereign hold over social life from the dawn of the country's history. Prado refers to the general atmosphere in the colonial period as having been "priest-ridden and religious," though this is not to be understood primarily in reference to the operation of the formal processes of the Church, and/or to deep commitment on the part of the population to Catholic dogma and a pattern of conduct directly oriented by this dogma, but most notably in reference to the absorption of a religious orientation that infiltrated the entire sphere of practical activity. Prado continues his discussion of this phenomenon, writing of "the all-pervading complex of beliefs and practices that dogged a man's footsteps from cradle to grave, confining all his deeds within the framework of their constant and powerful influence." Bastide (1951:335) writes about the way in which "the whole life of the *engenho* (the sugar plantation of the northeastern states), from the harvest festival to that of grinding, was placed beneath the one sign of Catholicism." In comparison with its operation in the Spanish dominions of Latin America, the coercive power of Catholicism in Brazil was less direct (as would be expected, given the aforementioned tendencies of accomodation and malleability that the Church exhibited in the Brazilian setting). However, as one observer (Elkins, 1976:233) has correctly emphasized, "it may be doubted whether the influence of Catholic values and Catholic practice was for that reason any the less pervasive." Azevedo (1950:147-8) tells of the way this cultural Catholicism was manifested in the behavior of the masses, and of how "[n]o one went without his rosary in his hand, or his beads about his neck; all punctually knelt in the streets upon the sounding of the Angelus ...".

In a previous chapter I reported on the distinctive character of Luso-Brazilian Catholicism. The distinctiveness of this Christian model was noticeable even when considered in the context of South American Catholicism as a whole. As might be gathered, it differed sharply from the ethically stern religions of the reformed countries of northern Europe; at the same time, it also lacked the flair for drama and passion of the Catholicism of Spain (Freyre, 1956; Ribeiro, 1956), being instead a highly ritualized, pragmatically-disposed, *cultural*, rather than spiritual, religious system, less attuned to the intimate meaning of its ritual forms than to the latter's "external color and pomp"; less oriented to formal ecclesiastical organization and doctrinal-ethical orthodoxy than to "sentiments and the senses...[and to] the exaltation of the values of cordiality and of the tangible forms of religion" (Holanda, 1973:110-12); a religion "of pretty words and exterior acts ... which does not live in the conscience of the people" (Thales de Azevedo, cited in Bruneau, 1982:21); a religion that expressed "more a climate of feeling than an education for spiritual life" (Bastide, 1951:336); a "household religion," as Bruneau (1982:24) describes it, "in which devotions are centered on a cult of saints, promises, communications with the dead, and so forth, largely to the exclusion of doctrinal matters and the sacraments." In short, its effect was stronger and deeper over the social body than over personal life.

These testimonies are remarkably consistent in their emphasis on the cultural, rather than ethical, underpinnings of this religion. Regarding the latter's overt shaping effect on collective thought and behavior, I return here to the idea that while the direct ethical impact of religion may diminish over time, in the degree that the society experiences modernization and secularization (as these processes are conventionally conceived), the cultural effect of religion will not. Instead, it tends to linger on, notwithstanding the fact that social change may be occurring in the material structures of the larger system. In this connection, we may invoke here again the notion of psychological sanctions, put forward by Weber. These sanctions, as we have seen, are deeply embedded in the collective way of thinking and find concretization in social practices. Whether in the case of the Protestant values eventuating in the material emergence of capitalism in the 1700s, or in the example tackled in the present analysis (i.e., of religious ideas establishing the character of interethnic life), we are looking at normative precepts that originate in religious belief, and remain in effect as underlying or subconscious guideposts for practical conduct, despite the fact that social behavior may have become outwardly *desacralized* with the passage of time. Therefore,

197

it is not simply to the formal collective adherence to religious doctrine and practice, but to the impact of religion as a *cultural system* (Geertz, 1973) and to the internalization of its value structure, that we need to devote our attention, in order to grasp the causal efficacy of these psychological sanctions.

As for the structural properties of universalism and particularism, it has long been recognized that in the U.S. the rigid doctrinal exclusionism of ascetic Protestant bodies virtually ruled out any possibility of syncretic reconciliation between the Christian and minority, or non-Christian, religious systems. This in turn did much to inhibit the unification of intergroup life along the dimensions of culture specified in this study. This was particularly the case during the 18th and 19th centuries in the Southern region, when ascetic-type Protestantism reigned supreme, and also the time when the non-Christian forms of religious life of the West African slaves came into direct contact with the Protestant core culture. By contrast, the greater doctrinal and procedural flexibility of Luso-Brazilian Catholicism occasioned its greater receptiveness towards the cultural contributions of the various ethnic communities, leading to their eventual integration into the total culture.

Slavery in hemispheric perspective

Slavery is a very complex and many-faceted subject, and its examination here will necessarily be limited to particular aspects. We will initially examine the way in which the hegemonic religious system and culture of the society worked to shape the material structures of the slavery institution, and then we will consider the social impact of religion, by identifying its effects on the assimilation and acculturation of the African element, both slave and free.

Religion impacted powerfully upon the architecture of New World slavery, materially as well symbolically, and modified its character by either lessening or aggravating the hardships of the "peculiar institution." Admittedly, this idea is not universally held as an article of faith among scholars of slavery. As a matter of fact, a *leitmotiv* and bone of contention in the historiography of New World slavery over the last three to four decades has been the issue of the relative mildness/harshness of plantation life across different slave societies, and of whether material or cultural factors weighed more heavily in the constitution of the character of slavery.

An important theoretical perspective first postulated in systematic and comprehensive form by Freyre (1922, 1956), and subsequently by

198

Tannenbaum (1946), Pierson (1967), Elkins (1976), among others, holds that slavery in Ibero-American societies was of a comparatively milder and more flexible sort than in Anglo-American settings, the reason for this being the different historical, institutional, and cultural circumstances of the settling groups of the Latin-American countries where slavery existed, namely, the Spanish and the Portuguese. Freyre (1956:185) states that the Luso-Brazilian master was "the least cruel in his relations with his slaves," and attributes this phenomenon mainly to the centuries-long (712 A.D.-1344 A.D.) Moorish domination of the Iberian Peninsula and the subsequent implantation in that area of the Moslem system of domestic, rather than industrial, slavery. These events in turn would have shaped the racial attitudes of the Portuguese, as well as their own conception of slavery. Freyre (1955) also gives credit to the monarchical (i.e., Imperial) regime which was in effect in Brazil until 1889 as an additional deterrent to the excesses of slavery. Tannenbaum (1946: 53) cites the Catholic heritage of Latin America as an ameliorating factor (see also Southey, 1970, orig. 1822;[1] Klein, 1969), as well as the fact that the Iberians brought with them to their New World colonies a legal framework, derived from Roman Law, which defended the moral status of the slave as a human being. Such a body of laws governing the status of the slave did not precede the entrance of the Africans into the British colonies in the New World, and therefore they were treated simply as chattels, without any juridical personality. Greenfield (1969) suggests that the social organization of the Iberian Peninsula, characterized by the extended family - a Roman legacy - as the fundamental unit, in contrast to that of northern Europe, structured around the nuclear family, was the determinant factor of the nature of slavery systems and slave status in the Portuguese/Spanish and Anglo-Saxon colonies of the New World. According to this view, the Luso-Brazilian plantation was set up in the same way as the Portuguese model of social organization, being characterized by an extended family, "headed by a *paterfamilias*, and composed of his mate, children, sons, and daughters-in-law, grandchildren, other relatives, unrelated dependents, and slaves" (1969: 47). In this model of organizational structure, as indicated, slaves were automatically absorbed into the extended family, along with other dependents, and thereby integrated into the wider society via this membership in the kinship system. The Anglo-American slavery system, on the other hand, was based on the small nuclear family, in the tradition of British social organization. Here was "neither a tradition nor a place for slaves ...". Instead of "being dependent members of the domestic group," as in the Luso-Brazilian system, the slaves became a "type of human capital equipment" (1969: 56).

Numerous reports of travelers in Brazil during the slavery era (e.g. Koster, 1816; Luccock, 1820; Graham, 1969/orig. 1824; Stewart, 1831; Gardner, 1973/orig. 1846; Marjoribanks, 1853; Codman, 1867; Agassiz, 1868; Burton, 1969/orig. 1869; Dent, 1886) tend to give support to the view that Ibero-American slavery was comparatively milder, and interracial relations comparatively more harmonious. A few of these may be cited here. John Luccock reported from the early 1800s that "[t]he laws ... respecting slavery are peculiarly mild in Brazil" (1820:591). Koster's observation from a decade earlier is that "the lives of slaves in Brazil have been rendered less hard and less intolerable than those of the degraded beings who drag on their cheerless existence under the dominion of other nations" (1816:402). In the latter half of the century (Sir) Richard Burton would conclude that "[n]owhere ... has the 'bitter draught' so little of gall in it" (1969:270-1, vol.I). Burton goes so far as to affirm that "[t]he slave in Brazil has, by the unwritten law, many of the rights of a freeman." More recently, Bastide (1959, 1978), never one to paint the Brazilian slavery regime or model of interethnic/interracial relations in rosy hues, asserted nevertheless that, in large part due to the paternalistic basis of plantation life, "[s]lavery in Brazil was relatively more humane than in other regions of the Americas" (1959:48).

Overall, then, it appears that cultural forces such as the dominant religion, the structure of the law, ideology, custom and tradition, in the American colonies of Spain and Portugal, combined to shape the general configuration of the system of bondage, mitigating its worst excesses as well as facilitating for the enslaved Africans the passage to the state of freedom. This is clearly an aspect of great importance for the historiography of slavery, yet one that is not always accorded sufficient attention. Tannenbaum (1946:53-4) gives a useful summary statement for the case of Brazil: "A hundred social devices narrowed the gap between bondage and liberty, encouraged the master to release his slave, and the bondman to achieve freedom on his own account."[2] In recent decades this viewpoint has increasingly come under attack by revisionist historians, sociologists, and social anthropologists (e.g., Mintz, 1961; Boxer, 1964[3]; Goveia, 1969; Sio, 1969; Degler, 1971; Toplin, 1971; Harris, 1974; Davis, 1969, 1975). These scholars insist that, as regards the general channels of oppression of the slaves, the Ibero-American slavery systems were not only remarkably similar to the British in the West Indies, or to that of the United States, but also, in some instances, Luso-Brazilian slavery may have been even more severe, particularly in the colonial (i.e., pre-1800s) era.

The issue is far from having been resolved. It has already been noted how, as an economic institution oriented basically to the requirements of a developing international capitalism, slavery functioned primarily to extract the maximum of labor and capitalistic profit from the slave force, and the methods utilized for achieving this goal differed little across slave societies in their systematicity and brutality. In this specific sense, very little beyond the geographical and sociocultural particularities of each slaveholding society could be used as a basis for differentiating one society from another. Such aspects as the harshness of slave labor, the system of punishments, the meager diet and shelter, along with the attendant implications of depersonalization and economic "commodification" of the Africans, cut across geographical boundaries, and lent uniformity to slavery regimes everywhere. The brutality or benevolence of the masters fluctuated, for the most part, in accordance with their own subjective inclinations, and this arbitrariness was a function and reflection of the very institutional workings of slavery *qua* socioeconomic system. It expressed the extreme inequality erected by this system between the ruling and subaltern classes.

At the same time, some differences *must* be discerned and taken into account in the broader hemispheric context, differences manifested in the material welfare of the slaves, their level of access to manumission, the greater/lesser horizontal and vertical mobility of the free blacks, the nature of dominant-minority interpersonal and cultural relations, and so on. There was sufficient variation among slave regimes to warrant more careful comparative analyses. Otherwise, the discourse remains hopelessly sterile. According to some authors (e.g., Elkins (1976:228), the various slavery systems of the New World produced such markedly dissimilar *social* consequences that attempts at "homogenization" of the slavery experience are unwarranted and counterproductive. When contrasting Ibero-American and Anglo-American slavery systems, revisionist writers, through what Elkins refers to as "a technique of citing exceptions," tend to blur these differential aspects, thus pushing aside "discriminations so strikingly gross as to have been perfectly obvious to every outsider who observed and wrote about slavery in nineteenth century Brazil" (1976:228). Elkins's remarks underscore the evidential validity and cogency of the documentation left by 19th-century travelers and chroniclers, and their value as a source of historical information about everyday life in New World slavocracies.

The fact remains that the larger spectrum of life under slavery cannot, should not, be reduced to its economic substratum. In this respect, the assumption that an economic category such as "slavery" would have produced identical socio-structural outcomes in every slave society is plainly untenable. The interaction between the economic forces of slavery and the particular cultural complex of the society produced sufficient variation in the character of the slavery system as a whole to warrant a rethinking of the economicist interpretation.

In any event, a more profitable approach to the study of slavery is to distinguish between the different dimensions of life on the plantation. Our principal interest here, of course, is not so much to weigh and determine the relative merits of each explanation, as to elucidate the role of cultural forces - most notably, the hegemonic religious sytem - in the constitution of the larger sociohistorical context. Thus, the specific issue of the greater harshness or mildness of Ibero-American vs. Anglo-American plantation systems is only peripherally pertinent to the central focus of this analysis, and will be addressed only in the measure of its heuristic usefulness to the latter.

In the first place, as we look at the example of Southern slavery in the United States, and at such aspects as the formative influence of ascetic particularist religion in the articulation of proslavery discourse, there can be little doubt that cultural factors figured prominently in the architecture of slavery in the Americas, and that religion was outstanding among those cultural forces. (We will consider the U.S. case more systematically in the next chapter). Furthermore, highly dissimilar kinds of effects on the material and cultural framework of slavery appear to have resulted in societies where Catholicism was the main religion vs. societies where this status was held by Protestantism. Specifically, the dominant religion was either an attenuating or aggravating force on the physical hardships of the plantation system, by having an impact on technical and administrative procedures, social practices, institutional arrangements, and various aspects of dominant-minority intergroup and interpersonal relations. The aspects of slave punishment, the level of access to manumission, and the absorption of liberated slaves into the institutional and cultural mainstream are all pertinent in this connection.

The African(-American) population in New World societies constitutes a minority contingent unlike all others, burdened as its members were by extraordinary constraints in their assimilative experience because of their circumstance of enslavement, and by the crippling effects from life under slavery, which haunted them long after emancipation. Therefore, it is important to look, if only cursorily, at the manner in which religion materially affected their life in bondage, as well as their passage to freedom, because of the interrelation of the processes and mechanisms linking servile status to manumission, and manumission to sociocultural assimilation. This sequence of events or stages can be better understood by considering the overall environment of plantation life. If we can accept the premise that sufficient elasticity was imparted to this environment by Catholicism to allow for a relatively untrammeled passage of the Africans to free civil status, then it follows that there were no objections or reservations on the part of the dominant religious ideology towards the idea of full social freedom and civil inclusion of the African element. The universalistic impetus of the dominant religion would thus be established, as well as the fact that this religious trait would have prevailed over considerations of "race." It is to this aspect, therefore, that we will now devote our attention.

The material amelioration of slavery may be briefly examined with reference to certain categories. One is the question of ownership of plantations and slaves by the Church in Brazil. Some 19th century reports suggest that the Church's involvement with slaveholding activity may have had an attenuating effect on the characteristic arduousness of the system, especially in certain areas of the country and during certain historical periods. Tollenare's report from the 1820s (1956:122) informs us that the management of some sugar mills in the Pernambuco state area by the Benedictine and Carmelite orders was distinguished by "much docility and moderation," and while this did not make these plantations as profitable as they should be as economic enterprises, it transformed their internal structure regarding the needs of production and consumption, to the point where the slaves there were "as contented as one can be in the shackles of bondage." Every year a few of them were liberated. We are further told (Southey, 1970:780-2, orig. 1822; Ribeiro, 1900:256) that the slaves of the religious orders thought of themselves as belonging to the saints themselves, and as a rule they were never sold.

Moreover, it appears (as discussed in earlier chapters) that the emancipation of the slaves itself was stimulated by the dominant Catholic environment in Brazil.[4]   One of the important mechanisms in this connection was the operation of the institution of *apadrinhamento* (godparenthood), which figured prominently in the Catholic tradition. As will be remembered, it was customary in Brazil for a slave child to be freed at the baptismal font, a practice known as *alforrias na pia* (manumission at the font). The amount to be paid was "insignificant," in the order of 5 to 50 *milréis* (Ribeiro, 1900:255), as a rule, twenty *milréis* (Southey, 1970:785, orig. 1822). This custom obviously worked to the advantage of Brazilian slaves, in the degree that social pressure enforced and maintained it, and all indications seem to be that public opinion and sentiment leaned towards its recognition and compliance. This aspect is borne out by chroniclers like, for instance, Koster (1816:407), who tells of the "considerable number of persons [who] are set at liberty [by means of this practice]," and of how "the smallness of the price enables many freemen who have had connections with female slaves to manumit their offspring ...". In this connection, the concern of a slave mother was to get a prominent white person to become the godparent for her baby, and this individual normally felt morally and socially compelled to abide by the tradition, and thus to put up the required amount to free the child. "It was both a meritorious and pious deed," says Tannenbaum (1946:57), "to accept such a responsibility and to fulfill its implicit commitments, and it bestowed distinction upon him who accepted them."[5]

The Catholic Church was also the source of a great many holidays enjoyed throughout the year, which slaves could use for their own purposes, "and for garnering such funds as their immediate skill and opportunities made possible" (Tannenbaum, 1946:61). A major goal of the slaves in this connection was the purchase of their freedom.

A strikingly different picture emerges for the U.S. South. There, the religious underpinnings of slavery provided the basis for "the denial of a moral status to the slave as a human being" (Tannenbaum, 1946:104). This generated a social climate that was not only extraordinarily restrictive regarding what the blacks could/could not do (see, e.g., Stampp's discussion of the stringency of the Southern slave codes, and of the judicial/police framework erected in the cities to enforce these codes, 1956:chapter 5), but also, and would be expected, intensely averse to the idea of manumission for the African bondsmen. On the whole, for the masses of U.S. slaves emancipation was apparently, as Stampp puts it, "little more than an idle dream" (1956:97). Both in the law and in custom the racial status of the Africans was equated with perpetual servitude, thus erecting a formidable barrier to emancipation. This same author reveals how in the Southern slave states "[n]o promise of freedom, oral or written, was binding upon [the] master." For example, the Arkansas Supreme Court declared: "If the master contract ... that the slave shall be emancipated upon his paying to his master a sum of money, or rendering him some stipulated amount of labor, although the slave may pay the money ... or perform the labor, yet he cannot compel his master to execute the contract, because both the money and the labor of the slave belong to the master and could constitute no legal consideration for the contract." Southern court records were replete with suits on behalf of blacks who claimed that they were being held in bondage illegally, since they had made themselves eligible for manumission either by having made full payment on their self-purchase, or through some emancipating clause in the will of the slaveholder (in Stampp, 1956:197).

As a result, the free African was truly an *avis rara* in the Southern region. Not only were free blacks a small minority - Degler (1971:43) reports that by 1860, when the black population reached a maximum in the Southern states, freedmen made up only one-sixteenth of this entire group - but also their freedom, as measured by the scope of physical and social mobility, was very limited, because of the multiple social and legal impediments imposed on it. The law was, in fact, particularly severe concerning the regulation of the physical mobility of former slaves. "The right to go from place to place without hindrance," wrote Russell (1969:106, orig. 1913), "might well be regarded as a right fundamental to real freedom, yet in few other aspects was the liberty of the free negro restricted as much as in this." In the final analysis, this phenomenon may likewise be traced to the effect of religion, specifically, to ascetic, Calvinistically-informed Protestantism, and its doctrine of election. (This will be the main focus of the next chapter, but some brief considerations will be made here). Taking into account the strict dichotomization of humanity into the two categories of elect and non-elect, a procedure which, when applied to the sphere of ethnic relations, translates into the polarization of the dominant and subordinate ethnic groups (i.e., the "whites" and the "nonwhites") into ontologically opposed categories, to be black and to be free in Southern society was a contradiction in terms, an aberration. It entailed the unimaginable fusion of fundamentally irreconcilable circumstances, namely, "election," understood socially as the superior state of freedom exercised by the white ruling population, and its conceptual opposite, "nonelection," understood as the inferior state of servitude, the naturally permanent state of the nonwhite subaltern group.[6] To be black was to be perenially locked into a subordinate position vis-a-vis the whites. It was, metaphorically, to be a member of the non-elect. Thus, Southern whites were intensely uncomfortable with, and resentful of, the idea of blacks in freedom, and did their utmost to curtail this freedom, and to re-enslave those who violated, in whatever form or degree, the stringent laws that regulated their conduct. It is not surprising, therefore, given this ideological background, that the life of the free Africans in the South was about as hellish as that of the slaves, and that, as Russell informs us (1969:104, orig. 1913), for many legal infractions they were punished in much the same fashion as the slaves were, in like circumstances. A clergyman made this observation in the 1840s: "Their freedom consists mainly in deliverance from compulsory labor" (Jones, 1969:120). The white plantocracy saw free blacks not only as a lazy, thieving, morally-degraded class, but also as potential disseminators of insurrectionary ideas among the slaves. In this latter capacity, they were perceived as a threat to the stability of the social order.

Legal strictures towards the free blacks in the South took various forms: any violation of formal law or social convention perceived to be serious enough could lead to their re-enslavement, association with slaves was strictly forbidden and attended with punishment, and manumission normally meant that the recipient had to sever ties with family, friends, and place of residence, since the law required that manumitted Africans leave the state within ninety days (Goodell, 1853:355-6) to six months (see Rose, 1976:188 for Alabama). This last provision applied universally in the South. Equally common was the law that prohibited the migration of free blacks to another state, as for instance the Charleston Act of 1835, which read that no freedmen were to enter South Carolina, or "be brought or introduced into its limits, under any pretext whatever, by land or by water" (*A Digest of the Ordinances of the City Council of Charleston from the year 1783-1844, 1844:378*).

The restrictions imposed on the physical movements of blacks in the urban context applied *equally* to free blacks as to slaves. Henry (1968:46) reports that in many cities of South Carolina, free blacks apprehended at large after the "beating of the tattoo" were sent to the "workhouse" for correction. In Richmond, a free black caught at large at any time without "an attested copy of his register" was either fined ten dollars or punished with stripes, "not exceeding thirty nine" (*The Charters and Ordinances of the City of Richmond*, 1859:197). At Mobile a fifty dollar fine was to be paid by free blacks at large after "the hour of ten o'clock at night" without special permission from the mayor or any of the city aldermen (*The Charter and Code of the City of Mobile*, 1859:120).

The association of free blacks and slaves was strictly forbidden by law. The Alabama Slave Code forbade fredmen to participate in any "unlawful assembly of slaves," an offense punishable with a fine, and, upon recidivism, with ten stripes. Rose (1976:184-5) elaborates on this aspect, writing that freedmen found "in company with any slave, in any kitchen, outhouse, or negro quarter, without a written permission from the owner, or overseer of such a slave" were punished with fifteen lashes for the first offense; thirty-nine lashes for every subsequent offense. And if any unlicensed free black preacher was found preaching or exhorting to an audience of free blacks and slaves, without the supervision of at least five slaveholders, the punishment was thirty-nine lashes for the first offense, fifty lashes for every subsequent one. In Richmond, a free black that allowed any slave to stay on his "lot or tenement" for more than one hour during the daytime, or for any length of time at night, without the written consent of the owner of the said slave, received thirty-nine lashes as punishment (1859:197).

In the postbellum period, Southern whites endeavored to maintain their control over a nominally-free black population, though intimidation and overt violence. The impediments to physical mobility naturally inhibited participation in mainstream institutional and cultural life, and deepened the castelike separatism that alienated the two ethnic-racial communities. This may be seen from the account of the Reverend Charles Stearns about a public event he watched in Georgia in the 1870s:

> Last Fourth of July the colored people marched through the streets, protected by the military, but the remark was made afterwards by the white people that it was a shame and disgrace to the whole country. I have not a doubt that if there had been no military there, this procession could not have passed through the streets (1969:162).

Religion and minority-group assimilation

Once freed from the shackles of life under slavery, the Africans were technically eligible to embark on the journey of assimilation into the main axis of society. The degree of difficulty that they would have encountered along the way may be seen as an index of how the dominant ethnic population defined and reacted to the presence of free blacks in their midst. It has, I believe, been sufficiently established in the present analysis that ethnic minorities in Brazil (this category referring primarily, though not exclusively, to individuals of African extraction) benefitted from a very favorable social climate insofar as their social and cultural assimilation was concerned, during both the slavery and postslavery periods. As pointed out before report upon report of foreign visitors to Brazil through the 1800s furnish evidence, first of all, of the very large number of freedmen, and then of their social (i.e., in the structural sense of occupational and political) integration. The following are representative. Agassiz commented in the mid-1800s on "[t]he absence of all restraint upon the free blacks, the fact that they are eligible to office, and that all professional careers are open to them, without prejudice on the ground of color ..." (1868:128-9).[7] Koster (1816:121), traveling through the province of Ceara shortly after 1800, and saw that in that region "rich mulattoes and negroes are by no means rare." Only a few years after Koster, the French merchant L.F. Tollenare reported that in Recife "[t]he number of mulattoes and free blacks is quite considerable. Among them one finds tailors, shoemakers ..." (1956:148). This chronicler also noted that the industry and enterprise of the free blacks gave them such an advantage over the idle *whites* that "the line of demarcation between the colors is almost destroyed, and with it, prejudice ... A white person here is certainly considered to be worthier than a black or a mulatto; but either of the latter, if free, sees himself/herself as worthy as any white" (1956:148; my translation). This last observation is very germane. Even if it is acknowledged that blacks during the slavery period in Brazil (or in any other slavery society) could not possibly have been entirely unhindered in their vertical mobility by ethnic-racial considerations, this remark by Tollenare still underlines the preponderance of *class* over *race* in the social integration of the minority element in Brazil, and, what is more striking, shows that the socioeconomic transformation of the individual enhanced the latter's status to the point of blurring the lines of ethnic-racial difference and inequality. This points to an *ontological* transformation, when it is considered that the physical marks of the minority element lost their restraining character in proportion to the degree that economic achievement increased.[8]

The cornerstone of this investigation is the idea that the social and cultural integration of the minority element in Brazilian society owed in large measure to the accomodating and incorporative attitude of the hegemonic Catholicism towards the presence of minority difference, an attitude which had theological and organizational referents, as pointed out earlier. In the preceding chapter we examined the ethical-doctrinal basis of Protestantism and Catholicism, with respect to the categories of universalism and particularism, so as to account for the differential posture adopted by each religion towards the problem of minority difference. Some additional aspects may be considered.

We have already seen how the Catholic Church in Brazil was a crucial mitigating factor concerning the material hardship of plantation life, and how it generally aided the process of manumission of the African slaves. This effect also extended into the next stage, namely, that of their wider social incorporation. To begin with, there was never in Brazil any official, systematic separation of churches for the dominant whites and for the ethnic minorities, as was the case in the antebellum South. This may be seen from the following accounts. "The Church is open to all," noted Luccock (1820:248), as he commented on religious life in Rio de Janeiro in the early 19th century. A couple of decades earlier, in the year 1800, Turnbull (cited in Elkins, 1976:233), passing through the city of Salvador, was struck by the intense religiosity of the people, and by the fact that the churches were "crowded with all ranks of people, from the meanest slave to His Excellency the Governor himself." Also from about the same time, the beginning of the Imperial era in Brazil, Koster reports on the disposition of churches in Recife, saying that "[t]he middle of the body of these churches is completely open; there are no pews, no distinction of places; the principal chapel is invariably at the opposite end from the chief entrance, recedes from the church, and is narrower; this part is appropriated to the officiating priests, and is railed in from the body of the church." The report continues, revealing gender distinctions, but not economic or racial ones: "The females, as they enter, *whether white or of colour*, place themselves as near the rails as they can, squatting down upon the floor of the large open space in the centre. The men stand along either side of the body of the church ... or they remain near to the entrance, behind the women; but every female, *of whatever rank or colour, is first accomodated"* (emphasis added) (1816:17-18).

The many public festivals of the Church were also structured in a way that encouraged social integration across all classes. This may be readily inferred from the account of Walsh (1830:387-88), who informs us from the early 1800s that on the occasion of the Procession of Our Lord of the Misericordia, which was always attended by the Court, and in which the Emperor himself carried the cross (in a re-enactment of the *Via Crucis*), "... no precaution is taken to exclude the mob. Close to the emperor, and pressing upon him, were blacks and whites, freemen and slaves, rich and poor, without distinction of persons." On another occasion, the festivities associated with the consecration of the Host on Holy Thursday (*Quinta de Endoenças*), the Emperor washed the feet of beggars.

All of these instances suggest the structural plasticity and universalism of Catholicism in Brazil, the factor directly behind the Church's determination early on that the condition of bondage was to be dissociated from the condition of "color," that is, from racial background (Ribeiro, 1956:66-7). The former condition was held to be injurious and stigmatizing, but not the latter. This had direct practical consequences, such as the possibility within the very context of slavery, as Ribeiro (1956:67) informs us, of "individuals of color ... and those recently manumitted ... [of assuming] ... the role of masters," a situation that would have been completely impossible in the Old South.

Also, as indicated in the previous chapter, making the sacraments universally available to the newcomers - whether the latter be the contingents of African slaves continuously arriving on Brazilian until the mid-1800s, or the 19th-century European immigrants - related to the premise of the dominant religion that all individuals were potentially eligible for incorporation into the Catholic ranks, hence, into the larger community. The principal barrier to admission into the social community as Freyre observed (1956:41), "the blot of heresy upon the soul and not any racial brand upon the body." If we consider that the erasing of religious difference was promptly achieved through the administration of the Catholic sacraments, and if we consider further that this process rested on the assumption of universal eligibility of individuals for Catholic membership, irrespective of ethnic, racial, or socioeconomic status, then it must also be granted that the elimination of religious difference would have meant the progressive dissolution of all manner of *non-religious* difference, which then paved the way for full social inclusion. *Culture* (in the form of religious status) therefore prevails here over *race* (or racial status) in the determination of the nature of the assimilative process.

Regarding the more direct contribution of the Church as a channel of social ascension, in terms of aiding the vertical (i.e., occupational) mobility of Brazilians of African descent, it is fitting to examine the latter's inclusion into the ecclesiastical hierarchy itself, and in subsidiary institutions, such as the lay brotherhoods.

The lay brotherhoods

The social and cultural integration of the minority element was greatly enhanced in the *irmandades* (the lay confraternities or brotherhoods, mentioned in chapter III). These religious organizations, the "most important branch of Catholic discipline" (Luccock, 1820:247), had their full flowering in Brazilian society during the first half of the 18th century (Boxer, 1964:135), and served a variety of social and benevolent functions, providing Africans in Brazil - particularly the freedmen, but also the slaves, in terms of facilitating their access to manumission - with opportunities for social advancement and prestige, as well as cultural integration. Luccock informs us (1820:248) that everyone (every adult white male, in any event) was expected to connect himself with some brotherhood, and "even Negroes were allowed to put on the habit of an order, to carry a silver wand, and to appear in processions with Princes and Priests, the nobility of earth and heaven." Even the slaves, we are told by another writer from the same period (Southey, 1970:784, orig. 1822), had their religious fraternities, "like the free part of the community: it is an object of great ambition for a bondsman to obtain admission into one of these, still more to be chosen one of the officers and directors; and he will even expend part of the money which he is hoarding for his own redemption in ornamenting Our Lady, that he may appear of some importance in the Brotherhood." It is true, of course, that the general stratification pattern of the society, which derived primarily from slavery arrangements but enduring beyond the slavery era, and was manifested in the differential standings of the ethnic components of the population (i.e., the whites situated at the top rungs of the social ladder, whites and a large number of mixed-bloods in the intermediary rungs, and the blacks at the bottom), affected the composition of the brotherhoods. In relation to this, it may be said that the latter were composed mainly on racial lines, whites, mulattoes, and blacks each having their own brotherhoods. Still, this was only a general pattern, not a rigidly codified principle of segregation. Many of these organizations made no distinctions of class or color, bond or free (Boxer, 1964:135), and on the whole the brotherhoods steadily advanced the social inclusion of the blacks.

Ribeiro (1956:67-8) and Verger (1981:218) identify as one of the key functions of the brotherhood that of functioning as a mutual-aid or beneficent society, through which funds were raised for the emancipation of slaves. Blacks were not only able to gain membership into these organizations on a large-scale basis, but also become elected officers and directors, with obvious economic and social advantages accruing therefrom. This aspect is instantiated in an incident involving Koster (mentioned earlier, in chapter 2), which shows that the social prestige and influence attached to the holding of ecclesiastical office in Brazil served to offset the power of racial stratification. This concerns his dinner with white and black members (the blacks were freedmen) of the brotherhood of Our Lady of the Rosary, based in Olinda (a city in the state of Pernambuco), in connection with some land, owned by the brotherhood, that he wanted to rent. The meeting proceeded amidst the greatest conviviality. A number of aspects may be highlighted here. First, the blacks appeared to Koster as being visibly conscious of their importance on account of holding administrative posts in the brotherhood. It is apparent that their advancement into this level of occupational mobility was made possible through membership in the brotherhood. Finally, this occupational status counteracted the handicap of color, as indicated by the general affability and lack of aversion displayed by the whites toward their company.

Despite some formal restrictions in Portuguese law during the colonial period in Brazil, which barred individuals with direct African ancestry from the occupying the higher statuses in the priesthood, this appears not to have been the case for the 19th century (Freyre, 1956:408). Travel accounts for that period disclose the fact that individuals of mixed ancestry, particularly those of lighter compexion, had relatively unencumbered access to ecclesiastical office. In the opening decade of the century Koster noticed that "the decided and unequivocal colour of the negro" was a basis for exclusion from the priesthood, as a general pattern. Yet, mulattoes, creole blacks, and all other varieties of hybrid types into which the product of the union between the EuroBrazilian and the African (or the EuroBrazilian and the Amerindian, or the Amerindian and the African) could branch, had relatively direct access to the holy orders and other institutional positions.[9] The signs of change were already apparent in the early Imperial era (the 1820s). At that time Walsh saw at the St. Francis de Paula Church in Rio de Janeiro a black priest celebrating mass, and commented that generally "blacks officiate in the churches indiscriminately with whites." (1830:336). C.S. Stewart also reported that

211

he had met in Rio individuals of high office "ordained to the services of the priesthood, of as jet a skin, and as pure African blood, as any in the country" (1831:99). And, in Debret's lithographic depictions of social life in Rio de Janeiro during the 1820s one finds a drawing of a black priest, standing at the entrance of a church, as some black children are brought in to be baptised.

A baroque religion

A ramification of the Portuguese colonial control of Brazilian society was the baroque quality of the dominant Catholic culture. A structural transformation in the Western arts regarding the trends of the preceding period (the Renaissance), the baroque movement roughly coincided with the 17th century. As philosophical, literary, and artistic movements will, it also spread itself over the broader social and institutional realm. It is in this connection that we may speak of a baroque Catholicism in colonial Brazil. The reference here is to the late colonial period, since in Brazil and other parts of South America the baroque did not attain its culminating achievements until the 18th century.

Briefly stated, the baroque movement emerged from the rejection of the neoclassicist rationalism and restraint of Renaissance art, and the exaltation of emotion. Some of its most frequently cited qualities are "grandeur, sensuous richness, drama, vitality, movement, tension, emotional exuberance, and a tendency to blur the distinctions between the various arts."[10] In Brazil the baroque style was not as fully realized in the architecture of the colonial churches as in the latter's internal ornamentation, in terms of what Bastide called the "sinuosity of the interior decoration" (1959:54). In the area of religious practice the baroque tendency was manifested in the triumph of the theatrical, liturgical dimensions of Catholicism over its formal dogmatic structure, concomitantly and in interrelated fashion with its interchangeable treatment of sacred and profane elements.

As analysts have pointed out, the baroque in Brazil adapted itself to the particularities of the ecological and sociological environment - more specifically, to the particular circumstances of the slaveholding areas, such as the sugar civilization of the northeastern coastal areas. In the rural context baroque Catholicism largely became a religion of the plantation, essentially subordinated to the authority of the *paterfamilias* of the Big House. As such, it reproduced the basic patterns of social stratification of slavery society, thereby reflecting the adaptation of the Catholic spiritual world to the social world (this was in fact, as already indicated, a process of reciprocal adaptation). The baroque churches of 18th and 19th century Brazil, for instance, functioned additionally as community centers. Their richly furnished vestries became an important gathering place for the masters of the sugar plantations, who would come with their families to socialize and discuss business (Bastide, 1959:55).

More fundamentally, in the baroque element of Luso-Brazilian Catholicism we see both a source and a reflection - a cause and an effect, one might say - of the incorporative or inclusionary character of the sociocultural system. In the churches, this meant the incorporation of the different social, ethnic, and cultural echelons of society, which, differentiated though they might be in the wider secular sphere, were all brought inside and integrated under the aegis of the Christian faith. Thus, we are told, "the same church may have the altar of the mulattoes (St. Ifigenia), the altar of the blacks (St. Benedict), and the altar of the Portuguese (St. Antonio)." In the public festivals and processions, this tendency was even more pronounced, bringing together "in fraternal association, in the same mystical or profane jubilation, the races and the social classes, children dressed up as angels, white angels, *moreno* (brown-skinned) angels, black angels, running after their mothers, laughing and screaming" (Bastide, 1959:56-8; my translation).

Bastide's reference to children dressed up as angels is germane to this argument. It concerns a conspicuous feature of the religious procession in 19th-century Brazil (and even in the present day, if to a lesser extent), one which expressed the democratizing effect that the dominant religion by and large exerted on the social and cultural life of the country. These were the *anjinhos* (literally, little angels), little girls, from eight to ten years of age, dressed up as angels, who would march before each group of images, led by a priest or a member of the brotherhood, scattering rose-leaves and flowers on the path. These young girls, as noted by Fletcher and Kidder (1867:151), "are a class created for the occasion [i.e., for the religious processions], to act as tutelary to the saints exhibited ... [They are] ... fitted out by a most fantastic dress ... [and they] ... fully comprehend the honor they enjoy of being the principal objects of admiration." Of greatest interest for our purposes is the fact that the young girls would not normally be barred from serving in this capacity on the basis of color (although *class* certainly must have had a bearing on the selection). In the operation of the brotherhoods the universalistic and equalizing tendencies of Luso-Brazilian Catholicism found a most effective outlet. (The active role of the lay brotherhood in organizing the religious processions is addressed more directly below). Writing from Recife in the early 1800s, Tollenare (1956:215) commented on the participation of the *irmandades* in the processions of the Holy Week, in which "young mulatto girls" played the role of the little angels. Half a century later Codman observed that in the processions "may often be seen little children dressed as angels; and very pretty, *though somewhat dusky*, are these tiny sprites, as they dance airily along" (1867;170-71; emphasis added).

As might be expected, this baroque Catholicism functioned not as a religion exclusively centralized in the temples, sacraments, and spiritual matters, but as one that permeated all social and institutional affairs. This defined the Church's treatment of the sacred and the profane as elements that could not only coexist harmoniously, but also be handled interchangeably, an approach that reflects the larger tendency in folk religion *in general* to mix religious and secular elements. This tendency prevented religious dogma from overriding the practical considerations of daily life. In this connection, Costa Lima (1988:104) registered the "mixture of theater and religious office" that prevailed in Brazilian colonial society, a phenomenon he interprets broadly as being associated with the elimination in that society of a distinction between "discourses." This is an important point to keep in mind, as we contrast patterns of contact between dominant and minority religious cultures in the New World. In the context at hand, it is linked to the way in which the universalism of the dominant Catholicism, together with the specific circumstances of Portuguese culture and history, led to practices that blurred the formal distinctions between the sacred and the profane, and between the magical and the religious. Thus considered, the dominant religion may be seen as a major stimulant of cultural unification, imbuing the faithful with a noticeably tolerant disposition toward religious, and otherwise cultural, difference. The report of Walsh on religious life in Brazil in the first quarter of the 19th century bears this out. He says that while the external aspects and doctrinal principles of Catholicism were adhered to by the masses, the latter were "almost entirely free from bigotry and intolerance towards those who differ from them ...". More recent observers, like Ribeiro (1956:58), have also supported this view, identifying the hybrid constitution of Portuguese folk Catholicism, which led in Brazil to a broad spectrum of religious syncretism involving Christian, Amerindian, and West African patterns, as a critical determinant of the cultural and biological consolidation of the larger society. "Were it not [for this factor]," he contends, "the mutual estrangement among the peoples that came together here would have been even greater." This religion thus lent itself admirably to the sanctification, or the absorption into the realm of the sacred, of a wide range of social reality, of "all the functions of life" (to use Bastide's apt phrase, 1959:56).

Towards cultural unity

At this juncture we can look more specifically at how Catholic universalism was conducive to the emergence of a pattern of national consolidation at the level of culture. It should be profitable, in this regard, to examine the key role of the brotherhoods in sponsoring, organizing, and staging the processions and traditional feasts of the Church. Their involvement with these events was time and again witnessed by visitors. Codman, for instance, saw the procession of St. George in Rio de Janeiro, in the 1860s, which "was composed of all the orders of ecclesiastical and lay brotherhoods" (1867:164). Several decades earlier, Debret (1989:31-45, Book III; orig. 1834) gave detailed descriptions of the pageantry and splendor of these celebrations, also mentioning the involvement of the various *irmandades* with them.[11]

The numerous religious feast-days constituted a striking feature of the life of towns and cities, an occasion in which all classes of the population enthusiastically participated. In the beginning of the 19th century Grant noticed that "[t]he chief amusements of the citizens are the feasts of the different saints, and other religious ceremonies and processions" (1809:231). Codman also tells of how "the frequent holidays and *festas* bring out the whole population into the squares and the churches" (1867:170). We have already noted the large-scale black participation in these events, and the resulting cultural exchange. This latter aspect may be focused on, again by appealing to Codman, who typically deplored how "[t]he Church in Brazil ... has allowed much of the African element to mingle with religion, as the people have mixed it with their blood. It adapts itself to [the ways and beliefs] of the blacks, and allows them to practise charms and rites of Fetish worship ..." (1867:166-67). I have referred elsewhere to the insertion of African dances and other ritual patterns into these religious events. In addition to the direct involvement of the brotherhoods in the public religious festivals, which in turn facilitated Afro-Brazilian cultural cross-fertilization, the structure of these organizations itself revealed this syncretic characteristic. Koster (1816:410) writes that the best known of the black brotherhoods were those that functioned under the patronage of Saint Benedict and Our Lady of the Rosary. The statue of Our Lady of the Rosary was, in this case, "even sometimes painted with a black face and hands."

In actively promoting these celebrations, in which the cultural ways of the African population were syncretically accomodated and absorbed, the brotherhoods had a revitalizing effect on African religious institutions, while at the same time bringing about the transformation of folk Catholicism. Although this process of cultural exchange was formally situated in the religious plane, it ultimately involved a wider range of cultural reciprocity. This may be understood more readily when we consider the fact that in traditional African societies the secular and sacred realms are not neatly marked off from each other. Thus, the impact of these festivities on the African culture of the blacks reached beyond the purely religious sphere, and promoted the resurrection (or at least reconstruction) of aboriginal African custom in the broader sense. Similarly, their impact on the dominant culture transcended the parameters of Catholic belief and practice. That is to say, in absorbing African religious custom the whites were in fact absorbing a wider range of minority cultural difference.

The element of dancing, for example, offers an excellent opportunity to document this latter point. As will be recalled, in the traditional African setting the dancing element is inseparable from religious worship, and the latter from social behavior in general. Thus, in the accomodating environment of Luso-Brazilian Catholicism this cultural pattern flowered and became one of the most salient characteristics of the cultural exchange between Brazil and Africa. (In the northernmost regions of the country, these considerations would apply mainly to the exchange with Amerindian populations). To be sure, African dancing styles were preserved in non-religious situations as well, but the public religious celebration was the venue *par excellence* for the meeting and fraternizing of the dominant and minority cultural traditions, the context in which the elements of racial and social diversity were gathered, to quote Bastide (1951:347), "into a single joyfulness." Tollenare (1956:136) observed how it was chiefly in connection with the religious *festas* that black entertainment took place, the latter consisting of "theatrical representations and dances." Fletcher (1867:152) was still able to observe in the latter part of the nineteenth century that "[n]o class enters into the spirit of these holiday parades with more zeal than the people of color."

The public religious festivity thus emerges as the centrally important context of cultural integration in the cities. As a result of this frequent exposure of the dominant population to the sacred-secular dances and other ceremonial patterns of the blacks, African cultural traits became steadily incorporated into and identified with Brazilian culture as a whole. This was noticeable as early as the opening years of the last century, as revealed, for example, in the report of Grant (1809:232). who describes in detail one of the emerging Afro-Portuguese hybrid dance styles (an early prototype of the *samba*), and noted that it was "indulged in by all ranks of the citizens." Tollenare also remarks on this phenomenon, stating that, when they danced, "the [white] men closely mimic the movements of the blacks, while the [white] women merely suggest them

..."(1956:139). And, we have already taken account elsewhere of Koster's comment, from the early 1800s, to the effect that Congolese dances were especially prevalent among the black population in Pernambuco, but they were rapidly becoming as much the national dances of Brazil as they were of Africa.

⸲ Religious life in the Brazilian *engenhos* greatly fortified and expanded a web of close interpersonal relations between the blacks and whites. (The peculiarly intimate character of dominant-minority relations in Brazil under slavery has been consistently noted in the literature.) This in turn led to a deep-going interpenetration of the dominant and minority values, sentiments, and traditions. Plantation Catholicism, even more than the folk religion of the cities, functioned in a rather distinctive and autonomous fashion vis-a-vis the orthodox version of Rome. The resident chaplain, for instance, was often the son of the *senhor de engenho* (the master of the sugar plantation), being in this capacity either a legitimate member of the family, or the offspring of the union between the master and a female slave. In either case, he was fully "integrated into the patriarchal system" (Ribeiro, 1956:82), thus constituting, from this standpoint - physically, administratively, symbolically - a subordinate element within the larger complex of the Big House.

Whether in the form of the general outlook and value system of the people; or the sacramental and ritual practices and observances; or the constant prayers, benedictions, and religious salutations[12]; or the blessing, by the chaplain, of the buildings and mechanical operations of the plantation[13]; or in the very physical structure of the Big House - the latter frequently had its own chapel, always its own sanctuary[14] - this religion entwined with virtually every aspect of daily life. This is confirmed, for instance, in the following passage, from Fletcher (1867:440-1). Visiting a plantation in the province of Minas Gerais in the second half of the 1800s, he came to witness and participate in what appears to have been a daily ritual of the household. "We were all sitting on the veranda," he recounts, "[when] the chapel-bell struck the vesper-hour. The conversation was arrested; we all arose to our feet ... the shouts of the children died away; the slaves that were crossing the courtyard stopped and uncovered the head. All devoutly folded their hands and breathed the evening prayer to the Virgin."

Freyre's comprehensive description of this phenomenon (1956:432-33) is also to the point and instructive, in showing how familial Catholicism held sway over the dominant and minority elements alike:

In the seventeenth and even the eighteenth century there was not a white gentleman [i.e., a master of the plantation], however indolent,

217

who would avoid the effort involved in the sacred duty of kneeling before the niches of the saints in prayer - prayers that were sometimes endlessly drawn out by negroes and mulattoes. The rosary, the chaplet of Our Lord, the litanies. They would leap from the hammocks to go and pray in the oratories; for this was an obligation that must be fulfilled. They would go, rosary in hand, and with holy medals, reliquaries, scapulars, St. Anthony hung about their necks, everything that was needed for their prayers and devotions ... Within the house they prayed in the morning, at mealtimes, at midday; and at night they prayed in the room set aside for the saints, slaves accompanying the whites in the rosary and the *Salve Regina* ... When it thundered loudly, whites and blacks would gather in the chapel or the sanctuary to sing the *Benedicte*, intone the *Magnificat*, and recite the prayers of St. Braz, St. Jerome, and St. Barbara. They would light candles, burn holy boughs, and recite the *Credo*.

The foregoing strengthens the impression that the religious acculturation of the blacks in the rural areas was direct and systematic. This aspect is also emphasized in the following passages. The first is from Southey (1822:781): "The children [of slaves] are carefully instructed in their [i.e., the masters'] religion, and the evening hymn to the Virgin is sung by all Negroes as a daily duty" (1822:781). Another is from the pen of the 19th-century historian of Brazilian slavery Perdigão Malheiro, who reported that "in the countryside in general the slaves are taught the prayers of the Catholic religion, and on the plantations they pray the Rosary at night, and on *Domingos de Guarda* (Holy Sundays or Sundays of Observance) they take part in the morning prayers, accompanied by the entire family, along with any guests that the family may have ..." (cited in Ribeiro, 1956:82-3; my translation).

Yet, on the plantation as in the urban setting, the reciprocity of cultural relations between the dominant and subaltern ethnic groups was a conspicuous phenomenon. The slaves, Koster observed, "imbibe a Catholic feeling" upon being brought to the Brazilian environment, an observation that denotes, it is true, the absorption of Catholicism at the formal level, but also, and principally, at the level of culture. That is, it underlines its internalization as a cultural system. At the same time, Koster continues, "the masters ... imbibe some of the customs of their slaves, and thus the superior and his dependant are brought nearer to each other" (1816:410-11).

In providing the conditions of possibility for the integration of the different ethnic-cultural groupings in Brazilian society, in the area of cultural relations proper - these conditions of possibility concern the ideological and structural circumstances discussed here: the baroque character of the dominant religion in colonial Brazil; the religious associations, such as the lay brotherhoods; the processions and festivals; the syncretic rituals within the churches; and the Afro-Christian hagiolatrical correspondences - the universalism of the dominant Catholicism also fostered the biological and psychosocial integration of the minority element, or, to state it differently, integration at the level of intermarriage and identity. That is to say, these two other areas (of the tripartite complex of cultural life, as postulated in this analysis) would necessarily have been affected by what was happening in the plane of cultural relations proper. But, we must not be guided solely by what can be inferred logically. The identification, however brief, of the specific manner in which Luso-Brazilian Catholicism affected dominant-minority patterns in the areas of intermarriage and identity formation must also be provided.

We have already laid much stress on the concrete and symbolic importance of the Catholic sacrament, during the colonial and Imperial periods in Brazil, as a "rite of passage" towards the religious and otherwise social inclusion of individuals. The Africans, Koster informs us (1816:409), though brought in as slaves, were nevertheless baptized before leaving their native shores for Brazilian ports. (This appears to have been the case particularly for the Africans from Angola, the area that supplied the greatest numbers of slaves to Brazil, from the late 1500s to the end of the 1600s, and then again during the 19th century, so that, all together, it is estimated that approximately one million Angolan blacks were imported; Pierson, 1967:33; see also Koster, 1816:418). Their entrance into the Catholic Church was "treated as a thing of course" (1816:410), and, at the same time that this was taking place, it also meant the removal of the principal obstacle to full social membership, as stated earlier.

The elevation of the minority element (and all persons) in Brazil to the status of member of society by means of sacramental induction has several implications. First of all, as has been seen, it translated a recognition of the basic humanity of the individual, even when the latter's civil status was the lowest in the social order, namely, that of slave, which precluded the enjoyment of an array of fundamental civil rights and privileges. This evinces the remarkably broad reach of Catholic universalism, the full measure of which was certainly felt in the Brazilian context. Clearly, too, this ideological orientation stood behind the formal sanctioning of slave marriages by the Church. The slaves, we are told (Koster, 1816:412),[15] were "regularly married according to the forms of the Catholic Church [and] the banns are published in the same manner as those of free persons ...". With institutional legitimation being extended by the Church in the vitally important area of marriage and kinship formation to the extreme case of persons (i.e., the slaves) who had been formally stripped of their citizenship status, and of the rights and freedoms thereof,[16] and reduced to the status of property, of "chattels personal," to use the language of the antebellum slave codes, it is plausible that where free persons were concerned, this legitimation process would have been automatic and even more directly applicable. Religious universalism, as a normative principle of social relations, stresses undifferentiation and inclusion, elements which are externalized in the manner in which the dominant religious body influences collective arrangements and affairs, and more to the point of this analysis, the arrangements and affairs of the minority ethnic communities. Since all individuals are rendered fundamentally equal in the sight of God (this equality being mediated by the sacraments), notwithstanding their diverse ethnic, racial, and socioeconomic backgrounds, no obstructions would in principle have been posed by the Church to the union of these individuals in families towards the goal of societal consolidation. Regarding the specific aspect of biological integration, this implies - and the historical record strongly confirms - that the Church implicitly and explicitly granted its *nihil obstat* to every kind of union between members of the dominant and minority groups, from the cases of lawful wedlock to the *de juras* marriages[17] to simple cohabitation. The Catholic religion in Brazil, though having remained formally subordinate to civil power, exercised an immense influence in the regulation of social life "right up to the Republic" [1889] (Prado, 1971:386). The Church and the State together produced a social climate that was very favorable towards the biological assimilation of the ethnic minorities (see, in this respect, Hollanda's discussion of the royal decree of 1755 regarding intermarriage, 1973:26), thus causing a tradition of interracial crossing and amalgamation to become firmly established in the colonial mores as early as the 16th century. The universalism of the Catholic religion was manifested, as has been shown, in an emphasis on community solidarity and the total inclusion of individuals through ritual-sacramental participation, and on this basis the Church endeavored to regularize into Christian marriage the interracial unions that lacked the benefit of the formal ceremony.

All that remains to be examined now is the psychosocial dimension of cultural integration, or that part of the assimilative process that pertains to the question of identity formation. To the extent that the dominant Catholic culture in Brazil shaped social thought and practices so that cultural unification and ethnic amalgamation were promoted, the psychosocial integration of the minority contingents would have emerged as a natural consequence of this process, that is to say, a consequence of the fusion of races and cultures. In more specific terms, as the members of the various formative ethnic-cultural communities - in addition to the Portuguese settlers, Europeans from other parts, Japanese, Africans, and Amerindians - commonly engaged in beliefs and practices that were perceived to be making up a cohesive cultural complex, applicable to the entire society, and as they also merged together biologically to produce a largely mixed and physically diverse population, they accordingly developed a cultural identity of which the primary referent was the society as a whole. They came to see themselves first and foremost in terms of the national identity, which overrode all forms of subnational membership - ethnic, racial, or socioeconomic. In the end, culture (i.e., cultural integration) triumphed over race and ethnicity.

Catholicism in Brazil may be said to have generated sentiments and values that had to do with class formation and class structure, in the specific sense that class standing in the society basically hinged on religious status: it depended on whether or not one was a full-fledged member of the Church. This was the fundamental prerequisite, as well as common ground, for everyone. Freyre (1968:244) draws attention to this point in the following terms: "Reds [i.e., Amerindians], blacks, and browns were as much the sons of God and the Virgin Mary as any white, as much the subjects of the King as any Portuguese...The civilized, Christian colored man could be socially as Portuguese as any Portuguese, as Christian as any Christian." Under the auspices of the dominant religion, then, these individuals enjoyed full eligibility for cultural assimilation, and, at least in principle, structural or institutional assimilation. And, if the structural integration of these minority segments has yet to be fully completed (i.e., socioeconomic inequality is still strongly *correlated* with ethnic/racial origin in Brazilian society), their cultural integration has proven hugely successful, creating equality in the sphere of interethnic cultural relations which, in turn, has generally favored the process of minority *structural* inclusion.

We have seen that the incorporation of individuals into Brazilian social life was accomplished, from the beginning, primarily on the basis of culture, and more directly still, of *religious* culture. In other words, this was accomplished on the basis of ritual. As befitted the brand of Catholicism described here, the unflagging effort of the Church to bring all the newly-arrived Africans - and, for that matter, *all* individuals: all the newcomers, slave or free, who entered Brazil from non-Catholic countries, or the different Amerindian groups, who were subdued into the status of minority groups - into the Catholic community via the sacrament of baptism, performed a function and conveyed a meaning that exceeded the strictly religious aspect. It went beyond the specific work of the

221

Church of saving souls, and expressed in a general way the work of the society of rescuing all the newcomers, the "pagans" - pagans not only in the specific sense of religious alienation and damnation, but, more broadly, of *social* alienation and damnation - from their outsidedness and into the social mainstream. Catholicism provided this basis of eligibility, a precondition for the eventual absorption into the social body. At this point of intersection between the society and the dominant religion, the two became so closely identifiable with each other as to combine into a single force. Religious assimilation is in this way transformed into the larger process of social assimilation. In being allowed participation in the collective ritual - baptism as a *particular*, that is, religious, principle of inclusion - the individual gains access to and becomes identified with the *general*, that is, social, principle of inclusion. The Church emerges in this way as a critical medium of assimilation and social advancement, a pattern observable at the very outset of colonization in Brazil, and, as Bastide informs us (1951:339), "increasingly so in the eighteenth century and under the Empire." This aspect goes far in clarifying the existential dimension of life for the Africans: their condition (leaving aside the slave status, which was not deemed intrinsic to them, and could therefore be terminated) was transformed from that of "inferior difference" to that of "normal members of society." This kind of ontological transformation has been shown to be untenable in biracially managed social systems, where the status of individuals, and their corresponding identity, are crystallized on the basis of permanently polarized racial categories. Such has been the ethnic developmental pattern found in the United States, as produced by the social dualism associated with ascetic, Calvinistically-grounded Protestantism. It is to that contrasting example that we shall move next.

Notes

1   Southey (1970:784, orig. 1822) remarks that "slavery has mitigations in Brazil ... [related to] ... privileges and harmless enjoyments connected with Catholic superstition, whereby the hours of bondage are exhilarated."

2   In contradistinction, the opposite could reasonably be asserted for the experience of slavery in the American South. There, "the presumption was in favor of slavery" (Tannenbaum, 1946:65).

3   As with other critics of the Freyre-Tannenbaum thesis, Boxer points out that claims of a milder Luso-Brazilian slavery are applicable "only

to nineteenth-century slavery under the Empire" (1964:173). However, he concedes that the possibility of emancipation for the African bondsmen, during the entire slavery period, was "much rarer" in the French and English American colonies than in Brazil; and that in the latter the slaves, for all the harshness of their day-to-day life on the plantation, were not entirely without legal protection (1964:177).

4   The same pattern was observed in other Catholic settings such as Cuba where, we are told (Tannenbaum, 1946:100), in 1827 there were 20,000 more free blacks than in all of the British Caribbean islands, where Protestantism was the dominant religion.

5   Through the *apadrinhamento* institution it was also possible for a member of the white community to intercede on behalf of a slave godchild, by protecting him/her from the worst excesses of a brutal owner, or by saving him/her from punishment for running away (Ribeiro, 1900:153).

6   The self-understanding of the Southerners as God's chosen people was deeply rooted in their Puritan (Calvinist) worldview, reaching back to the colonial beginnings of the country. Wright (1965:157) explains how this collective identity, the sense of being especially elected by God to carry out a divine plan, served important political purposes for the early English colonists in their relations with the resident Native-American societies. "The pioneers of New England," he noted, "were convinced that they were the children of God ... [t]heir sense of election operated to their material advantage and gave them a valuable assurance of right in all their endeavors."

7   These remarks may be considered as applicable to ethnic minorities in general. Thus, in the province of Ceará Koster noticed that the Amerindian population was being steadily assimilated, that "... the priesthood is open to them ..." (1816:120), and that in each village of that province there were "two *juizes ordinarios* or mayors ... one *juiz* is a white man, and the other an Indian ..."(1816:117).

8   In contrast, in U.S. Southern society the physical marks of the minority element were treated as the marks of perpetual social inferiority. As Tannenbaum put it, "being a Negro was presumptive of slave status" (1946:66).

9 This example foregrounds the particular character of the phenomenon of "whitening" in Brazilian society (an issue addressed in greater depth in chapter 2), regarding such aspects as the preponderance of class over race, distinctions of color (i.e., a little "white blood" makes for inclusion, in contrast to a multiethnic model in which a little "nonwhite blood" makes for exclusion), etc.

10 *The New Encyclopaedia Britannica*, 1995. vol.I, 1995:910-11. Chicago (Micropaedia).

11 Fletcher and Kidder (1867:146) noticed the following advertisement, in the 1860s:

> The Brotherhood of the Divine Holy Ghost of São Goncalo [a small village across Guanabara Bay, in the Rio de Janeiro area) will hold the Feast of the Holy Ghost on the 31st instant, with all possible splendor. Devout persons are invited to attend, to give greater pomp to this act of religion. On the 1st *proximo* there will be the feast of the Most Holy Sacrament, with a procession in the evening, a Te Deum, and a sermon. On the 2nd - the feast of the patron of São Gonçalo - at 3 pm there will be *brilliant horseracing!* [Fletcher and Kidder's emphasis], after which a Te Deum and magnificent fireworks."

12 Walsh's informative account of this practice is germane:

> The constant salutation of a baptised Negro, in the interior, is, 'Jesus Christo'; and the answer is ,'[Para] sempre - Forever'... Another answer is 'a Deos,' a contraction of the sentence 'Louvado seja Deos que faz santos - Praised be God who sanctifies us.' When I first met groups of negroes on the road, who all thrust out their hands at me, I thought they were beggars. It was merely this mode of salutation, which they never omit; whenever they return from work, or retire for the night, they all come into the family of their masters and give and receive this form of salutation" (1831:188-9).

13 Koster (1816:251) writes about the blessing of the sugar works, in which "the priest took his breviary and read several prayers, and at stated places, with a small bunch of weeds prepared for the occasion, which he dipped in a jug of holy water, he sprinkled the mill and the

persons present. Some of the negroes sprang forward to receive a good quantum of this sanctified water...".

14 Private residences also customarily had a specific area set aside for the practice of this domestic Catholicism, with an altar and various objects used in religious worship, as documented in Graham's description of a Brazilian residence she visited in the early 1800s:

> At one end of the room was a long table, covered with a glass case, enclosing a large piece of religious wax-work; the whole *praesepia*, ministering angels, three kings, and all, with moss, artificial flowers, shells, and beads, smothered in gauze and tiffany, bespangled with gold and silver, Saint Antonio and Saint Christopher being in attendance on the right and left..." (1969:127; orig.1824).

15 This pattern of slave marriage may be compared to that which generally prevailed in the antebellum U.S. South. In the latter, we are told (Genovese, 1976:475-81), slave marriages were also granted institutional sanction insofar as the ceremony (which sometimes could be quite lavish, in the more paternalistic households) was performed by a white or a black preacher. However, the accounts of these events by former slaves indicate that the formality and solemnity of the situation was often overpowered by a touch of the carnivalesque, in the sense that, as Stampp (1956:329) reports, slave weddings were mainly a show, a performance, for the whites. Oftentimes, the families from neighboring plantations would be invited to come and watch the spectacle. Also, in a great many instances a paternalistic master himself would officiate at these weddings, making it a "broomstick wedding," whereby the couple would jump over a broomstick, and this was the critical procedure lending symbolic legitimacy to the affair.

16 In the antebellum Southern United States, this deprivation meant the inability to enter economic contracts, to exercise a juridical personality (as, for instance, in being a party to a suit), to be elected to office, to have legally binding marriages, and so on; see, e.g., Stampp, 1956:196-201).

17 The *de juras* marriage was a simple ceremony in which, according to Herculano (cited in Pierson, 1967:113), "the mutual consent of both

225

parties was affirmed on oath before a representative of the Church without, however, the sacrament being given."

8 The church in the United States: Calvinistic Protestantism and ethnic assimilation

Dominant-minority relations in the antebellum South

When we compare the religious environment in Brazil and its effect on interethnic life with its counterpart in the United States, we find that the tendency of Luso-Brazilian Catholicism to open its doors to everyone, regardless of background, was as strong as the tendency of exclusion among the Protestant denominations in the United States - Baptists, Methodists, and Presbyterians, in particular - especially in the South. As concerns the African-American group, all through the slavery period, and even as early as the 1700s, the Protestant Establishment directly reinforced separatism in dominant-minority relations either by generally failing to reach out to incorporate this group, or by actively trying to push them to tend to their own religious affairs and needs (Tannenbaum, 1946:86-7; Genovese, 1976:235). The blacks, says one author, were simply "not welcome" in the white churches (Franklin, 1969:164). The practices of the Protestant churches, in fact (says the same author, 1969:200) supply the earliest examples of black-white segregation in U.S. society. There were, it is true, racially mixed churches in the Old South, but this does not refer to integrated congregations.[1] The organization of worship in those churches mirrored the rigidly separatist architecture of the larger society. Franklin describes it thusly: "When the slaves attended the churches of the planters they usually sat either in the gallery or in a special section ... In one instance the white congregation developed the ingenious scheme of constructing a partition several feet high to separate the masters from the slaves" (1969:200). Towards the end of the slavery era, or the decades immediately preceding the Civil War, the Protestant churches, through direct effort or by default, intensified this pattern of segregation (Genovese, 1976:235). The nature of religious interaction

227

between the dominant and subordinate classes was the pivotal factor behind the emergence and development of the independent black Church in the United States. Slaves and freedmen experienced growing dissatisfaction with the constraints imposed on their religious activity by white society. In the case of the slaves, their only options were either the white-supervised services on the plantation, where they were mostly subjected to exhortations and biblical injunctions by white (or black) preachers, urging them to remain obedient and docile; or the segregated services in the white churches. Increasingly, the slaves sought to develop an independent religious life by "stealing away" to secret religious gatherings, at the risk of severe punishment, if discovered.

To reiterate the basic points concerning the formal effect of Catholicism on the life of the Africans under slavery, we have seen that this religion proceeded from the official acknowledgement of the moral equality, or potential moral equality, of all individuals, a principle that was fulfilled through its ritual, or sacramental, structure. Human imperfection was accounted for, but as a temporary state, passive of transformation through sacramental intervention. Thus, slave status was treated as only a particular type of civil status, not an intrinsic, insurmountable ontological deficiency. While crippling the Africans socially, it did not constitute a barrier to their incorporation as full members of the Christian community. Ultimately, the admission into the Christian fold acted as a springboard to social assimilation. The informal level of Catholic practice, represented here by familial Catholicism, narrowed the ontological distance between the faithful, on the one hand, and the deity and the saints, on the other. As Holanda explains, "Christ, Our Lady, and the saints are no longer treated as privileged beings, exempt from any human sentiment" (1973:110). In this way, the familial Catholicism of rural Brazil undermined doctrinal orthodoxy and formalism, while encouraging the bridging of social boundaries and hierarchies, the idea of community. This created a very favorable terrain for the social incorporation of the minority segment, on the one hand, and for large-scale cultural integration at the national level, on the other. Regarding the latter, the reaction of the Protestant core culture in colonial and postcolonial U.S. society towards the minority modes of life presents a stark contrast. Evangelical or ascetic Protestantism in the United States stood in a consistently adversarial relation toward West African cultural manifestations (and, for that matter, toward the cultural manifestations of any group - such as the immigrant groups that came in the 1800s - that did not conform closely to the dominant Anglo-American Protestant model). In lieu of a disposition toward accommodation and syncretism, what prevailed was the methodical, harsh suppression of religious difference. In this way, the foundation was laid for the continuing separation of the dominant and minority cultural models. From the earliest phases of slavery, ascetic Protestant culture proved inimical to cultural interpenetration, and whether through the general governance of life on the plantation, or in the specific activities of the (mostly) Baptist and Methodist missionaries, it treated the cultural traits of the slaves with complete intransigence. I have elsewhere (1988) described this process as "the silencing of the drums," and this may be illustrated in the area of dancing and musical entertainment, which are undoubtedly the traits of greatest relevance for any analysis of culture in traditional African societies, since they permeate the wider context of social activity. We are informed (see, e.g., Mbiti, 1970), that the dancing theme is closely related to African religious mythology, religious initiation, and funeral rites. It is noteworthy in this connection that historical accounts consistently reveal that the dancing and musical expressions of the African slaves in the antebellum South met with fierce opposition on the part of the Protestant Establishment.

Writing about the Protestant influence in the nineteenth century, a time when Protestantism, particularly of the Methodist and Baptist variety, made great inroads among the African-American population, Phillips tells us that "in the evangelical churches dancing and religion were held to be incompatible. At one time on Thomas Dabney's plantation in Mississippi, for instance, the whole Negro force fell captive in a Baptist revival and forswore the double shuffle. 'I done buss by fiddle an' my banjo, and done fling 'em away,' the most music-loving fellow on the place said to the preacher when asked for his religious experiences" (1918:314). Another chronicler (Jackson, 1930:110) states that the conversion into the Baptist doctrine normally led them to quickly abandon "their banjos, fiddles, double-shuffle and break-down." Genovese (1976:569) writes: "On a number of plantations the slaves abruptly quit having dances when they got religion." In the Sea-Islands the slaves were taught, again by the Baptists, that dancing and instrumental music were sinful, but they managed to insert these elements into their religious worship in modified or "reconstructed" form, through the spirituals and what became known as the "ring shout" (see e.g., Johnson, 1930:150-1). The accounts left by 19th century visitors in the slave states tend to support these points. Sir Charles Lyell noticed on the Hopeton plantation in Georgia that slaves were "passionately fond" of dancing and music, but more than twenty violins had been silenced by the Methodist missionaries (1850:363). Traveling through antebellum South Carolina and Georgia, Fredrika Bremer writes about the amusements of the slaves, saying that in these states "the preachers have done away with dancing and the singing of songs" (1968:117, vol. II). This same observer was told by a planter that

229

"... the Methodist missionaries, who are the most influential and effective teachers and preachers among the Negroes are very angry with them for their love of dancing and music, and declare them to be sinful. And whenever the Negroes become Christian, they give up dancing, have preaching meetings instead, and empty their musical talents merely in psalms and hymns" (1968:290, vol.I). Writing in the 1850s, Olmsted comments on earlier times when "... the slaves were accustomed to amuse themselves in the evening and on holidays, a great deal in dancing, and they took great enjoyment in this exercise. It was at length, however, preached against and the 'professors' so generally induced to use their influence against it, as an immoral practice that it has greatly 'gone out of fashion' (1968:128). But, in fact, even in earlier times, the growing evangelical influence on secular entertainment among the slaves (and the general population as well) is revealed in reports such as that of Philip V. Fithian, who lived in Virginia as a plantation tutor in the mid-1770s. He tells us that the religious zeal of the (Ana)Baptists led to the "entire Banishment of Gaming, Dancing, and Sabbath-Day diversions" (in Farish, 1943:96).

The situation was made all the more problematic because the acculturative process was, as we have seen, rooted in racial considerations. Ethnic-racial minorities were faced with a situation in which, being denied the ability to preserve aboriginal custom, they could only opt for admission into the dominant cultural model. Yet, this admission was to be a limited one because their social classification as nonwhite precluded the experience of full-scale absorption into the mainstream culture. As a result, the progressive incorporation of the Africans and their native-born descendants into the Protestant fold did not prevent the emergence of a "black religion" and a "black culture," but the distinctiveness of the latter owed not to a persisting connection with the West African background -since that process of cultural continuity had been weakened early on - but to social alienation and marginalization. This point is emphasized by Frazier (1964:334), when he writes: "It appears from the historical evidence that the religion of the American Negro and his church organization grew out of his experiences on American soil." This notion would seem obvious, for it addresses the general principle that ethnic minorities develop cultural ways which reflect the structural circumstances of the host society, and how they collectively react to these circumstances. But Frazier is implicitly making an important distinction here, namely, between situations where the cultural traits of minority ethnic groups give evidence of large-scale cross-pollination between aboriginal custom and the patterns of the core culture, and situations where dominant-minority cultural relations are more clearly indicative of the complete submersion of the alien group under the hegemonic cultural system. In the latter case, minority-group members are systematically pushed into repressing their ancestral cultural and social heritage, and left with no option but to seek affiliation with the dominant mode of life, in the degree that this was made accessible to them. The dissociation of the African-American community in the United States from the African cultural matrix was observed early in the 1800s, as typically recounted in the narrative of the ex-slave Charles Ball. "The case is different," he states, "with the American Negro, who knows nothing of Africa, her religion, or customs ..." (1969:218; orig.1837).[2] Shifting now to cultural integration as linked to biological assimilation, that is, to the aspect of intermarriage and kinship relations, the evangelical churches in the United States were predicated, as mentioned previously, on the principles of individualism and particularism, principles which in fact invert the relationship established by Catholicism between the individual and the community. In other words, in Catholicism the individual acquires worth through participation in the ritual life of the community, a mode that can only promote unity and homogeneity. In the Protestant context, the community acquires meaning on the basis of being formed by individuals who are *inherently* worthy in their individuality. This mode naturally lays a premium upon diversity, which, instead of unifying the community, divides it into separate categories, and preserves it in terms of a framework of compartmentalization. The great diversity shown in the denominationalist basis of religious practice in American society testifies to the operation of this principle. Predictably, given its grounding in individual difference, Protestant practice and ideology during the colonial and antebellum periods translated into a fierce juridical opposition to miscegenation, as instantiated in the enactment of specific anti-miscegenation laws as early as the 1600s (see, e.g., Jordan, 1981:69-86). The impact of religious values and ideas is patently evidenced in the language of some of these laws. A Virginia resolution of 1630, for example, prescribed punishment to one individual for "abusing himself to the dishonor of God and the shame of Christians by defiling his body in lying with a Negro." A Maryland act of 1681 condemns interracial marriages as being a disgrace to "... Christian nations" (cited in Moore, 1941:179). Later, scriptural admonitions became a mainstay of proslavery arguments in the South, and a dominant theme of proslavery discourse as a whole was the divine rejection of racial amalgamation. One of the more prominent proslavery spokesmen of the South, Henry Hughes, insists in his "Treatise on Sociology: Theoretical and Practical" that the relations between the races must be strictly guided by the ideal of "hygienic progress" (by which he meant that these relations must be based on the

231

proper social and physical segregation and hierarchization of society's groups), that social and biological integration is "regress," that "hybridism" (i.e., amalgamation) is "heinous," the most horrible of sins. "Impurity of races," Hughes continues, "is against the law of nature. Mulattoes are monsters. The law of nature is the law of God" (1981:259-60). The redoubtable orator and statesman Henry Clay, of Kentucky, held the miscegenation of the "races" in the greatest contempt, insisting, in a famous address of 1839, that to endorse this intermixture was "to arraign the wisdom and goodness of Providence itself," and that "those whom He has created different, and has declared by their physical structure and color, ought to be kept asunder, should not be brought together by any process whatever of unnatural amalgamation" (in Ruchames, 1969:395). The explicitness of the religious mandate, so richly evident in these 19th century sources, admittedly fades as the society becomes secularized, and its institutions assume a more bureaucratic character. Thus, when the nation enacted into law the "separate but equal principle" a century ago (and three decades after the abolition of slavery), and accordingly erected the racial caste system known as Jim Crow, with the most stringent prohibitions of racial intermixture, the latter no longer overtly bore the religious imprint of legitimation.

This fact notwithstanding, the forces that animated this aspect of intergroup relations continued to derive basically from the ideological premises laid down by the dominant religion. From this perspective, in spite of the increasing prevalence of secularized social circumstances, religious ideas tend to remain the primary "dynamic impulse" (to use Giddens's phrase, 1991:871) behind social practices, in this case, behind the particular practices involved in the management of interracial crossing.

Finally, in a sociocultural system marked by ethnic separatism, the latter being erected on the basis of the larger framework of racial bipolarity, the integration of the population on the basis of a single (national) identity becomes virtually impossible. Of necessity, the incompletely assimilated segments of the population will be hindered in their ability to blend completely into, and identify fully with, the dominant mode of social and institutional life, and will therefore tend to rely primarily on their subnational identities, and only secondarily on the national, or citizenship, identity. The particularizing effect of the dominant Protestantism in this case, as has been indicated, contributed directly in this way to the fragmentation of cultural identity. This involved the process of identity formation, as well as the two other dimensions of cultural life outlined in this study (i.e., intermarriage and cultural relations), and we will explore this further as the discussion shifts next to a consideration of the proslavery defense of the Old South.

Southern social thought and the proslavery argument

In this second part of the chapter we will concentrate on the identification of the sanctions of ascetic Protestant ideology as manifested in formal writings. The body of writings to be examined is the proslavery argument, a comprehensive ideological framework consisting of essays, pamphlets, speeches, etc., by prominent Southern intellectuals - writers, clergymen, statesmen, public officials, scientists - and on the basis of which slavery was defended as the very cornerstone of Southern civilization. The aim of the analysis is to demonstrate the way in which the religious injunctions contained therein reinforced and crystallized a separatist ethos and mode of life in the South, and ultimately in the nation as a whole, thus setting the pattern for dominant-minority relations during the slavery era and beyond.

During the half century or so preceding the Civil War, ascetic Protestant ideology predominated in the Southern region of the United States, and had its impact felt in every nook and cranny of social life. This phenomenon may be understood in broader socio-historical perspective. The proslavery argument in the antebellum South - predominantly, but not exclusively, expressed in terms of its religious dimension - illustrates the way and degree in which ascetic Protestant ideology operated as a mainspring of social organization, providing the ideological underpinnings of collective thought and action, and legitimizing both formally and implicitly the patterns of intergroup relations in the Southern slavery order.

Starting in the 1830s onward, the apologists of slavery in the South developed a coherent and comprehensive defense of the institution, a body of ideology that came to maturity over the next few decades. Proslavery ideology was replete with contradiction, as ideological movements and discourses tend to be. In this case, a major contradiction was the simultaneous and dualistic characterization of the African slaves as beings who had the potential for being acculturated and assimilated into neo-European society, on the one hand, and as permanently inferior beings, unable to become sufficiently "civilized" to warrant full integration into the host society, on the other. The potentiality of the Africans for acculturation appears to have been universally hinted at, and even explicitly stated, by slaveholding classes in the New World, but the truly dominant theme of proslavery discourse was the idea of the inherent inferiority of the slaves. The oscillation between these two principles is the crucial process for understanding the dynamics of race relations during and after slavery, both in the context of the Southern states and in crosscultural perspective. It seems plausible that a fundamental attachment to, and formal enforcement of, one principle or the other would have produced sharply divergent patterns of black-white relations.

A cardinal concept implicit in the entire architecture of the pro-slavery defense is that of *difference*, which in turn I see as part of a larger conceptual framework involving the corollary notions of hierarchization, control, and boundary maintenance. The structural significance of each concept and how they are interrelated will be explored here. As a preliminary consideration, it may be proposed that the deepening level of involvement of the Southern plantation system with the process of international capitalist development, on the one hand, and the thrust of southern morality, on the other, converged to produce a particular mode of apprehension of reality, with direct implications for the question of difference.

There are two major theoretical coordinates undergirding the structure of the proslavery argument, and it is in relation to these coordinates that the principles of difference is dualistically revealed. They are the "mode of progress," as expressed in change, and the "mode of tradition," as expressed in stability. Though diametrically opposed, these principles sustained through their continuous tension the entire social and ideological edifice of the Old South. We need to recognize, first of all, that the African element, forcefully abducted and transplanted to neo-European settings in the New World, was universally perceived by the European as "difference" (the linkage between the idea of difference and religious thought is initially explored in chapter 6). This was a process initiated at the time of abduction on the African shores, then continued as the masses of black Africans entered their arduous life of bondage. The focus at this stage of interpretation is on this process of perception: how it comes to be, both concretely and at the theoretical level, how it continues, how it is affected in the direction of change or permanence. By exploring the dynamics of the perception of difference, the aim here is, in the first place, to achieve a grasp of the interconnections among the formal elements of the proslavery argument, or the intellectual categories that make up its fundamental structure. Secondly, to gain a better understanding of the process of classification of the African in the Southern slave society, and of the structure of intergroup relations.

The master-slave relationship and the problem of difference

At this point, it should be useful to consider, albeit in the briefest of outlines, what is involved at the level of intersubjectivity involving the dominant and subaltern social groups, in order to better elucidate the question of difference. Let us start with the subject and object. In the Hegelian analysis of the development of consciousness (Kojeve, 1980), two subjects meet initially as potential equals in the interactional arena and seek, through a reciprocal anthropogenetic Desire of the Other's recognition, to achieve selfhood. The idea of Desire is of utmost importance here, being linked to the fundamentak human need for self-affirmation through the objectification, appropriation, and "overcoming" of external reality. In the context of human relations, this pertains to the need for self-affirmation through being recognized by, and thus overcoming, the Other. Social interaction is thus predicated on a constant antagonism of consciousnesses which have not actualized themselves, but strive towards that goal, through the domination of other human Desires, that is, of other consciousnesses seeking to be recognized. To state the matter differently, there is in the social world a multiplicity of Desires struggling to impose themselves on other Desires.

The mention that humans are potential equals in this process of achieving selfhood is significant because, in the last analysis, the outcome will be one of inequality. Hegel essentially affirms that selfhood cannot be attained other than through the "death" of some Desires, and the preponderance of others. One must surrender his/her Desire, or his/her striving for recognition, in order that the Other's Desire prevail. In this sense, both organisms are alive, but in a frame of domination/subjection. Hence, as master and slave.

It is germane to this analysis that human reality be fundamentally affirmed here as *social reality*, in that the individual's subjective certainty of himself/herself can only be accomplished through the Other, through an entity that exists outside the individual. To be sure, the context is one of antagonism and perennial interindividual confrontation. In order to become human, individuals must confront themselves as "common objects," that is, as self-consciousnesses that theoretically carry the same potentiality for actualization, and exercise their sociability in a process that is inherently fraught with danger: the life-or-death struggle for recognition. Thus, we have the two moments in the Hegelian dialectic of consciousness which need to be clearly distinguished. In the first moment of the subject/object relationship, as indicated, the subject apprehends the Other *as subjectivity*, for it is only through the recognition of another human being like him/herself, realized in the confrontation of Desires, that the subject's selfhood is actualized. In this process, there is a reciprocal sharing of the symbolic world, and subjects could be said to be universally alike in their potential ability for transcending this pre-social stage of their existence, and for becoming fully human.

This process applies fundamentally to human interaction. And, while the confrontation of subjectivities will, according to Hegel, result inevitably and ultimately in a condition of inequality, (i.e., a Desire must assert itself over another), there must be a condition of essential equality in the first moment or phase of the dialectic - which is to say, individuals must be mutually apprehended as potential sources of recognition for other individuals *during the presocial stage* - before social life and social communication can take place. That in the second moment of the dialectic there is mastery of one subjectivity (Desire) over another is extremely important, but it does not invalidate the basis of "sameness" or equality that characterizes subjects at the initial moment of their confrontation. From this we derive the following: 1. the Other is not and cannot be apprehended as difference *a priori*. 2. the Hegelian formula parallels the Meadian model of symbolic interaction, in which the Other is apprehended in his/her *in-itself*, as a potential participant in a symbolic universe, and is not apprehended as abstractly reconstructed reality.

It is against this theoretical background that the concrete, historical situation of the master and slave in the American South shall be viewed. It is clear that here we are not dealing here simply with a dialectic of consciousness that involves the broader interactional process in the human community, but also with an objective condition of human inequality created by a specific arrangement of the relations of production. The fundamental separation between the master and slave can be taken as it presents itself: two beings that exist as unequals at both the objective and subjective levels. This relationship is affected not only in the context of the interactional dyad, but also in the wider context where the influences from other autonomous consciousnesses are asserted, such as the consciousness of progress manifested in the countertendencies stemming from European capitalism and from the capitalistic North. In both cases, these countertendencies tended to negate the Southern master's consciousness, and thus to affect the way the slave was defined and reatced to by the master.

Two questions of relevance may be raised at this time: How can the master's consciousness of the slave be characterized? To what extent did the countertendencies of capitalism and progress affect this consciousness? Hegel speaks of the problem of difference implicitly, as he develops his analysis of the evolution of consciousness. As explained, individuals meet in an *initial* context of equality until the moment when the Other is vanquished into submission by the Subject's Desire. Before this struggle occurs, humans are undifferentiated in their presocial existence, being thus perceived phenomenologically as beings of equal worth and like constitution. Otherwise, the Other's recognition of the Subject would not be valid and/or sufficient for the latter. Of course, after the struggle for recognition has taken place, and inequality is established (that is, after a dominant Consciousness-for-Itself and a subordinate Consciousness-for-Other emerge), the mode of difference is in effect. In the concrete situation of the master and slave, the African is fundamentally perceived as *thing*, or, in terms of what he/she can do. Which is to say, basically in terms of instrumental function. There is, therefore, an inversion of the Hegelian formula in the sense that the master comes to apprehend the slave not subjectively, as another human being and a potential source of recognition (for the master), but as moral order objectified, via the utilization of subjective categories (e.g. racial inferior, religious heathen, moral dwarf, economic commodity) that are external to the slave's *in-itself*. These categories are objectified as absolute reality. The relationship remains an objective one throughout the slavery period, and this is fully expressed in the proslavery defense. The African is never apprehended in terms of his/her organic totality, but only in terms of reconstructed reality.

One might think of the attempt to Christianize the Africans as the beginning of a process of recognition of their humanity. However, in the context of the Hegelian master-slave relationship, this perceptual oscillation that classifies the African somewhere between a thing and a full person, does not change the quality of the master's apprehension of the slave; it remains objective. It does not lead to transformation, to transcendence (by the slave) into a condition of equality. It continues to affirm the essential condition of the African as *difference*. This is where this principle of difference operates, and where it points to the inability of the slaveholding bourgeoisie to transcend its mode of responding to the world and to the slave class. In the proslavery argument, the progressive objectification of the African reaches its apex, as does the idea of tradition. The condition of the African as difference, as an expression of an internally differentiated human essence, is crystallized and ultimately reified. Again and again in the proslavery texts, we find evidence of this phenomenon. In the final analysis, it mattered little that economic conditions demanded the transformation of the master-slave relationship and the progressive recognition of the African as a being who was, in fact, only provisionally impaired, in terms of social performance in the slavery societies of the New World, by virtue of his/her cultural background and by the myriad barriers to social assimilation imposed by life on the plantation; a being, however, who had the potential for becoming assimilated into the Western cultural universe, for becoming fully human and equal with others. Throughout the years that led up to the Civil War *and beyond*, this relationship of differentiation and inequality between the Anglo-American and the African was maintained, with the Anglo-American consciousness emerging as a Being-for-Itself, that is, as absolute, exclusivist, monolithic, while the African consciousness was existentially negated so as to become a Consciousness-for-Other. Thus it was that the inequality between the dominant and the minority elements was perpetuated, beyond the parameters of life in slavery itself, and that, in the realm of cultural relations, the Africans were never able to assert their cultural identity, and engage, to any appreciable degree, in a dynamic process of exchange with the Anglo-American cultural model. This bespeaks a cultural imperialism on the part of the host culture that seriously hindered the development of interethnic cultural syncretism. Greater attention will be focused later on this last point.

The aspect of domination of this relationship will be linked to the mode of tradition, inasmuch as this mode expressed the perpetuation of the traditional structures of class dominance and subordinance prevailing in the South during the antebellum period. An element of paradox may be detected in this relationship, in connection with the opposing mode on which the slavery system was based, the mode of progress. Within the context of slavery, the growth of capitalist production was undeniably predicated on the apprehension and treatment of the African-as-difference, from the first moment of the subject-object dialectic, but in the context of a free-market society, certain capitalist tendencies, identified with the mode of progress, encouraged the recognition of the humanity of the African slaves. In the first part of the 19th century, as the South proceeded to expand its economy through the systematic cultivation and marketing of cotton, in order to meet the ever-growing demand for this staple in the international market, it set itself firmly on the course of material change and progress. In this way, the operation of the mode of tradition was constantly threatened by the pressures associated with the spreading influence of capitalism in Southern society. On account of this, the defense of slavery seems to alternate, to and fro, between a position in which the African is objectified as difference (i.e., as inferior being, as economic commodity) and thus permanently excluded from the human community, and a position in which his/her status as difference was merely provisional, and therefore passive of transformation. This latter position was frequently invoked as a basis for rationalizing the continuing operation of the system. Specifically, it implied that slavery was essentially a system of socialization or sociocultural training, and the Africans were potentially amenable to "civil improvement" (i.e., cultural re-training), and that in this training ground represented by life on the plantation they would build a valuable foundation which would pave the way for their eventual incorporation into the mainstream of social life.

To elaborate on this point. In the mid-1850s the economic analyst David Christy writes: "Slavery is not an isolated system, but is so mingled with the business of the world, that it derives facilities from the most innocent transactions" (1963: 113). Such a statement underscores the essential integration of slavery with the machinery of international capitalism, and the dynamic, historically-conditioned character of this relationship, while opposing this to the more static, ahistorical nature of slavery society as depicted in proslavery ideology. Christy's statement also shows the inevitability of a forward movement deriving from the integration of economic activity into the larger process of capitalist transformation of Western society, and implicitly emphasizes the vulnerability of the Southern plantation system, as a mere element of the "periphery" in a vast, global, structural network, to the various currents emanating from the "center." Thus, it opposes "progress" to "tradition," change to stability.

The economic praxis of the Southerner could not obviously be separated from the factor of increase - increase related, first of all, to the relentless spread of world capitalism and industrial technology, and then to the increasing structural complexity of the plantation as a system of production. It is true that slaveholding activity was uniformly portrayed in the economic arguments in favor of slavery as *progress*, progress realized in material terms, but, on a larger scale, it was also conceived in terms of progress as overarching the totality of social life. Christy (1963: 113) addresses precisely that equation between the practice of slavery and progress in the broader sense of human collective existence, when he says that all of the agencies associated with the manufacture and sale of cotton (this plant was the backbone of the Southern economy in the thirty years preceding the Civil War) manifestly promoted civilization and human happiness.

The moral basis of tradition

Why is the mode of stability of slavery designated here as the mode of tradition? Because it was in tradition that proslavery ideologues sought to legitimize and justify the continuation of the institution. Slavery was good and just because it had always existed. Furthermore, it had always existed under the auspices of Divine Providence. The ultimate justification was, therefore, tied to religious morality. In taking the moral route of justification the Southern planter class was apparently making provisions

239

for dealing more effectively with any possible collective sense of guilt. Edmund Ruffin points to the historical evidence: "Slavery has existed from as early as historical records furnish any information of the social and political condition of mankind" (1963: 69). Harper argues that "until within a very few centuries" the institution of slavery prevailed over "all those portions (of the earth) which had made any advances towards civilization" (1981: 79-80). And Reverend Thornton Stringfellow, possibly the foremost spokesman for the religious justification of slavery, contends that not only had slavery existed since the Patriarchal Age, and benefitted from "the sanction of the Almighty," but it had also been "incorporated into the only National Constitution which ever emanated from God," having therefore "its legality ... recognized, and its relative duties regulated, by Jesus Christ in His kingdom" (1981: 139). Stringfellow further invokes the language of Noah, in the Book of Genesis, to justify the permanence of bondage for all the Canaanites, or descendants of Ham, now identified in the proslavery argument as the modern African (see also Ross, 1969:50, orig. 1857). The latter therefore came to be not only singled out on the basis of ethnic/racial status (which is to say, it came to be identified as "difference"), but also cursed with the plight of perpetual enslavement. In the same text, the Old Testament book of Leviticus is cited as additional evidence of divine sanction of involuntary servitude: "Thy bond-men and thy bond-maids which thou shalt have, shall be of the heathen that are round about you: of them shall ye buy bondsmen and bondmaids. Moreover, of the children of the strangers that do sojourn among you, of them shall ye buy, and of their families that are with you, which they begat in your land. And they shall be your possession. And ye shall take them as an inheritance for your children after you, to inherit them for a possession, they shall be your bond-men forever" (1981: 151). Jenkins (1960: 202), calls this passage of scripture "the Rock of Gibraltar in the Old Testament case."

From this perspective, the principles of liberty and equality for all, which enjoyed ever greater vitality in the industrial nations of the world over the 19th century, were seen by Southerners as experimental kinds of notions, far more likely to bring about serious social imbalances and problems, than success and benefits for the whole of society. Various references, for example, can be found in the texts regarding the dismal condition of the working classes in free-labor commonwealths. "Liberty and equality," states Fitzhugh, "are new things under the sun" (1963: 34-35). Chancellor Harper adds that "of all things, the existence of civil liberty is mostly the result of artificial institution. The proclivity of natural man is to domineer or to be subservient" (1981: 85). And Fitzhugh reminds us (1963:35), that the plight of the masses of the poor in

European industrial-capitalist societies was a direct consequence of the injudicious application of these principles of universal freedom and equality, and that the underprivileged classes in those countries were, in fact, "far worse...than under the old order of things."

The association of tradition with religious morality is particularly relevant here in the light of the social and intellectual developments taking place in the American South in the early 1800s. It may generally be asserted that fundamentalist religion remained the mainstay of Southern morality throughout most of the antebellum period, but this status was dramatically enhanced in the beginning decades of the 19th century. At that time, the region experienced a departure from the Jeffersonian liberalism of previous years and from the egalitarian ideals of the Enlightenment, with a concomitant resurgence of evangelical Protestantism (Greene, 1984: 412-413). This was, according to Simkins (1959: 153), "the most significant development in the thinking of the Old South" during that period. An interesting illustration comes to us through the pen of Frederick Law Olmsted, noted chronicler of Southern culture in the 1850s, revealing the widespread popular hostility towards ideas of inequality, religious tolerance, liberalization of social mores, and social collectivism. While attending a religious service at a Georgia church, he witnessed the preacher go off on a "recurring cannonade upon French infidelity and socialism, and several crushing charges upon Fourier, the Pope of Rome, Tom Paine, Voltaire, 'Roosu', and Joe Smith" (1984: 207, originally 1861). Studies of religious history in the antebellum Deep South attest to the fact that the effect of the spread of revivalist religion did not stop at the level of spiritual revitalization, but rather, as Peterson informs us (1978: 15), this phenomenon "helped recast the Southern world view by increasingly grounding it in the Bible." The Southern animosity towards the intellectual currents in vogue in the Northern states at the time may be cast as an expression of a larger ideological resistance on the part of a prebourgeois Southern "periphery" against the capitalist encroachment of a Northern "center." The transformation of social and scientific philosophies in the hands of Southern religious fundamentalists will now be addressed in connection with the interaction between religion and science.

If the mode of progress can be broadly associated with the realm of nature, inasmuch as it involves the manipulation of the physical world for the betterment of human collective existence, the tradition mode can be associated with morality. In this sense, tradition exhibited a twofold aspect because, even though it stressed the principle of stability, it drew its impetus from opposing sources: religion, which stood for stability, and science, which stood for change. At the same time, religion and science

241

could be said to have had a dual effect on reality. We know of Max Weber's argument (1958) to the effect that ascetic Protestantism aided the expansion of capitalism, by virtue of its value structure. If this interpretation can be accepted, the mentality of evangelical Protestantism encouraged the consolidation of the mode of progress, while at the same time fostering the mode of tradition through the reinforcement of the *status quo* engendered by biblical literalism. The social conditions described in the Bible, when the latter is literally interpreted, are taken as givens, as absolutes. Science, in its turn, is generally associated with progressive material and technological change, hence, with the mode of progress. But we must consider science in a special light here. The emerging intellectual disciplines of the early 19th century which sought to explain the nature of human reality (i.e., geology, physical geography ethnology, anthropology), were significantly transformed or "reconstructed" by slavery apologists, whose major concern was to emphasize not the basic conflict between religious and scientific knowledge, but their potential compatibility. Among these disciplines stood out ethnology, rather broadly defined as a scientific orientation that not only concerned itself with the physical history of human populations, but also had a prescriptive aspect regarding the social ramifications of this developmental process. In the words of the editor of the *London Ethnological Journal*, ethnology was "a science which investigates the mental and physical differences of mankind, and the organic laws upon which they depend; and which seeks to deduce from these investigations, *principles of human guidance*, in all the important relations of social existence" (in McKitrick, 1963: 127; emphasis added). Through the interpretation of its most prominent Southern practitioners, people like the physicians Josiah Nott and Samuel Cartwright, ethnology became a useful additional source of moral legitimation of slavery.

In their effort to reconcile scientific research with biblical revelation, several Southern scientists, like Nott, emphasized the scientific explanation of the origins of mankind and of the processes of human differentiation, but continued to hold the great design of God in nature in the highest awe and reverence. Thus, while dismissing the biblical account of creation and human differentiation (i.e., monogenic creation through Adam and Eve, and differential lines of development coming down from Ham and Japheth, sons of Noah), and defending the plurality of species in the human race, Nott did not wish, however, to eliminate Divine Agency as the original source of all creation. The varieties of mankind had not occurred at random, but had descended from original stocks put on earth "by an All-Wise Creator" (1981: 227). Another scientist of the period, Matthew F. Maury, stated: "If the two cannot be reconciled the fault is ours, and is because in our blindness and weakness we have not been able to interpret aright either the one or the other" (cited in Eaton, 1964: 150-151). Yet another writer insisted: "There is no forked tongue in the language of learned men - whether physician or divine. Truth is the same uttered by one or the other - the phraseology may differ but truth is an unit" (Cartwright, 1981: 14).

The synthetic perspective was a difficult position to maintain. Nevertheless, for all the tension between them, religion and science came together to form a powerful basis of moral justification of human bondage. Their language might have been different, but the structural homologies were clear. The following points may be considered:

(a) the fundamentalist religion of the South, imbued with a Calvinism which effectively transcended the formal boundaries of religious belief and made its influence felt over the entire breadth of the social fabric, had as one of its constitutive elements the belief in predestination. It follows from this principle, as we have seen, that humanity must necessarily be divided into the chosen and non-chosen, the elect and the non-elect. Of theoretical interest here is the fact that the non-elect are treated as *difference*, a negative and inferior condition. The Africans were seen as the non-elect, hence, as difference, and unequal in their ontological status in relation to the neo-European element. The concept of difference has a broader meaning in that it encompasses not only the religious difference shown by the Africans, but also their overall cultural, psychological, and physical make-up. In the scientific world of the 19th century in which slavery apologists operated, there was also a division of mankind into two distinct groups, a natural "election" of the racially superior and "non-election" of the racially inferior. This phenomenon was not, however, conceptualized in religious, but in physical, terms. In this sense, the Africans and all other human groups classified as non-whites were seen as inferior in intellect and morality on the basis of a particular interpretation of perceived physical characteristics.

(b) the religious sanction for the historical development and prevalence of institutional slavery, through the centuries, was seen as deriving from God's early deliberations regarding how way the destiny of the different human groups (i.e., the different "races") was to be fulfilled. By assigning perpetual servitude as punishment to the descendants of Ham, God had "decreed this institution before it existed" (Stringfellow, 1981: 140). Similarly, the scientific sanction for black enslavement was seen to reside in the fact that the physical attributes which the Southerners considered to be indicative of inherent structural deficiency had been the basis for the logical placement of the black group in an inferior status "in all ages and

243

all places" (Nott, 1981: 233). Ancient paintings, sculptures, and inscriptions representing blacks as slaves or captives provided the irrefutable evidence, he continues (1981: 215-218), that this group was already physically different thousands of years before, that their collective existence was deemed barbarian by the ancients, and that they invariably occupied inferior status as "Plebeians, Servants, and Slaves". The end result here is a dual moral validation of tradition, one aspect of which stems from God, the other from Nature.

(c) in the orthodox religious viewpoint, while the association between the elect and non-elect will not purify the latter completely, and definitely will not transform their essence, it most certainly transforms the condition of the former. The slightest taint of the sinfulness of the non-elect weakens the spiritual and moral integrity of the elect. Understood more broadly, this means that these two groups are never to intermingle, but always to remain separate. The position of science in this regard is unequivocally parallel to that of religion, which may be seen in the universal condemnation in the South of the existence of the mulatto. In the dichotomous structure of Southern society, the mulatto was a very problematic category, an aberration, one that could not possibly have accomodated successfully. Again and again, Nott contends that invariably "the Caucasian race is deteriorated by intermixing with the inferior races ..." (1981: 237). In another instance he states: "Whenever in the history of the world the inferior races have conquered and mixed in with the Caucasian, the latter have sunk into barbarism" (1981: 219). The structural convergence between religion and science on this point is dramatically revealed in Harper's words: "If...the civilized European man be the most perfect variety of the human race, is he not criminal who would desecrate and deface God's fairest work, estranging it further from the image of himself, and conforming it more nearly to that of the brute" (1981: 131). The major idea here, therefore, is the impossibility of reconciliation between different groups, or, to state it in accordance with the earlier discussion on the master-slave relationship, the latter cannot be resolved on the basis of equality. The African must forever remain as difference, as inferior essence.

In the light of these considerations, it may be stated that the African as a category of inherent inferiority was validated on both moral *and* scientific grounds. Furthermore, it may be seen how the confluence of orthodox religion and reconstructed science placed into relief the element of difference and its correlate notions of hierarchization, control, and boundary maintenance. Stringfellow remarked in this regard to the effect that "... the divine Lawgiver, in guarding the property right in slaves among his chosen people, sanctions principles which may work the separation of man and wife; father and children," and God has always sanctioned slavery and "prescribed duties which belong to it, as he has other relative duties; such as those between husband and wife, parent and child, magistrate and subject" (1981: 153-154). The implications from these ideas are, first of all, that the use of "chosen people," a common theme in fundamentalist religion, suggests the ingroup/outgroup duality, as well as the negative evaluation of the outgroup from the standpoint of the ingroup. Secondly, it defines the pattern of power relations, insofar as, in a more general sense, this type of biblical exegesis appears to sanction social stratification at the most basic level. The aspect of difference, as operative here, emerges as the very bedrock of social inequality, establishing, as it does, the most fundamental criteria of human differentiation and domination. The same effect was had in the manner in which the science of the time, animated by racialist ideology, accounted for human difference. The medical-ethnological writings of Nott, Cartwright, and others, clearly disclose the tendency of this "reconstructed" science to treat human groups ("races") as discrete entities, sharply set off from one another by an array of racially-determined cultural and psychological attributes, on the basis of which they were accorded a higher or lower placement on the scale of humanity.

The structure of thought of the Southern ruling class

At this juncture, the structure of consciousness of the slaveholding class will be addressed, with particular attention being focussed on two pairs of interrelated categories, the conceptions of the individual and society on the one hand, and the conceptions of religion and science on the other. Each one of these notions has, in turn, its own internal dualism. This interpretative procedure sets the stage for the exploration of the homological correspondences between the internal elements of proslavery discourse and the worldview of the Southern collective subject. The manner in which human nature and social reality were defined in the antebellum South had, expectedly, a wide-ranging and powerful impact on proslavery discourse as a whole, and on the pattern of intergroup relations. In specific terms, the Southern conception of the individual and society was tied to the attitude towards the question of difference, and it determined whether the master/slave relationship was more deeply influenced by a conception of the African as a permanently inferior being, or as one that was potentially transformable and assimilable into the mainstream of social life.

It is fitting to begin by drawing a contrast between the liberal and conservative views regarding the nature of the individual and society. I have already mentioned how Southern thought in the early 1800s was characterized by a radical departure from Enlightenment philosophy and ideals. This phenomenon may be observe in the way the human being and the human collectivity were treated in the proslavery texts. The pivotal notions advanced by Enlightenment thought were, first of all, oriented by the factor of possibility, that is, by the possibility of perfection to be realized both at the personal and collective levels. Through the continuing development of his/her rational powers, the individual could manipulate and control internal as well as external nature, thus making possible the enhancement of the social welfare, the implementation of social equality, and the realization of progress. These are key themes in Condorcet (1976), who valued the power of rationality above all else. From this perspective emerges an image of the autonomous, free-thinking individual, unencumbered by what Kant (cited in Jones, 1975: 7) referred to as "tutelage," meaning, a managed form of thinking, or what Marx called ideology. An individual, moreover, who was in principle capable of providing for his/her needs by sole recourse to intellectual resourcefulness. "The time will therefore come," proclaims Condorcet, "when the sun will shine only on free men who know no other master but their reason ..." (1976: 259). This idea of universal human perfectibility differs sharply from the Southern conceptual models of (a) imperfect human beings who must relinquish all existential responsibility to a force outside of themselves, in this case, a Supreme Being who is considered the ultimate origin as well as master of every human thought and action; and (b) a humanity split dichotomously on the basis of positivity/negativity - which is to say, an imperfect humanity when considered in its totality - from the very beginning. It must be kept in mind that the explanation for this is a theological one, as indicated earlier in reference to the story of the sons of Noah. This process of differentiation necessarily leads to the formation of human societies that are imperfect, and because the constitutions of the two major groups (white and nonwhite) are assigned positive and negative values respectively, the ruling principle of social organization is hierarchization of power, reflecting the original patterns of development set down by the Creator.

Enlightenment thinkers believed that all individuals had innate intellectual abilities which fairly approximated a universal standard, and they all possessed what Descartes termed *bon sens*. Thus, through systematic education and the consequent development of their rational faculties people in general should be able to solve life problems successfully. Because in this view individuals are rational beings, capable of running their own affairs, the most suitable form of government for them is that which governs the least: a *laissez-faire* political system, exercising the minimum of political control, and predicated upon universal social equality. In contrast to this position, the intellectual orientation of the South called for an authoritarian system of government in order to keep the imperfection of individuals - in this case, the greater imperfection of certain segments of Southern society - under strict and permanent control. The Africans had to have permanent restraints over their lives because of their intrinsically imperfect nature. This imperfection originated in religion and morality (insofar as it had been determined by divine decree, in relation to God's curse on Canaan), therefore it must be equated with sinfulness. This idea of human imperfection being equated with sinfulness was a salient theme in the religious rationale of slavery.

Whenever proslavery texts dealt with the "moral" aspects of the institution, there was never any ambiguity regarding the particular conception of the individual and society that prevailed in the South in the historical period under investigation. In a famous essay of 1861 Stringfellow establishes the inequality that inheres in the human condition, by stating that one class of individuals (i.e., the "white race") are able, through socialization, to reach in mature life the full measure of rationality and independence in the handling of their affairs. The other class of individuals, namely, those classified as nonwhite, are, in contradistinction, forever impaired in their ability to become fully responsible, autonomous, rational human beings. As he puts it, "experience teaches us that the white race can be prepared in ... time to take charge of families, and perform the duties of citizens; while on the other, experience demonstrates that the black race cannot be prepared during a whole life to take charge of families, or perform the duties of citizens" (1861: 4). Inequality in the human condition must thus be treated as a point of departure. It has existed universally and throughout all time. It issues from "the Divine will" and it is "always an expression of the essential good" (Smith, 1856: 102). Finally, it is primarily manifested in the different levels of rational development of human groups.

Proslavery theorists pursue the idea of inherent human inequality by first rejecting the Lockean perspective of free and equal individuals in the state of nature, and then passing on to the exclusivist defense of the idea that human beings can only be considered as such in the "social state" (Smith, 1856: 68), that is to say, in a state of association with others. Properly understood, this means that individuals can only be considered as such in a dualistic context of social hierarchization. "Nothing is more obvious," affirms William Smith, "than that men are not equal in that intellectual and moral condition which would enable them to use certain social and political advantages for the benefit of themselves and others ..." (1856: 72). To reiterate a point already stressed: this state of inequality among the white and black races stems from determinations initially made by God regarding Noah's progeny, from whom descended all the peoples of the earth. The descendants of Shem and Japheth eventually became "distinguished for a progressive intelligence and a commanding influence upon the destinies of the world," and the descendants of Ham came to occupy a permanent position of inferiority as servants of the former (Stringfellow, 1861: 12). The Rev. Frederick A. Ross put the matter as follows: "Ham [i.e., the Africans] will share in the glory of God, as will Shem [i.e., the Asians] and Japheth [i.e., Europeans and neo-Europeans], but in a hierarchical order, in which Ham is at the lowest position" (1969:30-31, orig. 1857).

Such a conception of the individual leads to a model of an imperfect society, and to the requirement that civil government be instituted in such a way as to accommodate human differences, with power hierarchies organized for the administration and control of the inferior group(s). Thus it is that civil government can only be conceived as "submission and control by the will of another" (Stringfellow, 1861: 3; also see Smith, 1856: 69), otherwise there can be no progress for the human community as a whole. In this view, a homologous relationship is inevitably established between the totalitarian control of the master over his slaves, and the control exercised by the State over her citizens. And if this parallelism is brought out, as indeed it must be so that ideological orientation and objective praxis remain coterminous, the State will be conceived as a totalitarian entity. This consequence is corroborated in the words of Stringfellow and Smith, both of whom liken the level and quality of subjection of the slave towards the master, to the level and quality of subjection of citizens towards the State. "The State is master of the citizen," affirms Stringfellow, "and the man, who is master of the slave, is rightfully clothed with authority the world over to maintain dominion over both" (1861: 5). In this connection, slavery becomes on a smaller scale the functional correlate of the State. Smith maintains that "the great abstract principle of slavery is right, because it is a fundamental principle of the social state" (1856: 12). Masters become "special subordinate magistrates" (Hughes, 1981: 243), and their power is codified into law; the network of rights and obligations attached to the master/slave relationship is deemed derivative of the law. From this standpoint, the Enlightenment (Lockean) version of government, which originates in the consent of the governed, is nothing but a foolish scheme, since people are both neither free nor equal. Subjection to government from birth is "a universal necessity" and the State must be considered as "the opposite of freedom" (Stringfellow, 1861: 6).

Along with their implicit preoccupation with the question of the nature of human beings, proslavery authors explicitly affirmed the inferior nature of the African. As indicated below, even in essays that ostensively deal with political and/or economic aspects of slavery, the centrality of the issue of the nature of human beings and society is quite obvious. Dew writes in the 1830s, for example, of the impracticability and dire economic consequences that would result from the emancipation and deportation (to Africa) of the slaves in Virginia, from the disruption of population patterns, or from the emancipation without deportation. More specifically, the last procedure would cause the voluntary labor of the free blacks to be evaluated against the involuntary labor of the slaves, which was universally deemed in the South to be "vastly more efficient and productive than the labor of free blacks." The structure of this argument is, to all intents and purposes, economic. Yet, the African would not work well under coercion because, once freed, "the animal part of the man gains the victory over the moral" (1981: 52), an allusion to attributes of character presumed to be innate, an aspect that has nothing to do whatsoever with the economic process. In another instance, Dew points out that the expansion of commerce and manufactures in the western countries of Europe generated a middle class of freemen which acted as the absorbency context, so to speak, for manumitted slaves. The absence in the South of such a class to absorb and integrate emancipated blacks rendered abolition a highly impractical scheme, and the free black an anomaly. However, the real reason for the impossibility of absorption of the free black into a middle class is not connected with class considerations. Although, as Dew explains, slaves in Greece or Rome could, upon being freed, hope to join the ranks of free people on the basis of absorption of the cultural and civil virtues, in the South of the mid-1800s that was not to be, "nor ever will it be in all time to come." For, while the slave in antiquity bore only civil status as a mark of differentiation, the African "forever wears the indelible symbol of his inferior condition; the Ethiopian cannot change his skin, nor the leopard his spots" (in Faust, 1981: 58). This attitude is also clearly evidenced in Calhoun. His fear that the Southern slavery order might be overturned by an ascendance of the free black element recapitulates the basis of paradox of the argument: if the "rear ranks" of society are to be motivated to improve themselves in order to be able to catch up with the more civilized front ranks, how is this ever going to be achieved? The dissolution of Southern society, he fears, would automatically bring whites and blacks to a position of social and political equality, this being judged an abomination, one would assume, since the blacks would not have attained the necessary civil and moral development to justify this equalization. But, he cites the example of the British West Indies where, even after emancipation, blacks remained *de facto* slaves, no longer to individual owners, but to the community at large, representing a continuation of their former status, imposed upon them "by the bayonet of the soldiery and the rod of the civil magistrate" (1963: 15). He writes approvingly of these developments, thus confirming a basic fact: the social definition of the African as a being that was only provisionally deficient could be, and in fact was easily and frequently overridden by the definition of the African as an inherently - hence, permanently - inferior being. The former served best as a psychological crutch used by the bourgeoisie for rationalizing their enslavement of other human beings. The latter, on the other hand, was more in line with the exigencies of the antibourgeois, seigneurial, hierarchized structure of Southern society. After the slavery order was destroyed by the Civil War and the economic basis of human bondage removed, permanent subjugation of the black population still remained the desideratum in the South, at least in the degree that certain structures of consciousness of the Southern collectivity, the fundamental intellectual categories that made up the Southern world view, remained in effect.

But, again, we must not lose sight of the fact that in the progress mode there were continuous pressures towards the affirmation of the African as a being that was only temporarily handicapped. These pressures emanated from the economic activity of the Southern planter class in the context of international capitalism. As observed earlier, this form of classification of the African meant that he/she was seen as an assimilable being, capable of transformation and absorption of the social qualities necessary for eventual integration into civil society. Judging from the frequent attacks on capitalism by writers like Hughes, Ruffin, Fitzhugh, and others, there is no question that proslavery ideologues were keenly aware of the social implications of the capitalist transformation of their society. The focus of their concern was naturally the inevitable change in the social status of their African charges. Basically speaking, the more an economic system veered in the direction of capitalism, the more the life of individuals within that system would be affected by such tendencies as equality of opportunity, free enterprise, individual achievement, private property, and contract. The disadvantages of the African in a competitive and rationally-organized capitalist society would, theoretically, be conquered in time through systematic cultural training (i.e., through education and social integration). Thus, the condition of sociocultural "incompleteness," like that of the child, would only be temporary and explained by reference to cultural, not biological, factors.

What can be established here regarding the dialectical relation involving the master and the slave? Mainly, that an inversion has occurred, as stressed before, regarding the transformation of the *master* into the historical element of this relationship. This change signifies that it is now the consciousness of the master, and not that of the slave, that is being affirmed. To elaborate: the spread of industrialization, technological development and market relations in Southern society, during both the antebellum and Reconstruction periods should have produced a radical change in the master-slave relation, specifically bringing about the proletarization of the African. This would have occurred in conjunction with the larger structural shift in Southern society from the premodern condition of "community" to the modern condition of "society," and with the generalizing and standardizing effect on social relations that comes from the shift from affective to contractual relationships. This new dialetic would still be exploitative, to be sure, since the intensification of capitalist relations of production would have engendered a corresponding intensification of impersonality in the relationship between the capitalist and the proletarian. That is to say, the worker would continue to be apprehended in terms of his/her economic function and status as *thing*. Nevertheless, this new arrangement would have led to a radical transformation of the subordinate element. For our purposes, it is appropriate to note here that the capitalist-proletarian dialectic would have militated against the factor of difference, except for difference derived from economic asymmetry. Race-based difference or any other ascriptive form of difference tends to be weakened by the democratizing impulses of large-scale industrial capitalism. The latter facilitates the process by which individuals are rendered interchangeable, through being reduced to the common level of commodity. From this particular perspective, the African-as-difference would have been only a provisional formula, inasmuch any individual is theoretically as free as any other to pursue economic activity and function fully as *homo economicus*, this freedom being contingent mainly on personal industry and competitiveness. The experience of slavery, which slavery apologists defended as a training ground for absorbing the Africans into the ways of Western civilization, should, if this logic is pursued, have prepared the slaves for life in freedom, and given them a basis for participating in the marketplace and the body politic, as well as in cultural life. But, that was never the case, as may be readily ascertained from the experience of manumitted blacks during the slavery era, and of the black population as a whole after the Civil War. What unequivocally prevailed was a modified master-slave relationship. Both during and after slavery, the capitalist order of the South remained under the influence of seigneurial tendencies, and the conception of the black element by the dominant class remained essentially unchanged. As for the free black population in the antebellum period, we saw earlier how it was subjected to multiple restrictions regarding its physical and social mobility, restrictions so draconian and comprehensive as to parallel those that were imposed on the slaves themselves. This situation suggests the predominance of the mode of tradition, at both the symbolic and material levels.

In the mode of progress, the following considerations may be offered here concerning the nature of social reality. The dominant form of social organization encouraged by the expansion of capitalism was one characterized by increasing bureaucratization of institutional structures and social relationships. Social interaction was conceived in terms of increasing dependence on systems of abstract, rational rules derived from market mechanisms, and increasing independence from cultural forces (primarily religion). The main type of social control was representative government. Individuals were thus progressively liberated here from the constraints that ethnic affiliation, religious affiliation, kinship, etc., imposed upon them during the precapitalist era. They also had a measure of control over their lives through representative government. All of these aspects represent a legacy from the philosophical outlook of the Enlightenment.

But, these progressive notions, however sound they may have been in their abstract form, could only be pursued up to a certain point, before they began to clash with the ideological structure of the Southern slaveholding class. The idea of a dynamic social reality, a contractually-based society with its emphasis on culture, not race, and on individual achievement, rather than ascribed status, was directly at odds with the more static quality and rigidity of the mode of tradition. Thus, these notions were valid only in a relative sense. At the limit, they underwent reification. In this connection, equality and liberty, essential features of the mode of progress, were theoretically reconstructed in the degree required for maintaining the Southern system and its ideology. We find, for example, in Calhoun's "Disquisition on Government" (1963) the case being made for the necessary balance between power and liberty, so that social order and progress could be realized. Liberty was not to be considered as a precondition for human society, and to be enjoyed by one and all in limitless amount. For, if human beings have, from their primordial beginnings, been radically differentiated in their natural capacities, their best form of government must be one "adapted to their social and moral condition" (Smith, 1856: 50), and liberty must be dispensed by the State in the appropriate measure to each "community" of individuals within the society. As Calhoun puts it, "liberty ... when forced on a people unfit for it, would, instead of a blessing be a curse" (1963: 8). As abstract principles applied without qualification, liberty and equality "are not only destructive to the morals, but to the happiness of society" (Fitzhugh, 1963: 40). These statements are indicative of the tension between the ideas of progress and tradition, in the sense that the Africans were unfit socially either because of their innate constitution, or because they had not yet collectively advanced to the point deemed acceptable for civil integration. One may be left with the impression of the primacy of the classification of the Africans as beings that were only temporarily impaired, for Calhoun would have us believe that they might eventually be eligible for freedom (though their progress would be "necessarily slow.") This impression is short-lived, however. Although he speaks of the need to keep the principles of liberty and power in balance - liberty leading to progress, power leading to stability - the position of civil government is to prioritize order over "anarchy," the latter resulting from the misuse of freedom. The scales, therefore, were evidently tilted in favor of power or "protection." Clearly, too, the paternalism which pervades the entire argument is perfectly homologous to this conception of society predicated upon the "protection" of some of its groups. This is because paternalism may guarantee, through the exercise of power, a certain amount of freedom to the subordinate group, placing the members of this group above the level of thing or beast of burden, but, at the same time, through this protection it also promotes the perpetuation of subordinate status. This last aspect is, in the final analysis, the most pressing consideration, which is nowhere expressed with greater clarity than in Calhoun's assertion that "the existence of the race is of greater moment than its improvement ...". Change is acceptable, but only in an evolutionary sense, that is, only in the degree that it does not violate the ideological parameters of the ruling class or threaten its position within the social system.

From this point of view, individuals are definitely not born equal. They may be free to pursue their plans and aspirations, but in differing degrees, and in a relative sense. Specifically, those who possess the virtues of civilization in a higher degree are freer to do this, and freedom for the remainder can only be pursued to the point where it does not transgress the boundaries of communal order and security, the boundaries of systemic maintenance. Freedom is pre-determined. This unequal order of things is seen as determined by "some fixed law" (explicitly identified as Divine Providence), not by an artificial agency, such as civil government. From this we can glean the following: (a), because humanity was forever differentiated according to a higher determination, equality of freedom and equality of social condition cannot be mutually inferrable or deducible, and (b), the State must not interfere with social arrangements, for this would "effectually arrest the march of progress" (1963: 9-10).

The paradoxical definition of human nature and of society is, therefore, settled. Despite repeated assertions about the potentiality of the African for improvement under the slavery regime, and the need for this civilizing process to be necessarily slow, it is never clear that the *telos* of a high level of intellectual and moral development is ever going to be reached. In fact, the idea of an eventual levelling of the social condition, making blacks and whites equals in their exercise of social liberty, is invariably met with rejection. Hence, while the idea of continuous improvement for the African is deemed plausible, the logical consequence of such a process will not be entertained. In this respect, there is a conceptual reconstruction of progress, insofar as this relates to the condition of the subordinate group, a phenomenon best understood by keeping in mind the problem of difference, to wit, the fact that the pervasiveness in Southern society of the intellectual categories of "differentiated individual" and "differentiated society" countered the possibility of the eventual full-scale social integration of the Africans.

God and science through Southern eyes

The dramatic revitalization of evangelical religion in the South in the opening decades of the 19th century elevated religious knowledge to a level of unprecedented importance. The Bible was now the first and ultimate authority on all matters, sacred or secular. No less than Matthew Maury, a distinguished Southern geologist, affirmed that "the Bible is authority for everything it touches" (in Eaton, 1964: 151). Therefore, with the classification of the African as an inherently inferior being validated by scientific and moral sources, it was up to religion to carry through, as an essential feature of the mental structuration of the dominant group, the exclusion of the African from the human community. How was this to be accomplished? By recourse to the fundamental relation of orthodox religious thought, as embodied in the Southern model, towards the problem of difference. The only way that the status of difference of the African would have disappeared would be through full social integration, comprising assimilation at the level of culture, as defined by the threefold model of assimilation introduced in this study. This process was in turn contingent on the level of receptivity of the host society to syncretic interaction with the minority ethnic-cultural communities. The religious context from which was drawn the category of the African as an inherently inferior being, and which remained throughout the antebellum period the bedrock of the worldview of Southern society, was ascetic Protestantism. Within this broader philosophical orientation, I shall attempt to unveil the conception of God or supernatural power, and to show that it stressed the need for boundary maintenance as much as it rejected the idea of syncretistic fusion. These two principles must operate in unison. To begin with, it is worth repeating here that this theological enterprise was oriented by differentiation, hierarchization, control, and boundary maintenance. Jordan correctly points out, in this respect, that "the sectarian character of Protestantism fostered a spirit of tribalism, since sectarianism meant emphasis on distinctiveness from others and virtual, though inadmissible, abandonment of the ideal of Christian universality" (1981: 95). This phenomenon is fully manifest in the religious texts used in the defense of slavery. Let us look first at the issue of differentiation, by returning to a theme already discussed, namely, the peculiar convergence of the religious and scientific outlooks in the Old South. This trend was so pronounced that the lines of argumentation for the two perspectives were often parallel and fairly undistinguishable. In an important essay written in the early 1850s, "The Pre-Adamite Earth: Relations of Geology to Theology," R.T. Brumby expounds on the idea of God-as-differentiation by referring to the process of creation. Appealing to contemporary scientific theory, he seeks to show that the work of God, as the Great Architect, does not manifest itself in terms of continuity, but of *original diversity*. Citing the research of the celebrated geologist Sir Charles Lyell, he goes on to assert that the modern human being had not evolved *autonomously* from a lower species - a development which would have indicated the essential continuity of mankind - but, "each species is proof of a direct exercise of Divine Agency" (1852: 65). Two important points emerge here. First, that natural law is not spontaneous and self-regulating, but is fundamentally the expression of both the Agency and Essence of the Supreme Being. Thus, the objective world mirrors the nature of God. Secondly, the nature of God is posited as division or differentiation, and as stability, rather than as continuity and change. Another writer, William A. Smith, president of Randolph-Macon College, speaks of the essential inequality among human beings as representing "the will of God" (1856: 63) and "the law of Heaven" (1856: 64). Given that human beings were created in His own image (Genesis), we cannot escape the conclusion that the Divine essence is also one of differentiation and inequality. As concerns the aspect of eternity in God's nature, it follows that the structural patterns of life in the universe are also eternal, and that this naturally includes the inequality that prevails among human groups. This inequality stems not from the artificial creation (i.e., human creation), but from the original patterns of creation. Furthermore,

255

this condition of inequality demands the permanence of the dominance/subordinance pattern that is an integral part of civil government, both aspects emanating directly from "the will of God" (Stringfellow, 1861: 6).

The conception of God being dealt with here is that of Divine Power manifesting itself in nature, which, first of all, legitimizes things as they exist, and secondly, renders irrational and unjustifiable any artificial alteration of the *status quo*. Nature is where God is most concretely felt and manifested. Therefore, all natural phenomena are expressions of God's design of creation. Family government is such a thing. It is a "necessity of nature" (Stringfellow, 1861: 6). The system of relations of dominance and submission incorporated into slavery is construed as a functional counterpart of the family. More intimately still, it is "made part of the family relation" (Smith, 1856: 39). To ignore this fact is "perfect folly" (Stringfellow, 1861: 8). Thomas Dew (1963:32) reaffirms the principle that inequality inheres in the human community, thus rendering external attempts to alter this arrangement both futile and unnatural. He states: "The deep and solid foundations of society cannot be broken by the vain fiat of the legislator."

Finally, the question of power hierarchization, or control. That the Almighty is eternally just admits of no debate in the orthodox religious mind. In the religious justification of slavery, divine justice is presented as being inextricably bound up with the idea of *control*. God's chosen people must carry His principles of living and fulfill His expectations by bringing into effect "the moral and social control of the world." The control is temporary for some, such as children, who are still incomplete social beings, and permanent for others, such as nonwhites, who are intrinsically deficient creatures. Moreover, this fundamental separation and polarization of humanity into the white and nonwhite segments, and the permanent dominance of one over the other, are therefore not only expressive of the "Divine constitution of things," but also represent the very "cohesive element which binds us all together in the social body" (Stringfellow, 1861: 9).

As for the Southern idea of science, scientific knowledge played a singular role in the religiously orthodox South. In the abstract, science has been associated in this study with the mode of progress. This is because scientific and technological progress followed a parallel course to the expansion of market relations, with its accompanying effects of representative government and social egalitarianism. Considered in the concrete historical context of the antebellum Southern society, however, science appears as a reconstructed enterprise, a supportive structure for the conservative ethos of the region. The idea of science that springs from the writings of the proslavery intellectuals is often one that contradicts the basic premises of the scientific orientation. Specifically, the task of science was not seen as that of asserting the superiority of empirical investigation over scriptural revelation, but rather of serving as an adjunct or "hand-maid" to religion (Brumby, 1852:50). Southerners reasoned that the science-religion problematic ought to be encased in the framework of a "theological science," the latter idea implying the perfect harmonization of physical science with biblical doctrine. When treated in this light, science indeed "facilitated the diffusion of religious truth" (Brumby, 1852:48-50).

Whether in the progressive context of the Enlightenment or in the reactionary context of the antebellum South, science was an intellectual endeavor that was intimately connected with the realm of nature. What separated the Southern version of science from that of the Enlightenment was that in the South the force of Calvinist Christianity removed the dynamic character of the relationship between science and the natural world, whereby human beings can transform and manipulate nature through their rational powers. In other words, the individual's *internal* nature is treated as being dominant over *external* nature. The Southern model of reconstructed science, on the other hand, was one in which the individual was powerless in reference to immutable natural laws and circumstances, which had been established for all eternity by the Supreme Being.

The merger of reconstructed science and revealed religion led to the nullification of internal autonomy in the individual, and to the concentration of all authority in agencies or entities external to human deliberation. Rationality was reduced to the ability to adjust to, and function efficiently within, a context of domination and control, exercised by natural forces as an expression of divine will. Scientific progress was negated, as it became integrated with theological ahistoricality. From this, it followed that human groups were inherently unequal in their ability to *adapt* to control (i.e., unequal in their "fitness", to use the lexicon of social evolutionism), with the groups defined as nonwhite showing decidedly lower levels of fitness in this regard, and thus being inherently inferior.

A further aspect of the special relationship between religion and science in the antebellum South concerns the question of order, or tradition. Generally speaking, the Old South reflected the Romantic propensity to validate and uphold tradition. The dominant classes of the region were aristocratic and antibourgeois, and therefore cultivated an easygoing and genteel lifestyle, coupled with a marked aversion for the faster-paced, proletarian quality of life in the industrial North. William Russell noticed in the 1860s "the animosity evinced by the 'gentry' of South Carolina for the 'rabble of the North,'" a reference undoubtedly made to the ethnically-mixed, democratically-minded industrial population that was quickly filling the Northern cities. To the extent that science was perceived by Southerners as part of the global capitalist transformation of society, with its attendant features of maximization of efficiency and productivity and the relentless pursuit of progress, it was not generally held in high regard. Hence, the efforts of the men of science to make scientific truth subordinate to that of the Bible, so that the latter could grant legitimacy to the former. Next to old-time religion, Simkins points out (1959: 159), "the facts of science, and the allurements of earthly progress, were either subordinate or irrelevant."

Religious thought as worldview

Having looked at the secular influences arising from the religion-science linkage, I will now consider the sacred. The aspect of secularism attached to intellectual activity in the Old South paled before its theological, premodern orientation, a situation that may be largely attributed to the resurgence, under the auspices of Romanticism, of orthodox religion as the primary source of knowledge. Our concern here is to bring to light the manner in which this type of religious orientation affected the structure of consciousness of the Southern slaveholding class.

The preceding analysis of the conceptions of the individual and society in the proslavery texts has revealed that these elements were defined in accordance with the orienting principles of separation and hierarchization. The direct parallels between these conceptions of individual and social reality and the structure of orthodox, Calvinistically-informed religion should be readily apparent. One of the more ubiquitous notions in the texts is that slavery was necessary so that, with the existence of a subordinate class, the dominant classes would rise higher in the scale of civilization. For instance, in his famous "Speech on the Reception of Abolition Petitions," Calhoun states: "I hold, then, that there never has yet existed a wealthy and civilized society in which one portion of the community did not, in point of fact, live on the labor of the other" (1963: 13). Harper adds, in the same vein: "Slavery anticipates the benefits of civilization, and retards the evils of civilization;" it is, indeed, to be regarded as the "sole cause of civilization" (1981: 81, 91). Two important implications flow from these contentions. First, structured inequality was perceived as indispensable for the progress of civilized life. Secondly, the model of civil government found in the religious texts is authoritarian in

258

nature, and rooted in the design of Providence. The religious dimension can be easily verified, as, for example, in the essay by Rev. Thornton Stringfellow, "A Brief Examination of Scripture Testimony on the Institution of Slavery," in which St. Peter is quoted on this topic ("Servants, be subject to your masters with all fear, not only to the good and gentle, but also to the forward," and "Submit yourselves to every ordinance of man for the Lord's sake"). The author of the essay interprets this passage from the New Testament as enjoining "political subjection to governments of every form." This line of argumentation encompasses, all at once, the elements of difference, hierarchization, boundary maintenance, and control, and it finds its counterpart, first of all, in the actual substance of Calvinist doctrine. McNeil writes (1969: 258): "Most of what Calvin wrote on politics is marked by a deep respect for stable government and a cautious avoidance of any suggestion of resistance or revolution. Even under oppression the Christian is to submit and pray for deliverance." Legitimation for such a scheme of things was derived from the Almighty, inasmuch as civil obedience to instituted authority was an expression "of the Christian law of love."

These structural parallelisms, as may be recalled, are even more intriguing when it comes to the Calvinist doctrine of election, beginning with the fact that the belief in predestination affords believers the certainty of their salvation and of the complete inalterability of this outcome. By implication, this theological determinism, in sealing the fate of the elect for all eternity, has the same effect on the fate of the non-elect. Moreover, it permanently establishes the duality of humankind, which starts from a principle of differentiation of human groups but comes to apply, metaphorically, to the more general level of differentiation of these groups (i.e., the religious damnation of the non-elect becomes the symbolic analogue of the social marginalization of the ethnically different). Thus, divine election befalls the Subject, divine rejection befalls the non-Subject, that is, the Other. The condition of rejection becomes the lot of "the different," in reference to which the ethnic-racial modality of difference is the most relevant one for this analysis.

Furthermore, the inexorability of this process of human differentiation is grounded in the idea that God decreed slavery (understood as perpetual servitude) as a curse upon the Canaanites, from whom the African "race" was thought to have descended. This sharp division of ontological status between the "white" and "nonwhite" human categories thus reproduced in the social plane the impassable gulf between the communities of the elect and the non-elect, and the intense aversion of the former toward the latter (Weber, 1958), in the spiritual plane.

259

I have accentuated the feature of comprehensiveness of the concepts of election and non-election (rejection). To be one of the non-elect meant, properly understood, to have been excluded by divine design, and for all existence, from the membership of the saints. In broader context, however, the Calvinist orientation to the world affects the pattern of intergroup relations, shaping dominant-group perceptions and treatment of the subaltern group.

In the slave society of the American South, the African slave fit this category of the non-elect precisely, by virtue principally of his/her racial affiliation and skin color (as well as of other traits, such as language, culture, economy, and political system). No matter how much a black person might have been elevated through social training, economic and political advancement, miscegenation with members of the ruling group, or acculturation into the Anglo-Protestant mode of life, he/she could never hope to enter the membership of the elect, that is, to abolish servile status and to become a full-fledged member of society. His/her fate as difference had been perpetually sealed.

The election/non-election duality has been focused on here towards the goal of explicating the categories of difference and hierarchization. Now, the task ahead is to clarify the remaining categories of boundary maintenance and control, in reference to this theological coordinate. The conception of God drawn from the texts, as the following considerations will indicate, includes all four categories. For, while the non-elect are irrevocably separated from the elect, these groups do not exist in discrete and monadic isolation, but in dialectical interrelatedness. This means that if, on the one hand, the unbridgeable gulf between the two groups leads to the affirmation of the principle of boundary maintenance, on the other hand, their interdependence is a requirement. In being different, the non-elect deviate from eternally-established, monolithic norms and standards, and their difference takes on a quality of negativity. As such, negativity must exist vis-a-vis its negation, which is positivity. That is to say, it must exist in order for the standard of righteousness and holiness to be validated. This standard is conceived, in specific terms, as the state of grace of the elect, or, in general terms, as the elect's total model of existence: cultural, social, political, intellectual, economic. At the level of religious consciousness proper, the elect and the rejected express the rational segmentalization of reality that characterizes modern capitalistic society, and hierarchization. One writer states: "Rejection exists to realize election; rejection was necessary to bring the elect to the glory which God has ordained for them in His infinite love" (Hoeksema, in Berkouwer, 1960: 207). Calvin himself unambiguously stresses the fact that "there could be no election without its opposite reprobation" (1936: III, xxiii, 1).

260

Hoeksema restates this cardinal point, by saying that "rejection is the necessary antithetical side of election" (in Berkouwer, 1960: 208-209). That this logic underlay the existence and operation of the Southern slavery regime, there seems to be no question. Chancellor Harper's remark is quite *a propos*: "The tendency of slavery," he maintains, "is to elevate the character of the master" (1981: 116). The function and value of slavery as a form of social organization lay, therefore, clearly beyond its purely economic dimension. Proslavery theorists knew this well. To the extent that the superior, chosen race had the moral duty to advance steadily in their path of material and moral excellence (i.e., their path of holiness), and that this process depended fundamentally upon their being connected, via a system of relations of dominance and subordinance, with the imperfect (read: sinful) segments of the human race, slavery as abstraction and objective practice constituted a moral imperative in the Southern mind. Slavery was the essential structure for linking up the antagonistic elements of election and non-election, and for maintaining them in equilibrium.

Election and non-election must, therefore, remain perpetually interconnected and interdependent. Moreover, they must express a pattern of control and submission. The non-elect cannot be left alone in their imperfection, but have, instead, to be brought into the religious fold for the purpose of their supervised regeneration, even if this regenerative process is in principle limited and incapable of overturning the decree of eternal damnation settled by God. It is not difficult, I think, to perceive here the motivational basis for the proselytizing zeal of the religious fundamentalists of Calvinist persuasion. In a parallel sense, the inferior and heathen races must be brought, however forcefully, under the influence of Christianity and Christian society - even if it is recognized that the elevating effects of this experience will not change structural condition. The Africans were uprooted from native soil and brought over to work as slaves in a Christian setting for the glory of God. Their savage nature would be domesticated, their imperfection attenuated, their sinfulness attacked with the force of the Bible, but their structural deficiency would not disappear, and they could never hope to transcend divine rejection, that is, to achieve complete recuperation from an imperfect state which had been settled for eternity, and thus attain the condition of grace. In turning from the religious sphere to the categories of permanent inferiority and provisional inferiority involving the Africans, it may be said that the Southern slaveholding classes felt that the imperfection of their bondsmen and bondswomen could be combatted via the civilizing experience of slavery, but not to the extent of completely eliminating the condition of difference (or non-election), of liberating the

African from the staticism of permanent inferiority. This aspect discloses the operation of the principle of boundary maintenance, which acts to rule out mixture and undifferentiation. At the concrete level of society, this translates into the impossibility of complete cultural assimilation, involving the cultural, biological, and psychosocial aspects, and therefore, of full social membership, for some groups.

Viewed against this background, proslavery ideology in the American South may be characterized as having been fundamentally grounded in religious thought. It drew its constitutive categories from the underlying ideas and values of ascetic, Calvinistically-informed Protestantism, although, from a technical standpoint, the overall justification of the slavery institution was clearly argued on several distinct levels: economical, political, biological, ethical, *and* religious. Some additional points may be considered. First, proslavery ideas were a product of the Romantic shift to nonrationalist discourse and sources of truth validation. In the antebellum Southern United States, in particular, the dominant nonrationalist form of knowledge was ascetic Protestantism, consequently, the defense of the plantation regime was essentially anchored to religious sanction. Secondly, the general belief among proslavery theorists was that the form of authoritarian control exercised in slavery was structurally correlative with that which was exercised by the State. "The great abstract principle of slavery is right," insisted William Smith (1856: 12), "because it is a fundamental principle of the social state." Knowing, moreover, that the power invested in the State originates in God (Stringfellow, 1861: 6), and that the State is an extension of Divine Government in the sense that both essentially keep human imperfection (i.e., sin) as exhibited by the inferior segments of society, under a stricter form of control (Stringfellow, 1861: 8) we may proceed sylogistically as follows: Civil government is the structural counterpart of Divine Government as agencies for the containment and eradication of sin. Slavery authority is homologous to civil authority. Therefore, slavery is a religious office for the containment and eradication of sin. Finally, the presuppositions of proslavery ideology, elucidated here via a conceptual network comprising the elements of difference, hierarchization, control, and boundary maintenance, appear to be structurally homologous to the presuppositions of ascetic, Calvinistically-oriented Protestantism.

After the Civil War, with the economic and social basis of slavery destroyed, Southerners continued to appeal to the mediative effect of religious thought as they attempted to retain former patterns of dominance/subordinance in social relations, albeit in modified form. Following the post-Civil War decade known as Reconstruction, during which the African-American population experienced an amelioration of their social, economic, and political circumstances, there was a gradual and systematic reinstitution of white dominance across the South, both in the form of new legislation (i.e., the Black Codes), black political disenfranchisement, and direct intimidation and terrorism through the activities of groups like, for example, the Ku Klux Klan. This trend culminated in the 1896 Plessy vs. Ferguson Supreme Court decision, which established the Jim Crow system of segregation. Quarles comments thusly on this situation: "Whatever the southerner had surrendered at Appomattox, he had not surrendered his belief that colored people were inferior to white. Deeply imbedded in the regional culture, this view outlasted slavery. Much more than he feared the Negro, the southerner feared losing his grip on the world, almost a loss of his identity" (1976: 129).

The Civil War and the attendant destruction of the slavery system had removed the formal legitimation of the social definition of the Africans as permanently inferior beings. One would have expected, then, that their social definition as beings that had been rendered only temporarily impaired or deficient, but were now eligible for expanding social training and assimilation, should have gained progressively in importance. The unfolding events in the decades following the war, however, demonstrate precisely the contrary. That this was so may be interpreted largely as a result of the fact that, at the most fundamental level, a proslavery metatheory continued to be in effect. The basic Protestant ideas that structured the ways of thinking of Southerners with regard to the norms of interethnic and interracial existence before the Civil War, continued to exert this impact in the subsequent period, a pattern that has persisted down to present time. This effect, moreover, dominant though it may be in areas where Protestantism of the ascetic variety has been particularly entrenched (i.e., the so-called "Bible Belt" of the South and Midwest), applies to the society as a whole, in the degree that the latter can still be characterized as Protestant in its basic cultural orientation.

Notes

1   An exception to this pattern, as corroborated by Blassingame (1976:148), were the Catholic churches in New Orleans: "Most of the Negro Catholics [in New Orleans] continued to attend integrated churches throughout the Reconstruction period." Unlike the Protestant churches, Catholicism "was the only denomination which fought consistently against the proscriptive pew. Many observers noted the

lack of color distinctions among the communicants at the St. Louis Cathedral" (1976:199-200).

2   The dissociation of the African-American community in the United States from the African cultural matrix was observed early in the 1800s, such as evidence, for instance, in the narrative of the ex-slave Charles Ball. "The case is different," he states at one point (1969:218, orig. 1837), "with the American Negro, who knows nothing of Africa, her religion, or customs ...". It must be noted, of course, that slave dancing and entertainment remained a typical feature of plantation life in the United States throughout the slavery era, the opposition of the evangelical churches notwithstanding, and these patterns of behavior have generally been interpreted to have been carryovers from the African cultural heritage. However, the multiple - religious, legal, social - impediments to African culture shaped the pattern of slave dancing in the U.S. away from its African matrix, and towards the European end of the acculturation continuum. The prevalent use of the fiddle and the banjo (especially the former), as opposed to the African drum and other African instruments (see Southern, 1983, especially pp. 43-47, 182-3) was an important manifestation of this trend. Whereas in Brazil and in Caribbean settings, the African character of black dance and instrumentality was at once apparent to anyone familiar with West African dance forms, in the United States, it is pointed out (e.g., Herskovits, 1972:270), "pure African dancing is almost entirely lacking except in certain subtleties of motor behavior." The area of Louisiana may be an exception in this regard, but it must be treated separately because of the special character of its colonization.

As for the religious dimension proper, the Africans were able to insert their religious dances into the emotionally-charged atmosphere of the camp meeting revival. But, even in that special situation, they were not immune to the disapproval of the evangelists. Regarding the all-black, unsupervised plantation religious exercise, it may have retained elements of *style* (not content) from the African background (on this point, see Rawick, 1974; Blassingame, 1979; Escott, 1979; Raboteau, 1980), but it was also greatly inhibited by a very harsh and effective system of surveillance (see Henry, 1968, on the patrol system of the South).

Ecstatic religious expression emerges as the key feature of black folk religion, both during and after slavery. Black worshipping patterns, especially in the countryside, have indeed remained strongly emotional and experiential. Writers like Frazier (1964) believe that this is largely due to the white revivalist influence of the late 18th and early 19th centuries, who had a central role in the mass conversion of the Africans to Christianity, and set a model of religious behavior for them. Others, such as Raboteau (1980:67), argue that the whites themselves might have been influenced by the worshipping style of the blacks. Herskovits (1972) supports the latter view, and adds that blacks in the United States managed to retain the *form* of African religious excitement (i.e., rhythmic clapping, ring dancing, styles of singing, moving, etc.), and "reinterpreted" it in the context of evangelical Protestantism. Whatever the case may be, the fact remains that Protestantism hindered the survival on American soil of well-defined, readily recognizable, full-blown retentions of African worship.

9 Conclusions

After all is said and done, the key to a deeper understanding of the dynamics of interethnic and interracial relations in a multiethnic society may well reside in the sphere of *culture*, specifically, in the way the society under investigation has historically handled the problem of minority difference, symbolically and materially; that is to say, in the ideological apprehension of the principle of difference as such, as expressed in formal writings, dealt with in chapter 8; and in the actual practices and arrangements associated with the treatment of this difference (i.e., accomodation, rejection, etc.), as discussed in chapter 7. A culturalist form of analysis effectively unveils the mechanics of the dominant society's *relation* to minority difference, and thus has greater heuristic acuity and value than the more conventional and substantive political-economy or empirical approaches. The skepticism that sometimes surrounds the culturalist-interpretative approach regarding its fruitfulness for situations of intergroup inequality, together with the automatic reliance on "structural" approaches, recapitulates the false notion that the realm of aesthetics and symbolism (i.e., culture) and the realm of power relations are hermetically sealed from each other. This issue has already received a great deal of attention from (postmodern, feminist) analysts in the past couple of decades, who have stressed the political importance of the interpersonal and symbolic spheres. I have also called attention at several points in the analysis to the way in which political factors in U.S. society - I am thinking here of the major political and legal reforms since the 1960s - considered in isolation, have failed not only to eradicate interethnic divisions, conflict, and inequality, but also to explain the persisting ascriptive basis of this situation, as well as its recrudescence over the last decade or so. I have argued in this connection that cultural factors have greater explanatory power, and also that the material framework of interethnic life - the form and degree of ethnic stratification - is itself decisively affected by these factors.

The problematic of difference connects directly with the focus on religion. This study highlights the dynamic role of religion in society, including modern industrialized society, where social life has become secularized or non-religious. As noted in chapter 6, despite this overall secularizing effect, religious ideas are portrayed here as a set of normative principles that endure in the collective consciousness as a basic organizing template, conditioning collective understandings and practices accordingly. They continue therefore to influence social life at the nonreflective level of collective action, as absolute presuppositions, "doing their work in darkness, the light of consciousness never falling on them" (Collingwood, 1972:43). This interpretive stance calls for a reconsideration of traditional understandings of religion in social life.

I have attempted to demonstrate how the conception and treatment of minority-group difference, and the broader aspect of sociocultural formation, were fundamentally mediated by the dominant religion of the society. Religion furnished the basic ideological materials from which were formed the worldview of the collectivity and, ultimately, the society's cultural system. As concerns interethnic life, a particular understanding of minority-group difference evolved from the dominant religious ideology, that acted as an implicit normative force shaping collective thought and practice, and imparting a distinct character to the cultural system as a whole, and to dominant-minority ethnic relations in particular.

Contrasting the selected examples of Brazil and the United States, and the effect of the Catholic religion in one and the Protestant religion in the other, the analysis showed how these religious orientations led to the emergence and development of widely dissimilar systems of culture and intergroup relations. The models of culture have been treated here in terms of the interrelation of three components of the assimilative process, namely, dominant-minority cultural relations, intermarriage and miscegenation, and identity formation. In Brazil, Catholic universalism was shown to have stimulated the development of an integrationist type of ethnic-cultural system, in which minority difference was perceived and treated as being potentially transformable and assimilable into the general society. This means that this difference would eventually cease to be difference, and become part of the general standard. These perceptions, expectations, and associated practices regarding difference, were oriented by injunctions flowing from the hegemonic religion, in reference to which

267

minority-group difference was dissolved through ritual and symbolic means, that is, through the sacraments of the Church.

In the United States, by contrast, Protestant particularism was shown to have stimulated the emergence of a separatist type of cultural system. This it did, to my view, primarily in connection with the doctrine of predestination, Calvinistic Protestantism's "most characteristic dogma," according to Weber (1958:98). The rigid dualism of this doctrine shaped the structure of consciousness of the mainstream population, and more relevantly for our purposes, the manner in which it apprehended the "difference" of the incoming groups. Specifically, the aspect of difference as such was perceived analogically (and non-reflectively) as the condition of non-election. When what was involved in the concrete social context was merely cultural difference, the gulf between the latter and the dominant standard (which stood for the condition of election) was bridged by having this difference forcibly disappear under the core culture. When, however, it took the form of racial difference, it was deemed incapable of transformation into non-difference and, therefore, of reconciliation with the dominant pattern. It was thus preserved (and continues to be preserved) in isolation, in a sort of metaphysical permanence.

The case of the African-Americans is especially pertinent in this regard, as we have seen. Historically, members of this group, like those of all other groups maintained as ethnic-racial minorities in U.S. society, have been unable to shake off the status and stigma of "difference," no matter how much inclusion they may have experienced into the formal sectors of the society. When slavery ended in the U.S. in the 1860s and the civil status of the former slaves changed to that of free citizens, this formal change did not erase the societal perception of this group as "difference." Dominant and nondominant modes of life continued to be kept distinctly apart, intermarriage was tabooed legally and extra-legally, the minority identity was codified and reified. To make matters worse, the African-American community internalized (as a natural consequence of socialization) the separatist ethos and structure of the society, and their social construction as difference (this process was explicated in chapter 5), coming to defend vigorously their existence and cultural identity on this separatist basis. Naturally, this has hindered the larger assimilative process, while solidifying intergroup divisions, inequality, and conflict. This situation has abated only slightly in the present century, specifically, over the two decades following the dismantling of Jim Crow, but has been revitalized in recent years through the discourse and practice of difference associated with multiculturalism.

The focus on the religious mediation of this process situates the discussion squarely in the plane of culture, insofar as it emphasizes perspectives of social meaning, which are in turn a fundamental property of the world of experience, hence, of culture.

The recognition of the importance of this variation regarding these styles of culture, and of the interrelation of culture and ethnicity, should take us one step further toward a more solid grasp of the interethnic equation. Considering that, in varying degrees, multiethnic societies everywhere exhibit incomplete structural assimilation of minority groups, along with the persistence of ethnic and racial prejudice, it should be reasonable to claim that this problem may be significantly attenuated or aggravated, depending on the type of cultural structure of the society.

As will be recalled, in the concrete context of society the operation of cultural integrationism translates into the incorporation of minority-group difference via a complex of syncretically reciprocal associations with dominant cultural structures and traits, large-scale biological intermingling of all the groups involved, and their unification around a national (citizenship) identity. This model makes for the continuing enfeeblement and dissolution of the conceptual as well as concrete boundary lines that separate the various ethnic-cultural groupings, the fusion of cultural categories, and the formation of new products. Individuals see themselves equalized and unified chiefly on the basis of *culture* - the national culture - an identity that precedes and overrides all other considerations.

On the other hand, where cultural separatism is in effect, there prevails what might be called the compartmentalization of ethnicities, a process regulated ascriptively in U.S. society, on the basis of *racial* distinctions and determinations. This means that, notwithstanding the presence of assimilative impulses in the society, the prevalent pattern, as we have seen in earlier chapters, is to polarize the various ethnic communities in terms of a white/nonwhite distinction, while imposing structural and cultural separatism on the groups classified as nonwhite. The boundary lines that isolate the dominant from the minority ethnic communities are kept strong and unambiguous, and defended against tendencies of amalgamation. The cultural identity of individuals necessarily reflects this racial bifurcation of the population, and becomes indelibly associated with "race." Since race is treated in the society as a discrete and fixed category, this insures the inalterability of the minority status, irrespective of the degree of social advancement shown by the "minority" individual. To rephrase the matter, the minority condition is not eliminated by *any* amount of structural assimilation. Religious particularism animates this process by assigning greater value to the inherent attributes of individuals, and using these attributes as the chief criterion that shapes the way in which individuals will be treated in the collectivity. Thus, individual difference is perpetually maintained in its separateness and distinctiveness.

Under circumstances of full-blown cultural assimilation, as might be gathered, it is clearly impossible to continue to impose minority status on individuals who, though being members of groups marginalized as minorities, have experienced substantial vertical mobility. This means that the minority representation - its formal and informal recognition and establishment in the society - is a function of a separatist social organization. In the absence of structural separatism, there is universalization of identity, hence no need for the segmentalized representation and identification of individuals.

The cost-benefit assessment of the two models of culture may be approached in reference to the developmental framework of the societies under investigation, with a view to the effects of culture vs. social structure. In multiethnic contexts in general ethnic minorities suffer varying degrees of victimization at the levels of culture, depending on the extent of their exclusion from the cultural mainstream, and social structure, depending on the extent of their economic and political marginalization. In the integrationist model of culture, as exemplified by the Brazilian experience, the most serious aspect of intergroup stratification concerns "social structure," that is, class or economic stratification, which mainly has to do with the degree of modernization and rationalization (in the Weberian sense) of the social system. On the side of "culture," the ethnic groups in the population have been shown to be effectively unified by various integrative mechanisms around a common national identity. In the separatist model of culture, as exemplified by the U.S. experience, the structural rationalization of the society has made for a comparatively higher level of absorption of the minority segments into the bureaucratic (i.e., economic, political, educational) spheres of life, but in the area of "culture" interethnic divisions, exclusions, and enmities persist. In fact, the more rationalized the social system became, the more this led, unintendedly, to the hardening of patterns of intergroup separatism, a phenomenon that may be witnessed in the increasing bureaucratic identification and categorization of ethnic minorities, for the purposes of rectifying past discriminatory practices and bringing about a more equitable allocation of resources.

It has also been stressed that the official acknowledgement and classification of groups maintained as ethnic minorities in separatist multiethnic systems may be a valid measure in the *initial* phase of its application (i.e., after a period of *de jure* segregation and discrimination), as part of the set of formal measures taken towards the elimination of intergroup inequality in the economy, the polity, the educational system, and so on. Thus, it may be useful and even beneficial as a temporary corrective measure toward the rectification of past injustice. These benefits, therefore, should be pursued only as far as the point where parity is established between the disadvantaged groups and the rest of the population. If a politics of difference is pursued indefinitely, for its own sake, instead of provisionally, which is how it should be, the bureaucratic categorization and treatment of minority groups is sure to crystallize and reify minority status and inequality, permanently locking the minorities involved in a subnational status and mode of life, with all of the attendant problems, already discussed. In the final analysis, if the movement towards societal consolidation fails to absorb minority contingents at levels other than strictly structural ones, while allowing ascriptively-based exclusionary arrangements to go on, it will come to a halt and defeat its own purpose. The impasses and inconsistencies that have increasingly dotted the interethnic landscape in American society over the past decade, decade and a half, clearly bear out this viewpoint.

It might, of course, be argued that these minority individuals are likely to find refuge from their social victimization in their subcultural identity and way of life. This is surely true, up to a point, but the *ultimate* consequences of this mode of life are consistently harmful. Remaining a subcultural or subnational presence in the general society because of ascriptively-enforced interethnic differentiation and inequality, represents both the effect and the mainspring of continuing exclusion from the main axis of social life, and as such it cannot possibly be as much a refuge as it is a trap. In other words, the welfare of the minority element remains seriously compromised as long as the separatist arrangement endures.

In his pathbreaking analysis of American life in the first half of the 19th century, Tocqueville correctly reasoned that the rigidity with which the cultural and biological isolation of the subordinate ethnic minorities (i.e., Native Americans and African-Americans) was enforced would effectively preclude the possibility of complete societal integration in the future, even allowing for the eventual concession of political and economic rights to these populations. In fact, he saw that the extension of civil rights and equality to ethnic groups that were otherwise unassimilated only served to increase the animosity of the dominant group towards them, not to foster sentiments of solidarity between these groups. As long as the subordination of ethnic "difference" (i.e., that of ethnic minorities) had the seal of permanence or suffered no real challenge, as was the case during the slavery era, a certain degree of stability in intergroup relations was possible. But, as soon as minority-group members began to enjoy a measure of political and economic equality with the dominant white class, as in the developing industrial Northern regions, they increasingly became the target of social hostility. "In the United States," wrote Tocqueville, "the prejudice which repels the Negroes seems to increase in proportion as they are emancipated, and inequality is sanctioned by the manners white it is effaced from the laws of the country" (1945:374). This aspect was especially conspicuous in the Northern states, where "the white inhabitants ... avoid the Negroes with increasing care in proportion as the legal barriers of separation are removed by the legislature ..." (1945:390).

Observers since the late colonial period have recognized the problem inherent in having the dominant and minority ethnic communities coexist as "two foreign communities" (to use Tocquevilles's phrase), that is, as communities which, though being steadily equalized in the civil aspect, remain culturally and biologically separated. The dire consequences for the larger society stemming from this situation are obvious enough. Thomas Jefferson himself, for all of his firm conviction that the emancipation of the African-Americans from slavery and their subsequent admission into the larger social fold was an event "written in the book of destiny," feared nevertheless that "the two races will never live in a state of equal freedom under the same government, so insurmountable are the barriers which nature, habit, and opinion have established between them" (cited in Tocqueville, 1945:388-9). The barriers of "nature" and "habit" obviously refer to unresolved issues of racial intermixture and cultural blending. Of more recent date is the cogent remark by James Bryce, which addresses the same problem, and highlights the insufficiency of political integration when not buttressed by cultural integration:

A community in which there exist two or more race-elements physi- cally contrasted and socially unsusceptible of amalgamation cannot grow into a really united State. If the coloured people are excluded from political rights, there is created a source of weakness, possibly of danger. *If they are admitted, there is admitted a class who cannot fully share the political life of the more civilized and probably smaller element, who will not be consoled by political equality for social disparagement* (1968:247, vol. I, orig. 1901; emphasis added).

A key theoretical premise of the present study is the critical importance of social integration as built on the universal sharing of a system of culture. In light of the developments of the last twenty years in Western intellectual life (related principally to the "postmodern turn"), proposals for cultural unification such as this one are likely to cause passions to surge to a high tide. As the major theme and frame of reference of this study, cultural integration may be perceived as the quintessential "modernist," totalizing notion, rife with implications of authoritarianism concerning the imposition of the unitary identity and mode of life, ideological conservatism, and oppression. More concretely, it risks disavowal for its presumed disregard for structural diversity, dominant-minority power inequality, and so on. I should enter a *caveat* here, however. My advocacy of syncretically-produced sociocultural integration is not intended to disclaim the merits of structural pluralism, nor the need for liberal multiethnic societies to protect the right of their citizens to pursue the cultural modes of life that they find to be most congruent with their needs and aspirations. My contention is only that these societies ought ideally to provide the conditions of possibility for universal social and cultural inclusion, and that when this process occurs on a syncretistic basis, it not only allows diversity to be cultivated, but in fact requires it, because of the very nature of the syncretic integration of difference. In other words, the formation of the cultural *one* does not necessarily rule out the continuing dynamic presence of the *many* who contributed to this unification process. (I believe this has been satisfactorily dealt with in the earlier discussion on syncretism). But this outcome can never be reached in situations of ascriptively-grounded and mandated structural separatism, where pluralism becomes merely a function of this inegalitarian arrangement.

The essential prerequisite for pluralism, therefore, in my estimation, is that it be effected in a context of basic egalitarianism among the groups involved. (In the preceding section I noted that in integrationist systems this egalitarianism operates primarily in reference to intergroup *cultural* relations. The groups involved may still be noticeably differentiated on the basis of *class*). I referred earlier to the Swiss example of pluralism, designated as "corporate pluralism" in the literature, as an instance of this type of intrasocietal diversity. However, there is no need to appeal to this particular model of structural pluralism to demonstrate this point. Integrationist multiethnic systems, of the type I presented ideal-typically in this study, not only coexist with internal diversity - and therefore should not automatically be regarded as inhospitable to pluralism - but are in fact predicated on sameness *cum* diversity, aspects which operate simultaneously. Pluralism in this context refers to the ability of members of the different formative social groups to identify with the different cultural patterns and traditions that have blended into the total culture, while remaining an integral and indistinguishable part of the latter. Thus, these two "moments" of their cultural membership and identity are not mutually exclusive, but are, rather, two aspects of the same phenomenon of cultural integration. Pluralistic impulses thus arise, one might say, spontaneously, as an adjunct to the experience of full membership in the national life, not as a natural consequence of formally and informally prescribed intergroup cultural segregation. This phenomenon might also, to some extent, be seen in the experience of the "white ethnics" in the U.S., for instance, the Irish-Americans or German-Americans, who, having early on escaped the racial atributions that stigmatized and marginalized other immigrant groups, became fully absorbed - culturally, biologically, psychosocially - into the general society. That notwithstanding, they have remained, in varying degrees, attached to their ancestral heritage (refer, e.g., to Greeley's idea of *ethnogenesis*, in Feagin and Feagin, 1993), without this jeopardizing in any way or degree their full membership in the general culture.

Other groups, as has been shown, have had no choice but to remain closely aligned with their native cultures, relying primarily on their subnational identity, because of ascriptively (i.e., racially)-based impediments to their full asimilation into the social mainstream. It is one thing for, say, a Swedish-American family in Minnesota to celebrate its "ethnicity" by observing the St. Lucia ritual festivities in December, or to enjoy fish *gravad*-style. It is quite another thing for a Mexican-American family in California to do the same regarding Mexican customs. Not only are these two instances going to be perceived differently, from a symbolic standpoint, by the society, but also and more importantly, the "ethnicity" of the "nonwhite" groups is essentially a function and a symbol of their incomplete absorption into national life. In this connection, their "ethnic" celebrations might be said to be a sort of consolation prize for their permanent disenfranchisement. Considered in this context, structural pluralism or diversity stands merely as the expression of ascriptively enforced cultural segmentation: an inequalitarian pluralism, which is hardly worth pursuing (see, e.g., Burkey, 1978:107, on this aspect). In view of the foregoing, the idea of cultural integration advanced in this inquiry does not reflect the more conventional conception of assimilation, such as described by Gordon (i.e., the Anglo-conformity model of assimilation), involving the unilateral, unbending imposition of the hegemonic culture on the incoming groups, ruthlessly eradicating all manner of alien "difference." The idea of assimilation advocated here rests on a dominant-minority dialectical relation of exchange and complementarity, in reference to which the national culture emerges as the hybrid resolution of the tensions, antagonisms, as well as correspondences, among the various formative ethnic and cultural communities of the society. Thus, it is something that pertains to individuals from all of these communities, which they can all claim as their own, and with which they can all identify, since they see themselves in the overall mixture. It is, in a sense, like a Rousseauan *general will* in the cultural sphere, since it is based on universal participation, and formed from the contributions, made in roughly equal measure, of all groups -

syncretic mergers typically involve a rough equivalence of the cultural and ethnic items involved. Though this process may still be vulnerable to charges of the operation of "the tyranny of the majority," like Rousseau's formulation, it remains for the most part an egalitarian scheme of things. As such, it differs markedly from the assimilative situation mentioned above, in which the dominant culture reacts dualistically towards the alien communities: it imperiously absorbs those deemed absorbable, without any significant cultural reciprocity in the process; and it restricts the access of the remaining communities to the dominant mode of life, while preserving the distinctiveness of these groups - their "diversity" - in separate cultural compartments.

With U.S. society presently experiencing the waning of the integrationist impulses of the Civil Rights era and the ever more visible resurfacing of separatism across the institutional and interpersonal spheres, with the correlative increase in interethnic tension and inequality, it becomes particularly pressing to consider this issue in comparative perspective, insofar as that provides an awareness of alternative dimensions and possibilities in ethnic and racial arrangements, and therefore fresh insight into the daily problems of interethnic life.

Bibliography

Abbott, Andrew (1991). 'History and Sociology: The Lost Synthesis,' *Social Science History* 15:201-38.

Adorno, Theodor W. (1979). *Negative Dialectics.* New York: The Seabury Press.

Agassiz, Louis (1868). *A Journey in Brazil.* Boston: Ticknor and Fields.

Anderson, Charles H. *White Protestant Americans: From National Origins to Religious Group.* Prentice-Hall.

Andrade, Mario de (1989). *Dicionario Musical Brasileiro.* São Paulo: Editora Itatiaia.

Arbousse-Bastide, Paul (1940). Preface to Gilberto Freyre, *Um Engenheiro Francês no Brasil.* Rio de Janeiro: Livraria José Olympio Editora.

Azevedo, Fernando de (1944). *A Cultura Brasileira.* 2nd.ed. São Paulo: Companhia Editora Nacional.

_____ (1958). 2nd.ed. *Canaviais e Engenhos na Vida Politica do Brasil.* São Paulo: Editora Melhoramentos.

_____ (1950). *Brazilian Culture: An Introduction to the Study of Culture in Brazil.* New York: MacMillan.

Bailey, Kenneth K. (1964). *Southern White Protestantism in the Twentieth Century.* New York: Harper and Row.

Bakhtin, M.M. and P.N. Medvedev (1978). *The Formal Method in Literary Scholarship: A Critical Introduction to Sociological Poetics.* Baltimore: The Johns Hopkins University Press.

Ball, Charles (1969; orig. 1837). *Slavery in the United States: A Narrative of the Life and Adventures of Charles Ball, A Black Man.* New York: The New American Library.

Bastide, Roger (1951). 'Religion and the Church in Brazil.' in T.Lynn Smith and Alexander Marchant (eds)., *Brazil: Portrait of Half a Continent.* New York: The Dryden Press.

_____ (1959). *Brazil, Terra de Contrastes.* São Paulo: Difusão Europeia do Livro.

_____ (1971). *African Civilizations in the New World.* London: C. Hurst and Co.

_____ (1978). *The African Religions of Brazil.* Johns Hopkins.

Bastide, Roger and Pierre van den Berghe (1957). 'Stereotypes, Norms, and Interracial Behavior in São Paulo, Brazil.' *American Sociological Review* (December):689-94.

Berger, Peter (1969). *The Social Reality of Religion.* London: Faber and Faber.

Berkouwer, G.C. (1960). *Divine Election.* Grand Rapids: W.B.Eerdmans Publishing Co.

Blassingame, John W. (1976). *Black New Orleans.* Chicago: The University of Chicago Press.

_____ (1979). *The Slave Community: Plantation Life in the Antebellum South.* New York: Oxford University Press.

Blauner, Robert (1972). *Racial Oppression in America.* New York: Harper and Row.

Bluestone, Daniel (1991). *Constructing Chicago.* Yale Univ. Press.

Bosi, Alfredo (1993). *Dialética da Colonização.* Sao Paulo: Editora Schwarcz Ltda.

Boxer, Charles R. (1964). *The Golden Age of Brazil: 1695-1750.* Berkeley: The University of California Press.

Bremer, Fredrika (1968, orig. 1853). *Homes in the New World*, 2 vols. New York: Johnson Reprint Corporation.

Brophy, Beth. 1989. 'The Unhappy Politics of Interracial Adoption.' *U.S. News and World Report* (nov. 13)73-4.

Bruneau, Thomas C. (1982). *The Church in Brazil: The Politics of Religion.* Austin: The University of Texas Press.

Bryce, (Sir) James (1921). *South America: Observations and Impressions.* New York: The MacMillan Company.

_____ (1968). *Studies in History and Jurisprudence.* 2 vols. Freeport, NY: Books for Libraries Press.

Burkey, Richard M. (1978). *Ethnic and Racial Groups: The Dynamics of Dominance.* Menlo Park: Benjamin/Cummings.

Burns, E. Bradford (1993). *A History of Brazil*. New York: Columbia University Press.

Burton, (Sir) Richard (1969, orig. 1869). *The Highlands of Brazil*. 2 vols. New York: Greenwood Press.

Cable, George W. (1886). 'The Dance in the Place Congo,' *The Century Magazine* 31(Feb.) 517-28.

Caldcleugh, Alexander (1825). *Travels in South America*. 2 vols. London: John Murray.

Calhoun, John C. (1963, orig. 1854). 'Disquisition on Government,' in Eric L. McKitrick (ed.) *Slavery Defended: The Views of the Old South*. Englewood Cliffs: Prentice-Hall.

Calvin, John (1936). *Institutes of the Christian Religion*. Philadelphia: Presbyterian Board of Christian Education.

Camara, Evandro (1983). *Religion and Social Structure: A Comparative Analysis of African Religious Survivals in Brazil and the United States*. Unpublished Master's Thesis.

_____ (1988). 'Afro-American Religious Syncretism in Brazil and the United States: A Weberian Perspective.' *Sociological Analysis* 48 (Winter) 299-318.

Cartwright, Samuel (1963, orig.1857). 'The Prognathous Species of Mankind,' in Eric L. McKitrick (ed.), *Slavery Defended: The Views of the Old South*. Englewood Cliffs: Prentice-Hall.

Christopher, Robert Allen (1953). 'The Human Race in Brazil,' *Americas* (July) 3-31.

Christy, David (1963, orig. 1860). 'Cotton is King,' in *Slavery Defended: The Views of the Old South*. Eric L. McKitrick (ed.) Englewood Cliffs: Prentice-Hall.

Clark, Kenneth B. and M.P. Clark (1939). 'Segregation as a Factor in the Racial Identification of Negro Pre-school Children,' *Journal of Experimental Education* 8:161-63.

_____ (1950). 'Emotional Factors in Racial Identification and Preference in Negro Children,' *Journal of Negro Education* 19:341-50.

_____ (1957). *Prejudice and Your Child*. Boston: The Beacon Press.

Codman, John (1867). *Ten Months in Brazil*. Boston: Lea and Shepard.

Cole, Stewart G. and Mildred Wiese Cole (1954). *Minorities and the American Promise*. New York: Harper and Bros.

Collier, James Lincoln (1978). *The Making of Jazz: A Comprehensive History*. Boston: Houghton Mifflin.

Collingwood, R.G. (1972). *An Essay on Metaphysics*. New York: University Press of America.

278

Condorcet, Marie Jean Antoine Nicolas Caritat, Marquis de (1976). *Selected Writings*. K.M. Baker (ed.).Indianapolis: The Bobbs-Merrill Co.

Conrad, Robert E. (1983). *Children of God's Fire: A Documentary History of Black Slavery in Brazil*. Princeton: Princeton University Press.

Cooper, C.S. (1917). *The Brazilians and their Country*. New York: Frederick A. Stokes Co.

Copleston, Frederick (1985). *A History of Philosophy*. Book II. New York: Doubleday.

Coutinho, Afranio (1943). 'Some Considerations on the Problem of Philosophy in Brazil,' *Philosophy and Phenomenological Research* 4:187-193.

Cox, Oliver (1948). *Caste, Class, and Race*. Garden City: Doubleday.

DaMatta, Roberto (1983). *Carnavais, Malandros, e Herois: Para Uma Sociologia do Dilema Brasileiro*. 4th edit. Rio de Janeiro: Zahar Editores.

Davidson, Basil (1966). *A History of West Africa*. New York: Doubleday.

Davis, David Brion (1966). *The Problem of Slavery in Western Culture*. Ithaca: Cornell University Press.

Debret, Jean-Baptiste (1989; orig.1834). *Viagem Pitoresca e Historica ao Brasil*. São Paulo: Editora Itatiaia Ltda.

Degler, Carl N. (1971). *Neither Black Nor White: Slavery and Race Relations in Brazil and the United States*. MacMillan.

DeLerma, Dominique-Rene (1970). *Black Music in Our Culture*. Kent State University Press.

Dent, Hastings Charles (1886). *A Year in Brazil*. London: Kegan Paul and Trench.

Dew, Thomas R. (1963, orig.1832). 'Review of the Debate in the Virginia Legislature,' in Eric L. McKitrick (ed.), *Slavery Defended: The Views of the Old South*. Englewood Cliffs: Prentice-Hall.

_____ (1981, orig. 1832). 'Abolition of Negro Slavery,' in Drew Gilpin Faust (ed.), *The Ideology of Slavery*. Baton Rouge: Louisiana State University Press.

Dubois, W.E. (1990, orig.1903). *The Souls of Black Folk*. Vintage Books.

Durkheim, Emile (1965). *The Elementary Forms of the Religious Life*. New York: The Free Press.

Eads, J.K. (1936). 'The Negro in Brazil,' *Journal of Negro History* xxi (October) 365-75.

Eaton, Clement (1964). *The Mind of the Old South*. Baton Rouge: Louisiana State University Press.

Eisenstadt, Shmuel N. (1989). 'Introduction: Culture and Social Structure in Recent Sociological Analysis,' in Hans Haferkamp (ed.) *Social Structure and Culture*. Berlin: Walter de Gruyter.

Engels, Friedrich. in Karl Marx and Friedrich Engels: *Selected Correspondence*. Moscow: Foreign Languages Publishing House.

Escott, Paul D. (1979). *Slavery Remembered*. Chapel Hill: The University of North Carolina Press.

Evans-Pritchard, E.E. (1937). *Witchcraft, Oracles, and Magic Among the Azande*. Oxford University Press.

Ewbanks, Thomas (1856). *Life in Brazil*. New York: Harper and Bros.

Farish, D.D. (ed.) (1943). *Journal and Letters of Philip Vickers Fithian, 1773-1774*. Colonial Williamsburg Inc.

Feagin, Joe R. and Clarice Booher Feagin (1993). *Racial and Ethnic Relations*. Englewood Cliffs: Prentice-Hall.

Fernandes, Florestan (1971). *The Negro in Brazilian Society*. New York: Atheneum.

Fitzhugh, George (1963, orig. 1854). 'Sociology for the South,' in Eric L. McKitrick (ed.) *Slavery Defended: The Views of the Old South*. Englewood Cliffs: Prentice-Hall.

Flanagan, William G. (1995). *Urban Sociology: Images and Structure*. Boston: Allyn and Bacon.

Fletcher, James C. and Daniel P. Kidder (1867). *Brazil and the Brazilians*. Boston: Little, Brown, and Company.

Fogel, William R. and Stanley L. Engerman (1974). *Time on the Cross: The Economics of American Negro Slavery*. Boston: Little, Brown, and Co.

Foucault, Michel (1966). *Les Mots et les Choses*. Paris: Gallimard

Franklin, John Hope (1969). *From Slavery to Freedom*. New York: Vintage.

_____ (1997). 'Ethnicity in American Life: The Historical Perspective,' in Virginia Cyrus (ed.), *Experiencing Race, Class, and Gender in the United States*. Mayfield Publishing Co.

Frazier, E. Franklin (1944). 'A Comparison of Negro-white Relations in Brazil and in the United States.' Transactions of the New Academy of Sciences II, pp.251-69.

_____ (1969). *The Negro in the United States*. Toronto: The MacMillan Company.

Freyre, Gilberto (1945). *Sociologia*. vols.I and II. Rio de Janeiro: Livraria José Olympio Editora.

_____ (1947). *Interpretação do Brasil: Aspectos da Formação Social Brasileira como Processo de Amalgamento de Raças e Culturas*. Rio de Janeiro: Livraria José Olympio Editora.

_____ (1951). *Sobrados e Mocambos*. Rio de Janeiro: Livraria José Olympio Editora.

_____ (1956). *The Master and the Slaves: A Study in the Development of Brazilian Civilization*. Alfred Knopf.

_____ (1963). *New World in the Tropics: The Culture of Modern Brazil*. New York: Vintage Books.

_____ (1966). *Casa Grande e Senzala: Formação da Familia Brasileira sob o Regime de Economia Patriarcal*. 2 vols. (2nd volume published 1970). Recife: Imprensa Oficial.

_____ (1968). *The Mansions and the Shanties*. New York: Alfred A. Knopf.

_____ (1970). *Order and Progress*. New York: Alfred A. Knopf.

Gans, Herbert (1962). *The Urban Villagers*. New York: Free Press.

Gardner, George (1973/orig. 1846). *Travels in the Interior of Brazil*. Boston: Milford House.

Gardner, Robert W., Bryant Robey, and Peter C. Smith (1985). 'Asian Americans: Growth, Change, and Diversity.' *Population Bulletin* 40 (October) 1-43.

Gates, Henry Louis (1997). 'Black London,' in *The New Yorker* (April 28-May 5).

Genovese, Eugene D. (1967). *The Political Economy of Slavery: Studies in the Economy and Society of the Slave South*. New York: Vintage Books.

_____ (1969). 'The Treatment of Slaves in Different Countries: Problems in the Applications of the Comparative Method,' in Laura Foner and Eugene Genovese (eds.) *Slavery in the New World*. Englewood Cliffs: Prentice-Hall.

_____ (1971). *The World the Slaveholders Made*. New York: Vintage Books.

_____ (1976). *Roll, Jordan, Roll*. New York: Vintage Books.

Giddens, Anthony (1991). *Introduction to Sociology*. New York: Norton.

Goodell, William (1853). *The American Slave Code*. New York.

Gordon, Milton (1964). *Assimilation in American Life*. New York: Oxford University Press.

Gottfredson, Denise C. (1981). 'Black-White Differences in the Educational Attainment Process: What Have We Learned?' *American Sociological Review* 46 (October) 542-57.

Graham, Maria (1969. orig.1824) *Journal of a Voyage to Brazil*. New York: Praeger.

Grant, Andrew (1809). *History of Brazil*. London: H.Colburn.

Greene, John C. (1984). *American Science in the Age of Jefferson*. Ames: The Iowa State University Press.

Greenfield, Sidney M. (1969). 'Slavery and the Plantation in the New World,' *Journal of Interamerican Studies* 11 (Jan)44-57.

Griswold, Wendy (1992). 'The Sociology of Culture: Four Good Arguments (And One Bad One).' *Acta Sociologica* 35:323-28.

Guerra-Peixe, Cesar (1980). *Maracatus do Recife*. Recife: Irmãos Vitale.

Gulick, Sidney (1918). *American Democracy and Asiatic Citizenship*. New York: Charles Scribners.

Habermas, Jurgen (1979). *Communication and the Evolution of Society*. Boston: Beacon Press.

_____ (1994). 'Struggles for Recognition in the Democratic Constitutional State,' in Amy Gutman (ed.), *Multiculturalism: Examining the Politics of Recognition*. Princeton University Press.

Harper, William (1981, orig.1838). 'Memoir on Slavery,' in Drew Gilpin Faust (ed.), *The Ideology of Slavery*. Baton Rouge: Louisiana State University Press.

Harris, Marvin (1974). *Patterns of Race Relations in the Americas*. New York: W.W. Norton.

_____ (1997). *Culture, People, Nature: An Introduction to General Anthropology*. New York: Longman.

Hays, Brooks and John E. Steely (1973). *The Baptist Way of Life*. Prentice-Hall.

Hentoff, Nat (1975). *The Jazz Life*. New York: DaCapo Press.

Herskovits, Melville J. (1937). 'African Gods and Catholic Saints in the New World Negro Belief,' *American Anthropologist* 29:635-43.

_____ (1944). 'Drums and Drummers in AfroBrazilian Cult Life,' *Musical Quarterly* (Oct.).

_____ (1956). 'The Social Organization of the AfroBrazilian Candomblé,' *Phylon* (June) 147-166.

_____ (1964). *Trinidad Village*. New York: Octagon Books.

_____ (1967). *Cultural Dynamics*. New York: Alfred Knopf.

_____ (1972). *The Myth of the Negro Past*. Boston: Beacon Press.

Herskovits, Melville J. and Frances S. (1942). 'The Negroes of Brazil,' *The Yale Review* 32(Dec) 263-79.

Higham, John and Paul K. Conkin (eds.) (1979). *New Directions in American Intellectual History*. Baltimore: The Johns Hopkins University Press.

Hollanda, Sergio Buarque de (1973). *Raizes do Brasil.* Rio de Janeiro: Livraria José Olympio Editora.

Horowitz, Irving Louis (1964). *Revolution in Brazil.* New York: Dutton.

Hughes, Henry (1981, orig. 1854). 'A Treatise on Sociology, Theoretical and Practical,' in Drew Gilpin Faust (ed.), *The Ideology of Slavery.* Baton Rouge: Louisiana State University Press.

Hudson, Winthrop S. (1982). 'Baptists,' *Encyclopaedia Americana.* vol. III. Grolier.

Hutchinson, Harry W. (1963). 'Race Relations in a Rural Community of the Bahian Recôncavo,' in Charles Wagley (ed.) *Race and Class in Rural Brazil.* New York: Columbia University Press.

Jackson, Luther P. (1930). 'Religious Instruction of Negroes, 1830-1860, with Special Reference to South Carolina,' *The Journal of Negro History* 15 (January) 72-114.

Jenkins, William Sumner (1960). *Proslavery Thought in the Old South.* Gloucester: Peter Smith.

Jones, W.T. (1969). *Hobbes to Hume.* New York: Harcourt, Brace, and World.

Johnson, Guion G. (1930). *A Social History of the Sea Islands.* Chapel Hill: The University of North Carolina Press.

Jordan, Winthrop D. (1968). *White Over Black: American Attitudes Towards the Negro, 1550-1812.* Chapel Hill: The University of North Carolina Press.

_____ (1981). *The White Man's Burden: Historical Origins of Racism in the United States.* London: Oxford University Press.

Kallen, Horace M. (1970). *Culture and Democracy in the United States.* New York: Arno Press.

Kalm, Peter (1966. orig.1753). *Travels in North America.* New York: Dover Publications.

Kammeyer, Kenneth C.W., George Ritzer, and Norman R. Yetman (1990). *Sociology: Experiencing Changing Societies.* 4th ed.

Kasler, Dirk (1988). *Max Weber: An Introduction to his Life and Work.* Chicago: The University of Chicago Press.

Kennedy, Randall (1997). 'My Race Problem - And Ours,' *The Atlantic Monthly* 279 (May) 55-66.

Kidder, Daniel P. (1845). *Sketches of Residence and Travel in Brazil.* 2 vols. Philadelphia: Sorin and Ball.

Klein, Herbert S. (1969). 'Anglicanism, Catholicism, and the Negro Slave,' in L. Foner and E. Genovese (eds.) *Slavery in the New World.* Englewood Cliffs: Prentice-Hall.

Kluckhohn, Clyde (1962). *Culture and Behavior*. New York: The Free Press.

Koster, Henry (1816). *Travels in Brazil*. London: Longman, Hurst, Rees, Orme, and Brown.

_____ (1966). *Travels in Brazil*. C.H.Gardiner (ed.). Carbondale: Southern Illinois University Press.

Kroeber, A.L. and Talcott Parsons (1958). 'The Concept of Culture and of Social System.' *American Sociological Review* 23:582-3.

Lacan, Jacques (1977). 'Of Structure as an Inmixing of an Otherness Prerequisite to Any Subject Whatever,' in Richard Macksey and Eugenio Donato (eds.) *The Structuralist Controversy*. Baltimore: The Johns Hopkins University Press.

La Grande Encyclopedie, vol.VIII, Paris: Camille Dreyfus, 1886-1902.

Landes, Ruth (1940). 'Fetish Worship in Brazil,' *Journal of American Folklore* 53:261-70.

_____ (1955). 'Biracialism in American Society: A Comparative View.' *American Anthropologist* 57:1253-63.

Leite, Serafim (1938). *Historia da Companhia de Jesus no Brasil*. Lisboa: Livraria Portugalia.

Leonard, Neil (1970). *Jazz and the White Americans*. Chicago: The University of Chicago Press.

Levi-Strauss, Claude (1963). *Structural Anthropology*. New York: Basic Books.

Lima, Alceu de Amoroso (1956). 'Men, Ideas, and Institutions: Humanism and the Temperament of the People,' *The Atlantic Monthly* (February) 117-21.

Lindbekk, Tore (1992). 'The Weberian Ideal-Type: Development and Discontinuities,' *Acta Sociologica* 35:285-97.

LiPuma, Edward (1993). 'Culture and the Concept of Culture in a Theory of Practice,' in Craig Calhoun, Edward Lipuma, and Moishe Postone (eds.), *Bourdieu: Critical Perspectives*. Chicago: The University of Chicago Press.

Lisboa, M.P.A. de (1847). 'La Race Noire et La Race Mulâtre au Brésil.' *Nouvelles Annales des Voyages et des Sciences Geographiques*. Paris: Arthus Bertrand.

Lowrie, Samuel H. (1942). 'The Negro Element in the Population of São Paulo, a Southernly State of Brazil.' *Phylon* iii, 398-416.

Luccock, John (1820). *Notes on Rio de Janeiro and the Southern Parts of Brazil*. London: Samuel Leigh.

Ludwig, Theodore M. (1996). *The Sacred Paths*. 2nd.ed. Prentice-Hall.

Lyell, Sir Charles (1850). *A Second Visit to the United States*, 2 vols. London: John Murray.

Malefijt, Annemarie de Waal (1968). *Religion and Culture*. New York: MacMillan.

Malheiro, Agostinho Marques Perdigão (1944; orig. 1866). *A Escravidão no Brasil*. São Paulo: Edicões Cultura.

Manchester, Alan K. (1965). 'Racial Democracy in Brazil,' *The South Atlantic Quarterly* 54 (Winter) 27-35.

Maranhão, Walmyr (1960). 'Recife Carnaval.' *Americas*(March)17-21.

Marger, Martin (1994). *Race and Ethnic Relations: American and Global Perspectives*. Belmont, CA: Wadsworth.

Maritain, Jacques (1968). *Integral Humanism*. New York: Charles Scribner's Sons.

Marjoribanks, Alexander (1853). *Travels in South and North America*. London: Simpkin, Marshall, and Co.

Martí, José (1975). *Inside the Monster: Writings on the United States and American Imperialism*. Philip S. Foner (ed.) New York: Monthly Review Press.

Martineau, Harriet (1962, orig. 1837). *Society in America*. Garden City: Anchor Books.

Mawe, John (1978). *Viagens ao Interior do Brasil*. São Paulo: Livraria Itatiaia Editora Ltda.

May, Henry F. (1979). 'Intellectual History and Religious History.' in John Higham and Paul K. Conkin (eds.) *New Directions in American Intellectual History*. Baltimore: The Johns Hopkins University Press.

Mayntz, Renate (1992). 'Social Norms in the Institutional Culture of the German Federal Parliament,' in Richard Munch and Neil Smelser (eds.) *Theory of Culture*. Berkeley: University of California Press.

Mbiti, John S. (1970). *African Religions and Philosophy*. Garden City: Anchor Books.

McKitrick, Eric L. (ed.) (1963). *Slavery Defended: The Views of the Old South*. Englewood Cliffs: Prentice-Hall.

McNeil, John T. (1968). 'John Calvin,' in *International Encyclopaedia of the Social Sciences*. New York: MacMillan.

Merguson, R.W. (1915). 'Glimpses of Brazil,' *The Crisis* (November).

Moore, Wilbert E. (1941). 'Slave Law and the Social Structure,' *Journal of Negro History* 26 (April)171-202.

Morse, Richard (1953). 'The Negro in São Paulo, Brazil,' *Journal of Negro History* 38 (July)290-306.

Munch, Richard (1994). *Sociological Theory*. 3 vols. Chicago: Nelson-Hall.

Myrdal, Gunnar (1972). *An American Dilemma: The Negro Problem and Modern Democracy.* New York: Pantheon Books.

Nevins, Allan (1928). *American Social History: As Recorded By British Travellers.* New York:Henry Holt and Co.

Nina Rodrigues, Raimundo (1977). *Os Africanos no Brasil.* São Paulo: Companhia Editora Nacional.

Nogueira, Oracy (1959). 'Skin Color and Social Class,' in *Plantation Systems of the New World,* Pan-American Union Social Science Monograph n.7, Washington, D.C.

Nott, Josiah (1981, orig. 1844). 'Two Lectures on the Natural History of the Caucasian and Negro Races,' in Drew Gilpin Faust (ed.), *The Ideology of Slavery.* Baton Rouge: Louisiana State University Press.

Novak, Michael (1971). 'White Ethnic.' *Harper's Magazine* (Sept)44-50.

Ofari, Earl (1984). "'Whites' view of blacks' life too rosy," *Kalamazoo Gazette,* May 23, p.A7.

Olmsted, Frederick Law (1968, orig.1856). *A Journey in the Seaboard Slave States.* New York: Dix and Edwards.

_____ (1970; orig. 1860). *A Journey in the Back Country.* New York: Schocken Books.

_____ (1984). *The Cotton Kingdom.* New York: The Modern Library.

Otto, Rudolf (1958). *The Idea of the Holy: An Inquiry into the Non-Rational Factor in the Idea of the Divine and its Relation to the Rational.* New York: Oxford University Press.

Park, Robert E. (1964). *Race and Culture.* Glencoe: The Free Press.

Park, Robert E. and Ernest W. Burgess (1969). *Introduction to the Science of Sociology.* Chicago:The University of Chicago Press.

Pescatello, Ann M. (ed.) (1975). *The African in Latin America.* New York: Alfred Knopf.

Peterson, Thomas Virgil (1978). *Ham and Japheth: The Mythic World of Whites in the Antebellum South.* Metuchen: The Scarecrow Press.

Phillips, Ulrich B. (1909). *A Documentary History of American Industrial Society, Plantation and Frontier,* vols.I and II. Cleveland: The Arthur H. Clark Co.

_____ (1969; orig. 1918). *American Negro Slavery.* Baton Rouge: Louisiana State University Press.

Pierson, Donald (1944). 'The Brazilian Racial Situation,' *The Scientific Monthly* (May).

_____ (1948). *Cruz das Almas: A Brazilian Village.* Smithsonian Institution.

_____ (1964). *Teoria e Pesquisa em Sociologia*. Sao Paulo: Edições Melhoramentos.

_____ (1967). *Negroes in Brazil: A Study of Race Contact at Bahia*. Carbondale: Southern Illinois University Press.

Poppino, Rollie E. (1973). *Brazil, The Land and People*. New York: Oxford University Press.

Prado, Caio, Jr. (1971). *The Colonial Background of Modern Brazil*. Berkeley: The University of California Press.

Quarles, Benjamin (1976). *The Negro in the Making of America*. New York: MacMillan.

Quintanales, Mirtha (1981).'I Paid Very Hard for My Immigrant Ignorance,' in Gloria Auzalduá and Cherrie Moraga (eds.) *This Bridge Called My Back: Writings by Radical Women of Color*. Persephone Press.

Raboteau, Albert J. (1980). *Slave Religion: The 'Invisible Institution' in the Antebellum South*. Oxford: Oxford University Press.

Ramos, Arthur (1951). *The Negro in Brazil*. Washington,DC: The Associated Publishers.

_____ (1954). *Folclore Negro do Brasil*. Rio de Janeiro: Livraria Editora da Casa do Estudante do Brasil.

Rawick, George P. (1974). *From Sundown to Sunup: The Making of the Black Community*. Westport: Greenwood Press.

_____ (1977). *The American Slave: A Composite Autobiography*. Georgia Narratives. Westport: Greenwood Press.

Réclus, Eliseé (1862). 'Le Brésil et la Colonisation,' *Revue des Deux Mondes* 40. Paris.

Ribeiro, Joao (1900). *Historia do Brasil*. Rio de Janeiro: Livraria Cruz Coutinho.

Ribeiro, René (1956). *Religião e Relações Raciais*. Rio de Janeiro: Ministerio de Educação e Cultura.

Riesman, David (1967). *The Lonely Crowd*. New Haven: Yale University Press.

Rodrigues, José Honório (1962). 'The Influence of Africa on Brazil and of Brazil on Africa.' *Journal of African History* 3, 1:49-67.

Roosevelt, Theodore (1913). 'Rio de Janeiro,' *The Outlook*, Dec.20.

Rose, Willie Lee (ed.) (1976). *A Documentary History of Slavery in North America*. New York: Oxford University Press.

Ross, Frederick A. (1969, orig. 1857). *Slavery Ordained of God*. Miami, FL.

Ruchames, Louis (1969). *Racial Thought in America*. vol.I. The University of Massachusetts Press.

Ruffin, Edmund (1981, orig. 1853). 'The Political Economy of Slavery,'in Eric L. McKitrick (ed.) *Slavery Defended: The Views of the Old South*. Englewood Cliffs: Prentice-Hall.

Rugendas, João Mauricio (1976; orig. 1835). *Viagem Pitoresca Através do Brasil*. Trans.Sergio Milliet. Sao Paulo: Livraria Martins Editora.

Russell, William Howard (1861). *Pictures of Southern Life: Social, Political, and Military*. New York: James G. Gregory.

Schneider, L. and Charles Bonjean (eds.) (1973). *The Idea of Culture in the Social Sciences*. Cambridge: Cambridge University Press.

Schumpeter, Joseph A. (1976). *Capitalism, Socialism, and Democracy*. New York: George Allen and Unwin.

Schutz, Alfred (1944). 'The Stranger: An Essay in Social Psychology,' *American Journal of Sociology* 49 (May) 499-507.

_____ (1970). *On Phenomenology and Social Relations*. Helmut Wagner (ed.). Chicago: The University of Chicago Press.

Sheridan, Alan (1982). *Michel Foucault: The Will to Truth*. London: Tavistock Publications.

Sickels, Robert J. (1972). *Race, Marriage, and the Law*. Albuquerque: University of New Mexico Press.

Siegfried, André (1927). *America Comes of Age*. New York: Harcourt, Brace, and Co.

_____ (1955). *America at Mid-Century*. Prentice-Hall.

Simkins, Francis Butler (1959). *A History of the South*. New York: Alfred A. Knopf.

Smith, T. Lynn and Alexander Marchant (eds.) (1951). *Brazil: Portrait of Half a Continent*. New York: The Dryden Press.

Smith, William A. (1856). *Lectures on the Philosophy and Practice of Slavery*. Nashville: Stevenson and Evans.

Southern, Eileen (1983). *The Music of Black Americans: A History*. New York: W.W. Norton.

Southey, Robert (1970; orig. 1822). *History of Brazil*. 3 vols. New York: Burt Franklin.

Spix, J.B. von, and C.P.P. von Martius (1824). *Travels in Brazil in the Years 1817-1820*. 2 vols. London.

Stampp, Kenneth M. (1956). *The Peculiar Institution: Slavery in the Antebellum South*. New York: Vintage Books.

Stark, Rodney (1992). *Sociology*. Wadsworth.

Stearns, Charles (1969; orig. 1872). *The Black Men of the South and the Rebels*. New York: Negro Universities Press.

Stewart, C.S. (1831). *A Visit to the South Seas*. New York.

Streng, F.J. (1995). 'Rites and Ceremonies,' in *Encyclopaedia Britannica*, vol.26. Chicago: Encyclopaedia Britannica, Inc.

Stringfellow, (Rev.) Thornton (1861). *Slavery: Its Origin, Nature, and History*. New York: John F. Trow.

_____ (1981, orig. 1841). 'A Brief Examination of Scripture Testimony on the Institution of Slavery,' in Drew Gilpin Faust (ed.), *The Ideology of Slavery*. Baton Rouge: Louisiana State University Press.

Suttles, Gerald D. (1968). *The Social Order of the Slum*. Chicago: The University of Chicago Press.

Swanson, Guy E. (1992). 'Collective Purpose and Culture: Findings and Implications from Some Studies of Societies,' in Richard Munch and Neil J. Smelser (eds.), *Theory of Culture*, Berkeley: University of California Press.

Sweet, William W. (1952). *Religion in the Development of American Culture*. New York: Charles Scribner's Sons.

Tannenbaum, Frank (1946). *Slave and Citizen: The Negro in the Americas*. New York: Vintage.

Taylor, Charles (1977). 'Interpretation and the Sciences of Man,' in Fred R. Dallmayr and Thomas A. McCarthy (eds.), *Understanding and Social Inquiry*. Notre Dame: University of Notre Dame Press.

_____ (1987). 'Language and Human Nature,' in Michael T. Gibbons (ed.) *Interpreting Politics*. New York University Press.

_____ (1994). 'The Politics of Recognition,' in *Multiculturalism: Examining the Politics of Recognition*. Amy Gutman (ed.). Princeton University Press.

Tiryakian, Edward A. (1995). 'A Religion of Revivals,' in Andrew M. Greeley (ed.). *Sociology and Religion: A Collection of Readings*. Harper Collins.

Tischler, Henry L. (1993). *Introduction to Sociology*. 4th edition. Orlando: The Harcourt Press.

Tocqueville, Alexis de (1945). *Democracy in America*. 2 vols. New York: Vintage Books.

Tollenare, Louis-François de (1956). *Notas Dominicais*. Salvador: Livraria Progresso Editora.

Toplin, Robert Brent (1981). *Freedom and Prejudice: The Legacy of Slavery in the United States and Brazil*. Westport: Greenwood Press.

Tuch, Stephen A. and Jack K. Martin (1991). 'Race in the Workplace: Black-White Differences in the Sources of Job Satisfaction,' *The Sociological Quarterly* 32:103-16.

Valente, Valdemar (1976). *Sincretismo Religioso Afro-Brasileiro*. Companhia Editora Nacional.

Van den Berghe, Pierre L. (1976). 'The African Diaspora in Mexico, Brazil, and the United States.' *Social Forces* 54:530-43.

Verger, Pierre (1968). *Flux et Reflux de la Traite des Nègres entre le Golfe de Benin et Bahia de Todos os Santos.* Paris: Mouton.

_____ (1981). *Noticias da Bahia - 1850.* Salvador: Editora Corrupio.

Vilhena, Luis dos Santos (1969). *A Bahia no Século XVIII.* Salvador: Livraria Itapuã.

Wade, Richard C. (1964). *Slavery in the Cities: The South, 1820-1860.* New York: Oxford University Press.

Wagley, Charles (1948). 'Regionalism and Cultural Unity in Brazil,' *Social Forces* 26 (May) 457-64.

_____ (1963). (ed.) *Race and Class in Rural Brazil.* New York: UNESCO/Columbia University Press.

_____ (1964). *Amazon Town: A Study of Man in the Tropics.* New York: Alfred A. Knopf.

_____ (1971). *Introduction to Brazil.* New York: Columbia University Press.

Walker, Alice (1983). *In Search of Our Mothers' Gardens.* New York: Harcourt Brace Jovanovich.

Walsh, Robert (1830). *Notices of Brazil in 1828 and 1829.* London: Frederick Westley and A.H. Davis.

Weber, Max (1946). *From Max Weber: Essays in Sociology.* Trans. and ed. H. Gerth and C. Wright Mills. New York: Oxford University Press.

_____ (1949). *The Methodology of the Social Sciences.* New York: The Free Press.

_____ (1958). *The Protestant Ethic and the Spirit of Capitalism.* New York: Charles Scribners and Sons.

_____ (1978). *Economy and Society.* Guenther Roth and Claus Wittich (eds.). Berkeley: University of California Press.

White, Jack E. (1992). 'In African American Eyes,' *Time*, Sept. 7, p. 52.

Willems, Emilio (1949). 'Racial Attitudes in Brazil,' *The American Journal of Sociology* 14 (March) 402-8.

Williams, David R. (1987). *Wilderness Lost: The Religions Origins of the American Mind.* Associated University Presses.

Williams, Martin (1983). *The Jazz Tradition.* Oxford University Press.

Williams, Mary W. (1930). 'The Treatment of Negro Slaves in the Brazilian Empire: A Comparison with the United States of America,' *Journal of Negro History* 15 (July).

Williams, Raymond (1958). *Culture and Society: 1780-1950.* New York: Harper and Row.

Willie, Charles V. (1978). 'The Inclining Significance of Race.' *Society*. July/August.

Wirth, Louis (1938). 'Urbanism as a Way of Life.' *American Journal of Sociology*, 40:1-24.

Wissler, Clark (1923). *Man and Culture*. New York: Crowell.

Wuthnow, Robert (1987). *Meaning and Moral Order: Explorations in Cultural Analysis*. Berkeley: University of California Press.

Yetman, Norman R. (1970). *Life under 'The Peculiar Institution.'* New York: Holt, Rinehart & Winston.

Index

African culture
  convergences with Luso-
    Brazilian Catholicism
    75-82
  dances 85, 90
  instruments, Brazil 85, 93
  instruments, U.S. 88-89
  religion, features 74-75
The *anjinhos* 213
The *apadrinhamento* institution
  203, 223

Biraciality norm
  basis of ethnic relations in
    U.S. 94-98

Calvinistic Protestantism
  182-185, 227-263
  in the antebellum South
    183-184, 187, 233
  and cultural *angularity*
    178-179
  and cultural particularism
    172, 174-177
  and dominant-minority
    cultural relations 228-230
  and ethnic assimilation

185-187, 231
  ideological effect on behavior
    182
  overall effect on U.S. culture
    167, 184-185
  predestination and racial
    dualism 231-232, 244,
    259-261
  as theological matrix for
    U.S. evangelical churches
    182-184
Candomble 83, 92-93
Carnaval clubs 82-84
Catholicism
  a baroque religion in Brazil
    212
  and cultural integration 188,
    210-212, 215-218
  in the *engenhos* 196, 217-
    218, 224-225
  and ethnic identity 220-221
  and ethnic-social integration
    188-190, 195, 207-210,
    219-220, 263-264
  and ethno-cultural
    universalism 170-174
  and ethno-cultural